# Psychology
### General—Industrial—Social

*Third Edition*

# Psychology
## General—Industrial—Social

John Munro Fraser, M.A.
*Reader in Personnel Management*
*University of Aston in Birmingham*

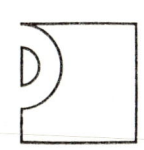

Pitman Publishing

*Third edition* 1971

SIR ISAAC PITMAN AND SONS LTD
Pitman House, Parker Street, Kingsway, London, WC2B 5PB
P.O. Box 6038, Portal Street, Nairobi, Kenya

SIR ISAAC PITMAN (AUST.) PTY. LTD
Pitman House, Bouverie Street, Carlton, Victoria 3053, Australia

PITMAN PUBLISHING COMPANY S.A. LTD
P.O. Box 11231, Johannesburg, S. Africa

PITMAN PUBLISHING CORPORATION
6 East 43rd Street, New York, N.Y. 10017, U.S.A.

SIR ISAAC PITMAN (CANADA) LTD
Pitman House, 381–383 Church Street, Toronto, 3, Canada

THE COPP CLARK PUBLISHING COMPANY
517 Wellington Street, Toronto, 2B, Canada

© John Munro Fraser 1963, 1971

*Cased edition* ISBN: 0 273 31497 1
*Paperback edition* ISBN: 0 273 41233 7

Made in Great Britain at the Pitman Press, Bath
G1–(MAN. 6/MAN. 109)

# Preface to Third Edition

Management in the final analysis is the management of people. This has become almost a cliché. Nevertheless it is worth repeating because the management of production, marketing, finance and the like, presents far fewer problems in the present-day world, with its rising standards of affluence and its increasingly egalitarian outlook. Human beings with their differences in ability and aspirations, their emotions and irrationalities, represent the major source of headaches to the present-day manager.

No one can ever manage anything until he has some understanding of it. Consequently, some insight into what goes on within the human personality and between one individual and another, is an essential element in the qualifications of the modern manager. Understanding depends on insight into cause and effect, and while we have acquired this to a considerable degree in the physical sciences, we are still at a relatively elementary stage in the behavioural sciences. This is why we can send men in rockets to the moon but cannot prevent unofficial strikes. The margin of error in the management of our human resources is much wider than in the management of our material resources.

The original intention of this book was to provide an introduction for students and managers to those aspects of psychology which can help in the understanding of the human problems of management. Since it was first written, my experience of industry has broadened through my work in the University of Aston and my contacts with managers and supervisors in various industrial and commercial organisations. I am very aware of my obligations to these friends and colleagues and I would like to acknowledge it here. As a result of this broadened experience, the book has been revised and re-written. I hope it will continue to fulfil the original intention.

JOHN MUNRO FRASER

# Preface to First Edition

IN 1947 the Committee on Education for Management recommended that psychology be included in the syllabus for a Common Intermediate Examination as a "background" subject. Its report sets out the reasons in the following terms, the aim being "to give students some training in the art and science of handling men," while the method is outlined in the succeeding sentence: "The content of the course is designed to provide an introduction to general psychology and to illustrate its application in dealing with the human problems of industry and commerce and the management of social groups."

It is with these terms of reference in mind that this book has been written. It is an endeavour to survey the fields of general, industrial, and social psychology from the manager's point of view and to draw the main issues together within reasonable space. Detail has been disregarded in order to present a coherent theme, and there will inevitably be passages where I have done less than justice to the complexities of the subject. The student who wishes to follow up any aspect in greater detail will find some guidance in the Notes on Reading at the end of the text.

The views I have put forward were acquired during the years I spent on the scientific staff of the National Institute of Industrial Psychology. They do not in any way constitute an official pronouncement by that body. I am glad, however, to acknowledge my debt to colleagues past and present, while reserving to myself the responsibility for any deficiencies in presentation.

JOHN MUNRO FRASER

# Contents

Preface to Third Edition                                          v
Preface to First Edition                                         vi

## Part I General Psychology

|  I    | From Classical Thought to the Scientific Method |   3 |
|  II   | The Senses                                      |  14 |
|  III  | Attention and Perception                        |  24 |
|  IV   | Imagery, Memory, and Thinking                   |  37 |
|  V    | The Learning Process                            |  54 |
|  VI   | Motivation and Emotion                          |  67 |
|  VII  | Individual Aims and Attitudes                   |  81 |
|  VIII | General Psychology and Psychiatry               |  93 |

## Part II Industrial Psychology

|  IX    | Introductory                                 | 107 |
|  X     | Individual Differences                       | 114 |
|  XI    | Impact and Relationships with Others         | 131 |
|  XII   | Qualifications and Innate Abilities          | 146 |
|  XIII  | Differences in Motivational Patterns         | 161 |
|  XIV   | Individual Patterns of Adjustment            | 171 |
|  XV    | Vocational Guidance and Selection            | 181 |
|  XVI   | Interviewing                                 | 197 |
|  XVII  | Training                                     | 215 |
|  XVIII | Incentives                                   | 228 |
|  XIX   | Work Study and Working Methods               | 244 |
|  XX    | The Physical Conditions of Work              | 268 |
|  XXI   | Accidents                                    | 284 |

## Part III Social Psychology

|  XXII  | Introductory                                 | 293 |
|  XXIII | The Social Anatomy of an Industrial Company  | 299 |
|  XXIV  | Leadership                                   | 314 |
|  XXV   | The Primary Working Group                    | 328 |
|  XXVI  | Entry into the Group and Group Attitudes     | 338 |

|        |                              |     |
|--------|------------------------------|-----|
| XXVII  | The Hawthorne Investigations | 351 |
| XXVIII | The Object of the Exercise   | 366 |
| Notes on Reading |                    | 379 |
| Index            |                    | 381 |

# Part I

# General Psychology

CHAPTER I

# The Study of Human Behaviour From Classical Thought to the Scientific Method

PSYCHOLOGY is the study of people—how they behave as individuals and how they react to each other in groups. It has been a centre of interest from the earliest times, and for hundreds of years writers have put forward theories about human nature. Some of these read rather oddly nowadays but in their time they carried a certain authority. Just what these theories were based on, however, is a question of some importance, for the methods of reasoning have undergone a considerable change in the last few centuries. For example, a question which occupied the minds of scholars in the Middle Ages was said to have been—

"How many angels can dance together on the point of a needle?"

In actual fact it is very doubtful if many of them ever really spent much time in it, but whether they did or not, it provides a useful illustration of how men thought five hundred years or more ago.

The reasoning used to answer this question was as follows—

1. An angel, as an incorporeal being, has neither limbs nor body and consequently takes up no room in space.

2. Nevertheless angels can occupy a position in space, for we think of them as being present in a particular place at any one time.

3. It follows, therefore, that an angel could be present on the point of a needle. But as he would take up no room there, there would be nothing to prevent him from being joined by another angel. Both being incorporeal, the two together would take up no more room than the first one alone.

4. In the same way, these two could be joined by a third, a fourth, a fifth and many more, until an infinite number had congregated.

Millions of angels, therefore, could dance together on the point of a needle without any danger of jostling or getting in each other's way, and if you follow the four steps in the reasoning carefully you will be bound to admit that this has the appearance of being a logical, though perhaps not a practically useful, conclusion.

### THE DEDUCTIVE METHOD

This is an example of *deduction* or reasoning from general principles to a particular conclusion. As we have seen, it starts off with two principles which were held to be self-evident, or acceptable to anyone without any need for further discussion or proof. They were—

1. That angels, having no solid bodies, take up no room in space.
2. That angels can nevertheless be located in space.

If these are accepted as true—and in those days when people were more inclined to accept the idea of angels than we perhaps are today, there was thought to be little need to examine them further—then the somewhat surprising conclusion that millions could dance on the point of a needle follows naturally and inevitably.

Up till about four hundred years ago most formal reasoning followed the deductive method. This is not to say that scholars were exclusively preoccupied with flippancies like these, but nevertheless it did result in our knowledge of the world about us being sadly imprecise and unsystematic. The ancient philosophers had built up a theory of the universe with the Earth at the centre and a series of concentric spheres carrying the various stars and planets grouped around it. The other "elements," Water, Air, and Fire, had their appropriate places in the scheme to which they were supposed to have a natural tendency to return. Ingenious and plausible as these theories undoubtedly were, they had little basis in exact observation. With the sweeping away of classical civilization by the Barbarian invasions the advance of knowledge slowed down; these theories were all that were left to explain the natural world, and they came to be accepted without further scrutiny. Conclusions were drawn from them which have only the most superficial relationship to the actual facts of experience.

For example, the four "elements" which were thought to underlie all matter, Earth, Air, Fire, and Water, were held

# FROM CLASSICAL THOUGHT TO SCIENTIFIC METHOD 5

each to have its characteristic "humour." Men's temperaments were thus supposed to be governed by the proportions of the different elements in their bodies. If a man had too much of the fiery element in his body, his temperament would be affected by the hot, dry humours which characterized it. He would be liable, in consequence, to fits of anger or irritation and thus would be known as a "choleric" man. Similarly with someone who had too much of the earthy element: he would suffer from the dull and heavy humours which characterized it, and would be "phlegmatic" in temperament.

No one had ever identified actual fire or earth in anyone's body, though they found substances which they believed partook of their nature. This did not prevent them from drawing such loose, though superficially plausible generalizations and treating them as explanations of everyday occurrences. Being based on unsound original principles, they were usually unsatisfactory and often misleading, though many hold sway in popular thought today.

## THE DECISIVE STEP

There was little chance of any real progress in our understanding of the natural world so long as these methods of thought dominated men's minds. In the sixteenth and seventeenth centuries, however, changes began to take place and new observations began to show that many of the older theories did not account satisfactorily for what was actually happening. The astronomers gained more knowledge of the movements of the planets, the physicians of what went on inside the body, others studied the qualities of various substances, while some began to deal with magnetic attraction. Developments in mathematics made it possible to see new relationships between these data and for a time it was obvious that the old theories were quite inadequate although no one had produced anything which was capable of taking their place.

It was at this time that an Englishman, Francis Bacon, Lord Keeper to Queen Elizabeth, pointed out the unsatisfactoriness of the existing state of knowledge. Most of what was accepted as self-evident, he said, had never been verified by observation of what actually takes place in nature. The so-called general principles were thoroughly unreliable, but nevertheless they had been exalted into a system of original causes which purported to underlie everything that happened in the world of nature. Most of the reasoning from these "first principles" was bound to lead to thoroughly unsatisfactory conclusions.

Now as most reasoning up till then had followed the deductive method there was little hope of progress. In this method everything depends on the principles from which we start and as these were unsound, because they were not based on exact observation, the conclusions were bound to be faulty. There is very little science, or natural knowledge, worthy of the name before the beginning of the seventeenth century.

Bacon's remedy for this unsatisfactory state of affairs was a quite simple reversal of the process. Instead of starting with general principles, he wanted to start with the facts—facts gathered from observation of a number of cases of the subject under review. Once enough cases had been studied, Bacon held, the similarities and regularities observed among them would quickly lead to the principles by which they were governed. This is known as the *Inductive method*, which starts with particular instances and works from them to the general principles.

### SCIENCE AND THE INDUCTIVE METHOD

Probably the first great natural scientist was Sir Isaac Newton, whose work illustrates the effectiveness of Bacon's method. Among other things, he collected many of the observations which had been made about the movements of heavenly bodies—facts gained by observation, as Bacon had said. The fall of the apple suggested to him that the earth was exerting a pull on smaller bodies around it, and this gave him the clue to the principle of gravitation which explained how the planets were held in their courses by the pull they exerted on each other. Applying this principle, he worked out the position of the stars and planets mathematically and decided where each should be in relation to the others. When he compared his conclusions with his observation of the actual positions, he found that each was in its right place and that therefore his theory fitted the facts.

From Newton onwards the scope of natural knowledge has

been constantly extended. Physics, chemistry, astronomy, biology, and many other fields have yielded up their secrets when subjected to systematic study by the scientific method. It is unnecessary to follow the development of science in detail, or to call attention to the mass of scientific knowledge now available which touches our daily lives at so many points, but a word may be said about the method.

Briefly, the scientific method falls into three stages—

*First*, as Bacon said, comes the systematic observation of what actually happens. Data must be assembled which must be exact and which should whenever possible be in the form of measurements, for only in such quantitative form can they be easily classified and their regularities studied. It was Lord Kelvin who said "Science begins with measurement."

*Secondly* comes the search for an explanation which will fit the facts. Several of these possible explanations, or *hypotheses*, may be tried, until one has been found which seems to account for everything accurately and comprehensively.

*Thirdly* comes the decisive stage of establishing whether this hypothesis is the correct one. This is done by *experiment*, or the devising of crucial situations in which the predictive value of the hypothesis can be tested. If it fits all the facts, the result of the experiment will be what would be expected according to that hypothesis. If it does not fit all the facts the result will be unexpected and another hypothesis must be found.

### HUMAN BEHAVIOUR

From the beginning of recorded history men have been interested in themselves, in human motivation, in the differences between individuals and in anything else which concerns human behaviour. Classical literature is full of speculations about why people do certain things, and a number of explanations and descriptions of certain areas of human behaviour are put forward.

Occasionally these are interesting and illuminating but in most cases they suffer from the defects we have referred to above. Lacking any adequate basis of observation they are usually no more than generalizations with some superficial plausibility but little real value as explanations of human conduct. The search continued, however, and each century has its quota of treatises about human behaviour, for it was felt that some understanding of the principles by which man's actions were governed would be of great practical as well as theoretical value.

We may note two trends, therefore. On the one hand, there is a continuing interest in human behaviour and a desire to find the underlying principles which would explain it. On the other, there is the development of the scientific method which had so greatly increased our knowledge of the natural world during the last three hundred years or so. Sooner or later someone was going to take this method, which had proved so useful in other fields, and apply it to those problems which had proved so interesting and yet so baffling for so long.

THE BEGINNINGS OF EXPERIMENTAL PSYCHOLOGY

It was in the latter part of last century that this development took place. First in Germany, then in other countries, laboratories were opened for the systematic study of human behaviour and data began to be collected about certain aspects of it. The questions mapped out for study were much more modest than those which had hitherto occupied the minds of scholars, but they were at least matters which could be observed carefully and systematically, and the results of these observations could be subjected to proper classification and analysis.

Gradually a body of knowledge began to be built up. It was concerned with undramatic matters like learning and remembering, with how we see and hear, and so on. There were many gaps—indeed there still are gaps—in the understanding of human behaviour, and there were many problems which did not seem to yield easily to scientific study. The great difference, however, was that the new knowledge was verifiable, that is to say, anyone who cared could repeat the experiments for himself and would reach the same conclusions. Experimental psychology might have been a late arrival among the sciences, but a science it remained none the less, for its conclusions were no longer the mere speculations of inspired individuals. They had been reached by the established processes of observation, hypothesis, and experiment, and though the principles so far uncovered might be relatively few, they could rank with the results of the older sciences as items of established, verifiable knowledge.

There are, however, difficulties, most of which arise from one or other of two sources. The first concerns measurement, to which reference has already been made. While the physical scientists could begin with the standard units already in existence for the measurement of dimensions, weight and so on, the early experimental psychologists enjoyed no such advantage. They had frequently to devise their own units of measurement for the phenomena they were observing and this in many cases proved a difficult task. The essential point about a unit of measurement is that it shall be objective and capable of giving the same results when used by a number of different individuals in a series of different observations. In observing human behaviour, however, it is not unknown for two individuals to record quite different happenings on the same occasion. Moreover, the behaviour itself can change as soon as it is subjected to systematic observation. The collecting of objective data about human behaviour, therefore, presents serious problems.

The second set of difficulties concerns the establishment of hypotheses by experiment. In the physical sciences it has proved possible, with the necessary ingenuity, to devise crucial situations which will prove whether or not a suggested explanation can be relied upon. But when studying human behaviour, this is not so easy. In an experiment it is normally essential that all the factors in the situation should be brought under exact control and only one allowed to vary at a time. In studying human beings, however, while some of the variables can be kept under control, can we be sure that all the people being studied are trying equally hard, that they are taking the situation equally seriously, that they each attach the same importance to every factor? This is by no means certain and there is, in consequence, a reservation in the minds of some people about the results of such experiments. Situations set up artificially in a laboratory are not real life, and the hypotheses established by these means are not always accepted universally as explaining human behaviour in the workaday world of ordinary life.

## THE SOURCES OF EXPERIENCE

All our knowledge of the outside world must come to us in the first place through our *senses*. In the early stages of psychological study, therefore, some time was spent in investigating how the senses work and how they convey their information to the brain. Some account of this is given in Chapter II. But it soon became obvious that only a few of the manifold happenings which pass before our eyes, ears and other sense-organs really make any impression on us. The phenomenon of *attention*, therefore, also called for investigation. Even those sensations to which we pay attention, however, have to be put together and fitted into the general pattern of our experience before they have much meaning, and consequently the transformation of sensations into *perceptions* had also to be studied. Sometimes, of course, we can attach the wrong meaning to what we see or hear because we have been influenced by a misleading *suggestion*. Attention, perception, and suggestion, then, form the subject-matter of Chapter III.

When the variations between human and animal behaviour came to be studied, it was soon apparent that one of the main differences between the two was that human beings had a much greater power of trying things out "in their heads." This links up with the study of *imagery* or calling up the impressions of sensations without our sense-organs actually being stimulated. When the traces of experiences we have had in the past are gone over again in this way we have the phenomenon of *memory*. Again when we try out our memories of what has happened in the past and our images of what might happen in the future in different combinations we are, in fact, *thinking*. Imagery, memory, and thinking are dealt with in Chapter IV.

Another difference between man and various animals is his much greater range and speed of *learning*. This was subjected to a great deal of systematic study and an outline of the various methods of learning and the conditions which govern it is given in Chapter V.

Nothing so far has been said about why an individual might want to learn one thing rather than another, or about the drives that *motivate* him. There has been some controversy about the instincts or urges which lie at the basis of all behaviour, and along with the feelings or *emotions* which follow the achievement or non-achievement of our goals, these have proved among the most difficult points to clarify. Some measure of agreement, however, has now been reached and these subjects are dealt with in Chapters VI and VII.

All the foregoing matters concern the normal person, and *general psychology* and its methods of study are concerned in the first place with normal behaviour. There is, however, a minority of abnormal persons who either through congenital defect or mental illness do not behave like others. The study and treatment of abnormal behaviour forms the subject-matter of *psychiatry* and a few details of this are given in Chapter VIII.

It is not suggested that the studies of psychologists followed this chronological order. Many of these subjects were being studied at the same time in different parts of the world, and at present research is being carried on in one place or another on all of them. Such a sequence, however, provides a reasonably logical order in which to arrange our knowledge of the individual, the sources of his experience, his methods of arranging and comprehending it, and his motivation and feelings. It will accordingly be followed in the first section of this book.

### SCIENCE AND VALUE JUDGEMENTS

The systematic approach to the physical sciences which began a few hundred years ago has led to a greater understanding of cause and effect in the physical world. We no longer think that storms and floods are sent by the Almighty to punish the wicked, but are rather the result of unbalanced natural forces. This deeper insight carries with it the possibility of influencing these cause-and-effect processes and making them work in the way which suits our convenience. As a result, we have gained a considerable degree of control over the natural world. We may not yet be able to prevent storms and floods, but we can at least predict that they are likely to happen and take action to protect ourselves. In other ways, we can control the processes of combustion to provide flexible sources of power; we can use these to drive trains, motor cars and aeroplanes. We can also talk to each other over long distances by means of telephones and wireless; and we have begun to explore areas of space beyond the Earth's atmosphere. We are, in fact, manipulating the forces of Nature to make life more comfortable and convenient for ourselves. And we are able to do this as a result of several hundred years study of the physical sciences.

In the social or behavioural sciences, however, we are much further behind. This is partly because systematic study in these fields began much later than in the physical sciences, and partly because of the difficulties in applying the scientific method that were touched on above. We are, nevertheless, beginning to uncover some of the cause-and-effect processes in human behaviour and we might be said to be in a similar position to the physical sciences at the beginning of the 18th century. We can now glimpse the possibility of influencing or controlling these cause-and-effect processes.

In some ways this can be an exhilarating prospect, but in others it can be rather frightening. Insight into the structure of the atom has made it possible to provide cheap electricity on a very wide scale, which could improve the standard of living of large numbers of people. But it also made possible the atomic bomb, modern versions of which could wipe out the whole human race. The scientific knowledge on which both these results depend remains neutral in itself, but the use to which this knowledge is put can be either constructive or destructive. The same will apply to the behavioural sciences. Our insight into the cause-and-effect processes in the human mind is beginning to deepen and to extend in range and will go on doing so with increasing speed. That we shall use this insight to make life a more satisfactory experience for more human beings does not necessarily follow. The means of doing so will be at our disposal, but whether we shall use these means for this purpose remains to be seen. It will be equally possible to turn them in the other direction, to limit the scope of the individual and control his thinking and actions in the way that suits the established authorities. Value judgements thus enter into the situation, and we must ensure that too great a concentration on the scientific method does not blind us to the fundamental importance of these.

## SUMMARY

1. What are the two principal methods of reasoning?

First there is the deductive method by which we start from generally accepted principles and reach particular conclusions, and second there is the inductive method by which we start with particular observations and work out the general principles which would account for them. Though science appears to rely mainly on the inductive reasoning, both methods are essential to constructive thought.

2. What are the essential steps in the scientific method?

First, the collection of factual data, their classification and analysis.

Second, the propounding of a hypothesis or possible explanation.

Third, the verification of that hypothesis by checking it against further data, usually in the form of an experiment.

3. How did experimental psychology come to appear as a science?

When the scientific method came to be applied to the study of human behaviour in the latter part of the nineteenth century. Only then did conclusions come to be reached which could be verified by repeating the observations and experiments.

4. Are there any difficulties in the application of the scientific method to the study of human behaviour?

One set of difficulties is concerned with measurement, for there are few standard units which can be readily applied in experimental psychology and it is not always easy to devise new methods of measurement which are objective. The other set arises from the difficulty of devising experimental situations which can be controlled so as to test hypotheses, and at the same time are adequate representations of real life. However, in the same way as we have assumed a good deal of control over Nature, we are beginning to understand some of the cause-and-effect processes in human behaviour. The eventual outcome, be it good or evil, depends on us and on value judgements.

CHAPTER II

# The Senses

THE individual person lives in a world which is occupied also by other human beings, animals, vegetable growths, and numerous material objects. He must, therefore, have some means of knowing what is going on around him if he is to keep out of the way of what is harmful and find his path safely among the other inhabitants of his living-space. Without some means of keeping in touch with his environment he would be an easy victim for those animals which are quicker and stronger than himself or even for such obvious dangers as falling off high places and breaking his bones.

Knowledge of the happenings in the outside world reaches us through our senses. The senses of sight, of hearing, of smell, and so on, enable us to receive news of certain kinds of happening and thus to keep in touch with what is going on around us. If we were to be deprived of any one of these senses we should have to live under a very grave handicap for we should lose one of our means of contact with the outside world. If we were to be deprived of all our senses we should indeed be in a sorry state.

The study of human individuals, then, might well begin with a survey of the kinds of impression they are capable of receiving from the environment in which they live. Most of this chapter, therefore, will be devoted to a description of the principal sense-organs and their workings.

### THE SENSE OF SIGHT

First, and in many ways most important, is the means whereby we receive impressions of the shape of things around us, their distance from us, their colour and the texture of their surfaces. These impressions come through our eyes which are like two cameras, each with lens, diaphragm and shutter, throwing images of the objects before them on to a sensitive plate behind.

In a camera the rays of light reflected by an object are concentrated by the lens and an image is projected on to the film or plate at the back. Should the light be too bright it can be modified by narrowing the aperture in front of the lens by means of a movable diaphragm.

Many of the parts in the human eye are much the same as in a camera. The lens catches the rays of light reflected by an object and concentrates them as in a camera, the only difference

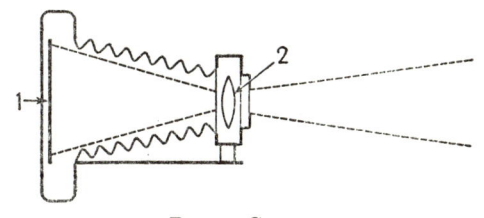

FIG. 1. CAMERA
(1. Sensitive film; 2. Lens)

being that in the human eye the lens can alter its curvature so as to focus on objects at different distances away. The place of the diaphragm in a camera is taken by the iris in the eye: this is the ring of grey, blue, or brown which surrounds the pupil, or black opening through which the light reaches the

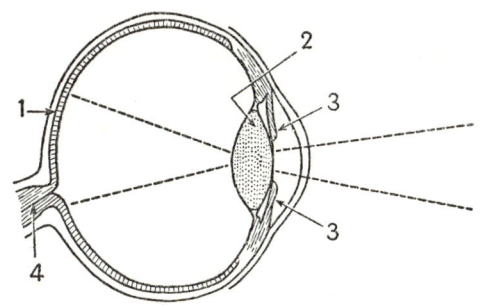

FIG. 2. THE HUMAN EYE
(1. Retina; 2. Lens; 3. Iris; 4. Optic nerve)

lens. When the light is dull and it becomes difficult to see, the iris shrinks to a narrow rim and the pupil becomes large so as to admit as much light as possible to the eye. In a bright light, however, as when we turn to face an electric light bulb for example, the iris will spread inwards leaving only a very small pupil and thus shutting out more of the light which might otherwise prove dazzling.

The place of the sensitive film in the camera is taken by a series of nerve-endings at the back of the eye-ball. These are known as the retina and are sensitive to different shades of light and dark, and to colours. When an image is projected on the retina by the lens, therefore, the reaction of the nerve-endings to it enables a record of its shape, outline, colour, and

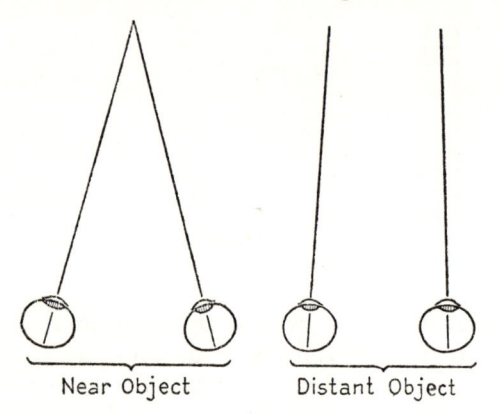

Near Object        Distant Object

Fig. 3. Focusing on Objects at Different Distances

so on to be transmitted to the brain by means of the optic nerve, to which all the nerve-endings in the retina are led.

This—a rather over-simplified description—shows how visual impressions of the appearance of objects around us can be conveyed through our eyes to the brain. We are thus able to "see" the outside world and to distinguish the objects which exist in it. We can also judge the distance of various objects from us partly by the differences in their size, and partly by the fact that we have two eyes which must turn inwards if they are to focus on an object which is close to us, and outwards when they are confronted by something further away.

### THE SENSE OF HEARING

In addition to the appearance of the outside world, however, there is the question of the noises which are found in it. When objects are struck or rubbed together or when air is forced through a narrow opening, sound-waves are set going which may be important as a warning of danger or as a means of conveying a message. It is advisable that human beings and indeed most animals should have some means of receiving or "hearing" these sound-waves. This means is provided by our ears.

Some distance within each ear there is a tightly-stretched membrane known as the ear-drum, to which is attached a small piece of bone known as the "hammer." When sound waves strike the ear-drum they cause it to vibrate and this in turn agitates the hammer causing it to beat upon another small

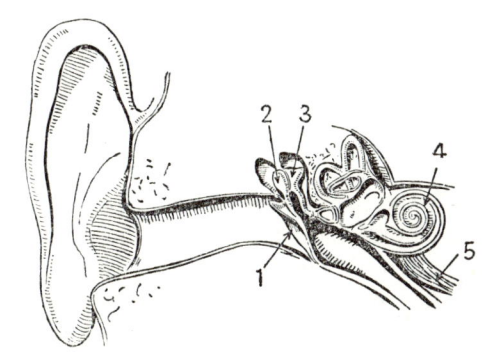

FIG. 4. THE HUMAN EAR
(1. Ear-drum; 2. Hammer; 3. Anvil; 4. Liquid-filled tubes; 5. Auditory nerve)

piece of bone known as the "anvil." This in turn is connected to a series of tubes filled with liquid in which small hair-like nerve-endings are suspended. As the vibrations from the hammer and anvil pass up and down these tubes they agitate the nerve-endings with the result that impulses corresponding to the original sounds pass up the auditory nerve into the brain.

Differences in the loudness of sounds can be distinguished and differences in the pitch or "wave-length" can be picked up by these nerve-endings. We can also decide where the sounds are coming from by the fact that they tend to strike our two ears in slightly different ways.

### THE SENSE OF SMELL

Another "long-range" sense, that is to say one that can tell us about objects at a distance as distinct from those which are actually in contact with our bodies, is the sense of smell. At the top of the inside of each nostril there are *olfactory* cells, and when small particles of gas are inhaled with the air we breathe these cells react to them and send a nerve-current along the olfactory nerve to the brain.

Thus if there is anything in the vicinity which gives off a gas, the particles of which are carried into our nostrils and excite the olfactory cells, we shall be aware of an odour, that is to say we shall "smell" the substance which is giving off the gas.

The sense of smell is not of anything like the same importance among human beings as are sight and hearing. We have, for example, very few names for smells and we have usually to describe them by reference to their source, such as the smell of violets, cigar smoke, or bad fish. At the same time our sense of smell is very quickly fatigued and thus becomes ineffective. It is the newcomer to a factory who remarks that a process has an unpleasant smell; once he has been there for some time he may no longer notice it.

Among animals it is probable that the sense of smell is more acute and more highly developed. In a dog's world the smells and their meaning are much more varied and exciting than in the world of human beings.

### THE SENSE OF TASTE

When we take certain substances into our mouths we become aware that they have a characteristic taste. This is due to their coming in contact with nerve-endings called taste-buds which are found in little pits mainly on the tongue, though there are a few situated on the soft palate and around the tonsils.

Any liquid in our mouth, or any solid which is sufficiently chewed and mixed with saliva to be semi-liquid, will run into these little pits and come into contact with the taste-buds. If it is a sweet substance certain of the nerve-endings will react to it and a message to that effect will be sent along a nerve-channel to the brain. If it is a sour substance, other nerve-endings will react and send a different message to the brain; similarly with salt and bitter substances, making up the four fundamental tastes.

Taste and smell are closely linked up, and many of what we imagine to be characteristic tastes of certain things, such as coffee, are in fact odours. If our nose is plugged and we shut our eyes we cannot distinguish coffee from a weak solution of quinine.

### THE SKIN SENSES

We are now familiar with the idea that our senses work by means of nerve-mechanisms which are made up of the following parts—

1. Nerve-endings, which are so arranged that they can receive a certain kind of stimulation such as light, colour, and shape in the retina of the eye, sound in the cochlea of the ear, gaseous particles in the nose, and so on. These are called the "receptors," or in simpler language the "receivers."

2. A nerve-fibre, which transmits the stimulation received by the nerve-endings to

3. The brain, where these stimulations are interpreted or understood.

In our skin there are also many nerve-endings, some of which respond to light pressure and some to deep pressure. These are quite separate from each other and send their messages along quite different channels to the brain. They are separate also from the nerve-endings which are sensitive to heat and cold. These can be stimulated separately, and when we touch one with a fine pointed pencil it will send word back to the brain that there is something hot touching the skin while if we touch another of these nerve-endings it will send a message back that it is in contact with something cold.

In addition to these there are also some fine nerve-endings which act as receptors for pain. Pain can result from the over-stimulation of any nerve-endings—think how unpleasant it is to be dazzled by a sudden blinding light or deafened by a very loud noise—but these additional receptors in the skin serve to warn us of any damage or injury to it.

### THE KINAESTHETIC SENSE

In addition to these easily recognized senses, we are able to know about the position or movement of our limbs by nerve-mechanisms which end in our muscles and tendons. By means of these we know whether our legs are bent or stretched out without looking to see. In the same way, when we make a vigorous movement such as swinging a hammer we get the feel of it by means of this "kinaesthetic" sense.

### THE SENSE OF BALANCE

Besides knowing about the position of our bodies in space, however, we are able to know about our balance from a series of nerve-endings suspended in the fluid which runs in a complex series of canals inside our ears. Any movement of our head causes this fluid to flow back or forward in these canals thus swaying the nerve-endings. From these, messages are conveyed back to the brain about the movement of the head and hence the angle at which it and the body are balanced.

If we are subjected to rapid swaying and changes of balance the movement of the fluid will be considerably greater. This may upset the sense of balance and can produce giddiness and nausea in some people. Those who dislike spending any time in a rapidly rolling and pitching ship are sensitive to these disturbances of the semicircular canals and in consequence suffer from "sea-sickness."

### OTHER SENSES

There are also nerve-endings in our digestive organs, sex organs, throat, and other internal parts of our body. Some of these convey information about our physical requirements, as when a sensation of dryness in the throat is associated with thirst or when stomach contractions are linked up with hunger. In other circumstances they tell us something about our bodily state and needs.

### OUR SENSORY EQUIPMENT

This discussion has perhaps led us rather a long way from the traditional "five senses"—sight, hearing, touch, taste, and smell. We have, in fact, added at least five more—heat, cold, pain, balance, and the kinaesthetic sense—without exhausting the list. All these senses definitely exist, for each has its own distinct and separate nerve structures, capable of being stimulated by a certain kind of activity and no other, and of conveying information about it to the brain. The brain is situated at the inner end of all these nerve structures and acts as a kind of control room. It has its outgoing channels of communication also, but these do not concern us here; we are thinking of the brain as a receiving station to which information about happenings outside our own body, as well as inside it, passes from the sense-organs along certain nerve-paths.

The workings of the human body are always fascinating to study, and from this aspect we have laid out the details of an interesting and complex picture. Let us put them together in terms of an ordinary person and his means of knowing what is going on about him. Protected by walls of bone in the top of his head lies his brain, at the centre of a complex system of nerves. In front are two eyes which he can move and focus in different directions, and which are constantly picking up visual information of the happenings around him and transmitting them back to the brain. On either side are his ears, registering any noises which are going on and sending them into the receiving station. Protruding in front is his nose, picking up any smells and passing on news about them to the same place. By means of these three senses he can find out about happenings which are some distance away from his body.

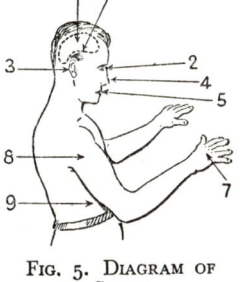

When our ordinary person comes close enough to touch anything he can bring more senses into play to find out about it. His skin senses will tell his brain if it is hot or cold, if it is pressing on him, or if it is damaging his skin and thus causing pain. He may put it in his mouth and thus bring it in contact with the taste-buds on his tongue which in turn will pass back news about whether it is sweet or sour, and so on. His brain will thus be kept informed about anything that is in contact with various parts of his body.

But his body is mobile, and his arms and legs can be swung in various directions; the kinaesthetic sense will keep his brain in touch with their movement and positions, while if his body swings away from an upright position, his sense of balance will send the appropriate messages to the receiving station.

FIG. 5. DIAGRAM OF SENSES

(1. Brain—receiving system;
2. Eyes—sense of sight;
3. Ears—sense of hearing;
4. Nose—sense of smell;
5. Tongue—sense of taste;
6. Semicircular canals—sense of balance;
7. Skin senses—heat, pressure, pain, etc;
8. Kinaesthetic sense—movement of muscles;
9. Visceral senses.)

Should any unpleasant pressures or discomforts arise in his internal organs, information will pass along "the usual channels" so that the brain is warned of any untoward development.

We are equipped, therefore, with a very remarkable series of mechanisms for knowing what is going on outside ourselves, between ourselves and the outside world, and within our own bodies. All our knowledge must come in the first place through the channels of our senses, so that our study must start with this brief sketch of their working. But while the senses provide the raw material, so to speak, a lot has to be done with the information they provide, before it is fully comprehensible.

## SUMMARY

1. What are the means whereby we know what is going on within and around ourselves?

All our information comes in the first place through our senses, sight, hearing, etc. Each of these has an end-organ (such as the eye or ear) which is designed to register certain kinds of happening. News of these passes along nerve-paths till it reaches the brain which acts as a kind of receiving station.

2. How does the sense of sight work?

The end-organ is the eye, in which images of the objects in front of it are thrown by a lens on to a sensitive surface composed of nerve-endings at the back (the retina). This can register light and shade, movement and colour, and pass these impressions back to the brain by means of the optic nerve.

3. How does the sense of hearing work?

The end-organ is the ear, within which is a piece of membrane (the ear-drum) which vibrates in sympathy with any sound waves which may strike it. These vibrations are passed by means of small pieces of bone (the hammer, anvil, etc.) into tubes filled with liquid. Nerve-endings suspended in this liquid translate the vibrations into nerve-impulses and pass them to the brain by means of the auditory nerve.

4. How does the sense of smell work?

The end-organs are nerve-endings at the top of each nostril. These react to any gaseous particles in the air which is breathed through the nose, and transmit information about them to the brain through the olfactory nerve.

5. How does the sense of taste work?

Taste-buds located in pits on the tongue and other mouth surfaces form the end-organs. Liquids flowing into the pits cause these buds to react to their taste. The taste-buds then send messages to the brain by means of the appropriate nerve.

6. What does the sense of touch consist of?

There are a number of different kinds of nerve-ending in the skin. Some of these respond to heat and some to cold; some respond to light pressure and some to heavy pressure; some again respond to pain. Each of these end-organs passes its information along an appropriate nerve-channel to the brain.

7. What senses tell us about the position and movement of our bodies?

Nerve-endings in our muscles act as end-organs for the kinaesthetic sense. These transmit information about the position of our limbs or about their movements. Within the ear, there is a complex system of canals filled with liquid which reacts to alterations in our balance. These form the end-organs for the sense of balance.

8. Are there any other senses?

Certain of our internal organs (bowels, bladder, etc.) have nerve-endings in them which can transmit information about changes in them along appropriate nerve-channels to the brain.

CHAPTER III

## Attention and Perception

Now that we know something of how an individual keeps in touch with the outside world we have a picture of him receiving a continuous stream of information from his sense-organs, all of which is conveyed to his brain along the appropriate nerve-channels. It may be worth while to pause here for a moment and think what your sense-organs are telling you about what is going on just now. Your eyes will be seeing this line of type; your ears, are they hearing any noises in the room or beyond it? Your nose, can it smell anything cooking, or is it giving you any information about the cigarette you may be smoking? Have you anything in your mouth and if so, what does your tongue tell you about its taste? What about your skin sensations? Your fingers will probably be in contact with the cover and the pages of this book. What temperature are they? Are the pages cooler than the cover? Can you feel the weight of your clothes on different parts of your body, and are you aware of the pressure of your own weight on the chair you are sitting on? Have you any painful spots on your skin, such as where you cut yourself shaving?

Your kinaesthetic sense will be telling you something about the position of your limbs and whether they are in motion or at rest. What do your semicircular canals tell you about your balance? Are you sitting upright or leaning back so that you need support from the cushions behind you? Is there any news from your inside? Or do the nerve-endings there report that all is quiet and comfortable?

If you have carried out this survey of the information given by your senses—or sensations as it is more accurate to call it—you will realize that there is too much of it for you to deal with all at the same time. If you try to think of all your sensations at once, you may succeed in keeping several of them in mind but you will probably be unable to concentrate on what you are reading.

In day-to-day life, however, if all this mass of sensation is being passed continuously along the appropriate nerve-channels to your brain, how do you in fact deal with it?

MAKING SELECTIONS FROM AMONG OUR SENSATIONS

The answer is, of course, that we remain largely unaware of a great many of our sensations in normal life. Until you stopped to think of the noises, smells, tastes, and pressures about you just now, you had been to a great extent unconscious of them. It was only when you began to pay attention to them that they came into your consciousness.

This brings us to the next question we must consider. Out of the mass of sensation which is presented to us at any one time we make a selection by turning our "attention" on certain items. We single out these sensations and bring them fully into the centre of our awareness, while we allow the remainder to pass unheeded or at the most we let them remain in the margin of consciousness. That is to say, we may be paying attention mainly to what we are reading while at the same time we are pleasantly aware of the taste of a piece of chocolate we happen to be sucking, though we are not giving much attention to it. We may be just aware of the light beside us, but we may be largely unconscious of the warmth of the fire and the position of our limbs as we lie comfortably stretched out in an armchair.

Of course, all this may change quite drastically and suddenly. If the telephone rings we shall shift our attention to lifting it up and answering it, and forget about our book. If a spark leaps out of the fire and sets light to our trousers our attention will move at once to the heat and pain on our skin. And if the fire begins to smoke our attention will be caught by the unpleasant odours which thus assail our nose.

This matter of "paying attention," therefore, means that we make a selection of the sensations which are being presented to us, bringing some into the centre of our consciousness, while others remain on the edge, or outside altogether.

*Why do Things Catch our Attention?*

In some cases we do not have to make any effort to direct our attention to certain sensations. They call attention to themselves so that it becomes impossible to disregard them. Is it possible to classify the kinds of sensation which do this and the reasons why they do so? In other words, can we classify the attention-catching qualities in sensations? If we could, our classifications would have considerable practical significance. In advertising, for example, it is important to know how to catch the attention of passers-by.

Broadly speaking, the intensity of a sensation will have a great deal to do with its attention-catching properties. We might disregard a slight noise beside us, but when someone begins to operate a pneumatic chisel or throw sheets of corrugated iron off a truck they catch our attention without difficulty. The loudness of a sound, the brightness of a light, the keenness of a pain, the strength of a smell—all these have a lot to do with the amount of attention they attract. It is possible to imagine cases where such sensations are of so overpowering an intensity that they leave us practically no attention for anything else. Severe pain, for example, can come near to blotting out our awareness of most other sensations.

Change or movement has a lot to do with attracting our attention. This is illustrated most obviously in the sense of sight, for when we are looking at a landscape any animal or bird which moves catches the eye at once. Nor has this escaped the attention of advertisers or display experts, for a great deal of ingenuity is exerted in devising mechanisms to produce some kind of movement in shop windows—electric signs that change colour, figures that jump about or perform little contortions. An illuminated legend that can switch itself off and on will attract far more attention than one that remains on all the time.

In other cases also, change in the sensation will attract attention: a sound that grows louder or softer, one that starts and stops or changes its note will force us to take notice of it when a continuous unbroken sound might remain outside our consciousness. This fact is known to the accomplished speaker, who continually varies his tone, sinking his voice to a whisper then suddenly raising it on a note of urgency. In this way he can hold the attention of his audience much better than someone with a monotonous delivery who never pauses or changes his tone. Lecturers with this kind of delivery ought not to be surprised when they become aware that their hearers' attention is straying.

Repetition also will attract attention, provided it does not have the opposite effect of becoming monotonous. A single tap might escape notice, while a series might force themselves on our awareness. Continued repetition, on the other hand, might cause them to become so familiar that they would fade into the background of consciousness.

Things which have some kind of systematic arrangement tend to call attention to themselves, whereas those which are merely a jumble will be passed by. Symmetrical patterns and closed figures gain attention—facts which make it worth while to take trouble over advertising layout to ensure that it is well spaced, neatly set out, and surrounded by a border.

Lastly, any novel sensation tends to catch attention. We notice at once any unfamiliar object in a well-known background in the same way as we notice a familiar object in an unusual setting. A policeman's helmet on our family hat-rack would at once catch the eye, while if we are attending a public ceremony the sight of a colleague on the platform will evoke the involuntary remark, "Look, there's old so-and-so."

*The Direction of Attention*

Attention does not entirely depend, however, on particular sensations attracting it to themselves; to some extent it can be consciously directed. We can say to ourselves, "I am going to listen or watch closely for the next half-hour," and we can be to some extent successful in doing so. Of course, if there is something else going on which tends to distract our attention this will be more difficult, and the greater the distraction the greater the effort needed to keep our attention fixed.

It is easy to over-estimate our powers of consciously directing our attention. In World War 2 it became apparent that radar-watchers were missing a certain proportion of signals while they were on watch. A series of experiments were carried out in which a pre-planned programme of signals was shown over a two-hour period to a number of subjects, this being the normal "watch." The subjects of the experiment noted down the signals they observed and when these were compared with the programme, the number of missed signals could be accurately determined. It became apparent that after a comparatively short time, say twenty minutes or half an hour, the proportion of missed signals began to mount up. Accordingly the timing of the watches was reorganized so thas full use could be made of the period during which the watcher could concentrate his attention successfully.

At the same time, attention can be unconsciously directed so that we notice anything which links up with what touches us closely. Birth and death, our own advancement, the fear of disease, these are practically universal in their appeal. We shall be on the look-out, unconsciously but continually, for anything which refers to them.

This fact is of use again in the advertising world. Suggestions that a product appeals particularly to men of distinction will fit into our continuous interest in putting ourselves into that category and we shall be unconsciously on the look-out for anything that supports it. Fear, again, is never far from our minds and we shall tend to pick out and attend to anything which might contain a threat to our security. Horror stories in magazines or newspapers never lack readers.

Temporary attitudes and moods will also affect the direction of attention. When we are feeling rather inadequate and sorry for ourselves we shall be quick to notice any slight or fancied insults. We attend, in fact, to anything which happens to fit in with our interests or attitudes of the moment, and we may remain quite blind to sensations which do not make any such appeal.

*What Happens when we Pay Attention?*

The actual manner in which we bring our attention to bear on something, or bring a sensation into the focus of consciousness, is fairly complex. If we think of a terrier standing in front of a rat-hole we shall have a good overall picture of attention which we may analyse into the following component parts—

In the first place the receptors of the sense-organs are adjusted so as best to catch the sensations to which attention is being paid. The terrier will be turned to face the hole so that its eyes will be focused on it and its ears will be pricked so as to catch the slightest sound from it.

Secondly there will be postural adjustments: the terrier will stand with its forelegs spread out and its head and shoulders lowered towards the hole. This will involve the third element in attention which consists of certain muscle tensions. If you listen carefully for a few moments you will find that your neck and shoulder muscles have become tensed up and when you stop listening you will be aware of a distinct relaxation in them.

Lastly, and to some extent involved in the foregoing, attention implies an increased clarity of sensation in the area we are attending to. We may be gazing idly about us, but as soon as our attention is fixed the objects in our view will be more exactly focused and will become sharper and clearer. We may be listening to nothing in particular, aware of a vague jumble of sounds about us, but when our attention is caught we shall distinguish the individual sounds more carefully from the background.

### PERCEPTION

Knowing what is going on in the outside world, however, is not merely a matter of paying attention to certain sensations. Something must be added before the result has any meaning. These sensations must be organized into *concepts*.

In the first place, we shall probably have several different sensations from an object at the same time. Suppose we are presented with an apple: our eyes will inform us that it is approximately spherical in shape and that it is green, yellow, and red in colour; our fingers will tell us that it has a smooth skin which is cool to the touch and that the indentations in either end have a harder, slightly brittle substance in them.

When we put this object to our nose we shall be conscious of a sweet but rather sharp odour from it, while if we shake it beside our ear we may hear something rattling inside. If we bite the object we shall find that beneath the skin there is firm flesh from which some drops of liquid run and which has a pleasantly sweet, tart taste.

All of these sensations added together constitute our experience of the fruit, though they came from different groups of sense-organs. The first thing that happens to simple sensations, then, is that they must be given some sort of organization, and those which emanate from the same source must be grouped together, whether they come through eyes, ears, nose, and so on.

This process of organization starts in babyhood and goes on with increasing speed and variety throughout childhood and adolescence. It is an essential element in our understanding of the outside world and is an active process; that is to say, it is something we ourselves do to the sensations singled out for our attention. We shall get an entirely wrong idea if we think of our minds remaining passive while information comes to them along the sensory nerves. We are, in fact, busy all the time putting different sensations together, comparing them with each other, moving our heads to get a better view and adding more sensations to complete the organization and make it more meaningful.

*Relating Sensations to Past Experience*

But in addition to this grouping and organizing of our sensations there is some reference to sensations we have had in the past and to the ways we have represented them to ourselves.

For example, when we have arranged the sight, smell, feel and taste of the object referred to above we shall say to ourselves "This object is substantially the same as the ones which have given me the same set of sensations in the past. These objects I have been accustomed to think of as 'apples,' for I have heard other people speaking of them in that way." This classification of new sensations in relation to those we have had in the past is the process of conceptualization. It depends largely on the formation of *concepts*, or mental models which we form in our minds to provide a framework into which we can fit our sensations. It is the concepts we form in our minds which give meaning to what our senses tell us about the world around us. Unless we can add a concept to a sensation picked out by our attention, that sensation will be meaningless. And unless we share common concepts with other people we shall be unable to communicate with them. An Englishman uses the word "apple" to denote the concept we have been describing. A Frenchman, however, would use the word "pomme" and if each were confined to his own language, neither would know what the other was talking about.

The process of singling out sensations by means of attention and interpreting them in terms of concepts is known as "perception" and it is going on all the time. To a great extent it depends on past experience, or on the equipment of concepts we already have. We interpret our new sensations in terms of these concepts, for even though we have never had exactly the same set of sensations before we are likely to say to ourselves "Here is something which looks red and spherical, it has a fruity smell and feels cool and smooth. When bitten it is softer and more liquid than an apple and has rather a different taste." We learn in due course that this object which in many ways resembles an apple though it differs in others is called a "tomato." We have thus acquired a new concept with which to interpret these new sensations.

In many cases, of course, we work on only a limited number of sensations from an object. The mere sight of an apple will be enough for us to apply the right concept to it, and it will enable us to call up for ourselves images of the other sensations we should expect to get from it. Similarly, when we recognize a house, we only see the near side of it and perhaps one end and part of the roof. We supply the far wall and the other end from our existing concepts of houses as well as the space inside which we should expect to find split up into rooms. This can go wrong of course, and some practical jokes depend on presenting a sensation which triggers off the wrong concept. Suggestion plays a large part in this and an example is given when this is discussed in a later section.

## *The Perception of Wholes*

It is important to emphasize that we do not add up our individual sensations one by one and make sense of the total but rather that the concept clicks into place as soon as the pattern establishes itself. The organization is implicit in the perception, not something which is added afterwards. Take, for example, Fig. 6 on page 32.

We do not see eight small circles and then arrange them in the form of a diamond; we rather perceive a diamond-shaped figure, and then note that it is made up of eight small circles. This has been made clear by the investigations of the *Gestalt* school of psychologists.

The word *Gestalt* is German and means "shape" or "form." It has come to be used in psychology in the sense of a whole-made-up-of-parts, and emphasizes that the whole has a quality which is over and above the sum of the individual parts. Perhaps the word "pattern" or "configuration" would convey the meaning just as well, but the original word *Gestalt* continues to be used.

The distinctive contribution made by the *Gestalt* school is to correct the tendency towards thinking of perception as a process of adding sensations together one by one until the total picture emerges. This tendency is probably inevitable when one tries to explain the perceptual process or to describe how sensations are organized by our minds. It is necessary to be clear, however, that what we perceive first is the organization of the sensations; we see a pattern or hear a tune. The separation of the different colours or the splitting up of the individual notes is something that happens later.

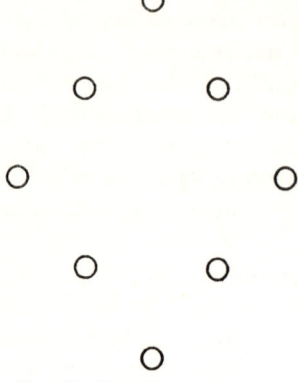

FIG. 6. THE PERCEPTION OF WHOLES

*Mistakes in Perception*

This habit of supplying the missing parts sometimes leads us into mistakes. When we see a large jug standing in a basin on the wash-stand of a rather old-fashioned hotel we usually assume it to be full of water and thus fairly heavy. If we go to lift it up and it turns out to be empty we shall get a slight shock when its weight proves to be so much less than we had expected. There has been a fault in the perceptual process, that is to say we have organized our sensations about the jug and related them wrongly to our past experience of such objects, the result being that we thought we were confronted by a full jug, when in fact it was an empty one.

Such mistakes happen when the context leads us to supply qualities to an object which in actual fact it does not possess. There are a few well-known illusions which illustrate this, such as the Muller-Lyer illusion of two horizontal lines with "whiskers" on the end. The one below appears longer to most people because of the context, i.e. the "whiskers"; these being differently arranged in the line above tend to make it appear shorter.

An equally fruitful source of mistakes in perception is our own expectation or mental set. If we are expecting a particular bus for example, and another with superficial similarities turns up instead, we may step aboard without noticing the difference.

In the ordinary way of life, however, such mistakes are relatively infrequent, rather surprisingly so when we realize how far our normal perceptions depend on a limited number of sensations, a familiar context, and a particular set of expectations. If we went through life examining everything from every angle before we made up our mind whether it was a chair, a table or a bookcase, we should never be able to compete with the mass of sensation which is presented to us. There is no time for all this, and in point of fact we arrive at most of our perceptions by a very few sensory cues related very quickly and at times superficially to our previous experience.

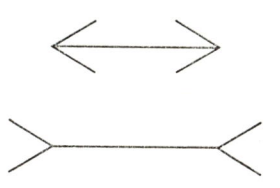

Fig. 7 The Muller-Lyer Illusion

## SUGGESTION

There is, however, one point about these mistakes in perception which we might consider further: this is the question of suggestion. When we are led to assume the presence of something which is not actually there it is due to our adding up our sensations, relating them to our previous experience and getting the wrong answer. Sometimes this happens when the cues are so arranged that we are led to expect the wrong total situation, and sometimes it is due to the wrong mental set in ourselves. Either way the wrong answer has been *suggested* to us.

Suppose, for example, we are walking across a moor and we see a patch of green vegetation which appears to be growing on solid ground. When we step on it and it sinks beneath our weight we realize that our assumption was wrong and our new and more correct perception is of a piece of marsh. The original and misleading perception of solid ground was suggested by the appearance of the vegetation and our own eagerness to get across the moor.

Many of the practical jokes which so amused the last generation depended on this process of suggestion. Sir Osbert

Sitwell describes a chair, purchased by his father for the entertainment of visitors, which presented an appearance of great strength and solidity; it suggested, in fact, that it would be capable of supporting the weight of any normal person who wished to sit down on it. The chair was, however, so constructed that when sat upon it collapsed at once, a situation which Sir Osbert's father thought vastly amusing until by mistake he sat on it himself. Any "joke-shop" will furnish examples of similar bits of apparatus designed to suggest a misleading total situation.

*The Role of Other People in Suggestion*

The intervention of another individual, however, opens up wider possibilities of suggestion. When the sensory stimuli are vague and indefinite it is sometimes possible to make people see or hear what is not there by judicious prompting. The same happens when experience becomes difficult to classify. To some extent the prestige of the person making the suggestion will affect the situation; if the managing director sees a small fault in something there is usually a number of others who will quite sincerely see it also.

At the same time, individuals vary in the degree to which they are suggestible. Various tests have been designed, one of which consists in playing a gramophone record which repeats the words " You are falling, you are falling forward," in an urgent and insistent tone. Some people can be made to sway noticeably back and forward when listening to this record and even to lose their balance. Others remain quite still and unaffected.

Past experience can be distorted by means of suggestion and people can be made to remember things that never happened. Situations have been arranged where someone comes into a classroom while a lecture is going on; such an incident will be noted by most people but few will pay much attention to the details. If they are asked later "How many books was he carrying?" such a question will suggest that he had at least two. The members of the class will therefore reply with random numbers, such as "three," "four," "two," and so on, though in fact the intruder was empty-handed.

## SUMMARY

1. Can our brains deal with all the sensations which are being transmitted to them at any one time?

No. Our various sense-organs are pouring in too great a mass of information for them to deal with. We must make some kind of selection, bringing certain sensations into the centre of our awareness, while certain others may remain on the edge. The remaining sensations are largely disregarded. This process of selecting certain sensations is called attention.

2. What causes certain sensations to catch our attention more easily than others?

Attention depends to some extent on—
(*a*) the intensity of a sensation (loudness of a sound, brightness of a light, etc.);
(*b*) whether it changes in intensity or position;
(*c*) whether the sensation is repeated;
(*d*) the systematic arrangement of sensations;
(*e*) whether the sensation is novel or unexpected.

3. Does the catching of attention depend solely on the sensation?

No. We can direct our attention consciously on certain things. At the same time it may be directed unconsciously by our desires, our fears or our particular interests.

4. What actually happens when we direct our attention in some particular way?

Our sense-organs will be so directed as to catch any sensations which may come from that particular quarter, and our posture will be adjusted so as to facilitate this. Certain muscle tensions will develop in the effort to focus our sense-organs in the desired direction so that any sensations will be as sharp and clear as possible.

5. Is our understanding of the outside world simply a matter of receiving sensations?

No. Crude sensations by themselves are of very little use. They must be organized into concepts, those from the same source which come through different sense-organs being put together, and related to our previous experience. This process is called perception.

6. How far is perception an active process?

Very largely. Our minds must constantly be at work on our sensations; otherwise they will have little or no meaning. In normal life we work on a surprisingly small number of sensory cues, supplying a large part from the context or from our previous experience.

7. Are our perceptions always accurate?

Not necessarily. By relying so much on the context and by supplying the missing elements for ourselves we may occasionally make mistakes. This is particularly so when the context is misleading or when our own expectations lead us to supply evidence which is not in fact there.

8. Can these mistaken perceptions be influenced by other people?

It is possible so to manipulate the context that an individual is encouraged to supply incorrect additional evidence for himself. This process is known as suggestion.

9. What factors cause suggestions to be effective?

The strength of an individual's own expectations will cause him to respond more easily to suggestion, though here there are wide differences between individuals. The prestige of the person who makes the suggestion will have a lot to do with its effectiveness.

CHAPTER IV

# Imagery, Memory, and Thinking

WHILE we rely on our senses to tell us what is happening in the world around us, not all of our experience depends on our senses. It is possible to lie with our eyes shut in a sound-proofed room and have quite an exciting time, though none of our sense-organs is actually stimulated. We can, for example, imagine the tinkle of a mandolin, or the rumble of an approaching train, we can smell again the perfume of a rose or call up the image of a mountain landscape before our closed eyes. This power of experiencing sensations without the stimuli being actually present before our sense-organs—of smelling a rose when it isn't there—is known as "imagery" and is a very important element in our mental life. It plays an important part, for example, in the formation of concepts.

## IMAGERY

Images are of various kinds, some being straightforward recollections of what has already happened. We can call up an image of old so-and-so's face when he realized he was drinking the managing director's coffee; or of the crashing noise we heard when a bus hit a lorry broadside on. These images are simply a repeat of sensations we have already had.

But we can also call up images of things that have never happened, or which are never likely to happen outside a cinema. We can imagine a dog saying "Blimey! Call this a bone?" or an all-in wrestling match taking place in Westminster Abbey. We have never seen or heard of these occurrences, though we may have experienced their constituent parts—an all-in wrestling match in a sports stadium and a service in the Abbey. We have put the parts together into a different pattern in our imagination, and so, to a certain extent, we have created something new.

Since images are rather like sensations which happen without the appropriate sense-organ being actually stimulated, it follows that we can have as many different kinds of images as we have different kinds of sensation. This is, in fact, the case and we have talked above of visual images, when we call up a picture of something we have seen or might see, such as the wrestlers or the Abbey service. We have also talked of auditory images, when we imagine a sound such as the crashing of glass. We can also have kinaesthetic images, as when we think of swinging a golf club or aiming a blow at someone we dislike, and we can have images of pain, heat or cold as when we reproduce the sensation of putting our hand into very hot water, and feel again that split second's delay before the pain really makes itself felt. We can also have olfactory images as when we think of the smell of flowers or of food being cooked.

*Individual Differences in Imagery*

When we try to study the imagery of different people we come across various difficulties. In studying sensation, for example, it is not difficult to control the stimulus, say by increasing the temperature of two metal plates each by so many degrees at a time. We can then say to an individual "Which of the two is the hotter?" with some expectation of getting a fairly precise and sensible reply. But images do not depend on the actual stimulation of sense-organs, in fact they are quite independent of them, for some people can imagine a symphony of Beethoven's through the din of a pneumatic drill. At the same time, images are much less steady and distinct than sensations and if, having persuaded someone to imagine the smell of orange blossom, you ask him if the image is still strong and distinct, he may have to confess that the elusive perfume of the flowers has turned into a strong odour of fried onions.

With all these difficulties, however, it has proved possible to find out a little about imagery and to compare the relative clarity of different images and the frequency with which they occur in our mental life. Visual images seem to come first on the list, being both clearer and more definite, and occurring more often than others. This is not unexpected, because of the great importance of sight to man and because images in other senses are frequently accompanied by visual images as well. If we try to imagine the taste of a fried potato chip we shall usually think of the appearance of one at the same time.

Auditory imagery seems to come next on the list. Again this is not unexpected, for sounds play the next most important part to sight in our sensory experience. The least clear and the least frequent images in human experience seem to be those of pain and smell. The latter sensation plays only a minor part in our ordinary life, though in the life of certain animals it is of much greater importance.

But the studies of imagery have brought to light another fact of great practical importance: this is the difference in individuals' power of imagery. While to most people visual imagery is important, there are some to whom auditory or kinaesthetic imagery is of much greater importance. Such people will tend to think in terms of the sound of peoples' voices rather than their appearance, the "feel" of tools and movements rather than their shapes or the drawings from which they are made. When a highly skilled workman happens to think of his job in these ways he may find it very difficult to pass on his knowledge to others and indeed when we talk to such people we may be aware by their halting speech and continual gestures that they are having great difficulty in expressing themselves. It is not uncommon to hear a tradesman say, "Oh, I can't explain exactly what I mean, but if I had my tools here I could soon show you."

*Cases where Images can be Confused with Real Life*

In ordinary life there is not much danger of mixing up images with actual sensations of what is happening around us, though at times faint sensations can be confused with images. If someone is made to listen to an irregular succession of very low sounds he can sometimes be persuaded, by such questions as "Wasn't that one now?" or "Did you catch that one?" to hear what is not actually there. Similarly with very faint pictures on a screen, people will sometimes mistake one of their visual images for reality. This links up with what we were saying about suggestion, but such examples are of little significance in ordinary life.

When people do begin to confuse their images with happenings in the real world, we think of them as ill in some way or other. There is a certain condition, much beloved by music-hall comedians, in which an individual who has been drinking seriously over a long period imagines that he is being pursued by long slimy snakes and may even see and feel them crawling over his body. Such images are called hallucinations, and while they may be very tragic and distressing when they occur, they belong to the realm of mental or physical illness rather than to the ordinary experience of the normal person.

There is, however, one type of imagery in which images are so sharp and distinct that they seem almost to have the steadiness of real sensations. This is known as *eidetic imagery* and is quite usual among children between the ages of ten and fifteen, though it is not very common among adults. If we look at the following arrangement of letters for about a minute—

|   |   |   |
|---|---|---|
| X | R | B |
| L | J | Z |
| C | F | Q |

the normal person is usually confident that he can repeat the letters in the order in which they are normally read (XRB LJZCFQ, beginning at the top left-hand corner and reading each line in succession from left to right). He would, however, be quite confused if he were asked to read the letters off from right to left, without looking at the square. Anyone with the power of eidetic imagery, however, will have such a steady and distinct image in front of him that he will have no difficulty in reading them from right to left, from top to bottom, diagonally, backwards, or in any order desired.

*The Place of Imagery in Mental Life*

How far is imagery important in our mental life? It may seem rather a waste of time to try to call up a picture of a tree when we are sitting indoors, or to reproduce in imagination the flavour of chocolate on our tongue. In effect, however, it is upon this capacity to experience things in their absence that all mental life ultimately depends. If we had no powers of imagery we should have no awareness of anything except what is actually present to our senses; we should be confined to the immediate present without any ability to recollect the past or to anticipate the future. Our powers of invention would be negligible, and we should be unable to solve any problem that was not immediately present to our senses.

Images are to a great extent the basis for ideas, and we find it difficult or impossible to conceive of anything without some kind of image of it in our minds. Abstract thought, therefore, is greatly facilitated by the use of images, and we can communicate these thoughts to each other by means of them. In many cases we can make use of our images as a means of communication in the shape of maps or diagrams; indeed the more use we make of these in teaching or lecturing the easier will it be for others to understand what we mean and the more certain that they will remember it accurately.

## MEMORY

Memory has a certain connexion with imagery, for it can be thought of as the power of calling up images of what has happened to us in the past. An experience, such as a series of sensations forming the basis of a perception, does not just happen and then pass away. It leaves some kind of trace of itself behind in our minds. These traces may be fleeting, as when the experience has attracted little attention to itself, or they may leave a deeper impression.

Traces of previous experience remain in our minds for a surprisingly long time; occasionally one realizes that events in remote childhood are still present somewhere in one's consciousness along with happenings of more recent date. Some people have gone so far as to say that everything that has ever happened to us has left some kind of trace behind it which is still somewhere in our minds.

These traces can be brought to mind, sometimes with considerable vividness. This is what happens when we recall certain experiences; for example, when a friend says, "Do you remember that delightful day we spent together on the moors?" we call up images of the feel of the sun and the wind, the vista of heather and gorse, the smell of flowers and the sensation of physical fatigue after a long day's walking. His remark has caused us to experience something of these sensations again in the absence of the original conditions and some time after the event.

It is in some manner like this that memory works. Filed away in our minds are the traces of all kinds of experience. This *retentive* process is largely unconscious and sometimes causes surprise when we realize how much is stored away. When we *recall* any of these traces, we bring an image of the original experience into our consciousness and in a manner we go through it again. When something in our actual experience links up with a trace in our minds we *recognize* it and can thus relate it to the original experience. What is called "remembering" in ordinary speech involves some or all of these processes.

*Recall and Recognition*

Recognition is a much simpler process than recall, for if we see or hear something that links up with a trace in our minds recognition takes place automatically. Most people are familiar with the experience of meeting someone after an interval; recognition takes place at once and the images of where and how previous meetings took place come into the mind by themselves. Likewise one hears people frequently saying "I can't just call it to mind, but I should recognize it if I saw it."

When we try to recall something, that is to say when we voluntarily make an effort to call up an image of the original perception, we sometimes have difficulty. For example, if someone were to say to us "What was the name of the lady who was concerned in the early development of radium?" we might have to cast about for some time before we could recall it. We might go through any experience of hearing lectures or reading articles about the subject, we might perhaps recall that it was a French name, and that French ladies are called Madame or Mademoiselle, until finally we hit upon the name "Madame Curie." All this might happen quite quickly or it might take some time, depending on a number of factors.

*Factors Influencing Recall*

For example, if we worked in the radiology department of a hospital and during our training had heard continual reference to the work of the Curies we should probably be able to recall the name at once. This would be due to the fact that we had heard the name repeated many times, because *repetition* of an experience makes it easier to recall.

At the same time, if we are radiologists, the name "Curie" will have a great deal of *meaning* for us, because so many of the early developments, and possibly parts of the modern technique, will derive from their work. To a radiologist the name "Lester Piggott" will have little or no meaning (unless he happens also to be a racing man) and it would be correspondingly difficult to recall.

Another factor which makes things easy to recall is the *intensity of the original stimulus*. If we have ever been in a position of great danger, when we were thoroughly frightened and were only extricated after almost having given up hope, we shall have little difficulty in recalling the experience. When we hear people saying "I shall remember this to my dying day" they are probably speaking the truth, provided that the incident has really had a powerful effect on them.

In one way, however, recall of such experiences is not quite so simple. We may find no difficulty in recalling the general form of the incident but the details may become blurred and distorted. This will be illustrated when we hear witnesses giving an account of an accident—that it was all very terrible, but as to whether the cars were above or below the crossroads, which side of the road they were on and which one was turning in which direction, there will be little or no precision and very slight agreement. The psychology of witness or testimony shows how difficult it is to get an objective and accurate account of the facts some time after.

*Forgetting*

When the traces of previous experience fade in our minds we "forget." To some extent this happens when we have no cause to recall them, but there are too many curious examples of people recalling events in remote childhood for us to be certain that they simply fade out through time until they are not there any longer. It seems more likely that the traces are covered up or blocked by other traces of a similar nature. We may remember a business or home telephone number when we are using it every day, but if we move to another number this second number will overlay the first one until we no longer remember it.

Our mental life is so lively that we are constantly gathering traces of many different kinds; when these follow thick and fast one upon the other there is little chance of any remaining clear and undisturbed in our minds for long.

There are also emotional elements in forgetting, and some experiments suggest that we forget those experiences which have been unpleasant or damaging to our self-esteem. Shock, illness, or emotional disturbance may also have an effect in obliterating, covering up or distorting the traces in our minds.

The process of forgetting can be measured by making people learn various kinds of material off by heart and having

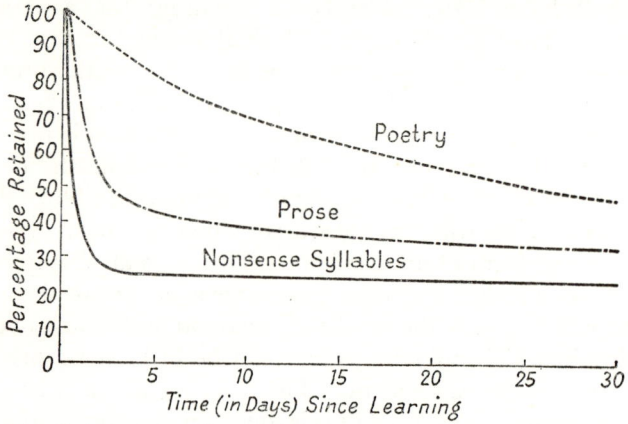

FIG. 8. RETENTION CURVES FOR DIFFERENT TYPES OF MATERIAL
(After J. P. Guildford: *General Psychology*)

them repeat what they have learned each day after. The amount retained can then be measured and plotted on a graph as above. These curves show that forgetting happens quickly immediately after the event and then more slowly; also that the more meaningful the material the less is forgotten.

*Memory Training*

Some of the foregoing can be put to use in improving one's ability to remember certain things. For example, in study it is advisable to read with concentration so that the original experience of the material will be fairly intense. Passive staring at the words on a page will be of little value.

Next, it is well to practise recalling the material you are studying. Rehearsing the main points or writing up summaries will make it easier to recall what you want to learn. This may be facilitated by the use of mnemonics or jingles in which the key points can be memorized by rote, such as those which are, or were, used by Latin masters—

"A dative put remember, pray,
 After envy, spare, obey, . . ." etc.

### THINKING

As we have seen, we are provided with a number of ways of dealing with experience, over and above the actual happenings about which our senses inform us. We have memories of what has happened in the past and images of what might happen in the future and we can fit these together in different concepts so as to try out what might be useful in different situations. This is the process which we might call thinking, and it can vary from mere day-dreaming in which we imagine ourselves as having become suddenly wealthy, to realistic and purposeful reasoning-out of a solution to a particular problem.

In its simplest form reasoning can be seen among certain animals. Presented with a series of doors, several of which open at the same time with food being found always through the middle one, they can remember enough of their previous experience and interpret it sufficiently accurately to go directly after a while to the middle door when a new set is placed before them. So long as the connexions between experiences remain thus simple, obvious and immediate, some animals can work them out for themselves quite as well as small children up to the age of four or five. As soon as the situations become more complex, however, the very limited powers of the animal become apparent and it fails to be able to deal with them.

*Thinking to Some Purpose*

Purposive thinking or reasoning is generally called into play when we are confronted by a difficulty of some kind. So long as we can carry on in our routine manner, meeting the usual situations in the ways that have proved adequate before and living by means of our habitual modes of response, we are not called upon to reason, and most of us do not do so. As soon as these habitual modes of response let us down, however, and we must find a new solution to our problem, we are forced to begin reasoning.

One important step is usually the putting forward of hypotheses, or possible explanations. These will probably be in the form of questions. If a motor-car suddenly stops we ask ourselves "Has it run out of petrol?" thus putting forward the possible explanation that it lacks the fuel on which the engine must run. If people look surprised at our appearance we shall ask ourselves "Have I a smut on my face? Is my hair tousled, my dress in disarray, or have I forgotten some essential article of attire?" thus running over a whole series of such hypotheses.

These hypotheses usually depend on past experience, and their number and adequacy will be largely determined by how much we know about the subject in question. The man who knows a lot about motor-cars will be able to produce many more possible explanations of a stoppage than he who merely knows how to drive and where to put in the petrol, oil, and water.

*Checking our Hypotheses Against the Facts*

Our possible explanations are next evaluated and checked. Much of this can be done symbolically or "in our head." When thinking about our motor-car which has stopped we can say to ourselves, "It can't be short of petrol because I had it filled up yesterday, unless perhaps it's sprung a leak or someone's syphoned some out. It can't be the battery because the horn's still working. There might be a stoppage in the feed pipes or perhaps something's gone wrong with the petrol pump. I'll have to look." Thus before we begin investigating we may have discarded several hypotheses and produced others which we can set about checking by experiment.

This interaction between symbolic processes and real life experience is characteristic of human thought and vastly increases the range of experience that can be dealt with. If we were confined to the actual sensory experiences before us we should have only a limited range of possibilities to try out, while if we had no contact with the facts of experience at all we might become unrealistic and impractical. When we alternate between trying things out in practice and thinking of new possibilities in our heads we begin to forge ahead rapidly and to increase our range of action.

*Mental Set*

The problem about which we are reasoning gives direction to our thought, and ensures that we shall recall experiences that are likely to be relevant. When we get stuck in a motor-car we call up all we ever knew about its workings in an effort to hit on the right explanation for the stoppage. This happens to some extent automatically, for the "mental set" engendered by the problem will ensure that everything relevant comes to the surface. The solution of the problem thus becomes more easy to find, for our mind is crowded with material to work on and we put together various bits of experience and pull them about until we get the right answer.

There may be times, however, when our direction may be the wrong one, and a misleading suggestion at the start may throw us off on the wrong track and make the solution harder by calling up all the wrong associations. This can be illustrated by the Radio programme "Twenty Questions," when occasionally an answer, given in perfectly good faith, creates a misleading impression and sets the questioners off on a wrong track. In the same way, when we are thinking something out we may make a mistake, call up the wrong sort of memories and experiences and go a long way down a blind alley before we realize the mistake and retrace our steps.

*Language*

This process of trying things out symbolically is greatly facilitated by the use of language which in a sense forms a vehicle for thought. More particularly it enables us to express concepts in which are summed up common aspects of things. The word "tree," for example, sums up a great number of things we have experienced, many of which differ quite considerably from each other. Unless we could file them all away neatly in our minds under that heading we should have great difficulty in dealing with such concepts as "That green thing with branches in the churchyard which is like the other green thing in the field which is like the other green thing in the orchard only it is a little smaller," and so on. When all these green things with branches can be grouped together into one concept and given the name "tree" they become much easier to deal with.

The more similarities we see among our experiences the more ideas or concepts we form and the more words we need. These concepts are in a sense condensations of experience, by means of which we isolate the same aspect of a number of different things. Think of the colours for example: we have all seen hundreds and thousands of brown things—brown boots, brown bread, brown cows, and brown earth. This word "brown" isolates and brings together the common aspect in all these things and enables us to apply that concept to various new or imagined experiences.

The more complex our appreciation of experience becomes, the more concepts we shall have and the more words we shall need. This is the difference between the child's simple "Man go in house" experience, and the grown-up's deeper realization that a well-dressed stranger with an air of importance and an assured manner has entered the Town Hall where all the municipal business is transacted, presumably to pay his rates, get a licence for something, or confer with the town clerk about some important development.

## The "Private World" in which the Individual Lives

It will already be obvious that what we are aware of at any one time is no more than a *selection* from the sense impressions that are crowding in upon our nerve-endings. The processes of attention by which this selection has been made have already been discussed, and it will be realized that we are disregarding a great deal more than we are actually taking in. But, in addition to making this selection, what we are aware of is also an *interpretation* of these sense impressions in terms of the concepts which are called up by them. The sense impressions by themselves have no meaning, for they are no more than stimulations of certain physiological mechanisms in our bodies. "Meaning" is something we add for ourselves and it depends almost entirely on the concepts which are brought into play by the sense impressions. Thus, the green things with branches referred to above are only meaningful when they are interpreted by the concept which we have formed in our mind and labelled "tree" and which we know is also used to interpret the same kinds of sense impression by the people among whom we live.

Two people, therefore, presented with the same range of sense impressions, may not each make the same selection and interpretation. The attention of one may be directed or manipulated in a different way from that of the other, while each may attach different concepts to these sense impressions. Thus, each may have an entirely different experience in that same external situation, for each one is having that experience in his own "private world" of selections and interpretations of what is going on around him. This concept of the "private world" is an extremely useful one in the understanding of one's fellow men, for it not only calls attention to the impossibility of entering fully into the experience of another person, it also opens up the subject of differences between the "private worlds" of different people. The dweller in a primitive community, where the concepts in common use are simple and practical and concerned with the routines of everyday life, will have a vastly different experience from the sophisticated Londoner if the two meet on the escalator in the Piccadilly Circus Underground Station. Moreover, the difficulties which each will have in communicating with the other will be considerable, for language is only effective if one can be sure about the concepts which each word will call up in the mind of the other person.

*Communication between "Private Worlds"*

The word "communication" is cropping up with increasing frequency nowadays and when things go wrong, it has become fashionable to describe the difficulty as simply a "failure in communication." This may be true enough, but ought we not to be paying more attention to the prevention of these failures? One way is to keep in mind the private world of the individual with whom one is trying to communicate and to make some effort to find out the meaning he is attaching to what one says to him. This meaning is more important than the words that are used, for even the best phrased and most comprehensive "communication" will be a waste of time if no meaning or the wrong meaning has been attached to it. The only way to keep a check on it is to draw him into discussion, or encourage him to comment on it. If his comments are to the point, then we can be reasonably sure that he has interpreted our words as we had intended him to. If, on the other hand, his comments are wide of the mark, then he has a distorted interpretation of what we have been saying and this must be corrected before going any further. Communication should thus always be a dialogue between the communicator and the recipient if the communicator is to retain any control over the meaning which is attached to what he has said.

Some people's "private worlds" are very simple straightforward places, for they only use a limited range of fairly obvious concepts to interpret their experience. If such a person begins to extend the range of his concepts, however, and if he learns to use more subtle and sophisticated ideas, he will begin to be aware of a great deal more of what is going on around him. The process of education ought to have this as its major aim—to increase the range and subtlety of the concepts which the individual can use and so widen and deepen his awareness of the world and of his own potentialities. One of the functions of art and literature is to enable ordinary people like ourselves to share the experience of the artists and writers and others of great sensitivity and deep awareness by looking at their interpretations in the shape of pictures or writings.

The solving of problems also is carried out in one's "private world." Faced with a difficulty, as has been pointed out above, one calls up all the concepts which bear upon the situation and juggles them around until the right interpretation appears. This is the process of human invention for, by such jugglings around, sometimes the flash of insight happens which leads to a new development. A very long time ago, one of our remote ancestors had such a flash when he got the idea of pushing a stick through a hole in a round piece of wood. This is basically the concept of the wheel, and one does not need to stress its importance in human development. It seems so obvious to us now that we take it completely for granted, but still, no other animal has had that particular flash of insight. The "private worlds" of human beings, therefore, are much more complex and interesting places than those of even the most advanced animals, though again there are considerable differences between one human being and another. It is an interesting and perhaps useful exercise to try to enter in imagination into the "private worlds" of some of our more intellectually distinguished contemporaries. For one of the things which it is within our power to do, and which makes a vast difference to our personal development, is to increase our equipment of concepts, improve our ability to manipulate them and generally make our "private worlds" more interesting and exciting places in which to live.

## SUMMARY

1. What is imagery?

Imagery is the power to experience sensations without the sense-organs being actually stimulated. We can have images of sensations which have happened in the past or of things that have never actually happened. We can have as many different kinds of image as we have senses.

2. Do we all have the same kind of imagery?

This is difficult to say, for images are vague and shifting and tend to disappear when we try to examine them closely. Generally speaking visual and auditory images seem to predominate but different people seem to find one type of imagery coming more or less naturally to them.

3. Are images ever confused with real-life happenings?

Only in cases where we are dealing with very faint indistinct sensations or in illness when we see hallucinations. Children sometimes have very sharp distinct images (eidetic imagery) but they do not confuse them with real life occurrences.

4. What is the use of imagery?

It enables us to experience things in their absence, either re-living past events or anticipating future happenings. Without imagery our mental life would be confined to what is immediately in front of our senses.

5. What are the three elements in memory?

(*a*) Retention, through which traces of our previous experience remain in our minds.

(*b*) Recall, when we bring these traces back into our consciousness and to some extent re-live the experience.

(*c*) Recognition, when we realize that an experience we are having now is similar to one of which there is a trace in our minds.

6. What makes an experience easy to recall?

(*a*) The intensity of the original sensation.
(*b*) How much meaning it had for us.
(*c*) How often it was repeated.
(*d*) The general form which may remain in our mind, though the detail may be forgotten.

7. What are the causes of forgetting?

(*a*) The fading of the original traces.
(*b*) The covering up of them by traces of other similar experiences.
(*c*) Shock or their association with unpleasant experiences.
Forgetting happens rapidly at first and then more slowly.

8. How would you describe the process of thinking?

When we rearrange the experiences we have had into different patterns and by seeing resemblances between them, try out various possibilities and new conformations "in our head" we are thinking.

9. What is the point of thinking?

When our routine methods of dealing with a situation prove ineffective we must think out a new way of dealing with the situation. But not all thinking is purposeful; it may be mere day-dreaming.

10. How do we think out a solution to a problem?

By working out possible explanations or hypotheses and trying them against the facts either in real life or in our heads. The more we know about the problem the more useful hypotheses we shall be able to produce.

## IMAGERY, MEMORY, AND THINKING

11. What gives direction to our thinking?

Usually the problem before us sets us thinking along certain lines, calling up experiences which seem relevant, enabling us to produce suitable hypotheses, and in other ways enabling us to find the solution. Sometimes, however, a wrong mental set will make it more difficult for us to find a solution.

12. Has language anything to do with thought?

We can only deal with experience in thought if we can classify its different aspects under various concepts. We need words to express these concepts precisely. The more concepts we have the more words we shall need.

13. What is the "private world" in which the individual lives?

Each of us makes his own selection from what is coming in through his sense-mechanisms by the process of attention. We also make our own interpretation in terms of the concepts in our minds. Not every one makes the same selection and interpretation, so that what we are aware of at any one moment is a personal and private experience and it is vital to remember this when we are trying to communicate with another person. Those having a wide range of concepts will live in a more interesting "private world" than those whose equipment of concepts is simple and obvious.

CHAPTER V

# The Learning Process

BABIES come into the world puny and unprotected, completely at the mercy of circumstances. Yet in a few years' time they are able to look after themselves to a remarkable extent. This development is in great measure a matter of learning.

Primitive peoples can only provide for their elementary needs by methods which are generally unreliable and inefficient. Their life together is poor and simple compared to the modern industrial community with its high material standard of living and its complex social and cultural life. Part of the difference may depend on the latter's greater resources of technique and materials, but mostly it is a matter of modern man having learned more about how the resources of nature can be exploited and more of the skills on which this depends.

Human development, therefore, is largely a matter of learning. Each year of his life the individual learns more about what goes on around him, while each stage of a community's development depends upon its members learning new skills and ways of thought, new and more complex relationships. If we are to understand human behaviour, therefore, we must know something about the learning process, for learning goes on more or less continually throughout the life of individual and community alike.

## THE CONDITIONED REFLEX

Probably the simplest form of learning is found among animals. By a process known as "conditioning," new behaviour-patterns can be grafted on to those which already exist.

This is probably best illustrated by the experiments of Pavlov, a Russian who was engaged some years ago on the study of digestive processes in dogs. He noticed that the sight and smell of food stimulated the secretions which assist digestion, that is to say when a hungry dog is presented with a savoury-smelling plate of food, saliva will dribble from its mouth, while certain gastric juices will flow in its stomach.

Anyone who has had any acquaintance with dogs will know that this is so, at least so far as the saliva is concerned, for it is an automatic reaction, or reflex action, which happens with any hungry dog whenever food is presented to it.

Pavlov found that if something else happened every time a dog was presented with food this other happening would become so associated with food in the dog's experience that after a time the other happening would be sufficient by itself to start the dog salivating. For example, every time a dog was fed a bell was rung; the dog naturally salivated when its dinner appeared, but after a few days the dog would salivate as soon as the bell was rung, even though no food was presented to it. The dog had, in fact, learned to associate the sound of the bell so closely with the appearance of food that the reaction which the latter automatically brought forth was now called into action by the former. The dog had, in fact, been conditioned to salivate at the sound of a bell.

In case this sounds rather a futile pursuit for a scientist to spend time on, we must, in justice to Pavlov, point out that he used the conditioned reflex mainly as a means of exploring the perceptions of animals and of finding out what they can see and hear. His method consisted in conditioning a dog to dribble at the sound of a bell in the key of A, and then sounding a bell in the key of C. If it dribbled at the new sound this would suggest that the dog noticed no difference between the two bells. If it failed to do so, however, it would be obvious that the dog could discriminate between the two different keys. By means of this method Pavlov found out that dogs' ears can pick up sounds that humans cannot hear. He also found out that dogs are colour blind.

*The Significance of Conditioning*

It is important to be clear about what actually happens during the conditioning process. We start with an already-established pattern of reactions, such as a dog salivating at the sight of food, flinching when hurt, or snuggling against anything warm and comforting. All these reactions follow automatically on particular stimuli, such as the sight of food, pain, or a warm fire. What is to be learned is presented in close association with the original stimulus until it is so linked up with it that the response follows automatically, even when the original stimulus is withdrawn.

This could be shown diagrammatically as follows—

 *Original Stimulus*       *Original Response*
 (The pain of a blow)   →   (Flinching or crying)

This is automatic and inevitable. When, however, pain has been inflicted several times by means of a whip the situation will be as follows—

 *New Stimulus*        *Original Response*
 (Seizing of a whip)
 Associated with    →
 *Original Stimulus*
 (The pain of a blow)   calling forth (Flinching or crying)

When the conditioning is fully established the diagram could be simplified into the following—

 *New Stimulus*       *Original Response*
 (Seizing the whip)   →   (Flinching or crying)

As time goes on the animal may come to associate certain tones of voice or even certain words with the seizing of the whip, and it may show signs of apprehension when it hears these. This is a case of even more remote conditioning from the original stimulus.

Most animal training depends to a great extent on the conditioning process, the right response on the animal's part being associated with rewards, and the wrong responses with the fear of punishment. By degrees more and more complex behaviour-patterns can be built up in this way until the turns produced at the circus are finally perfected. Whatever one may think of these aesthetically, it is interesting to see how the trainers never run any risk of the conditioning breaking down. Each successful trick is rewarded by a suitable titbit, while every time an animal fails it is made to try again and is threatened by gestures or whip-cracking until it achieves the desired performance.

*Conditioning in Human Learning*

In early life a great deal of human learning is probably a matter of conditioning. The baby left alone in a room with an electric fire may crawl towards it in order to play with this pretty brightly-glowing object. If it succeeds it will burn itself more or less severely and from that moment onwards it will distrust brightly-glowing objects in general and electric fires in particular, having associated them with the pain suffered from the original burn.

In the same way its mother represents a source of infinite reassurance and comfort to a small baby, but soon it will appear that certain types of behaviour may cause even the mother to stop being comforting and reassuring. The baby learns to avoid these so far as it can understand and control them. During the first few years of life learning may be largely a matter of sorting out "things that have pleasant results" from "things that have unpleasant results," with moments of frightening bewilderment when behaviour which was expected to have pleasant results unaccountably turns out to have unpleasant results.

Many of our attitudes grow out of this learning process, and many uncritical people will approve of things simply because their early conditioning has taught them to do so. Perhaps we should not over-emphasize the importance of conditioning in human learning, even among small children, because there are other methods, but at least the conditioning process does bring to light one aspect of learning which we cannot overlook, that of motivation.

No one will ever learn anything unless he sees good reason for doing so, and the stronger the reason for learning the quicker and more efficient will the learning process be. Dogs pay little attention to electric bells until they begin to associate them with food. Then they will learn to distinguish between one and another without difficulty. Children have no interest in personal cleanliness until dirty hands become associated with disagreeable consequences. Then they will learn to take some care of their appearance in order to avoid the unpleasantness of a rupture in the good relations with their parents.

### THE DEVELOPMENT OF SKILLS

It may take a little time to establish a conditioned response in an animal, and in the same way it may take some time for a human being to develop a particular skill. Practice or repetition frequently bulks large in the learning process.

This is most clearly seen in the development of some manual skill, such as playing scales on a piano. At first the fingers are clumsy and ill-controlled, the notes are struck unevenly and with differing weight, and the scales are jerky and inaccurate. Gradually, however, control develops and the notes are struck more accurately, the scale becoming smoother and more rhythmic in consequence. The improvement is gradual and continuous, and leaving out the question of learning scales of different keys, it depends entirely on practice.

Any activity which depends on the formation of muscular habits, therefore, such as the playing of a musical instrument, is largely a matter of repetition. One would expect improvement to be directly associated with practice in the sense that every trial was a little better than the one before it. Shown diagrammatically this would mean the following learning curve—

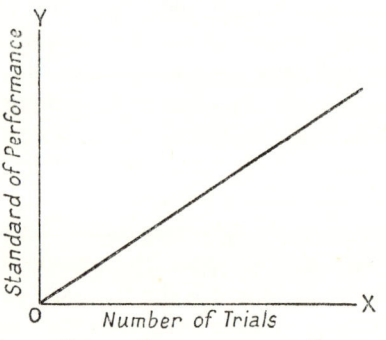

FIG. 9. STEADY IMPROVEMENT BY PRACTICE

If it were possible to find a learning situation which depended solely on the acquisition of simple manual skills, such a curve might be found.

### LEARNING BY INSIGHT

There is, however, another kind of learning which is of great significance in human affairs. This is learning to understand things, a purely intellectual or "ideational" process, which might occur when one is presented with a railway time-table,

# THE LEARNING PROCESS

and asked to find out from the mass of figures and letters the next train for, say, Manchester.

Now the first time we may have to do this it may take us quite a time before we can sort out the connexions between the index and the page numbers, between the stations on the list and the times of the trains. But having got all this clear, the second time we consult a time-table it may take us no time at all to find what we want. The whole thing has become child's play because we have developed enough insight into the time-table to understand how to use it.

Now in a situation which depends entirely on insight, our first trial may take quite a long time, but our second will take no time at all. Our third trial may be only a little better than our second because we may already have reached nearly the limit for that kind of performance. In this case our learning curve will look quite different, showing a quick improvement after the first trial, but very little after the second.

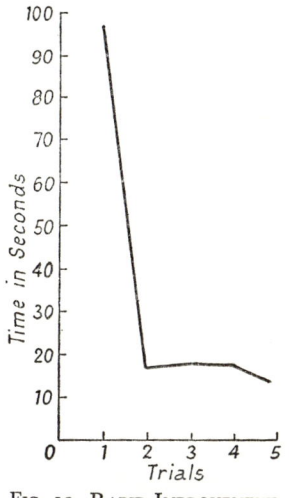

FIG. 10. RAPID IMPROVEMENT BY INSIGHT

Most people can probably identify these two learning processes, practice and insight, from their own experience, and can think of situations where skill is built up slowly by repeated trials, and also of situations where what is to be learned breaks upon one "in a flash." If we could find cases of pure practice learning and pure insight learning we should probably have the two characteristic curves in an extreme form.

### MIXED LEARNING SITUATIONS

In ordinary life, however, we do not find learning situations which depend solely on practice or solely on insight. There may be a bias in one direction or another, but most of them are mixed, practice accounting for a certain amount of steady improvement with insight developing every now and then to produce a sudden leap to a higher standard of performance.

This is borne out, for example, in the ordinary person's experience of learning to ride a bicycle.

At the start one has to learn a number of things at the same time. The pedals must be driven by one's feet smoothly and with the right amount of pressure on each alternate downstroke. One learns to balance by leaning from one side to another to compensate for the varying distribution of weight, and by turning in one direction or another to avoid falling off as the machine wobbles. At the same time one must steer the machine in the direction one wishes to go, put the brakes on when one wishes to slow down, pedal harder uphill or to increase speed, and so on. It is difficult to keep all these things in mind at the same time and so we start off on a level surface with a friend to hold us upright while we master one set of muscular movements, such as pedalling. Practice will soon bring this under control and as the muscular habits develop we can turn our attention to steering the machine and keeping our balance. All the time insights will be developing about the relation of our speed and balance, and of the effect of balance on steering.

As we go on the various muscular movements will form into habit-patterns and will cease to require much of our attention to keep them going. Once the pedalling movements have integrated into a muscular habit-pattern they will drop out of sight, so to speak, and the same will happen to the movements involved in steering, balancing, and so on. More integrations are formed, more insights develop and gradually the whole complex of skills involved in riding a bicycle is built up.

Improvement in such a case will go in fits and starts. There will be periods where little is noticeable and when one is, in fact, wrestling with the pedals and trying to make them go round smoothly. There will also be periods of very rapid improvement, when one discovers that by getting up enough speed one can keep one's balance without difficulty. Practice will indeed make perfect, but there will always be flashes by which we improve more in ten minutes than we have done in the previous week's steady application.

### THE TYPICAL LEARNING CURVE

This process can be shown in the form of a learning curve. A graph is laid out with the number of trials along the X axis and some measurement of performance on the Y axis. It may call for a certain amount of ingenuity to devise an objective criterion of performance. Where the time taken gives an adequate measure, improvement will be shown by the learning curve dropping until the physiological limit is reached, below which it is impossible for any human being's performance to

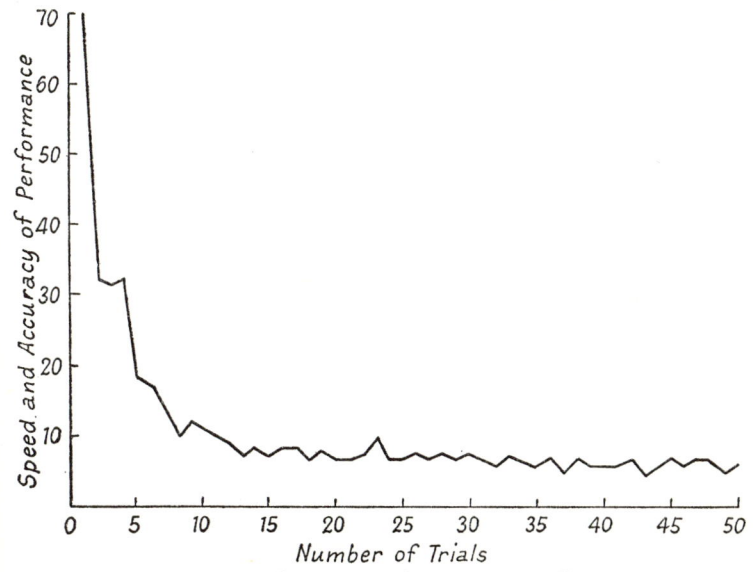

FIG. 11. LEARNING CURVE FOR MIRROR-DRAWING EXPERIMENT

drop. Where, however, the performance must be evaluated on some other basis such as accuracy or smoothness, then improvement will be shown in larger numbers of marks being awarded and the curve will rise until the limit of performance is reached. But whether the nature of the task compels the curve to have an upwards or a downwards tendency the same characteristic form will be found.

Above, for example, is a typical learning curve, built up on mirror-drawing study in a laboratory.

In this case performance has improved rapidly in the first few trials as insights into the unfamiliar task developed. Then it levelled off while practice in the new muscular habits went on. After a little, new insights appeared and the habit-patterns integrated with a consequent rapid improvement in performance. So the learning process proceeds, with flat periods where little or no improvements take place interspersed with rapid jerks where a new level is reached quite suddenly.

Learning curves can most easily be built up in the laboratory on tasks which can be evaluated easily on an objective basis. In case these should look artificial and unconvincing, however, here is a curve for the learning of morse by telegraph operators over a period of weeks.

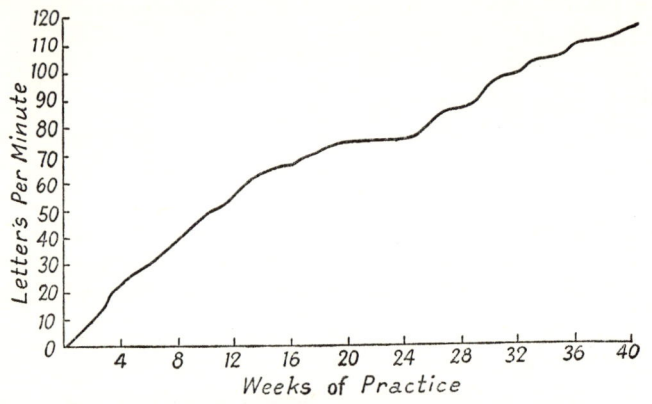

FIG. 12. LEARNING CURVE FOR TELEGRAPH OPERATORS

Here again the characteristic pattern appears.

### DIFFERENCES IN SPEED OF LEARNING

The ability to achieve insight into what has to be learned can have an important limiting effect on the learning situation. In some animal-learning studies several years ago, dogs and cats were shut up in boxes which could be opened by pulling a string or moving a lever while food was displayed to them outside. They responded by making random efforts to open the box, shaking the door, pawing the lock and plunging about until by accident their paw happened to catch in the lever and make the movement necessary to open the door. This became known as "trial-and-error" learning and is indeed characteristic of a situation where insight is inadequate to what has to be learned. A second trial showed the same random behaviour except that the necessary movement might be made a little earlier in the proceedings. Further trials would show further improvements until the animal had understood which movement was necessary to open the box and could make it first time by deliberate intention.

Trial-and-error learning was thought to be characteristic of animals in contra-distinction to man who could short-circuit this process by making many of the initial moves in his head. This view, however, was modified when animals came to be studied in circumstances which were a little more natural than puzzle-boxes in a laboratory. It was found, for example, that dogs could achieve insight into certain situations and solve them first time. For example, if a dog were placed in front of a fence behind which was a plate of food, it could find its way round the end of the fence or through a gap some distance along it. There was little or no random trial-and-error in such a situation for the dog could learn by insight how it should be dealt with.

When a hen was confronted with the same situation it was unable to achieve the necessary insight into it. The hen fell back at once on trial-and-error behaviour, flying against the wire and fluttering about in random undirected trials. Various studies have shown that different animals are capable of achieving insight into situations of different levels of complexity, and it seems apparent that they only fall back on trial-and-error learning when their insight is inadequate.

Of the same nature as trial-and-error learning is learning by imitation. Movements can be copied without any real understanding of their purpose and sequence, as when children or certain animals mimic adult activities.

Some things can be learnt fairly effectively by imitation, as they can by trial-and-error, but these processes always have limitations. Only cut-and-dried routines or "drills" can be learned in this way and without real insight into the situation the learner will always be at the mercy of unexpected happenings. There will always be the danger that the "drills" are put into practice in unsuitable circumstances.

### DANGERS OF CLASSIFICATION

We have described various different aspects of the learning process and it is to be hoped that the reader will find that most of these, on reflection, strike an answering chord in his own experience. But we must not expect to find that any learning process can be neatly described as involving "conditioning," "practice," "insight," "trial-and-error" or "imitation" alone. Most learning situations will depend on some or all of these processes going on at the same time.

Motivation is fundamental to the learning process so that from this point of view there will always be an aspect which recalls the conditioned response. Learning will only take place when what is learned presents itself as a means of obtaining something we already desire. Likewise practice or repetition comes into most learning situations to a greater or less degree; indeed in many cases when a skill is being learned it is only after a certain amount of practice that some insight can be developed at all. Few of us when learning about mechanical things have escaped the humiliating experience of trying all the adjustments we can think of in the hope that one may prove to be right, thus falling back on the trial-and-error learning when our understanding of the situation is defective. Again many of us have gone through motions that we have seen other people use at one stage or another, thus showing how imitative learning can play its part.

But probably insight is most fundamentally important in human learning. This is what has been called the "Aha-experience," when all of a sudden everything clicks into place in our mind and we see the activity to be learned quite clearly and simply. Such an experience is not confined to ideational learning; it can be equally valid when a manual or muscular skill is approaching perfection and one understands exactly how the tool should be used to get a certain effect or how the arms must be swung to bring off a certain shot in golf.

Probably also this method of learning is characteristic of humans with their greater power of trying things out in their head or going over the situation in symbolic terms (see previous chapter), rather than in actual practice. And certainly many of the things that people must learn in a modern industrial community require the exercise of insight before they can be learned effectively.

So many things have to be included in our consideration of the learning process that the reader may find himself being asked to consider incongruities simultaneously. If, however, he thinks of an ascending scale of learning, from animals with rudimentary minds learning simple routines up to human beings with their highly developed powers of perception and thought learning difficult and complex intellectual tasks, he will find that most of the processes described in this chapter will fit in quite easily somewhere in the picture.

## SUMMARY

1. What is the simplest form of learning? How does it work?

Conditioning is the simplest form of the learning process. It takes place when something new is grafted on to an already-existing stimulus-response pattern, such as when a dog is conditioned to salivate at the sound of a bell which is rung at the same time as food is presented.

2. What is the significance of conditioning in animal and human learning?

The training of animals is almost entirely a matter of conditioning, what has to be taught being associated with food or other rewards, while the wrong reactions are associated with punishment or the threat of it. In the earliest years of human life most learning is probably very largely a matter of conditioning.

3. What are the relative parts played by practice and insight in human learning?

The learning of most skills depends largely on practice or repetition which results in the steady but gradual improvement in performance. Learning by insight results in sudden flashes of comprehension which lift the performance at one leap on to a higher level. As most learning situations are mixed the typical learning process shows periods of gradual or even imperceptible improvement through practice, interspersed with rapid improvements when new insights have been achieved.

4. What is a learning curve?

A learning curve is a graph showing the improvements in performance during a learning process. The number of trials or time-scale is laid out on the horizontal axis and the scale of performance on the vertical axis. According to the task to be learned the curve will have different shapes, but in most cases it shows the typical "plateau periods" with periods of sudden improvement.

5. What is trial-and-error learning?

When insight fails, the learner may fall back on random movements, trying everything he can think of until by chance he hits on the right thing to do. This is typical of animal learning whenever the task is beyond the animal's level of insight, but it can also be seen in similar circumstances among human beings. Learning by imitation is also seen when insight fails, the learner copying movements blindly with no comprehension of their purpose or meaning.

CHAPTER VI

# Motivation and Emotion

In our consideration of human behaviour so far we have confined ourselves mainly to *how* things happen, how the senses work, how we remember, how we learn, and so on. We have not yet paid much attention to *why* things happen, why an individual wants to learn something, why he thinks about this or that, and so on.

Yet without considering the "why's" of behaviour we shall be left with a very one-sided and incomplete understanding of human beings. In particular we shall have no clues as to which course an individual is likely to take, because though we may know something of the workings of his mind we shall know nothing of the direction in which he is moving or the goals towards which he is aiming. Any understanding of these goals or directions must depend on some study of the motives of behaviour.

Let us suppose that a small child were presented with a tray on which were displayed a copy of Plato's *Republic*, the connecting-rod of a motor-car engine, a hank of grey wool, and a chocolate. It is practically certain that the child's attention would be attracted first by the chocolate and that left to itself it would pick it up and eat it. It is also highly probable that the child would make an effort to overcome obstacles in order to get at the chocolate, while it would not do so in order to get at the other objects.

If this be accepted as a likely development of such a situation, then it becomes obvious that there is a bond of attraction between the child and the chocolate. We may look at this from two different angles. On the one hand the chocolate has certain properties which make it an attractive object to the child, while on the other, there is something in the child which makes it want the chocolate and which will cause it to make some effort to take it and eat it. In other words, the chocolate is an attractive object to the child, while the child is motivated towards taking and eating the chocolate.

Thus in our understanding of motivation we can, and indeed we must, approach the subject from two points of view. We can think of the objects, or properties of objects, which attract an individual and we can think of the elements in the individual—desires, wishes, and appetites—which will move him towards various objects.

### FUNDAMENTAL HUMAN URGES

In such an obviously complex and intricate field—for all around us people are striving to achieve all sorts of things—our first task must be to try to simplify the issues by getting down to fundamentals. Are there any motives which are sufficiently simple and widely felt that they can be taken to be universal among human beings? In other words, if we take a number of people chosen at random and put them into any situation, is there anything we can be quite certain that they will all do without exception?

There are obviously a few such things that one can be certain of. The desire for food, for example, can be relied on to make itself felt in anyone after about six hours without a meal, and the same will apply to the desire for drink. The same may be said in this climate about a desire to keep warm either by putting clothing on our bodies, or finding warm and sheltered places where we can sit in some protection from the elements. Likewise the desire to sleep will make itself felt in everyone after many hours of activity, while everyone, at one time or another, will feel a desire to associate with other people and at times with the opposite sex.

These simple basic urges—to provide oneself with food and drink, with clothing, rest and shelter, to associate with other people—are universal among human beings because they are necessary to support life. Unless we are conscious of these urges as individuals and are capable of satisfying them we shall starve or freeze to death, and unless as a community we can provide for them we shall cease to exist after a generation or so.

Nor are these urges peculiar to human beings only. Animals also are motivated by them because their survival depends equally on providing for them.

*Variations in the Means of Satisfaction*

The satisfaction of these urges, however, is not always so simple as in the case of the child with the chocolate. In the long run a great deal of planning and forethought will be required to satisfy them and the motivation, to be effective, must provide also for the means of satisfaction of the basic urges. This, of course, is the point at which variation steps in, because while we can be sure that all animals including humans will desire food we cannot be sure what kind of food they will desire or what means they will use to satisfy that desire.

Among the animals the kind of food desired and the means of procuring it tend to become specialized and fixed, and the behaviour-patterns involved become rigid and unvarying to such an extent that the animal's anatomy becomes modified to make it better adapted for the purpose. Cows have satisfied their hunger by eating grass for so many generations that they have developed mouths and digestive organs which are adapted for that purpose only. Tigers, on the other hand, prefer animal food and their bodies and habits are adapted to the pursuit and slaughter of suitable beasts. Both animals desire food and both can provide themselves with it, but it is as fantastic to think of a cow chasing a goat and eating it as it is to imagine a tiger lying happily in a pasture chewing the cud. Moreover, neither animal would want to.

This rigidity and specialization in the means of satisfying their basic needs is characteristic of animal behaviour and at times it is carried to very remarkable lengths. In the provision of a safe environment in which to bring up their young, for example, some insects go through a complicated series of routines such as digging an underground chamber, leaving a paralysed victim for the family to feed on, or laying eggs which will be eaten and pass through the digestive system of another animal. Weaver-birds, for example, build an extraordinarily delicate and intricate nest of leaves and other materials in which to hatch out their eggs and bring up their young.

None of these behaviour-patterns seems to have been learned by the creatures concerned, for each can set about its particular routine and produce the correct result at the first attempt.

Indeed in some cases it is quite impossible that the creature has even seen the complete series of activities carried out in its entirety. Animals in such cases seem to be acting from some inner urge, quite blindly and automatically, and with no comprehension of the outcome. Their behaviour, however, seems to be quite effective in achieving the particular purpose for which it was designed.

These blind, uncomprehended, but effective motivational patterns are known as *instincts*, and this term should be kept for use in describing animal behaviour. Instinctive behaviour has been defined in the following terms—

(*a*) It is the performance of complex trains of activity which involve the whole organism.

(*b*) These trains are of biological value to the species (i.e. they serve to keep it alive).

(*c*) They are similarly performed by all members of the species.

(*d*) They do not have to be learned, but are performed perfectly, or at least adequately at the first attempt.

### HUMAN MOTIVATION

Has instinctual behaviour any place in human life? Does a small child, in other words, begin suddenly to provide for any of its basic needs without having been taught? There may be some examples, such as a baby sucking or getting rid of its waste products, but these are very few. The characteristic thing about human life is that so few behaviour-patterns appear ready-made or are performed similarly by many members of the species. Most behaviour-patterns have to be learned and there are very wide differences between different individuals in them.

Think, for example, of the provision of food. The basic drive is common to all the human race, but people eat meat, vegetables, cereals, fish, fruit, and many other comestibles, down to seal blubber and bird's-nest soup. The balance between these products will vary according to the time of year and the part of the world, while each individual will have his own preferences among what is available. At the same time people will eat in different ways, some with knives and forks, some with chopsticks, and some with their fingers. In providing themselves with food different communities will make different arrangements, some taking up hunting and fishing, some raising flocks and herds, some cultivating the soil, and some trading and exchanging.

All these different methods of satisfying the basic urge for food have to be learned by the individual as he grows up in a community. Thus a small child in the Far East will probably be introduced to rice as soon as his digestion can cope with it, and by the time he is adult his ideas about eating will be expressed in a complex series of behaviour-patterns which may begin with ploughing and planting in the paddy fields and end with a bowl and a pair of chopsticks with some bits of highly spiced fish and vegetables to give some relief to the bulk of the main dish. A western child, on the other hand, will develop an appetite for a whole range of foods, will eat them in a different manner and will think of procuring them in shops and markets for money which he has earned by engaging in quite different activities.

*Motivational Patterns*

What seems to be characteristic of human motivation, then, is that while the basic urges necessary to sustain life remain the same, the means of satisfying them are extremely variable, and have to be learned as the individual develops. This presents quite a different picture from animal motivation because the influence of the community and the individual will make itself more widely felt.

It also makes human motivation very difficult to explain except in the most general terms. We may start with a number of simple drives necessary to maintain life, such as hunger and thirst, a drive towards self-protection which makes us seek warmth and shelter, and a drive towards self-assertion which makes us try to make some impression on our environment. To these we may add simple drives necessary for the continuance of the community such as the sex impulse and an urge to be among other people. Everyone would probably admit that the basic motivational pattern of human beings and of many of the higher animals is something like that, any disagreements being mainly confined to matters of nomenclature.

As soon as we begin to think of the motivation of a particular individual, however, the trouble begins. It is of little interest or value to say that he will feel these basic simple urges; what we want to know is his motivation at this particular moment in terms of the directions and goals he sets himself and the objects which will have an attraction for him. Such a problem will be a highly individual one because it will depend on the following matters—

(*a*) The natural environment which will make certain things possible. A tropical islander will not seek fur from polar bears.

(*b*) The culture-pattern which will have provided certain means of satisfying basic urges and taught him to like them.

(*c*) The immediate social group which will hold out certain values and discourage others.

(*d*) His own pattern of abilities which will make certain things easy of attainment.

(*e*) Habit which will cause him to repeat certain behaviour-patterns.

*Basic Needs and Culturally-determined Methods of Satisfaction*

Can we provide ourselves with a simple framework for the understanding of human motivation? This will run us into the dangers of over-simplification but it is nevertheless necessary if we are to grasp this fundamental problem in psychology. Bearing in mind the essentially complex nature of the issue and making every allowance for individual variations, we might lay down the following categories for the classification of basic human needs. These are—

MATERIAL NEEDS, or everything necessary to maintain our bodies in health, such as food, shelter, means of keeping warm and dry and so on. These are obvious and straightforward, for if we fail to supply them we shall cease to exist, while if we only succeed in partially supplying them, if our diet is inadequate and if we are not properly protected, we shall suffer from deficiency diseases or the other unfortunate accompaniments of a low standard of living.

COMPANIONSHIP NEEDS, or everything associated with living with other people and interacting with them. If the individual does not succeed in satisfying this need, he will feel lonely and unhappy; in the longer term also, this need is important for the survival of the species. If we do not live together, we shall not have families, and if we do not have families, the human race will die out. Moreover, the family is an essential unit in providing children with the protection and affection which is essential to their development in the early stages of life. This heading, therefore, covers needs which are of fundamental biological importance even though they may not be so immediately obvious as the material needs outlined above.

Ego Needs, or everything associated with being an individual as distinct from other individuals. This is quite as fundamental and universal as the other two categories and it can be taken to cover all that the individual does to have some impact on his environment, every attempt to set higher standards for himself, every refusal to be submerged in the mass. Again, if the individual feels that he does not matter or that nobody cares about him as a person, he will feel unhappy and deprived, while in extreme cases he may become pathologically depressed or even run the risk of suicide.

Accepting these three categories for what they are worth, as a means of classifying basic human needs, we should turn our attention mainly to the means of satisfaction. As a generalization we could say that every activity which the individual sets about is undertaken because it appears to him a means of satisfying one or more of these needs. Similarly, every institution in a community owes its continued existence to the fact that it is seen by the members of that community as a satisfaction-pattern. But the way of life of different individuals and communities is so varied that we must make some effort to understand how these needs are being satisfied. The primitive agricultural village with its rather inefficient cultivation of the surrounding soil will provide a low standard of material satisfaction, but the intimate contact with other members of a small social unit may provide a much higher standard of satisfaction for the companionship needs. Similarly, it is not difficult to be a person in a small unit, to satisfy one's ego needs by knowing that one counts for something as an individual and is recognized by other people for one's skills, one's knowledge or one's personal worth. The modern industrial way of life, on the other hand, offers a much higher material standard of satisfaction through its vastly more complex and efficient economic system, but whether it offers the same companionship and ego satisfactions to the ordinary person is a matter for conjecture. A big city can be a very lonely place and the individual can be a very small and insignificant unit in it. Whether the ordinary person has the same overall degree of satisfaction in an industrial city with its high standard of living as he had in the village with its closer companionship and greater opportunities for being known as an individual is a question worth pondering.

## EMOTION

The detached study of human behaviour always risks giving the impression that individuals move about like specimens under a microscope, with this or that characteristic, learning things according to a predetermined method and speed, and moving towards predictable goals in a manner which can always be foreseen. There is something inhuman about it all, something mechanical and predictable which is remarkably uncharacteristic of human life. Something is missing which ought to be taken into consideration if we are to get a true picture of human behaviour. What is it?

In the language of everyday life, we have paid no attention to a person's "feelings." We have allowed no place for that which always accompanies every one of an individual's activities, we have forgotten that whatever he may be doing he will have some feelings about it. It is to this "feeling-tone" if we may call it that, that we must now turn our attention. What do we know about it?

Apart from the fact that some feeling-tone accompanies all our waking and some of our sleeping experiences, we may say in the first place that it has a varying quality. At times it may be pleasant or even very pleasant; at other times it may be unpleasant or acutely so. Then again it may be neither noticeably pleasant or unpleasant, but rather neutral in quality.

We can, of course, establish this fact by observation of ourselves or other people. At any one moment we may think of our feelings and decide whether they are pleasant, unpleasant or neutral, or we may look at another person and make a fairly accurate guess at the state of his emotions by observing his facial appearance, gestures, or voice.

We can also decide, in general terms, the kind of things which will cause a pleasant feeling-tone, and which an unpleasant one. The right degree of fatigue, an armchair by the fire and agreeable companionship usually result in the former, while physical discomfort or the threat of it in the latter.

## The Accompaniments of Emotion

As has been mentioned above, feelings are accompanied by characteristic gestures and behaviour. When we see someone smiling quietly to himself, whose posture is upright with head held high and chest out, we can say with some certainty that his feelings are pleasant. If a child breaks out into fits of laughter and hops and skips and dances, we suppose that its feelings are acutely pleasant. But if we meet someone whose posture has slumped, whose head is bowed and whose shoulders droop, who says little and whose mouth and facial expression have a downward tendency, we can be pretty sure that his feelings are unpleasant. If a child, whose emotions are usually more vivid than those of an adult, breaks down into tears and moans we shall say that its feelings are acutely unpleasant.

All this is a matter of common observation, for such expressions and gestures can be seen among our friends and acquaintances in the course of our daily life. But there are other physical accompaniments of emotion which cannot be seen by ordinary observation because they are concerned with the internal organs of the body. Strong emotion will cause changes in the rate of breathing and also in the pulse rate and blood pressure. These can be measured by the appropriate instruments. Rather curiously, emotion will also cause changes in the electrical resistance of the skin, due to the sweat glands coming into action. These changes can be measured by passing a small current through a portion of the skin and linking it up with a galvanometer. The so-called "lie-detector" depends on instruments like these, for it is simply a means of studying emotional reactions which are not visible to ordinary observation or subject to conscious control.

There are other accompaniments of emotion which depend on rather intricate parts of the nervous system which link up with the "ductless glands." When these glands are stimulated they discharge fluids into the blood stream which cause the digestive processes to be interrupted, counteract fatigue in the muscles, and open wide the air passages in the lungs. All these changes would enable the individual to fight or run away more effectively if he were to be attacked. In ordinary life, however, emotion-provoking situations can seldom be solved by such actions and consequently these changes in the body serve only to interfere with its normal functioning. This is the reason why emotional strain is linked up with various kinds of ill-health such as stomach and digestive ailments—the "psychosomatic" complaints.

*What Causes Emotion?*

A small baby will show emotions in a very simple and easily understood form; its range of emotion will be from pleasant on the one hand, through a neutral state to unpleasant on the other. There will be little more differentiation than this, the emotions being simply a matter of general excitation of feeling. There will be happy feelings, there will be unhappy feelings, or there will be no feelings at all. Beyond this, the emotional life will have no further complications.

The causes of these feelings will be equally straightforward and will in most cases be concerned with the baby's physical comfort or discomfort. When it is warm and well-fed it will be happy and when it is cold, hungry or in pain it will be unhappy.

As we grow up, however, our emotional life becomes more complex. The kinds of situation which arouse emotions increase and become rather more subtle. Pleasant emotions no longer depend on physical well-being alone, but can be aroused by the approbation of our fellows, the successful execution of something we have planned for some time, or the carrying out of some intricate activity at which we are particularly good. Unpleasant emotions can be called out, not only by actual physical discomfort but by the threat of it, by losing the good opinion of one's associates or by the inability to comprehend a situation or to manipulate it in the way one wants. Particular individuals will react differently to the same situation, one experiencing pleasant emotions from it, another remaining quite neutral, while a third experiences unpleasant emotions from it.

*What Different Emotions are There?*

As the situations which provoke emotion develop and become more complex, do the emotions we experience become differentiated into various types? In other words is the simple "happy—neutral—unhappy" pattern of the baby replaced by a number of different "happy" emotions, such as "pleasure," "excitement," "satisfaction," and so on, and a number of different "unhappy" emotions such as "fear," "anger," "hatred," "frustration," and the like?

This is a very difficult question to answer. In ordinary speech we have a large number of words indicating different emotional states and it is generally accepted that, say, "fear" and "rage" are quite distinct and separate. When these come to be studied in the laboratory, however, it has proved impossible to lay down such a clear distinction between them. The behaviour-patterns which give them expression can easily be confused so that when one is presented with a series of records of an individual's behaviour including those of his breathing, pulse rate, and other internal changes, it is possible to say "This person has been suffering from a strong unpleasant emotion," but not to define that emotion as "fear," "anger," "hatred," or anything else, without knowing what caused it.

In the same way the gestures with which we express our emotions depend on the manners of the people we live among. In this country, clapping the hands would generally be interpreted quite correctly as a sign of pleasant emotions, but in China it is a sign of worry or disappointment. Likewise in some families the means of expressing anger is to stamp and shout, whereas in others it is rather to become silent and icily courteous in what few words have to be said.

Attempts to differentiate emotions, therefore, have proved unsatisfactory, and it is difficult to be certain that we have a number of separate ones, each labelled neatly "fear," "love," "horror," and so on. Yet obviously there *are* differences between our emotions, otherwise these different words would not have appeared in the language, nor would they convey a meaning from one person to another. How then can we sum the situation up?

*Conclusion*

We may begin by saying that every experience in life is accompanied by some kind of feeling, or by an awareness that it is happening. In many cases, this feeling will be quite unremarkable and approximately neutral in tone. In such cases we may say that the experience will have aroused no emotion.

In other cases, however, the experience will arouse an emotion, the feeling or awareness which accompanies it being sufficiently strong to draw attention to itself and to have a very definite tone. Such emotions will be accompanied by gestures or expressions which can be seen by other people, and also by changes in the digestive processes, pulse rate, etc., which cannot be seen.

The kinds of experience which call forth emotion will vary with the individual according to the kind of people he has lived among, his own aims, values and ambition, and his own stage of emotional maturity and control. In general, however, emotion will probably be aroused by experiences which threaten or enhance his integrity.

The kinds of emotion we feel can be subdivided broadly into pleasant and unpleasant (those feelings which are merely neutral we shall not consider as emotions). According to the kind of experience which has called them out we may further subdivide them as, for example, a pleasant feeling following close association with an individual to whom we are attracted would be called love or affection, while a similar feeling following the recognition of our achievements by people we respect might be called gratification. Similarly an unpleasant feeling accompanying a threat of physical harm against which we cannot fully protect ourselves might be called fear, while a similar feeling following the discovery of something we had done which was considered unworthy by those we respect might be called shame.

These subdivisions of the pleasant and unpleasant emotions,

however, do not appear to have their own characteristic and distinct behaviour-patterns, and it seems very doubtful whether they can be distinguished one from the other except in terms of the experiences which call them forth.

## SUMMARY

1. What do we mean by motivation?

We are concerned here with what causes one individual to direct his efforts in any particular direction. We may consider it from two points of view—
   (*a*) The external objects which have an attraction to him.
   (*b*) The inward urges which move him in different directions.

2. Is there any common element in motivation?

Basically all human beings and many animals are affected by a few simple fundamental urges which they must satisfy if they are to sustain life. These are food, drink, clothing and shelter, companionship, and the like.

3. What are the characteristics of animal motivation?

Rigidity and specialization seem to be typical of animals in this direction. So much so that highly complex trains of activity emerge in the behaviour of all members of the species, which keep them alive and which seem to be performed adequately at the first trial without being learned.

4. Has this type of instinct any place in human motivation?

Very little. What seems to be characteristic of human motivation is its flexibility in devising means to reach its end, its need to be learned, and its subjection to individual variations.

5. What causes the variations in human motivational patterns?

Such things as the natural environment which makes certain things available; the culture-pattern which leads to certain things being generally accepted; the immediate social group, its attitudes and values; the individual's abilities and habits.

6. What do we mean by emotion?

Emotion is the feeling-tone which accompanies almost all of our activities. It ranges from acutely pleasant, through a neutral zone, to acutely unpleasant, though probably the neutral zone should not accurately be called emotion.

7. What are the accompaniments of emotion?

There are overt signs and gestures such as smiling, crying, clapping the hands or adopting a drooping posture. There are also internal changes in blood pressure, breathing rate, sweating, or in the discharges of ductless glands. These latter cannot be consciously controlled.

8. What causes emotion?

Basically, pleasant happenings cause pleasant emotions and unpleasant happenings cause unpleasant emotions. In childhood the emotional life is simple and is concerned largely with bodily well-being. In adult life the emotional life becomes more varied in consequence of the more varied social existence we lead.

9. Is it possible to differentiate between different emotions such as fear, anger, and the like?

Emotions can be classified broadly as pleasant and unpleasant, for the bodily changes accompanying these are quite clear and distinct. Beyond this, however, it is perhaps impossible to classify emotions except in terms of the situations which have called them out.

CHAPTER VII

# Individual Aims and Attitudes

If we accept the classification of basic human needs outlined in the previous chapter, then each one of us is presented with the same basic problem. We have to find means of satisfying our material, companionship, and ego or "self-actualization" needs in the circumstances in which we find ourselves. If we live in a modern industrial community, the means of satisfying the first will be quite simple and obvious. Money makes it possible to buy any material thing in the local shops, so that if we can provide ourselves with pounds and new pence, this need will be taken care of. The obvious corollary to this, of course, is that anything that will provide us with money will acquire a significance as a means of satisfaction. This explains why people can be persuaded to work at all sorts of tasks, some of which may have little meaning in themselves but serve their purpose as a means of earning a living. In some factories, for example, one can see girls assembling little bits of electronic apparatus, the purpose of which is too technical for them to understand. Nevertheless, they continue applying themselves to their allotted tasks and observing the levels of accuracy demanded, because this means a wage-packet at the end of the week which pays their digs, buys their clothes, and leaves something over for make-up and hair-do's and the occasional evening out. Money is such an infinitely flexible means of material satisfaction that it can be adapted to give a significance to practically any task. If you can get paid for it, it must be worth doing. If you can get paid a bit more, then it's worth working a bit harder.

### NON-MATERIAL NEEDS

There is a certain danger, however, that when we are trying to enlist people's motivation in a task, our thinking stops there. It is not so simple as that, however, as some of the rate-fixers or work-study engineers have found to their cost. We must bear in mind the other needs besides the material ones, which are not always satisfied in such a straightforward manner.

The means of satisfying our companionship needs in the modern world, for example, are fairly complex. When we lived in small village communities where everyone knew everyone else and shared the same ideas, this was simple enough. The individual was born into the community, lived there all his life, belonged there and in fact, had his companionship satisfactions handed to him on a plate. A modern town or city, however, is no longer a community in that sense, but is split up into a number of different groupings—family groups, working groups, spare-time clubs and so on. Each of these is capable of satisfying one's companionship needs, but each will only do so on its own terms. That is to say, each will only give one a feeling of belonging if one conforms to the way of life of that grouping. To be accepted as one of the boys in the local folk-club, one must dress and behave in a certain way, use the appropriate type of language and be knowledgeable about certain performers and certain songs. To be accepted in the local Rotary Club, on the other hand, one must dress quite differently, talk and behave in a manner which the folk-club would described as "square," and have opinions about a number of things which would be similarly unacceptable there. The likelihood of conflict between these various groups becomes immediately obvious.

Each individual also finds himself a member of a number of different groups and is dependent on them for his companionship satisfactions. He must therefore adapt himself to the way of life in each of these groupings. In many cases, this will not be difficult for there may not be much difference between the accepted values in the various groupings which make up his life-pattern. In other cases it may present problems. There will, however, nearly always be one group whose values seem to him the fundamental ones or the "right" ones. This is known as his "reference group" and in some cases may be his family, in others a political or a religious grouping. It will have a considerable influence on his values and opinions on a number of subjects, these being favourable if they accord with the way of life in his reference group, or unfavourable if they clash with it. This individual's reference group is usually the one from which he has derived the maximum companionship satisfaction.

These groups also play a large part in satisfying peoples' ego or self-actualization needs. A few of us may obtain a considerable feeling of personal achievement from our work or other self-directed activities, but to many the job is little more than a means of earning money. A fair proportion must therefore depend on "status" for this kind of satisfaction. Status, however, is always status in a group and in our "pluralistic" society each group will only grant status on its own terms. These involve attracting attention to oneself for some activity of which the group approves. To be an important chap in a street gang, for example, one would have to excel at a number of activities which would be considered delinquent or antisocial by more conventional groupings. Nevertheless, some young people put a great deal of effort into these because they are what cause them to be respected and admired in that group. The fact that they may sooner or later bring them into trouble with the police is entirely irrelevant; this may even raise them still further in the group's opinion. Other people, or course, may out a similar amount of effort into keeping the garden tidy, cleaning the car, taking part in local charitable activities and other bourgeois pursuits, because their feeling of importance in the groupings which make up their life-pattern depends on activities like these.

## PATTERNS OF SATISFACTION

The need to earn a living, to feel that one is liked and accepted in the various groupings to which one belongs, and to achieve a certain significance as an individual, these are the basic elements in everyone's motivation. Where the differences appear is in the methods of satisfaction, for in the modern pluralistic society there are all sorts of activities for which one can be paid, all sorts of different groupings each with its own way of life, and all sorts of activities which will make one important in one or other of these groupings. Each individual will have his own pattern of satisfactions, or his own range of activities which give him a financial, companionship or status dividend. This will be personal and peculiar to the individual and may never accord exactly with that of another individual. The two might, in fact, be entirely opposed, the activities which provide satisfaction to the one being non-satisfying or frustrating to the other. Differences in ability, background, previous experience and many other factors enter into this very complex picture. A further complication arises from the fact that no one can ever be completely satisfied for more than a short time. Our ego or self-actualization needs are always pushing us onwards towards higher standards. Once we have achieved these, however, we soon take them for granted and feel just as hard up after our rise of a hundred a year as we did before we got it. This dissatisfaction with present standards and continual desire for higher things is the condition of human progress.

A further problem presents itself when the individual fails to find a rational means of satisfying his basic needs. Instead of disappearing, these needs then become more pressing and he is driven to do something about them, even though this may not be entirely rational. This is the "frustration" process and in its extreme forms it can become almost pathological. A typical example is the castaway on a desert island where the means of survival are at their most primitive. He may end up by eating and drinking things that he would find utterly revolting in a normal situation, for these are the only means available for satisfying his hunger and thirst. As soon as a need gets out of control, the possibility of irrational behaviour will make itself felt. Only when a need is satisfied does it cease to be pressing.

In our way of life there are very few people who are actually below the breadline in a material sense. There are many however, who have never gained much satisfaction for their companionship and self-actualization needs because they failed to be accepted and admired in conventional groupings. These are the people whose frustrations manifest themselves in aggressive or even anti-social behaviour. The teenage delinquent, for example, is frequently the young man whose family has given him little affection or support, who has never gained any feeling of achievement from his school work or been any good at games or other accepted school activities, and gets no sense of belonging or significance at work. What is more natural, then, than for him and a gang of similarly deprived adolescents to build up a way of life where to be one of the boys, one must share anti-social attitudes, and where to be important, one must model oneself on the tough figures who are given so much regrettable publicity in the mass media? This self-image provides a vehicle for the expression of hostility to a social pattern which in the main has been a source of frustration.

#### THE SELF-IMAGE

The concept of the "self-image" is extremely useful in understanding individual motivation. Everyone has at the back of his mind an image of the kind of person he thinks he is. It is not particularly rational nor is it even very conscious. But it exercises a considerable influence on what he will do willingly because it accords with his image of himself. It also helps to determine what he will resent because it challenges his self-image. Thus the teenage gang leader will get a lot of satisfaction out of the "punch-up" because he can then express himself as the tough, dangerous figure on whom he is modelling himself. He would find the routine of a semi-skilled job frustrating because it provides no scope for the expression of the personal qualities on the possession of which he prides himself. Obtaining an insight into an individual's self-image is not difficult and it provides perhaps the quickest short-cut to understanding his motivation.

How the individual builds up his self-image is a further question. Basically there are two processes at work, one concerning the kinds of activity which have given him satisfaction, and the other involving the figures who have been put before him as people to be admired. Think, for example, of a not-very-intelligent boy who is not much good at class-work. Book-learning and all that this implies will this become a source of frustration to him. On the football field or in the school sports, however, he may make a much better showing, scoring goals and winning races of various distances. These athletic activities thus provide him with the sense of achievement which is essential to him and consequently his motivation will be channelled in that direction. In the newspapers and on the television he is continually presented with football and other games heroes, athletes and jockeys, as important figures around whom widespread adulation centres. Consciously or unconsciously he begins to model himself on these so that a self-image is built up which enables him to express himself on the football field or the race-track. It will handicap him still further, however, in any intellectual or bookish activities.

Contrasting self-images could be envisaged among young people who were no good at games or athletics but whose class work provided a much more satisfying field for self-expression. They might have more difficulty in finding figures admired for their intellectual achievements in the mass media, for the popular appeal of this kind of activity is considerably less. Somewhere in their environment, however, there would be someone on whom they could model themselves. As in so many other aspects of motivation, we have an interaction between the individual's abilities and the way of life in which he finds himself. The self-image is the resultant of this interaction, and the degree to which it is influenced by the figures put forward to be admired at the present day can be a source of some concern.

### ATTITUDES

One way of explaining motivation is to think of the individual as having a kind of build-up of pressure inside him. If this pressure can find an outlet in satisfying and socially acceptable activities, it will provide him with the energy which he puts into these. If, on the other hand, such activities are not available to him, or he cannot find them for himself, then the pressure will begin to get out of control. Either it will push him into activities which are neither satisfying in themselves not acceptable to the community at large, or it will be bottled up inside and find the strange twisted outlets which accompany emotional disturbance. We should keep in mind a picture of energy flowing freely into a range of activities which are satisfying to the individual, which do not interfere with those of other people, and which lead on to a widening scope for self-expression. This is the healthy life from the motivational point of view.

Our present-day pluralistic society with its multifarious groupings offers a wide variety of activities. Not everyone, however, will find that all of these offer equal scope. Some will find certain groupings and activities satisfying and rewarding, while others will find them a source of frustration and failure. Each individual, according to his pattern of abilities, background and pre-conceptions, will gravitate in certain directions and away from others. Similarly each grouping will have its own "clientele" who find it rewarding and satisfying, this being balanced by others who have never gained any satisfaction from it. We thus have a complex picture of rewards and frustrations varying from individual to individual and group to group.

When anyone has had a satisfying experience in the sense that he has derived a financial, companionship or self-actualization reward from it, that experience will become the focus for positive attitudes. That is to say, there will be a favourable feeling-tone surrounding everything associated with it. This will not be thought out in logical terms, nor will the individual always be able to justify it entirely rationally. If, for example, someone who has found games and athletics a satisfying means of self-expression gets involved in an argument say, about professionalism in sport, he may fall back on remarks like "I don't care what you say. I think games are a jolly good thing." He is thus expressing an attitude, rather than giving a reasoned judgment.

In our society there must obviously be a very wide range of attitudes, both positive and negative. Different ways of earning a living, from productive work to administration; different levels of income offering higher or lower standards of living; varying levels of education and opportunity; political parties with different interpretations of public policy; these and other elements in our way of life will have been a source of satisfaction to some people and of frustration to others. Some will thus be in favour of certain aspects and will seek to perpetuate and extend them. Others will consider them unjust and will wish to see them changed or brought to an end. Argument will be continuous as everyone tries to justify his attitudes or impose them on other people, and the emotional element in these arguments may frequently outweigh the rational.

*The Assessment of Attitudes*

If we are ever to understand the individual, some insight into his attitudes will be essential. This can be obtained if, in conversation, we listen to the notes of approval or disapproval in what he says about various subjects. If, for example, he talks enthusiastically about the introduction of new plant and production processes at work, we can assume that his attitude to industrial progress and development is favourable. This will probably link up with a satisfying work career and a self-image of a rising young executive. But if, on the other hand, he refers to such developments as new-fangled nonsense, change for the sake of change which doesn't really do any good except to create jobs for clever chaps who couldn't recognize a decent day's work if they saw one, then we can assume that his attitudes to such developments are negative or unfavourable. This again may link up with a self-image of a skilled and experienced chap who prides himself on his knowledge of how things have been done for the past twenty years. Such a self-image will feel itself threatened by change and will consequently be hostile to it.

In addition to the attitudes of the individual, there are shared attitudes which will cause a number of people to react in a similar way. These may be very important for if one makes a change that becomes the focus of shared negative attitudes, that change will arouse widespread hostility. This could be embarrassing and in some cases even damaging, so that it can be worth while to try to assess attitudes beforehand. Various ways are available, the simplest being the questionnaire which puts forward a series of statements and asks the recipient to agree or disagree. An example might be—

*Women should have equal pay to men.* Agree. Don't know. Disagree.

When a number of these have been collected and analysed, the proportions in favour or against can be worked out.

Attitude surveys have become a regular feature of present-day life and the papers are continually quoting the results. We can learn whether opinion is swinging in favour of the government or against it; whether trade unions are considered to be doing a good or a bad job; whether the majority think conscription should be re-introduced, and so on. There are, of course, dangers in that the sample surveyed may not be representative or that questions can be misinterpreted. The surveying of attitudes now has its own technology which has become fairly complex. When systematically followed, however, it can provide a useful guide to feelings that command support among groups of people.

### DIFFERENT ASPECTS OF MOTIVATION

The study of motivation is perhaps one of the most interesting aspects of psychology but is is an aspect which presents certain difficulties. Prominent among these is the problem of measurement, for there are no standard units available. In the study of sensation, for example, experiments can be conducted where subjects are exposed to lights of measured brightness or sounds of measured pitch. Their reactions can be assessed objectively and hypotheses proved or disproved according to the accepted methods of science. In studying motivation and attitudes, however, it is difficult to find experimental situations which can be controlled and where the reactions of subjects can be objectively assessed. We are thus thrown back on theories which can be partly substantiated by studying particular situations but can never be proved in the same manner as the laws of physics or chemistry. We can suggest that some of the people will be motivated in a certain way some of the time, but never that the same theory will apply to all of the people all of the time.

One view that has been put forward has a certain fairly obvious validity. This suggests that needs are arranged in a hierarchical order and that until the more mundane ones are satisfied we shall not be conscious of those that are higher up the scale. Thus, if anyone's material needs are unsatisfied and he is short of food, warmth and shelter, then nothing else will matter to him except a square meal and a safe place to sleep. As soon as he achieves these satisfactions, however, his material needs will fade into the background and he will be concerned with being accepted by other people to satisfy his companionship needs. Once he becomes one of the boys and these needs are thus satisfied, they will also be taken for granted and he will become aware of his ego needs or the desire to have some status and significance. Whatever level he achieves, however, there will always be one stage higher, and on this interpretation, it will be the higher stage that matters to him. The satisfactions he has already achieved will count for little or nothing because, having obtained them, he will take them for granted.

Another theory separates human needs into two distinct categories, the "satisfiers" and the "dissatisfiers".[1] This is rather more complex but suggests that if anyone is deprived of his material and companionship needs, or if these are only met on a minimum standard, he will be dissatisfied. When these dissatisfactions are removed by improving his living standards, however, he will not necessarily be satisfied. The "satisfiers" depend on meeting his ego or self-actualization needs. This can be illustrated by thinking of someone who is working under hygienic conditions and earning a wage or salary which makes possible a high material standard of living. Such a person, however, may suffer a sense of frustration because his job is rather a meaningless routine which offers little or no scope for personal achievement. In present-day industry it is not uncommon to find people in work-situations where there is little or nothing to be dissatisfied with, but where there is a similar shortage of things that make for real satisfaction.

Such people can be contrasted with those who are earning comparatively little and working under poor conditions but who feel they are doing something really worthwhile. The picture of the artist starving in a garret while he produces a great masterpiece may be somewhat overdrawn. Examples can nevertheless be found in everyday life where someone has found a greater satisfaction in less well-paid work which provides him with this feeling of personal achievement and social significance.

## SUMMARY

1. What are the means of satisfying our material needs?

In the western industrial communities, money enables us to buy any material thing we may want. Thus, any task that can be made into a means of earning money becomes significant to the individual.

[1] *Work and the Nature of Man*, F. Herzberg, (Staples, 1968)

2. What are the means of satisfying our companionship needs?

In our way of life, by becoming a member of various different groups. Each of these will have its own way of life, however, to which we must conform if we are to be accepted in that group. Most people have a "reference group" which to them represents the "right" way to think and behave.

3. How do we satisfy our ego or self-actualization needs?

Mostly by acquiring status in one or other of the groups to which we belong. Status, however, is always status in a group, and depends on being successful at the activities of which that group approves. These may not always accord with the way of life of other groups.

4. Can we generalize about the means of satisfaction in the present-day world?

No. Each individual must find his own pattern of satisfactions among the means available to him. This will be entirely unique and personal to himself.

5. What happens when the individual fails to find means of satisfaction in conventional or socially accepted activities?

His fundamental needs will become more pressing and may drive him to unconventional or anti-social activities. This is the "frustration" process and can be illustrated among teenage delinquents who have never had any sense of belonging or being significant in the home, at school, or at work.

6. What do we mean by the self-image?

This is the figure which the individual has unconsciously at the back of his mind as the kind of person he thinks he is. It is influenced by the kind of activities from which he has obtained satisfaction and the kind of figures he has regarded as people to be admired. Insight into the individual's self-image provides a quick clue to his motivational pattern, for he will be keen to do anything which accords with his self-image, while he will resent anything which challenges or attacks it.

7. How are attitudes formed?

Anything which has been a source of satisfaction will be the focus of positive attitudes, while anything that has been a source of frustration will be the focus of negative attitudes. In present-day society with such a wide range of groupings and activities, some of which are satisfying to certain individuals but frustrating to others, there is inevitably a wide range of attitudes and possible conflicts between them.

8. How can attitudes be assessed?

By listening to the favourable or unfavourable tones when an individual is talking about different things, or by questionnaires which invite a representative sample to agree or disagree with certain statements.

9. Are we always conscious of our basic needs all the time?

One theory is that they are arranged in a hierarchical order, and when the simpler food, warmth, and shelter needs are satisfied, we forget about them and become conscious of our needs (*a*) to be accepted and (*b*) to feel significant. Another theory is that when our simpler needs are not met we shall be dissatisfied, but when they are met we shall not necessarily be satisfied. It is the needs to feel significant and to gain some sense of achievement that are the "satisfiers."

CHAPTER VIII

# General Psychology and Psychiatry

PSYCHOLOGY is the study of normal human behaviour, and the main aspects have been touched on in the preceding chapters. It has a physiological side, for much depends on an adequate knowledge of how our bodies work, of the nervous systems which bring information from the sense-organs and which initiate the movements of our muscles, and of the more abstruse reaction systems which control the internal secretions and other processes which accompany various states of feeling and activity. It is concerned with cognition, which is the name given to all the processes which begin with the sensations from the outside world, their perception, comprehension, and the memory of them. It is concerned also with learning and with the development of skill, while it also has a dynamic side in its preoccupation with the motivation of behaviour and the feelings and emotions which accompany it.

## THE METHODS OF PSYCHOLOGY

Originally, these matters were studied mainly through men paying attention to their own experience, reflecting on it and trying to give a connected account of what went on in their own minds. This method is called introspection, or the observation of one's own experience, and it must always occupy an important place in psychology. There are, however, obvious difficulties in its application partly because each individual's experience is very private and personal to himself and partly because as soon as we begin to study our own experience we find that it becomes very elusive and difficult to grasp.

To make up for the deficiencies of introspection other methods were brought into use by experimental psychologists. Some of these were aimed at giving greater precision to introspective data, such as by asking an individual to decide which of two lights was the brighter, then narrowing the difference in intensity until it was clear from his confused responses that he was unable to distinguish between them, and some were aimed at substituting actual behaviour for them. If one were studying memory, for example, it was obviously more satisfactory to give the person being studied a list of words to remember and to ask him to write down the number he recalled after various intervals than merely to ask him whether he thought it was easier to recall meaningful words than syllables which didn't make sense.

As the science progressed knowledge was accumulated about what happened under various conditions, and theories began to be put forward as to the underlying laws. When these theories were formulated they had to be tested against the facts and this made it necessary to devise crucial situations which would show whether or not they were correct. These situations were known as experiments and were set up so that all the factors were under control, to eliminate chance influences. One factor could then be varied at a time and the results noted.

As an example of the experimental methods in psychology we might think of Weber's work on the perception of differences in intensity. If, for example, someone were shown into a room illuminated by one candle and another candle were lighted, even without seeing the actual candles he would perceive that there had been an increase in the brightness of the light. But if someone were in a room illuminated by five hundred candles and another one were added the increase in brightness would not be noticeable. Why was the addition of one candle enough to produce a perceptible increase in the intensity of the illumination in one case and not the other?

Weber worked on this problem by exposing people to lights of a calculated brightness and then increasing them to the point where the individual just noticed the difference. At different brightnesses he found that a different amount had to be added before it was noticeable; but when he calculated the amount added as a fraction of the original brightness he found that the ratio was constant. In other words, no matter how bright a light may be, if one-hundredth extra brightness is added to it the difference will be just perceptible.

In this way Weber's Law, which holds for perceptible differences in brightness, loudness, temperature, smells, and other sensations was established. Briefly expressed, this states that one stimulus will be noticeably different in intensity from another stimulus in the same sensory mode only if the ratio of the difference to the original stimulus is greater than a known constant. Since this law was first established, however, considerable differences between individuals' reactions have been noticed, and the law has been found not to apply uniformly throughout the whole range of intensities.

It was always possible, however, that such situations set up in the laboratory and carefully controlled might be so divorced from the circumstances of real life that their results would be meaningless. To guard against the influence of these artificialities, field observations were carried out where a situation could be studied under real-life conditions. In such cases it would obviously be impossible to control all the factors which might influence the individual, but at the same time one would see more natural behaviour without the constraints of the cut-and-dried laboratory situation. A judicious alternation of introspection, laboratory experiment, and field studies probably leads to the quickest and most effective expansion of knowledge.

## PSYCHIATRY

In addition to the large mass of normal people, however, there is a minority whose behaviour is abnormal and who must be regarded as suffering from some form of mental illness or handicap. The study and treatment of these abnormal people is the subject-matter of psychiatry or, as it used to be called, medical psychology. In former times those who were in any way abnormal mentally were classified as "mad" or "insane" and were locked up and either neglected and left to themselves, or treated with considerable cruelty in order to drive out the evil spirits which were supposed to possess them. The ratio of cures was usually low.

Recent and more imaginative treatment, however, has led to a better understanding of mental illness and it now becomes possible to separate those who are suffering no more than a temporary maladjustment from those who are utterly and incurably unfitted for ordinary life and who need to be looked after for their own protection and that of others.

Among the latter type of case we may note two briefly. The first of these is the mental defective whose powers of comprehension are so limited that he cannot deal with the ordinary affairs of life and who remains for most of his life at the intellectual level of a child of three or four years old. This kind of person has to be given a simplified life for his own protection and is normally put in an institution or educated at a special school where everything is taken very slowly and simply.

The second type is the person who is suffering from severe delusions or hallucinations. This is the conventional idea of "madness," when the individual exists in a world of his own believing either that he is the Emperor Napoleon or that he is made of glass and mustn't risk getting broken. Such cases are very tragic, the more so because frequently nothing can be done with them; but along with the very low mental defectives they are comparatively rare.

Apart from these serious disturbances of personality, however, there are a number of manifestations of mental ill-health of a temporary and less grave character. Prolonged emotional strain or fatigue can result in symptoms of mental disturbance or even of complete breakdown, without it being necessary for the sufferer to spend the rest of his life in a lunatic asylum. In some of these cases rest and relaxation will often effect a cure by themselves, while in others treatment by a psychiatrist will bring the patient back to normal.

*Neurosis and Conflict*

Perhaps the most frequent cause of neurosis, as these curable maladjustments may be loosely called, is conflict between two opposing impulses. Such conflicts are not infrequent; indeed they are the normal currency of life. For example, we would all like to save money, though at the same time we like to smoke cigarettes. Quite often, therefore, when we fork out our hard-earned money we are conscious of two impulses, one saying "This is a ridiculous price, you really can't afford it, you know," while the other cries "You must have enough cigarettes in your pocket, for if you run short you'll be miserable, nervy, and you won't be able to stop thinking about smoking." We solve the conflict by telling one or other of the two voices to keep quiet—usually the one which says we can't afford it.

But in some cases the conflict is more serious and we find it impossible to resolve on the spur of the moment because the two impulses are more deep-seated and the issue is of greater real importance. We may continue with both somewhere present in our consciousness for some time. Such a state of affairs may impose a serious strain and will certainly make our behaviour less effective. In some experiments with animals conflicts have been produced artificially. They were trained, for example, to expect to find food behind a trap door of one colour and to anticipate an electric shock if they approached another. Once this conditioning had been well established, the colours were changed and the animals were put into a state of conflict between their desire to get at the food they had been trained to expect and their distrust of the changed situation in which unexpected electric shocks were somewhere in store for them.

Their reactions to such a conflict were most extraordinary. Some would sulk and refuse to try, ending up, when forced, in a kind of sleep-like trance from which they could not be roused for some time. Others became hysterical—whining, struggling, and refusing to eat. Others again ran in circles about the floor with great rapidity, varying this with convulsive hopping and twitching and finally allowing themselves to be rolled into balls or moulded this way and that without showing any more resistance than if they were pieces of clay. Obviously, therefore, severe conflict can result in serious behaviour disturbances, while milder conflicts often result in such hesitation and oscillation between two impulses that neither is adequately dealt with. If an animal is presented with a plate of food while at the same time a hostile animal is produced, the first one will hesitate between the food and the enemy, making ineffective attempts to eat and ineffective attempts to drive the intruder away and so doing neither job properly.

*Methods of Dealing with Conflict*

Conflict is unavoidable in human life, for the satisfaction of our basic needs (see Chapter VII) is always in danger of bringing us up against the needs and wishes of other people. There is therefore a continual need for adjustment, and we have frequently to say to ourselves "I would like to do so-and-so very much, but if I went straight at it I should be most unpopular with the people about me, and might even get involved in behaviour that I would be very much ashamed of. I'd better give up the idea, or try to find some way of doing what I want that other people will not take exception to." Most of us can manage to make these adjustments for a large part of the time by taking a reasonably objective view of our own desires, the convenience of other people, and the type of behaviour which is considered acceptable by the people we live among.

A process called *sublimation* frequently helps in this, for by its means the energy behind an urge which would lead to unacceptable behaviour is, so to speak, drained off into more acceptable channels. A man who has great ambition to dominate others and to be recognized as an outstanding figure among them may, if he puts the energy behind this drive into artistic or literary activity, achieve his end of being recognized and at the same time contribute creatively to the community in which he lives.

But there are some cases where an individual cannot achieve any reconciliation between his conflicting impulses, with the result that they continue to exist side by side at the same time. This results in what is called *dissociation*, or the splitting off of a system of ideas into a sort of water-tight compartment in the personality. In some cases this may cause the patient to go into a "trance" in which he carries on a sequence of activities which bear no relation whatever to his normal life. The most frequently quoted case of this concerns a patient of Dr. Janet's who was unable to make an adjustment between her sorrow at her mother's death after a particularly distressing illness, and the need to continue her normal life. She would go on as usual for a period with no reference whatever to the tragic event, giving an impression of complete callousness to it; from time to time, however, she passed into a trance-like state in which she went through the scenes of her mother's death with the most intense emotion.

Apart from some cases like these, however, many quite normal people allow conflicting impulses which they cannot reconcile to exist side by side. Desires to do as well as we can for ourselves often cause us to do things of which other people might disapprove and consequently they come up against our desire to stand well with our fellow men. When this conflict is forced on our attention we show the greatest ingenuity in explaining it away to our complete satisfaction. This process is called *rationalization*, or finding reasons for the apparent discrepancy, and can perhaps be seen at its best when a fox-hunting man is endeavouring to reconcile the satisfaction he gains from this exciting sport with the suspicion that it is more than a little cruel and not quite up to the standards of kindness to animals to which he endeavours to live up in other ways. He is generally quite sincerely successful in showing that the danger to the fox is infinitesimal as compared with the thrill it derives from the chase, and, in fact, that the fox really enjoys being hunted as much as the field enjoys hunting him.

In other cases, however, conflicting impulses cannot exist side by side and one or other has to be *repressed*. This happens when we refuse to admit the existence of a disturbing impulse and thrust it down out of sight in the hope that it will disappear. It is a harmful process, for the impulses do not disappear, and it is quite different from the conscious suppression which follows a rational adjustment to conflict. When we feel like calling attention to ourselves at a party by rather too hearty behaviour but restrain ourselves because our host and hostess are rather quiet retiring people, we do ourselves no harm at all though we may have a less enjoyable evening than we had hoped. But if, for example, we attach guilt or shame to our strong interest in the opposite sex and instead of recognizing that this desire is perfectly normal and healthy, repress it, we may be initiating deep-rooted emotional problems which are rarely easy to resolve.

When we repress such an impulse because it conflicts with our idea of delicacy or with the standards we have been brought up to accept we set up a barrier against its normal expression in consciousness. This barrier will usually take the form of an exaggerated distaste for anything which has the remotest connexion with the repressed impulse. But the impulse will find ways round this barrier and will show itself in consciousness in a disguised and sometimes rather unpleasant form. The ridiculous prudery which until quite recently was attached to anything which could be remotely suggestive of the sex organs, combined with a morbid interest in the hunting out and degradation of those whose sexual conduct had been irregular, serves as a common enough example of the process of repression and its results.

*Phantasy*

The continued need for adjustment in our mental life imposes a considerable strain on everyone, and the individual's capacity for enduring this strain varies. Some people can adjust to the most trying conditions without any outward difficulty, while others show the various symptoms touched on above to such an extent that they become mentally ill and have to be treated in hospitals. There are, however, ways of escape which may have a limited effectiveness.

One of these is to retire into a day-dream and to find there the satisfactions which ordinary life denies. Everybody indulges in phantasy to some extent and real life might become too discouraging for words if we could not occasionally launch off into the unknown as the captain of an imaginary space-ship, dine at the best restaurant in town with the girl of our day-dreams, or show the boss, in a phantasy conversation, that we are not to be trifled with.[1]

When the return to real life becomes too difficult, however, there is a danger that we are finding an unhealthy amount of satisfaction in our day-dreams and are using them as a retreat from the realities of ordinary life. It is still more dangerous when we begin to use alcohol to assist our day-dreams and blur the edges of reality. Very frequently the drunkard is one who cannot cope with the adjustments which real life calls on him to make, and who retires into his private world where, accompanied by a few kindred spirits, he can achieve effortless satisfaction.

In the same category is the individual who develops some crippling symptom which makes it impossible for him to stand up to ordinary life. This is known as "conversion hysteria" and may appear as paralysis of the limbs, asthma, digestive disorders and other complaints of nervous origin.

*Anxiety*

Much of the strain involved in these continual adjustments will make itself felt as anxiety, a great deal of which is entirely normal and universal. Paying our bills, making do on our

---

[1] James Thurber's *Secret Life of Walter Mitty* is perhaps the best-known example of this.

salary, passing examinations, the disastrous results of illness, keeping our jobs—at one time or another these are everyone's problems and everyone gets worried about them. As we succeed in coping with the situation, however, so do the anxieties disappear and in such cases no one is seriously the worse. Worry of this type, though unpleasant at the time, leaves no permanent after-effects.

But there are forms of anxiety which are much more serious and which do not disappear with the cause. These are usually due not to what is going on in the real world around us, but to something unacknowledged or repressed in our own minds. For example, someone who has set very high standards for himself, or who has had them imposed on him in childhood, may be constantly worried that he may not be living up to them. Moreover, his anxiety will probably have rather a guilty tinge about it, made all the more real because he does not acknowledge it to himself. Anxiety of this type will find its outlet in all sorts of individual ways.

Roughly speaking, so long as one is anxious *about* something, and if that something is sufficiently serious that it might have grave effects on our well-being, then the anxiety is quite normal and need cause no fears about mental ill-health. But as soon as the anxiety becomes generalized and out of proportion in duration and depth to its apparent cause, such as, for example, when "bomb-happy" people continue to be paralysed with fear even after their removal to a safe area, then it is a symptom of some more serious and deep-seated failure in adjustment.

Human life involves a continual series of adjustments between what we would like to do and what we can do; between what other people expect of us and what we expect of ourselves; and between our own powers and resources and the pressures of the external environment. Each one of us has a breaking point and the toughest can be reduced to pulp after a long period of hardship, fatigue, and discouragement. Some unfortunate people have such limited powers of adjustment that their breaking point is reached after the comparatively mild pressures of ordinary life. So long as our powers of adjustment are adequate to what is demanded of us, we may be worried and depressed at times but never out of proportion to the causes. And we shall recover as soon as the cause is removed.

As soon as we begin to fail to make an objective adjustment to the demands made upon us the signs of strain will appear. These may either be in the form of uncontrollable anxiety which fastens on matters other than its real cause, or they may be one or the other methods of dodging the issue mentioned above—repression, dissociation, or phantasy. Rest and an honest attempt to face up to the situation and accept one's own limitation may help at this point, but as soon as the individual finds that he can no longer compete with ordinary life, the services of a psychiatrist should be sought.

## SUMMARY

1. What is the subject-matter of psychology and what are its methods?

Psychology is the study of normal behaviour among human beings or animals. It first used the method of introspection or observation of one's own thoughts and reactions, but as this has limitations it was later supplemented by controlled observation and experiment. Situations can be set up in the laboratory in which one factor can be varied at a time and the results noted. These can at times be supplemented by field observations of individuals in ordinary life situations.

2. What is the subject-matter of psychiatry? Is it only concerned with "mad" people?

Psychiatry is concerned with mental illness or abnormality. There are comparatively few forms of this which render people "mad" or completely unfitted ever to take part in ordinary life. Mental defectives are of such limited intelligence that they cannot look after themselves in the normal world, while people with severe delusions have to be shut up for their own protection.

3. What less serious forms of mental illness are there?

Various forms of neurosis may handicap an individual quite seriously, but these are usually temporary and curable. Most neuroses spring from conflict, or the existence of two incompatible impulses in the mind at the same time.

4. What are the means of dealing with conflicts?

When a conflict arises in the mind of a normal person he may either *suppress* one of the two impulses or *sublimate* it and so resolve the situation. Unresolved conflicts, however, may lead to *dissociation* or the splitting off of one part of the personality, any incongruities being *rationalized* or explained away to the individual's own satisfaction. In other cases one of the impulses may be *repressed* or forced down out of sight and its very existence denied. This can be dangerous, for the repressed impulse often makes itself felt in indirect and unpleasant ways.

5. What other symptoms are there of inability to deal with the adjustments required in ordinary life?

*Phantasy* is one means of escaping from real life into a day-dream, and *psychogenic illness* produces symptoms which make it unnecessary for the individual to go on trying. Disproportionate anxiety also shows that the strain of the adjustment called for is becoming too much for the individual.

# Part II

# Industrial Psychology

CHAPTER IX

# Introductory

By now we have a fair idea of what the experimental psychologist has to tell us about the individual human being. We have seen how man acquires information about the outside world through his senses—sight, hearing, and the like—and how he organizes that information into meaningful perceptions; we have seen how these perceptions are stored in his memory and how new experiences can be classified with them either in the real world or in thought. The learning process, the motivation of the individual, and his feelings and reactions to situations—all these have been dealt with in objective terms by experimental psychologists who have assembled a considerable body of knowledge about them. There are still gaps in that knowledge as has been pointed out above, but the conclusions so far reached are reliable and valid because they have been arrived at by the methods of science. They can be verified by anyone who cares to repeat the experiments and observe the same facts.

But so far this "individual human being" we have been thinking of remains an anonymous abstraction rather than a living person. He has been the subject of innumerable experiments on sensation and perception but he seems to have no life of his own and no real existence outside the laboratory. He has, in fact, little in common with the ordinary people we meet from day to day.

In real life people are usually seen in the context of some meaningful activity. They are fathers of families, taking their place in the life of the home; they are members of cricket clubs, collaborating in the playing of a game during their leisure time; they may be shop assistants, machinists or farm labourers, earning their living by taking part in the economic activities of the community. Each of these activities forms an area in the existence of a man (or woman) and it is within this that his significant life is lived. If we wish to understand individuals outside the laboratory we must consider them in one or other of these phases of activity and study their behaviour in that particular environment. The environment which concerns us at the moment is that of industrial work.

### THE DEVELOPMENT OF INDUSTRIAL PSYCHOLOGY

One result of the Industrial Revolution was to make a wider separation between people's working life and the rest of their activities. Formerly a great deal of productive work had been carried out in the home during the less busy seasons of the farming year. Tasks had been shared out among the members of the family and work, home life and relaxation had been informally intermingled. With the advent of power-driven machinery, however, more and more people came to be assembled in factories where they worked together for a fixed number of hours in the day. Particularly in the early stages there were many unfortunate aspects of this setting up of work-communities which cut off people's economic activities from the rest of their lives. These must be balanced against the astonishing increases of productivity by which the factory system was enabled to turn out enormous quantities of relatively cheap goods.

From the psychologist's point of view the Industrial Revolution meant that most work was carried out in special environments, and that many individuals were engaged on definite tasks which were repeated with little variation throughout the working day. Industrial work had taken on its present-day character, losing the variety and informality of the self-contained village economy and throwing up the characteristic problems of large-scale repetitive production. New skills were called into being and new adjustments were demanded of those who practised them.

The first incursion of the experimental psychologist into industry in this country was in 1917. During the war which was then in progress the development of barbed wire for strengthening field fortifications and of automatic weapons firing hundreds of rounds a minute had lent an enormous accession of strength to the defence. Attacking infantry could be mown down from virtually impregnable positions, unless these were subjected beforehand to heavy bombardment by artillery. Fire-power had to be increased rapidly and substantially and this meant an enormous expansion of the munitions industry at home. New factories were set up throughout the country and thousands of workers, many of whom had never worked in industry before, were recruited into them. Long hours were worked, processes were broken down and jobs simplified, and the shells and cartridges began to roll out in the required numbers.

Unfortunately, however, there were other results also. Sickness began to increase among the workers, accidents multiplied, and public attention came to be drawn to the fact that all was not well within the munition factories. A committee was set up under the name of the "Health of Munition Workers Committee" to study the subject. Some of the members of that committee had been trained as experimental psychologists.

### THE METHODS OF INDUSTRIAL PSYCHOLOGY

The immediate problems which were presented to the Health of Munition Workers Committee were twofold. Briefly they had to find out—

1. Why there was so much sickness and other difficulty among munition workers.
2. How it could be reduced.

The methods at their disposal were greatly improved by the experience of the psychologists among them, for they brought with them all the techniques, which had been developed in psychological laboratories, for observing human behaviour. They were thoroughly conversant with the applications of the scientific method in this field as it had been developed over the last thirty or forty years.

The result was that instead of dealing in windy generalizations about the effect of factory work on women previously unaccustomed to these conditions, the Committee started by the painstaking collection of facts—facts about hours of work, facts about output, and facts about the actual incidence of sickness. As one would expect from the history of science, regularities began to appear and fluctuations in the rate of output began to link up with certain variations in the hours and conditions of work. Soon it became possible to devise situations in which hours were experimentally altered in order to prove or disprove certain hypotheses about their effect on the rate of output.

In this way a body of verifiable knowledge began to be

built up, most of which remains reliable and valid today. In the early stages it dealt mainly with hours of work and other factors which tended to induce fatigue, and when it was decided that the Health of Munition Workers Committee should continue its work and extend its scope, its name was changed to the "Industrial Fatigue Research Board." Gradually, however, other matters came to be studied, such as posture, methods of work, the design of machinery, heating, lighting, and ventilation, and the name was changed to its later title of the "Industrial Health Research Board." Most of this Board's valuable work consists in the application of the methods of the experimental psychologist to the study of human behaviour in the work-situation.

In 1921, Dr. Charles S. Myers, who was then Director of the Cambridge Psychological Laboratory, became convinced that the young science of experimental psychology had an important contribution to make to British industry. With the collaboration of a committee of business men, headed by Mr. H. J. Welch, he set up the "National Institute of Industrial Psychology," a scientific body operating on a non-profit-making basis, to make available the results of psychological knowledge to industry and commerce and to undertake further research in these fields. During the next thirty years or so the development of industrial psychology in this country was carried out largely through the agency of these two bodies.

### THE SUBJECT-MATTER OF INDUSTRIAL PSYCHOLOGY

Industrial psychology is the study of human beings in the work-situation, but the issue is complicated from the start by the fact that there are many different kinds of work-situation. The reader is probably already aware of the complexity of the industrial and commercial scene and of the wide variety of jobs which exist within it. But there is a further problem peculiar to the industrial development in this country, in which the typical firm is the small one. The majority of firms engaged in productive industry employ less than 250 employees, while well over half the working population still earns a living in firms of that size or less. Each of these firms has its own methods and its own standards, so that the already wide range of jobs is further extended by the large number of firms in which they can be done. It is unrealistic therefore to think in terms of a given number of standard work-environments; we must consider an almost infinite number of variations.

This variety, added to the fact that the individual tasks to be carried out within these job-situations are usually specialized and often repetitive, has drawn attention to the importance of putting the right person into the right job. The variations between individuals are just as great as those between jobs. If we look around we shall see that some are tall and some are short, some are pleasant and some disagreeable, some are quick in the uptake and some are slow, and so on. Many of these differences have been studied systematically by psychologists and this knowledge can be of considerable service in matching up people with the kind of work for which they have the capacity, aptitude, and temperamental qualities, and in which they are likely to find success and satisfaction.

*The psychology of individual differences*, which is dealt with in Chapters X to XIV, provides the theoretical foundation for *vocational guidance*—advising individuals about the kind of work they should enter—and *vocational selection*—choosing the most suitable person for particular types of employment (Chapter XV). The methods involve the testing of various human attributes which have proved to be measurable—intelligence, attainments, and special aptitudes—and of estimating others which are more difficult to reduce to an objective basis. More important, perhaps, is the investigation of an individual's past history during an *interview* and from it predicting the main lines of his future development. This is dealt with in Chapter XVI. Recent developments in methods of vocational selection are also discussed.

Once we have decided on the most suitable job for a particular individual we have to consider how he can be *trained* most economically and effectively in the necessary skills. Here we draw on the psychology of the learning processes and deal with it as the problem of industrial training in Chapter XVII. By utilizing this knowledge in the drawing up of a training scheme we shall avoid wasting time and effort.

Motivation is an important element in training as indeed it is in every aspect of the work-situation. Here again variations are apparent, for people respond differently to different *incentives*.

There are various ways of compensating extra effort and encouraging individuals to aim at satisfactory standards at work. Many of these aim at linking up remuneration with performance on the job, not always with complete success. Some account of the question is given in Chapter XVIII.

The study of work has revealed many variations in method, some of which are effective, while others impose a disproportionate strain on the operator. The *methods* of studying and recording different kinds of job are dealt with in Chapter XIX, along with the conditions which govern the most effective application of human effort to work. This leads on to the *physical conditions of work*, for the recording of output rates has revealed variations which link up with the arrangement of hours, the lighting, heating, and ventilation of the work place, the incidence of noise, fumes, and other unpleasant conditions. Fatigue and boredom are also considered under this heading in Chapter XX.

Lastly there is the question of *accidents* at work (Chapter XXI). When these are adequately recorded they are seen to centre round certain places and types of machinery which are recognized as sources of special danger. Measures can be taken to reduce this danger, but these are not always as effective as they might be on account of the human element.

## SUMMARY

1. Can we achieve an adequate understanding of human beings by studying them in the laboratory?

No, because the most significant aspects of an individual's life are lived in contact with others while engaged on some common activity. Industrial psychology is the study of human beings in the work-environment.

2. What are the principal characteristics of the work-environment?

In an industrial country most work is carried on in specialized groups by highly developed, subdivided processes in which the individual's task is only a minute part of the whole. Such tasks in these specialized work units demand new adjustments on the part of the individual.

3. When did industrial psychology emerge as a special study in this country?

In 1917, when the Health of Munition Workers Committee was set up to consider sickness among women war workers. This body has continued to study the subject under the title of the Industrial Health Research Board. After the 1914–18 war the National Institute of Industrial Psychology was set up by Dr. C. S. Myers for a similar purpose.

CHAPTER X

# Individual Differences

THERE is no need to draw special attention to the fact that human beings differ one from the other. To stand in a busy thoroughfare and watch the crowds passing is to see a continual variety of features and expression, of stature and build. No two are exactly alike and if an acquaintance appears among the passers-by we recognize him at once, without any danger of confusing him with any of the hundreds of others. This uniqueness of the individual has been shown to hold in certain unexpected characteristics like fingerprints, no two of which have been found to conform to exactly the same pattern.

Such differences, however, are variations between certain definite limits. Human beings, apart from the very occasional monstrosity, have the same number of eyes, ears, and limbs, and their features are arranged in the same general pattern upon their faces. In stature men are seldom much less than, say, five feet in height as adults, nor are they frequently found more than six-feet-three tall. Their weight, girth and other measurements will also be found to be restricted within a certain range of variation.

We are dealing, therefore, with variations within certain limits, and these limits are often quite surprisingly narrow. How is it, then, that the individual remains unique when his range of variation in any one characteristic is limited?

The reason is, of course, that human beings can vary in many different characteristics. Some of these can be measured in inches or in pounds and ounces, while some are concerned with less tangible matters. Scales of variation have been established for some of these characteristics and we know, for example, what is the average height of adult males in this country. But if we have two men, both of whom are exactly average in height, they may still be quite different, even in physique. One may be fat and the other thin, one may be dark and the other fair, one may be symmetrical in build while the other may be misshapen or ungainly. And when we come to take their mental characteristics into account, the differences between the two may be even more strongly marked.

## THE EXPERIMENTAL APPROACH TO INDIVIDUAL DIFFERENCES

To make sense of these differences between individuals, we must obviously approach them with some caution. Two questions are involved. The first concerns the variations between individuals in certain definite characteristics, and the second deals with the arrangement of those variations in each individual which makes up his unique personality. (We are using the word personality to mean all the characteristics which make up the complete individual.) It will be easier to deal here with the first of these questions and to leave the other until later in the chapter. This will not only follow the logical order, but it will enable us to deal with the studies which have been made on the subject in their historical order as well.

In the later years of the last century a number of scientists, among whom was Sir Francis Galton, became interested in human measurements. They gave their studies the somewhat clumsy name of *anthropometrics* and they set about collecting as many measurements of human beings as they could. It was soon apparent that when they concentrated on any one characteristic among people of the same race and sex, regularities in the distribution of differences were beginning to appear.

In studying the heights of adult males, for example, the following scale might be drawn up—

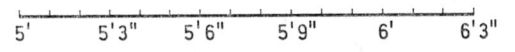

```
|___.___|___.___|___.___|___.___|___.___|___.___|
 5'    5'3"   5'6"   5'9"   6'    6'3"
```

FIG. 13. SCALE OF HEIGHT FOR ADULT MALES

As they were collected, cases would be placed in the appropriate measurements on the scale. When a hundred observations had been made the distribution would look something like that shown in Fig. 14, each case being represented by an O.

When we join up the tops of these columns as on a graph, the curve will look like that shown in Fig. 15.

This bell-shaped curve kept making its appearance whenever these human measurements were studied, provided that a substantial number were recorded, and provided that they were adequately representative of the same racial and cultural group. If African pygmies were mixed up with tall Zulu

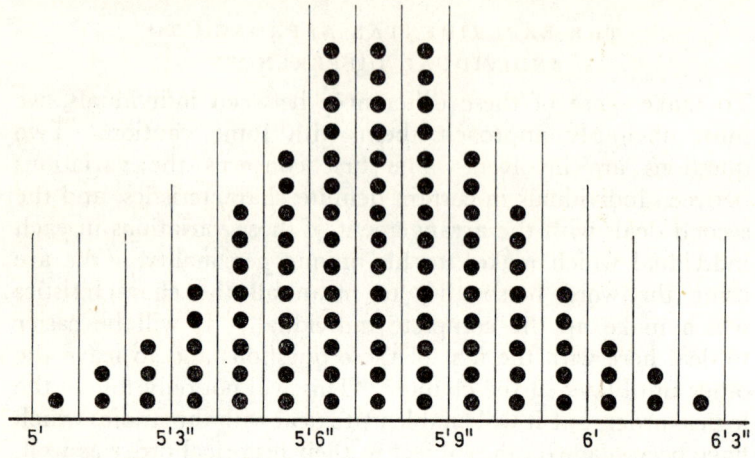

FIG. 14. A Hundred Cases Arranged in the Scale

warriors the results, as one would expect, would not show the same regularities.

*The Curve of Distribution*

Physical measurements, such as height, weight, length of arm, girth, and so on, when studied systematically among people of the same race and culture showed this regular bell-shaped

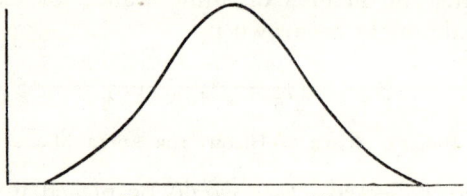

FIG. 15. Normal Curve of Distribution

distribution. Such a curve shows that the measurements were grouped round a central tendency, most of them being in an average category—in the hump of the curve—and the remainder tailing off fairly symmetrically above and below the average.

Now certain other studies, for example in the fields of botany and zoology, had shown similar distributions within a species. In certain kinds of plant, for example, there might be a maximum and a minimum number of leaves. Within that range, the actual distribution of the number of leaves among many specimens would show the same bell-shaped curve.

Is there any reason why this should be so? If we pause for a moment to consider the theory of probability we shall find that there is. Take, for example, a situation where there is a certain number of possibilities such as in the tossing of pennies. If we have two pennies and toss them, there is one chance that they may both fall with their heads up, and one chance that they may both fall with their tails up; there are, however, two chances that they may fall one heads and one tails. (Shown diagrammatically in Fig 16.)

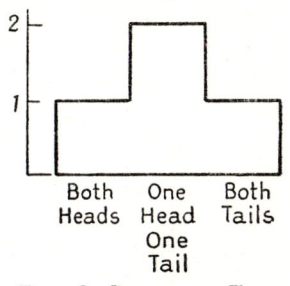

FIG. 16. CHANCES OF TWO PENNIES FALLING HEADS AND TAILS

Suppose we have six pennies, the chances will be as follows—

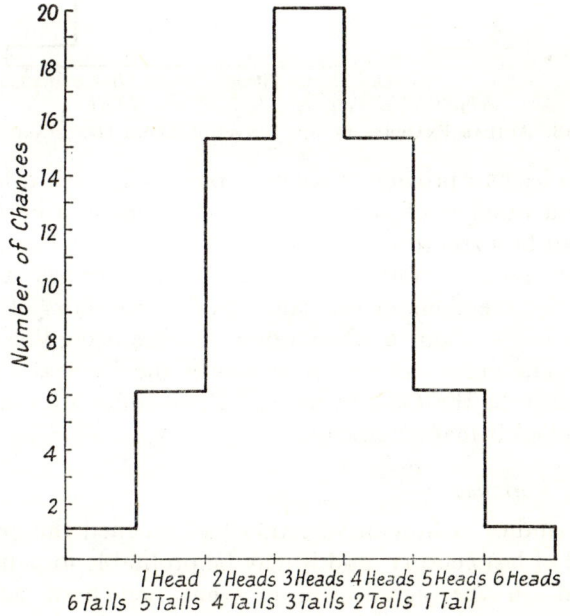

FIG. 17. THEORETICAL CHANCES OF SIX PENNIES FALLING HEADS AND TAILS

In both these cases the same bell-shaped curve is making its appearance again. Here is an actual example from tossing six pennies 100 times—

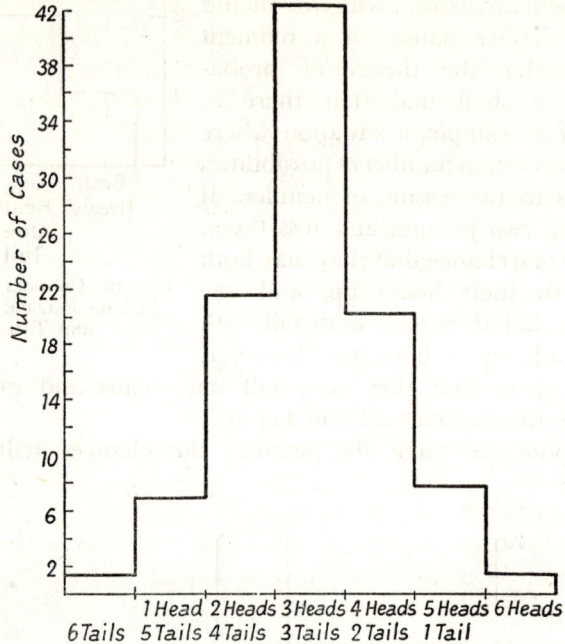

FIG. 18. ACTUAL EXAMPLES OF SIX PENNIES FALLING HEADS AND TAILS

The reader can provide other examples for himself if he cares to take a number of pennies, shake them up in a box, throw them out and record the results.

If we have a range of variation, therefore, as we have within the members of the same species, the laws of chance tend to bring about a distribution of cases according to this curve. The curve actually is known as the Normal Curve of Probability or the Gauss Curve of Error, after the man who first studied it mathematically.

*Scales of Variation*

The studies in human variation had reached this point by the end of last century, and it may be profitable to pause for a moment on the significance of what had been achieved. Up to this point we have been concerned with tangible measurements which could be expressed in inches or in pounds and ounces.

In each of the physical dimensions studied, the same regularity of distribution had been found. When individuals in a homogeneous and representative group were ranked for height they would be found to be arranged more or less symmetrically around the average with decreasing numbers above and below. A scale for height could then be established and if any new individual were produced his height could be measured against it and shown to be above average or below, very much above or very much below. The same process could be repeated for weight, colour of hair, girth, and many other physical characteristics. All of these were found to conform to the expected law for the distribution of variations within a species.

The first of our two questions, that of the variations of individuals in terms of certain characteristics, seems to be approaching an answer, at any rate in the sphere of physical measurements. What was happening in the sphere of mental measurements?

Several attempts had been made to give quantitative expression to mental differences, mainly in the sphere of perception. But it was not until 1906, when a French physician, Alfred Binet, was charged with the duty of deciding which of the Paris school children were too dull to profit by education in the ordinary schools, that the matter began to take a recognizable shape. Binet began by asking the children a series of simple questions, the answers to which did not depend on special knowledge, such as "What is your name?" "How old are you?" "How many pennies have I got here?" When he recorded the number of correct answers given by children in any one age group, he found that the same bell-shaped curve of distribution was appearing again.

There is something rather dramatic about this moment in the development of science, for it marks a new departure in our understanding of individual differences. Rules which had already been established in the field of tangible physical measurements which could be expressed in inches or in pounds and ounces were making their appearance in the field of intangible mental measurements which it had not been possible in the past to express in objective terms at all. Binet's work is notable for two reasons. In the first place it suggested that the regularities already observed among physical measurements were to be found among mental measurements also; and in the second place it showed that an objective means could be devised for measuring some mental attributes.

### MEASUREMENT IN TERMS OF SCALES

We may now take it for granted that differences between individuals on any one characteristic are likely to be distributed

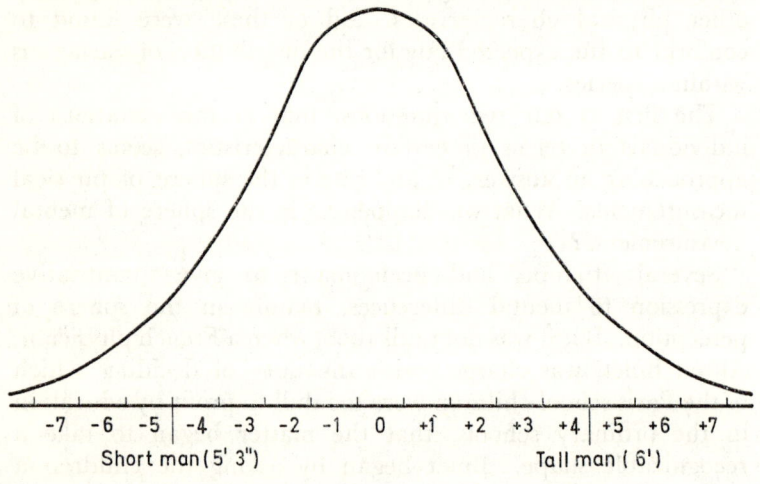

FIG. 19. MEASUREMENT IN TERMS OF AN AVERAGE

according to the Normal Curve. We can thus utilize these Normal Distributions to set up scales of variation for each of these characteristics. Taking the height of adult males in this country as an example, we know that the distribution will be as illustrated in Fig. 14. If we alter the scale along the X-axis of the graph to that shown in Fig. 19, this will enable us to express heights in terms of their relation to the average. Taking this as 5ft. 7½ins. we can now say that a man of six feet tall will be plus 4½ inches from this average. This means that he will be a fairly tall man, because there will be rather less than 10 per cent who will be further above the average than he.

Similarly, a man of 5ft. 3 ins. would be minus 4½ inches from the average. He would be a fairly short man for again there would be less than 10 per cent further below the average than he.

Measurement in terms of averages is the key to the setting up of scales for human characteristics. It is less important to know, for example, that a man is six feet tall than to know that he is in the top 10 per cent of the distribution. "Tallness" is really a relation to the average, for if the same man were to be

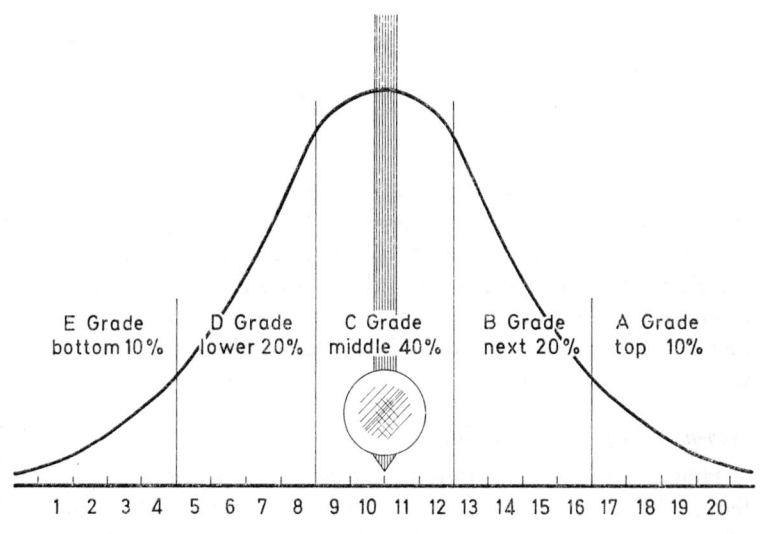

| E Grade | D Grade | C Grade | B Grade | A Grade |
| bottom 10% | lower 20% | middle 40% | next 20% | top 10% |

1  2  3  4   5  6  7  8   9  10  11  12   13  14  15  16   17  18  19  20

FIG. 20. POINT SCALE ILLUSTRATING THE "PENDULUM GIMMICK"

moved into a community where the average height was six feet three (assuming that one could be found) he would no longer be tall. He would, in fact, be rather short—not that he had shrunk but rather that the average or reference-point had moved up considerably.

The same point is even more important in tests of intelligence or other mental characteristics. It is of no practical use whatever to know that an individual has got 60 items right out of 100. Such a figure is insignificant in itself, for if the average of the people who had done the test under the same conditions were 75, then it would be a low, or below-average score. If, on the other hand, the average were 45, then it would be a high or above-average score.

In setting up a scale for a human characteristic, therefore, we must first of all find out as much as we can about the distribution of that characteristic in the population with which we are concerned. We know, for example, that the heights of adult males in this country vary according to the curve shown in Fig. 14. We can then divide this distribution up in any manner we find convenient. The simplest is to set up a five-point scale as follows—

|         |        |             |
|---------|--------|-------------|
| A Grade | top    | 10 per cent |
| B Grade | next   | 20 per cent |
| C Grade | middle | 40 per cent |
| D Grade | lower  | 20 per cent |
| E Grade | bottom | 10 per cent |

It may, however, be necessary to subdivide these five grades to provide finer shades of difference, in which case a 20-point scale will be useful. This is illustrated in Fig. 20 and has proved satisfactory in practice. It provides more subdivisions than the five-point scale, but these are not so minute that they suggest a degree of accuracy greater than the method of assessment which is being used.

*Non-measureable Characteristics*

Height can be measured in the accepted standard units of feet and inches and tests can be scored in terms of the number of items done correctly in a given time. There are many human characteristics, however, which cannot be reduced to such figures or scores, but which are important if we wish to make an assessment of an individual. One way of dealing with this is to establish an average for that characteristic in the population as a whole. This may sound difficult, but in fact is not impossible. If a few knowledgeable people sit down to consider their experience, they can usually agree on a description of the average person from this point of view.

Taking this as a reference-point, we can then set up a scale in terms of the Normal Curve. A gimmick which has proved useful over the past few years is to think of a pendulum hanging in the middle of the curve with its tip between 10 and 11 on the 20-point scale. If an individual is considered to be average from the point of view of this characteristic, then the pendulum will continue to hang at its point of rest, and he will be given a 10–11 rating. If an individual is considered to be above the average, he will push the pendulum upwards along the scale. If he is just a little above the average it will go to 12–13, but to push it up to 15–16 will require rather more weight of evidence. To push it up to 17 or beyond will require very much more, for this would mean putting it into the A grade which we consider to be the "something-extra" grade, for which only a comparatively small proportion of the population qualify.

In the same way, if the individual is rather below the average the pendulum would be pushed down to 9–8. Rather more weight of evidence would be required to push it down to 6–5, while a great deal more would be needed to push it down to 4 or below. This would mean the E grade, or very much below average grade, which applies to only about 10 per cent of the population.

It is hoped that this method of scaling makes sense to the reader for it has proved to be of considerable practical use in summing up human characteristics. We shall discuss its applications in greater detail to particular characteristics in due course, but at this stage, it is important to establish the essential points. These may be summed up as—

*First:* separating out a particular characteristic or a group of characteristics which have something in common.

*Second:* determining an average for the population for these characteristics and using this as a reference-point.

*Third:* making use of the "pendulum gimmick" on the Normal Curve of Distribution to measure upwards or downwards from this reference-point.

One of the problems in making judgments about our fellowmen is that of subjectivity. Everyone has his own standards for different characteristics, usually based on his own experience or back-ground, his own attitudes and prejudices. As a result it is very difficult for two people to agree on their judgments about another person. Not only is each thinking in terms of his own standards, the words they use to describe the personal characteristics they have in mind have never been objectively defined. Thus, when someone says of another "He is a good chap" we don't know exactly what he means by good, nor do we know the standards on which he is judging goodness. Once we have agreed on a scale as described above, however, we are at least in sight of dealing with this latter point. We shall be sharing the same reference-point, and if, for example, one says "He is a tall man" he other will know that he means someone who measures at least six feet. We can now deal with the former point which concerns the characteristics for which we set up our scales.

*How Many Scales?*

There are many different aspects of human personality and if we tried to set up a scale for each we should probably end up in a state of confusion. Moreover, some of these aspects might be of little practical importance in everyday working life. On the other hand, if we were to confine ourselves to "Good chap—Bad chap" or "Efficient—Inefficient"—such over-simplifications would overlook many essential factors.

The problem is therefore to decide how many aspects of personality we need to consider if we are to sum up an individual adequately. It will be an advantage if we can reduce these to as small a number as possible, but we must be careful not to leave anything out that might be important. One approach which has proved useful in practice has been to think of an individual from five separate points of view. From each of these a rather different aspect of his make-up will be seen and can be scaled in the manner described above. Once the individual has been considered from each of the five points of view in turn, little of importance will have been missed out.

What we are suggesting is that the personal qualities of the individual human being can be grouped under five general headings. And that scales of difference can be set up under each of these headings based on the Normal Curve of Distribution for the appropriate qualities in the population as a whole. This may sound rather a large claim, but we shall discuss it in detail in the following chapters. If it proves practicable and acceptable on a wide scale, it would have several advantages. One of these would be to reduce the margin of error between different peoples' judgments on their fellow-men. If two people were thinking of the same aspect at the same time, and if there were something in common between the standards on which they were judging, there is at least the likelihood that their judgments would be rather more objective and consequently more in agreement. If these judgments were borne out in practice, they would help to solve many problems of selecting people for jobs, of appraising the qualities they were showing in these jobs, and in considering them for further promotion.

These five aspects and the relevant scales form the subject-matter of the following chapters. At this stage, however, a brief summary may be useful.

1. *Impact on Others*

This aspect covers everything that can be seen and heard in the first fifteen or twenty minutes of contact. It concerns the individual's appearance and turnout, his speech and manner, his self-confidence in dealing with other people and his sensitivity to their reactions. All of these, of course, are superficial qualities and there is a general tendency to dismiss them as of comparatively little importance. What must be emphasized, however, is that this is the aspect of the individual to which other people react, and consequently it plays a large part in what they think of him.

People must live and work among other people and many of the difficulties which arise in everyday life stem from their reactions to each other. If the impact which an individual makes upon others brings out uniformly hostile or otherwise unfavourable reactions, this will make it difficult for him to express himself among them or to make the most of his potentialities. Similarly if in an interview an individual makes an unfortunate impact on the interviewer, this will bias the latter's judgment of his other personal qualities. There is everything to be said therefore, for keeping this aspect of a person separate from the others, for trying to make our judgments on it as objective as possible, and not allowing these to influence our judgments on his other personal qualities.

Health and physical fitness along with any disabilities, can also be included under this heading. As these involve professional advice in the shape of a report from a medical man, we shall deal with them fairly superficially. It is a waste of time for a layman to try to make judgments on these matters which can only be dealt with by a qualified specialist.

### 2. *Qualifications or Acquired Knowledge*

Under this heading we consider everything that an individual knows. It can be subdivided into General Education or that which is not directed towards equipping him for any particular trade or profession; Specialist Training, which provides skill or knowledge which will be of practical use; and Work Experience, or the time he has spent on different kinds of job.

This aspect can be of considerable importance, but it presents fewer problems than some of the other headings, because we have objective standards available. General education can be assessed in terms of examinations passed or certificates obtained, such as G.C.E. "O" or "A" levels, while the same applies to specialist training which may rise to University degrees or membership of recognized professional institutions. Work Experience can be assessed in terms of how long an individual has been in a particular job or how long in another type of position. Problems of judgment are therefore simplified by the existence of these standards which can be commonly accepted among the people concerned.

### 3. *Brains or Innate Abilities*

Here we are concerned not with what the individual knows or has done, but with what he is capable of doing. In everday terms this heading covers "quickness on the uptake" and aptitudes for particular types of task. These are aspects of the individual which can be made the subject of psychological tests and a considerable amount of knowledge and research can now be called on which we shall discuss later. We can scale individuals under these headings with a certain degree of accuracy by means of these established methods.

What these tests do not tell us, however, is how much use the individual will make of his abilities. This leads on to the fourth and most important heading.

### 4. *Motivation*

We have already discussed the needs which are fundamental and universal in the human personality and the problem which is presented to each individual in finding means of satisfying these needs. Quite obviously there are differences here, for some succeed in living active and satisfying lives which give them plenty of scope for self-expression. Others seem never to find these opportunities and in consequence carry on in a somewhat dull and frustrated existence. In our way of life it is unfortunate though inevitable, that some people will have a better start than others and will have more chance of building up a life-pattern which provides an adequate range of satisfactions.

Nevertheless, whatever their start in life may have been, there are some individuals who always seem to be able to create opportunities for themselves. These are the ones whose Motivation appears to be high up the scale, for whatever situation they find themselves in, they succeed in making something of it. This can only be accounted for by greater build-up of pressures within them. Other people in a similar position will feel less urgency, will try less hard, and will consequently find smaller scope.

Over and above the degree of Motivation in the individual there are the different directions in which it can find its outlet. Certain types of activity appeal to some people and provide them with satisfying outlets. These may not appeal to others who seek different kinds of outlet but who may strive equally hard in their own particular directions. This Motivational heading is perhaps the most interesting and certainly the most important aspect of the individual and it plays the greatest part in the kind of life-pattern he will build up for himself.

5. *Adjustment or Emotional Balance*

Our final heading covers the emotional make-up of the individual which in day-to-day terms, shows up in the amount of stress he can put up with. Once again there are differences, for some people remain calm and collected in very trying situations, while others lose control under comparatively little pressure and become childish and irresponsible in quite normal everyday life. Similarly, some individuals seem able to put up with certain kinds of stress while others react emotionally to them.

Generally speaking, living among other people provides the

kind of pressure which most of us have to put up with most of the time. Practical problems can usually be solved, given a little time and the requisite technical knowledge and experience. Moreover, once they are solved they usually stay solved. Problems involving people, however, are not always soluble. Very often they have to be lived with and though we may think we have solved them in one way, they frequently crop up in another. How the individual fits in with his fellows and the degree of responsibility he can cope with among them, is usually a manifestation of his emotional Adjustment in action.

These five headings are put forward as a framework in which to organize our ideas about personal qualities. The reader is invited to consider them and to decide whether any major aspect of human personality has been omitted. One way of doing this is to think of as many words as possible which are used in everyday speech to denote attributes of the individual. Then to consider which heading they can be fitted under. One result of this sort of exercise is to show up how imprecise many of these terms are, also that they may carry an element of approval of disapproval. "Leadership" for example, is a term which is always being bandied about, and is universally regarded as a Good Thing. It can apply to the individual whose technical knowledge, experience, motivation and emotional adjustment make him an effective supervisor on the factory floor. But it may also apply to the militant shop steward whose frustrated aggressiveness makes him the leader of an unjustified "wild cat" strike. Here we have the same term being used to describe two totally different sets of personal qualities.

Individuals differ from each of our five points of view and we shall discuss scales for these differences in the following chapters. One person may be high on some of these scales and low on others. This means that we can cover a very wide range of differences between people, but still keep them within the same framework. We could find someone who made a very good Impact on Others, good-looking, well-dressed and with a charming manner, who had normal education, was quite bright but completely idle and irresponsible. He could be contrasted with a highly-qualified research worker with a quick and active mind, whose slovenly turnout, sarcastic manner and outbursts of bad temper made an unfortunate Impact on Others, but whose dedicated Motivation to his work made him an invaluable, though unpopular, employee. These two would be utterly different from each other, but their contrasting personal make-up could still be contained in the same Five-Fold Framework.

## SUMMARY

1. What is a Normal Curve of Distribution?

It is a bell-shaped curve showing that most of the cases fall into a middle or average range and that diminishing proportions tail off above and below. It represents the probabilities of how a number of chances will fall out.

2. How does the Normal Curve apply to human beings?

Differences between human beings on any measureable attribute are usually distributed according to the Normal Curve. This can be verified by studying measurements of height, weight, etc., and it has also shown itself when certain mental attributes have been subjected to objective tests.

3. Can the Normal Curve be used to scale human attributes?

Once an average has been established for an attribute, individuals can be scaled upwards and downwards from this reference-point. A twenty-point scale can be put on the curve and the idea of a pendulum hanging at the average which can be moved upwards or downwards from this point (10 or 11 on the scale) helps to make judgments on the attribute more objective.

4. How many scales do we need to cover all aspects of an individual?

There are very many different attributes but these can be grouped fairly comprehensively under the following five headings:

(a) *Impact on Others* covering appearance, speech and manner, and everything else about the individual to which other people react.

(b) *Qualifications or Acquired Knowledge*, or everything that the individual knows, his general education, specialist training and experience.

(*c*) *Innate Abilities or Brains,* quickness on the uptake, aptitudes and other attributes which can be measured by appropriate tests.

(*d*) *Motivation,* or how successfully he can apply his abilities and achieve results.

(*e*) *Adjustment,* or the amount of stress he can cope with, usually showing in the amount of responsibility he can take among other people.

CHAPTER XI

# Impact and Relationships with others

WHEN two people begin to interact with each other, a process takes place which is not entirely rational but which has a certain significance of its own. This is the formation of a relationship, which is based on mutual awareness and expectations.

Suppose, for example, we have two people alone together, perhaps in a waiting room or a railway compartment. Neither has seen the other before nor have they ever spoken together. They are two strangers who have not yet made contact and are, in fact, two isolated entities with nothing at all between them.

After a few minutes, however, conversation begins, perhaps with a remark about the weather or some other non-committal comment. This leads to a response which calls out a further contribution until the two are talking freely together. Consciously or unconsciously each is becoming more aware of the other and forming impressions of him. Moreover, each is building up expectations of how the other will respond, these impressions becoming more definite as they are progressively confirmed in the continuing conversation. These mutual awarenesses and expectations are the essential elements in the relationship between the two, and this relationship forms the channel along which they communicate with each other.

We live our lives in a network of relationships with other people. Some of these are comparatively short and transitory like a casual conversation on a bus; others are long-term and more significant as in the groupings at home, at work and in our spare time, which make up our life-pattern. There are, however, variations in the quality of these relationships which can make them more or less satisfying experiences and better or worse channels of communication.

Suppose, when our two strangers are thrown together, one remarks, "Nice day, isn't it?" and the other responds, "Yes; Very pleasant to see the sun again. Days like this always make me feel better." This kind of exchange will cause one to think of the other as an agreeable person and to expect courteous and friendly responses from him. If these expectations are confirmed by further similar responses, then the relationship which comes into being will be of good quality. It will be a satisfying experience from the companionship point of view and will be the source of other satisfactions in the sense that one feels that the other is taking him seriously and paying attention to what he says. Each will enjoy the other's company and will be glad to prolong the relationship as far as is practicable. It will provide an effective channel of communication between the two, with little danger of distortion through emotional reactions arising from threats to the self-image.

If, on the other hand, a casual remark about the weather is met by "O.K., O.K. So you think it's a nice day. That's just fine, isn't it. Now will you for God's sake shut up!" or a similarly discourteous response, a diametrically opposite process will come into effect. One will become aware of the other as a disagreeable so-and-so and will form expectations of ill-mannered and insulting responses from him. If these expectations are progressively confirmed in further exchanges, then the relationship which comes into being will be of poor quality. It will be a frustrating experience which they will be only too glad to bring to an end as soon as possible. If, however, the situation demands that they continue interacting over a period, the prolonging of the relationship will become increasingly irritating. As a channel of communication it will be extremely unsatisfactory, for it will be the cause of all sorts of distortions. Each will feel his self-image challenged by the other and may well be more preoccupied with defending himself than with understanding what the other is saying. As these defence-mechanisms are usually far from rational, the chances of effective communication between the two will be minimal.

### SOCIAL ROLES

We live our lives in continuous interaction with other people, and the groups to which we belong are networks of interpersonal relationships between the members. These usually form a pattern or structure arising from the mutual awareness and expectations on which the relationships depend. Thus, if in the family group, mother continually meets expectations of sympathy and understanding, she will be the one to whom it seems natural for the others to pour out their troubles. Once this is well established, mother will have taken a definite "role" in the family group. If, however, she suddenly becomes too busy to listen and sympathize, there will be some shock and surprise, and a feeling that she has let the family down. She has, in fact, failed to meet the demands of the role which the others have come to expect of her.

A social role could be described as the kind of behaviour which sums up the expectations which are implicit in the relationship between one individual and the others with whom he interacts. In groups where the structure is well established, this will be quite obvious and taken for granted. When the comic comes on the stage, for example, he and the audience know exactly what to expect. His role is to make jokes and theirs is to laugh and applaud. If the turn is successful each will stimulate the other into putting more and more energy into these roles, ending up with the audience rocking with laughter and the comedian becoming more confident and daring in what he puts over. An unsuccessful turn is one where these mutual expectations are not met, little or no energy is enlisted in the roles, and the whole thing falls flat.

In some groups the mutual expectations embodied in the roles are quite clear and definite. Theatrical performances, formal lectures, parade-ground drills—these are typical examples where everyone concerned knows exactly what is expected of him and what he can expect from other people. Such groups are known as "secondary groups" and are characterized by a rigid structure of relationships and a narrowly restricted definition of the members' roles. In some ways membership of such groups is a reassuring experience, for people know where they stand and can rely on each other to behave in the expected manner.

There are other groups, however, usually small in size, where the situation is more flexible and the expected roles less clearly defined. These are known as "primary groups" and provide more scope for the individual to express himself as he feels inclined. They involve certain risks, however, in that the individual may misinterpret his role or may exceed the rather vague limitations that are placed upon it. He may thus bring the group into danger of collapse, for no matter now informal it may be, there must still be some structure of roles and relationships if the group is to continue in existence. Perhaps an example will help to make this clear.

A football game is an artificial conflict between two primary groups. There is a certain structure of relationships represented by the rules of the game, while the players accept their roles of centre-forward, half-back, goal-keeper and so on. These roles offer plenty of scope for active self-expression in passing the ball, tackling the opposing player, making openings and scoring goals. They can thus enlist the maximum motivation of which fit young men are capable on a Saturday afternoon. There are, however, limitations on these roles, such as no player except the goal-keeper handling the ball, no player being off-side and so on. The referee is there to enforce these restrictions which are embodied in the rules. There are, however, other limitations which can be less definitely laid down as, for example, those to prevent rough play or tackling in such a fashion as might injure another player. So long as these limitations are accepted and the referee's decisions taken as final, the game can proceed and the two teams can have a hard afternoon's exercise with plenty of exciting competition. But if the players do not understand or accept these limitations on their roles, the game will degenerate into a free fight and will be a waste of time for all concerned. The structure of roles and relationships on which a game of football depends will have collapsed, its place being taken by a different structure. This might be described by some as a "punch-up," or by others as a disgraceful lack of "sportsmanship," this being the term used in ordinary speech to describe the proper understanding of the roles on which games and other sports depend.

*Skill in Recognizing the Roles Available*

Awareness of the kind of role open to one in a social situation seems to come naturally to some people. They can move into an unstructured primary group and in no time at all play an active part in it, at the same time appearing to behave quite naturally and acceptably. There are others, however, who seem ill-at-ease, who call out unfortunate responses by ill-judged remarks, and who tend to lower the quality of relationships in the group. Such people lack insight into the scope and limitations of the roles open to them and are consequently at a disadvantage in their interactions with other people. Differences in the self-image also make themselves felt here, for the latter person probably thinks of himself as a plain, blunt man, with no time for the fashionable fripperies, who says what he thinks straight from the shoulder. The former has a rather more sophisticated self-image, feels that he knows something of the world, and can adapt himself to a wide range of situations.

These differences may not matter in a rigidly-structured group, particularly one where authority can be supported by threats of punishment. It was once a common experience for people to find themselves in a group where the boss did not think it necessary to consider the reactions of his subordinates. He said what he thought and they could like it or lump it. If they didn't like it, they had no means of expressing their dissatisfaction, for disagreement could quite easily mean the sack, and with high unemployment making the prospect of another job fairly remote, it was as well to keep one's mouth shut when the boss was laying down the law. Communication in such groups would have obvious limitations, but what was perhaps more serious, they encouraged an indifference to the reactions of others which had wider repercussions.

Now that a much lower level of unemployment has made the maintenance of authoritarian relationships more difficult, these communication difficulties are becoming more apparent. There is thus a greater demand for the kind of skill which can handle social roles in such a way as to build up better-quality relationships with those who interact in them. This is not a sentimental matter based on a rosy dream that we should all become a big happy family. It is rather a matter of practical down-to-earth importance in the present-day world with its full employment and its increasing spread of egalitarian self-images. Social roles are interdependent, and if in a one-to-one interaction an individual takes an authoritarian approach, he is forcing the other into a subordinate role. The other can either accept this on a "Yes, sir. No, sir. Three bags full, sir" basis, or he can resent and rebel against it. Neither of these interpretations of his role will facilitate effective communication.

All of this should make clear the importance of the Impact on

Others heading in our Five-Fold Framework. There are certain types of job which involve continuous interaction with others, in which effective communication plays a very large part, and which are, in fact, social roles rather than tasks. Examples of these are sales jobs where the reactions of prospective customers play a large part in success, and management jobs which involve meetings with subordinates and superiors as well as with others on the same level. This element is also important, though little recognized, in factory-floor supervisory jobs which involve continuous communication upwards, downwards and sideways, and the sorting out of many day-to-day problems. In present-day industry the amount of authority that can be effectively exercised at this level is minimal, consequently the demands on this interpersonal skill are at their highest.

### LEVELS OF IMPACT ON OTHERS

The foregoing discussion has been intended to make clear the practical significance of our Impact on Others heading. We can now turn to the different levels of skill that can be seen in the population and consider how these match up with the demands of various jobs. First of all, what is the average?

So far as his appearance is concerned the average man in this country seen about the streets, is wearing a suit which he bought from a multiple tailor and which has cost him approximately twenty pounds. At this price it will have been a mass-produced job and the amount of individual fitting and adjustment will have been fairly limited. As his average income, indicated by the Department of Employment and Productivity's index of earnings, will be in the region of £25[1] per week, and as his family responsibilities will be a wife and two children, it is unlikely that his budget will rise to a new suit every year. He will, therefore, be wearing what was a fairly low-cost suit to begin with, which has been to the cleaners a few times, and which has lost something of its pristine freshness. His collar will probably be a little creased as he wears his shirt for more than one day, and the remaining details, such as tie, shoes and so on, while reasonably presentable, will not indicate any great care and attention. He will, in fact, be

[1] This was the figure in 1970.

a rather nondescript figure, neither well-dressed nor badly-dressed, and unlikely to attract a second glance so far as his appearance and turnout are concerned.

This is where the appearance pendulum hangs in the middle of the scale in this country. If the reader wishes to verify this for himself, let him observe his fellow-men in that part of the town where the multiple stores are to be found. He will see a great many average men there to whom the above description will apply, that is to say if they are dressed for the street. Working clothes must be disregarded for our purpose at the moment, for they are determined by the kind of job in which the individual is engaged.

Continuing to observe people in the street, there will be a few who have paid a little more attention to detail and who give the impression of a rather better turnout. These will push the pendulum upwards along the scale into the B or 13–16 grade. He will also see a few who have a rather scruffy, run-down appearance, whose hair is unkempt, whose suits badly need pressing and whose shirts have been worn longer than they should. These will push the pendulum downwards into the D or 8–5 grade. He may also see the occasional tramp, dressed in a selection of other people's cast-off clothing, down-at-heel and badly in need of a shave and a haircut. These will provide the extra push which carries the pendulum down to the E or 4 and below grade. These differences among the dress of men in ordinary life will be comparatively easy to recognize. There will also be differences in the turnout of women, but we shall make no attempt to describe these, partly because of the continual changes in fashion and partly because we know our limitations!

Appearance and turnout are factors in anyone's Impact, but they are not necessarily the most important. So long as the individual is not below the average from these points of view, speech and manner will play a more important part. Here we are presented first of all with the problem of accent. The average person in this country speaks with the accent of his locality. That is to say, we should be able to tell as soon as he opens his mouth whether he comes from London, the Midlands, Lancashire, Yorkshire or further north. This accent, which will be enough to betray which part of the country he comes from, will however not be sufficiently marked to render him difficult to understand or make him sound comic. He will make minor grammatical slips which will only be noticeable if one pays close attention to what he says, and he will have a rather limited vocabulary. This will manifest itself when he is trying to explain something complex, for then he will tend to repeat himself, stumble to find the right word, and fall back into the clichés, "see what I mean," "you know," and the like. This is where the pendulum hangs in terms of speech, vocabulary and use of the language.

Most important of all, of course, is the handling of interpersonal relationships, self-confidence among other people, sensitivity to their reactions and the ability to exercise some sort of control over these. From this point of view our average man is all right in a familiar situation. Among people he knows and with whom he feels on level terms, he shows no lack of confidence and can express himself to the maximum of his vocabulary. It is when he is placed in an unfamiliar situation that his limitations become apparent. Either he becomes silent and reserved and isolates himself from the group, or he overdoes it and tries unsuccessfully to dominate the others. He cannot find the right role in which to express himself and consequently strikes the wrong note and tends to embarrass the others.

There is always a danger that one appears to be laying down the law in these matters, and if this becomes real, then the exercise defeats itself. It is therefore essential that the reader should review his own experience on these matters and consider whether this tallies with the descriptions which are here suggested. Exercises have been conducted with students and other groups in which they have been invited to grade recordings and demonstration interviews. After a little practice and discussion, it is surprising how closely their judgments approach each other, which suggests that the element of objectivity in these judgments is increasing. The idea of the average person, from the Impact on Others point of view, appears to provide an acceptable reference-point at which the pendulum hangs in the middle of the Normal Curve.

*Demands of Jobs from the Impact Point of View*

What kind of job would the average person be capable of in terms of its demands on the qualities we have been discussing under this heading? A moment's reflection should make it clear that he could cope with anything which involves no more than routine interaction with the same group of people during working hours. There are lots of jobs like this on the factory floor or in the office, where there is no responsibility for other people and where communication takes place mainly on everyday matters which are well understood by all concerned. In this kind of work-situation, the average person can handle his interactions with others quite adequately most of the time.

It is when a job demands more than routine relationships that the Impact aspect of the individual begins to acquire a certain significance. Some of these do not rank particularly high on the job evaluation scale and consequently attract little attention. A milk roundsman, for example, has a fairly modest job, but it is one which involves him in continuous relationships with a number of people. Each of these will have his, or more probably her, requirements in how many pints are to be delivered from day to day, where they are to be left if she is not about, whether she wants any cream or other extras, how often she pays her bill and so on. There will be a continuous round of small-scale arrangements, each of which can be carried out on a mutually friendly and helpful basis. Each on the other hand, can become an issue over which a rather bad-tempered argument arises if the milkman's tact and savoir-faire falls short of the demands of the job.

There are many other examples of jobs which make slightly more than average demands from this aspect. Receptionists, telephone operators, retail salesmen, petrol pump attendants, storemen, minor public officials and the like; each of these provides the opportunity for making routine interactions with others either a smooth and unremarked experience for them, or a minor source of frustration. The cumulative effect of these will show up in the sales figures, the numbers of small complaints, and the public image of the organization. It is an unfortunate but inescapable fact that to many people a visit to the Town Hall, the Employment Exchange or the Social Security office is associated with these small irritations and frustrations. This suggests that a slightly higher standard on the Impact on Others scale in the selection process might improve the relationships between these institutions and the public.

## A JOB AS A SOCIAL ROLE

When we consider supervisory or management posts, however, interaction with others assumes an even greater significance. Such posts place an individual at a focal point in the pattern of relationships within an organization. The first-line supervisor, for example, must deal with the operators under his charge, and also with the second-line supervisor or manager to whom he is responsible. He must also interact with some functional specialists, work-study men, maintenance mechanics, progress chasers, personnel officers and the like. He will have dealings too with the shop steward. Many of these interactions will involve matters of considerable importance and may rouse some feeling on the part of those concerned. This is the kind of job which is much more a social role than an actual task, and things can go seriously wrong if the demands of this role are not adequately met. We must therefore set a standard rather higher up the Impact scale.

Dress and appearance play a certain part in this but rather in the negative sense. If the individual looks scruffy and unkempt, this will handicap the initial impression he makes, though it may be overcome later. Self-confidence will be essential if he is to take the initiatives which the role demands, for if he cannot speak up for himself, important points will be overlooked because he has not commanded sufficient attention when these are brought up in discussion. At the same time, however, he must be able to listen, which may mean subordinating himself to the other person as the situation requires. Perhaps most important, however, will be a sensitivity to the reactions of the people with whom he is interacting. If he remains unaware of these, he may fail to communicate effectively because he is not encouraging the feedback on which this ultimately depends.

The social role demanded by this level of post is not static, like that of a routine job. It is constantly changing, and to be successful in it the individual must be capable of adapting to changes. He must switch from being the encouraging and sympathetic listener to being the chap in charge giving instructions about what's to be done and how it's going to be done. At one moment he may be disarming opposition by discussing possible difficulties in a reasonable manner; while at another he may be making it clear that he's standing no nonsense. He must cope with a range of situations, each of which makes its own demands on his self-confidence, his sensitivity and his powers of expression. Each will also have its measure of success, usually in terms of how effective the communication has been between the parties involved.

When discussing this aspect of Impact on Others with students, one occasionally encounters rather negative reactions. Typical of these is the question "Does this mean that we must always be acting a part? If so, it's a horrible idea. Surely a person can just be himself, without worrying all the time about whether he's meeting the demands of a social role?" Admittedly there are some unpleasant connotations in this concept of social roles and the idea that we must always be putting on an act has its distasteful aspects. Nevertheless, if one faces up to the realities of life among other people, one must accept the fact that one must adapt one's behaviour if one wishes to deal effectively with one's interactions with them. These adaptations can, of course, be made in an entirely cynical and calculating fashion with the sole intention of manipulating other people for one's own selfish advantage. If this is so, they will probably defeat themselves, for the smooth talker may get away with it once. As soon as other people realize this, however, he will be at a disadvantage, for the more he tries to put himself across, the more suspicion and distrust he will encounter.

Meeting the demands of interpersonal situations and recognizing the social role expected of us, is something which we must face up to in our pluralistic society. That there are different levels of skill in meeting these demands and coping with these roles is one of the facts of life. Success in certain types of job depends to some extent on the acquisition of this skill, though this is only one aspect of the job and the individual who carries it out. A high level of Impact on Others will not make up for a lack of Qualifications, low Motivation or inadequate Adjustment. It is, however, one aspect which should be separated out and considered by itself.

### LOWER LEVELS OF IMPACT

We have already mentioned the kind of dress and turnout which would push our pendulum downwards from the average.

Similar considerations apply to speech and manner for one can encounter local accents which are so marked as to be incomprehensible to anyone unfamiliar with that part of the country. Grammatical faults can also become more pronounced with a heavy sprinkling of "we was," "he done," "don't know nothing" and similar breaches of the rules. Vocabularies also can be limited and here is it interesting to note how often the deficiencies are made up by swear-words. These can sometimes serve the purpose of giving emphasis to what one is saying. When they pop up before every other word, however, it is pretty obvious that the speaker's vocabulary is under some strain.

As is usually the case, however, it is the individual's self-confidence in interacting with others which plays the most important part in his Impact. And what pushes the pendulum down from this point of view is a shut-in manner which inhibits the making of contact with other people. The below-average individual is continually on the defensive, takes the most casual remark as a challenge, cannot relax in conversation and in consequence is practically impossible to communicate with. His ability to establish good-quality relationships is virtually non-existent while his skill in recognizing the role expected of him is similarly deficient. If this kind of person is placed in a position which demands communication and interaction with others, he will leave a trail of misunderstanding and ill-feeling behind him. And it will be the task of some other poor sucker to tidy up the mess!

There are, of course, jobs where relationships with others are of comparatively little importance. Many factory-floor production jobs fall into this category along with unskilled or labouring jobs. They can never be entirely ruled out, however, for there must be some communication about what is to be done, who is going to do it, and what happens when he's finished. There will also be some minor difficulties to be sorted out in the course of the day. It is here that the limitations of those of below-average Impact will make themselves felt, for their limited skills in interaction will make it possible for any of these minor difficulties to build up into a major crisis with its accompanying bad feeling. The person immediately in charge must therefore, be sufficiently well up the Impact

| 1-4 | 5-8 | 9-12 | 13-16 | 17-20 |

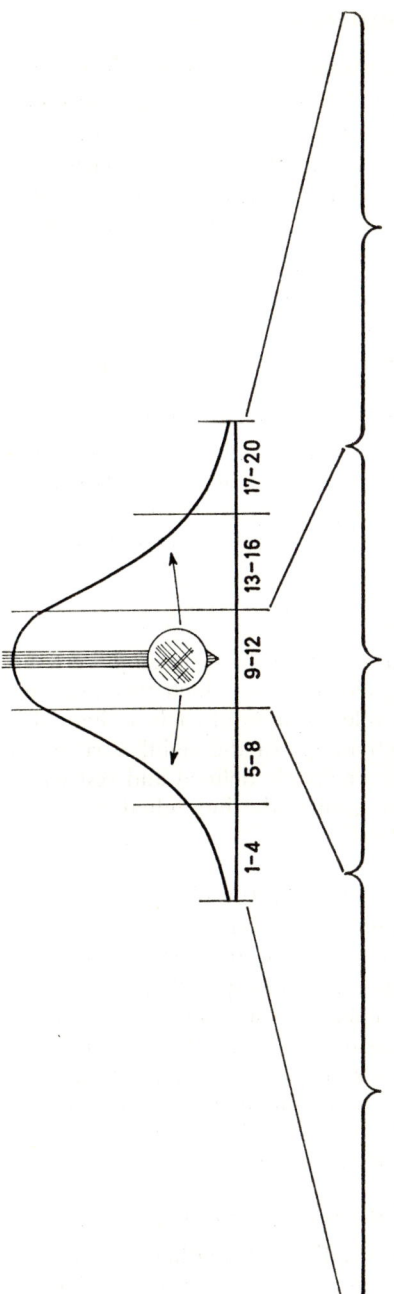

Scruffy turnout, and accent so marked as to be at times incomprehensible. Grammar and vocabulary inadequate to normal conversation. Manner inhibited and self-confidence so shaky as to make the establishment of effective relationships difficult or impossible.

Suitable only for jobs where communication and interaction with others is of little importance.

Unremarkable and rather nondescript in dress. Noticeable but not incomprehensible local accent. Minor grammatical slips and vocabulary limited to everyday communication. Self-confidence adequate to routine interaction but rather under stress when placed in unfamiliar situations. Limited initiative in expressing himself or making the most of social roles.

Suitable for jobs involving no more than routine interaction with the same group of people.

Turnout showing more attention to detail. More adequate command of language and ability to express himself. Self-confidence adequate to a wide range of situations with ability to seize opportunities offered by social roles and make the most of them. Some control over reactions of others.

Suitable for jobs where effective communication and interaction with others plays a significant part.

FIG. 21 SCALE FOR IMPACT ON OTHERS

Showing where pendulum hangs for the average of this aspect and the kind of evidence which would be needed to push it upwards or downwards from this point.

scale to make up for these limitations, sort out these difficulties before they become acute, and deal effectively with the communication problems presented by this kind of situation.

The scale shown in Fig. 21 is an attempt to draw together the aspects of the individual with which we are concerned under the Impact on Others heading, and to relate these to the demands of different jobs.

## SUMMARY

1. What constitutes a "relationship" between people?

A relationship is the mutual awareness and expectations which come into being when two people interact together. It can be of good quality and form a satisfying experience to those involved; or it can be of poor quality, in which case it will be a frustrating experience.

2. What is a Social Role?

Any grouping is a network or structure of relationships between the members. The expected behaviour on which this structure depends constitutes the social role required of each individual if the group is to continue functioning. In the rigidly-structured "secondary group" these roles are clearly defined and restricted. In the more flexible "primary group" the individual has more scope in how he interprets his role.

3. Is there a skill involved in recognizing roles?

Some individuals with a sophisticated self-image can quickly recognize the roles open to them, express themselves effectively in them, and draw other people into corresponding roles which are co-operative and lead to effective communication. Others lack this skill and are ill-at-ease or tend to fall back on authoritarian roles with a complete lack of sympathy for the feelings of colleagues and subordinates. In a fully-employed, egalitarian society, it is difficult to support these authoritarian roles, with the result that others tend to rebel against them.

4. What is the average under the Impact on Others heading?

A rather nondescript-looking individual, neither well-dressed nor badly-dressed; speaking with a recognizable but not incomprehensible local accent; making minor grammatical slips and with a slightly limited vocabulary. His self-confidence will be adequate to familiar situations, but he may be rather at a loss in a strange environment.

5. How does the individual's Impact on Others relate to his job?

In jobs which involve no more than routine interaction with others, the average person is perfectly adequate. In jobs where this aspect plays a more important part, a rather higher level of Impact may be advisable.

6. In what sort of jobs is Impact on Others more important?

In supervisory or management jobs which involve continuous interaction and communication with others. Such jobs are social roles rather than tasks, for they are at the focal point of a number of important relationships. These roles, moreover, will be constantly changing according to the situation, hence the demands on the individual's skill will be correspondingly greater.

7. Is below-average Impact on Others a handicap?

There are some jobs where this may be of little significance, for communication and interaction with others play only a limited part in them. It is important, however, that those in charge of such jobs have sufficient skill to make up for the limitations of those with below-average Impact.

CHAPTER XII

# Qualifications and Innate Abilities

THE division we have entitled Qualifications or Acquired Knowledge can be important in determining one aspect of the demands of the job and the kind of person who can meet these demands. It presents comparatively few problems of judgment, however, for we are involved here in an area where objective standards are available. These are represented by examinations, certificates, membership of professional institutions, years in a job, and the like. Doubts have been cast on the value of examinations as a test of knowledge and there are obviously problems in the maintenance of examination standards. While accepting the validity of these doubts, however, one can still say that to pass an orthodox examination, the individual must display a certain standard of knowledge in the subject-matter on which he is being examined. Whether or not he will apply this knowledge effectively in practice is a separate question, and one which will crop up under our Motivational heading. It may well be a more significant question, but at the moment we shall disregard it and accept the examination result for what it is worth under our Qualifications heading.

If we decide that a post requires a Higher National Certificate in Production Engineering as a minimum standard of Qualifications, then from this point of view the decision as to whether the candidate is acceptable or unacceptable makes itself. If he has obtained this certificate he is acceptable in terms of Qualifications. If he has not obtained it, he is not acceptable—unless, or course, he reaches such a standard under the other headings as to justify modifying this minimum requirement. For the moment, however, we shall leave this complication to one side.

### A SCALE FOR GENERAL EDUCATION

At the moment the average person in this country leaves school at fifteen and probably without any certificate of General Education. This is a year later than was the case twenty-five years ago, and is a year earlier than will be the case some time in the 1970's. We are thus presented with a curve of distribution which is moving upwards along the X-axis. It is therefore necessary to bear in mind that the standards applicable at any one period may have to be modified in a few year's time. We can say at present that under half of the school population achieve any kind of recognized certificate by the end of their full-time education. Certainly a *good* Certificate of Secondary Education (C.S.E.) or General Certificate of Education (G.C.E.) Ordinary level lies beyond the reach of all but a minority, while those who obtain G.C.E. Advanced level ("A" level) are progressively fewer still. The proportions who go to University or continue their full-time General Education at other institutions are less again, though the increasing number of places available will change this proportion substantially in the next few years.

It is not difficult therefore, to rough out a scale upwards from the average for General Education. This may not be accurate in the sense that the numbers included in each stage correspond exactly to the percentages of leavers who pass that level of examination. It nevertheless provides a simple means of relating different educational levels to each other. Where problems present themselves is in the lower half of the curve. When about three-quarters of the population went to Secondary Modern schools, the method of "streaming" used in these provided a series of steps. The average of the population usually ended up in the "A" stream, while lower down the scale would be found in the "B" or "C" streams. As the Comprehensive system becomes widespread, however, it will be necessary to take a further look at the standards for estimating achievement in General Education. For everyday use at the moment, however, the accompanying table should provide a simple but adequate means of ranking.

20 Outstanding achievement at University with first-class honours degree, prizes or other evidences of distinction.
19 Upper second-class honours degree.
18 Lower second-class honours degree.
17 Third-class or pass degree.
16 Three or more "A" levels with grades in the higher brackets.

15  Two "A" levels.
14  Four or more "O" levels with grades in at least the middle brackets, or four or more Grade 1 C.S.E. passes.
13  Less than four "O" levels or Grade 1 C.S.E. passes.
12  Lower standard C.S.E. or R.S.A. Examinations.
11 ⎫
   ⎬ No publicly recognized certificate but at least average in the "A" stream of a secondary modern school.
10 ⎭
9   Below average in the "A" stream, as shown by place in class, or above average in "B" stream.
8   From here downwards lower "B" stream or "C" stream would apply.

### SCALES FOR SPECIALIST OR TECHNICAL TRAINING

This division is concerned with education or training which is designed to equip the individual for work of one kind or another. At the higher levels there may be difficulties is deciding just what is "education" and what is "training." A degree in mathematics with a specialization in statistics—should this be classified as general education or as training for a professional career? These and similar questions could lead us into a discussion on the purpose and philosophy of education, but however attractive this might be, we shall avoid it and stick firmly to our brief. In the majority of cases the distinction will be quite apparent.

Once again we are confronted with rising standards. Up till a short time ago one could say with confidence that the average person in this country might get some systematic training on the job but would not attain any certificate which would be publicly recognized. With the advent of the Industrial Training Boards, however, more apprentices are spending periods at local technical colleges where they are following a recognized course. This may lead to a City and Guilds Certificate, and Ordinary National or even a Higher National Certificate or Diploma. While we can lay down objective standards, therefore, we may under-estimate the proportions of the population which should be included in each.

A further complication is the proliferation of courses and certificates in different areas of training. Business studies, for example, appear in the syllabuses of many colleges, and diplomas can be obtained after periods of full- or part-time study. A National Examinations Board for Supervisory Studies has recently been set up which awards an ordinary and an advanced certificate. Attempting to rank these in an objective manner presents problems, but a relatively simple answer is to consider the length of the course and the standard of entry. If, as with the N.E.B.S.S. certificate, it can be taken part-time over one academic session and requires no evidence of previous educational achievement on the part of the entrant, it could be placed in the lower half of the B grade, 13–14. If, however, a course were to last for two or three academic sessions part-time, or one full-time, and the equivalent of G.C.E. "O" level were required for entry, then it could be placed in the upper half of the B grade, 15–16. Courses which approximate to graduate standard, requiring the equivalent of G.C.E. "A" levels for entry and lasting more than one academic session full-time, could be placed in the A grade, or 17 and upwards.

Professional or quasi-professional associations have made their appearance in increasing numbers in the past few years. Many of these entitle their members to put letters after their names, implying that they possess qualifications of some significance. The intentions behind these bodies have usually been initially to bring together individuals engaged in the same kinds of activity and to provide a forum for the sharing of experience and the exchange of views as to future developments. Sooner or later the question of qualification for membership crops up and some decision must be taken as to what this shall be. Sometimes it may be laid down as a certain period of experience; sometimes a formal examination may be required. Standards vary from the well-established Engineering or Accountancy Institutions, membership of which provides a qualification of graduate level in our A grade or 17 and upwards on the scale, to more modest bodies which would be placed in our B grade or 13–16 on the scale.

It will be apparent that the setting out of a scale for specialist, technical or professional qualifications is rather a hazardous project. Nevertheless, if we are to achieve any comparability of standards the attempt must be made. The following may serve as an outline framework—

20 — This grade covers university qualifications which could be classified as professional training, scaled as for General
19 — Education, 1st class honours, 2nd class, pass, etc. It also involves the qualifications awarded by recognized pro-
18 — fessional associations which are the equivalent of graduate level. These would include the Engineering Institutions,
17 — the senior Accountancy bodies and others of similar standing.

16 — These would include qualifications which require more than two sessions of part-time study and are publicly recognized, such as Higher National Certificates or Diplo-
15 — mas. Also, membership of associations which require formal qualifications of less than graduate standard.

14 — These would include qualifications requiring two sessions or less part-time study and membership of associations which require few formal qualifications but rely rather on
13 — experience.

12 — and below. It is unlikely that from here downwards there would be any qualifications other than experience on the job.

### SCALES FOR DIFFERENT LEVELS OF JOB

Under this aspect of our Qualifications heading we are concerned with the individual's work experience. This will naturally be related to the job for which he is being considered and can be laid down with some degree of accuracy in the specification. If, for example, we are looking for an assistant personnel manager, we shall be concerned not only with his General Education and his formal Professional Training, but also with the kind of experience he has obtained of Personnel work and the amount of responsibility he has undertaken. But even though the requirements may be specific to the particular job, it may still be necessary to relate jobs to each other. For this reason we must consider a scale on similar lines to those we have already discussed.

Where, then, does our pendulum hang in terms of the average job? Several sources of information are available here, perhaps the most useful of which is the Index of Weekly Earnings published every six months by the Department of Employment and Productivity. This is based on a representative sample of adult male workers in manufacturing industry and shows the average take-home pay including overtime, bonus, piecework earnings and the like. At the moment this stands at something over £25 per week for the country as a whole. When broken down geographically it works out rather higher in the Midlands and the South-east, and rather lower in the more Northerly areas of the country. Different variations also appear when analysed by industry, but all these details can be found the appropriate publications. From our point of view, however, this figure gives a broad indication of what the average man takes home at the end of the week. What kind of job does it represent?

Generally speaking it means a semi-skilled job which has been organized as a stage in a production process and has a set level of expected output. Such a job will demand a fairly high tempo throughout the day but will not require much in the way of training or experience. There are, however, some jobs designated as skilled which would also fit into this category. These demand little in the way of formal training but depend rather on experience, and can be carried out at a fairly leisurely pace. At this level the differences between "skilled" and "semi-skilled" work are rather blurred for some so-called skills have been overtaken by mechanization, while some other jobs which have never been included in the traditional apprenticeship system make demands which are at least equal. We could sum up, therefore, by saying that if a job demands a limited degree of knowledge and expertise and commands a wage equal to the average current earnings, it can be said to leave the pendulum hanging in the middle of the scale.

To push our pendulum upwards we need evidence of a higher degree of skill which can only be acquired by formal training and planned experience. Highly-skilled jobs at this level involve the individual in planning his own work and making decisions as he goes along. In engineering, a toolmaker working from drawings would move the pendulum upwards to perhaps 12 on the scale while in other industries similar examples could be found. Another type of job which would justify this grading is one on which several others depend. Such jobs may not necessarily be highly skilled but they involve a certain responsibility for several others throughout the day. Such jobs have been designated as "semi-supervisory" and though they still involve working on the job they call for a wider scope than the others around them. "Relief hands" or "service hands" would fall into this category.

Jobs which involve formal responsibility for the supervision of others would push the pendulum definitely into the B grade, 13 or 14 on the scale. At this level it is unlikely that the individual would work on the job itself except in emergency, but would rather be involved full-time on supervision. Higher-level supervisory jobs would come next, while in the upper end of the B grade, 15–16 on the scale, would come managerial jobs. In these the intellectual element would be more obvious in forward planning, the setting of objectives and the provision of resources. Higher management jobs concerned with longer-term planning would come into the A grade, 17 or upwards.

To push the pendulum downwards, we would be concerned with lower-grade semi-skilled jobs, while still further below would come the unskilled and labouring jobs. As mentioned above, the level of earnings may be useful as a guide but this should never be taken entirely at its face value. Piecework, bonus incentives and regular overtime, can push up the earnings of some jobs well beyond their fairly modest demands in training and skill. There are also different bargaining advantages among certain groups which can be exploited to raise the levels of earnings. It is not unheard of for a supervisor to take home less at the end of the week than the pieceworkers who are formally under his charge. Such disadvantages can to some extent be offset by "staff" conditions and a greater security of employment, but they nevertheless tend to confuse the situation. Figure 22 sets out a rough scale for different levels of job.

## SCALES FOR INNATE ABILITIES

We have referred briefly to Binet's work on the measurement of mental abilities among Paris school-children in the early 1900's. This opened up a wide field of research on "intelligence testing" which has since been developed in Europe and the United States and has resulted in a well-established body of knowledge about the Innate Abilities heading of our Five Fold Framework. To summarize this in the space at our disposal would be an impossible task but we may attempt to describe

| 1-4 | 5-8 | 9-12 | 13-16 | 17-20 |

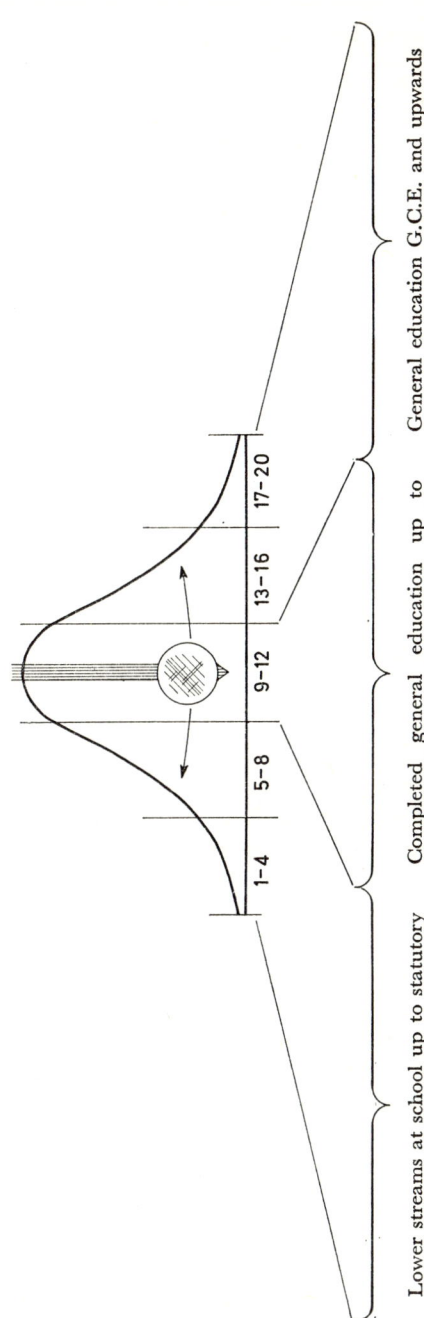

Lower streams at school up to statutory leaving age. No formal training except what is picked up on the job. Lower-level semi-skilled jobs, downwards to unskilled and labouring. Earnings below average or spasmodic.

Completed general education up to school-leaving age, perhaps obtained a certificate. Some systematic training at work, but no formal qualification. Higher-level, work-studied semi-skilled job on fast tempo, or lower-level skilled job learned mainly by experience. Earnings somewhere near national average.

General education G.C.E. and upwards to University. Technical training shown by formal qualifications. Jobs from highly-skilled, upwards through supervisory level to management. Earnings rising appropriately.

FIG. 22. SCALE FOR QUALIFICATIONS

Putting together general education, specialist training and work experience, though these are not always on the same level.

briefly what an intelligence test is, and what practical use can be made of it.

An intelligence test is a standardized perceptual task which can be given to a number of people under identical conditions. It does not demand previous knowledge, being made up of items which are equally familiar to all those who are being tested, such as words or figures, or equally unfamiliar, such as diagrams or shapes. It is designed so that it can be scored objectively, leaving no room for judgment as to whether the answers are right or wrong. To meet these requirements in designing a test calls for a certain expertise, while the application of intelligence tests demands a certain standard of training if the results are to be relied upon. The little puzzles which appear in newspapers or on the television should always be treated with suspicion, for they are not "intelligence tests" in any real sense of the term.

After the test has been designed it must be calibrated. This involves applying it to a representative sample of the population and obtaining enough scores to set up a curve of distribution. When a test is thus tried out in practice there is usually one person who achieves the highest score and one who achieves the lowest. Between these extremes a Normal curve will build itself up around a central tendency or average. Once this has been established, scores can be expressed in terms of this distribution in the manner which has already been described. The 20-point scale can be used, or the more statistically sophisticated method of Standard Deviations or "sigma units."

While it is comparatively simple to express the test scores of adults on such a scale, a certain difficulty presents itself when testing children. Their scores on a test will rise with age until adolescence is reached, a child of twelve years old gaining a higher score than a ten-year-old simply because it is two years older. In these circumstances therefore, the scores of children of different ages cannot be compared directly with one another. The way around this difficulty is to work out an average score for each age-group, eight years old, nine, ten and so on. Once these have been established, any child's score can be expressed in terms of these age-groups. Thus, if a child gained a score which was exactly the average of twelve-year-old children, this could be taken as representing a "mental age" of twelve.

But if the child's age in years, or its "chronological age" was only ten, then it would be obvious that it was the equivalent of two years ahead in mental ability. This difference can be expressed in the form of a ratio known as the "Intelligence Quotient" or "I.Q." viz—

$$\frac{\text{Mental Age}}{\text{Chronological Age}} \times 100 = \text{Intelligence Quotient.}$$

Thus, in the case just noted this would work out as

$$\frac{\text{Mental Age}}{\text{Chronological Age}} \frac{12}{10} \times 100 = 120 \text{ I.Q.}$$

A child whose ability is above the average for its age group will have an I.Q. of more than 100, while one whose ability is below will have an I.Q. of less than 100. One whose ability is exactly average will have an I.Q. of 100. There is nothing in the least mysterious about Intelligence Quotients; they are simply a means of expressing a child's test-score in relation to its age and thus making it possible to compare children of different ages. When adults' I.Q.'s are quoted, this simply means that their scores are being placed on a scale which has been so widely used for children that it has become common parlance.

### THE PRACTICAL UTILITY OF INTELLIGENCE TESTS

Intelligence tests provide a very useful means of ranking people in terms of their Innate Abilities. The research work which has been carried out over the past sixty-odd years suggests that, so long as allowance is made for age, an individual's test-score remains on much the same level. This would indicate that there is a certain standard of perceptual or mental demands which the individual could meet without difficulty, while there are others with which he might find it less easy to cope. To establish this conclusion, studies have been carried out in which test-scores were compared with performance in other areas.

These studies depend on a statistical device known as a "coefficient of correlation." If we have two curves of distribution say, one made up of scores on an intelligence test and the other of marks in an examination, we can compare the relative positions of the individuals concerned. If we found that these were exactly similar, the individual with the highest test-score getting top marks in the examination, the second highest next, and so on down to the lowest scorer on the test coming out bottom in the examination, then the correlation coefficient would be $+1$. If, on the other hand, we found that the lowest scorer on the test got top marks in the examination, the next lowest second, and so on until the highest scorer in the test came out bottom in the examination, then the correlation coefficient would be $-1$. If we found that there was no relation whatsoever between the test-scores and the marks in the examination, then the correlation coefficient would be 0.

Most of the studies that have been carried out in this field have shown positive correlations. These however, have never been near $+1$, or completely positive. This raises a further question of what level of correlation can be considered really significant. If the coefficient worked out at $+.2$ would this mean that there was a real relationship between the test-scores and the examination marks? Or $+.3$? or $+.4$? The answer lies in a test of "significance" or a statistical technique which indicates at what point the correlation could have occurred by chance and above which it represents a real relationship. Many of the studies referred to show correlations which are over the borderline of significance, but there are very few where the chance element can be completely dismissed. This suggests that, while what is represented by the test-score plays a part in performance, it is not the sole determinant.

There is, of course, no reason to be surprised at this. Any individual may have high Innate Ability, but it is the use he makes of this in practice which determines his actual performance. Our Motivational heading will thus play a part, and consequently the indirect use of intelligence tests is often more significant than the actual result. What is frequently found in practice is that the test provides a cut-off point, or a level below which there is very little chance that the individual will be successful at the task. Above this minimum, however, while the individual may possess the Innate Ability required, it is his Motivation or the degree to which he applies this ability in practice which determines his performance. Thus, if two people reach the same level of performance and one has a high test-score while the other has a lower one, then it is fair to assume that the latter has shown more Motivation than the former.

Intelligence tests can rank people with a fair degree of accuracy under the one heading of Innate Abilities. But real-life situations call for other qualities as well as brains. They involve interaction with others which brings the Impact aspect into play; they may call for experience, knowledge and other aspects of the Qualifications heading; and they demand varying degrees of Motivation and Adjustment. It is always a mistake to isolate any one of the five headings and attach an exaggerated importance to it. While intelligence tests can provide valuable information about one of these, it is nevertheless important not to let them get out of focus.

*Other Types of Ability Test*

Intelligence tests can be made up of verbal material, that is to say they will call for quickness in seeing relationships between words. They can also be made up of non-verbal material, where those undergoing the test must see the relationships between different forms of diagram. Numerical tests can also be devised where the problem is to see relationships between sets of figures. As none of these tests depend on actual knowledge, they call into play a fundamental "quickness on the uptake" and show the different levels which appear characteristic of each individual. Some individuals however, gain relatively higher scores on the different types of test, and we can be presented with high verbal scores and low non-verbal and numerical scores. Similarly, we can find low verbal scores offset by high non-verbal and numerical scores. These differences suggest that certain individuals find that the various kinds of material are easier or more difficult to deal with, and this can raise problems. In many jobs, communication with others plays an important part and thus a low verbal score could be a handicap. In other jobs of a more practical nature, where communication is less important, this might be of little significance and a high non-verbal score might be an indication of future success.

It is also possible to devise tests for special aptitudes. Some people are quicker than others in their understanding of mechanical things and these differences can we shown up in tests which consist of diagrams illustrating wheels, levers, gears, and the like. When asked what will happen when one or other of the points in the diagram is moved, some people get the right answer straight away, while others find it difficult to think out how the relative movements will affect each other. These differences will show up in the scores which usually have some correlation with performance in mechanical training or on jobs which involve dealing with machinery. There are also differences in manual dexterity or the ability to manipulate things with the hands or fingers. These can be measured by tests which involve moving small objects around according to a set pattern, placing pegs in holes, or similar manual tasks. Below certain scores it often works out that the individual is too "ham-handed" to be any good at an assembly job or others which demand quick and deft manipulation of components.

There are certain abilities which can be considered "general" in the sense that they show themselves is a wide range of mental or perceptual activities. There are others which are more "special" in the sense that they can be recognized only in activities of a more restricted nature. These latter could be thought of as "aptitudes" as they equip individuals to learn certain types of task more quickly than others. Research work on test-scores suggests a kind of hierarchical arrangement of abilities, with the more generalized ones higher up the tree and the more specialized at the lower levels. The demands of different jobs under this heading can usually be set out as a series of minimum standards.

A further type of test can be devised which is specific to a particular job. This consists of a sample of the activities, laid out so that it can be carried out under standard conditions and the individual's performance scored objectively. "Sample" or "analogous" tests for small assembly jobs can be set up on these lines and when they are tried out on a representative group of untrained individuals a curve of distribution can be built up. When subsequent performance on the job is compared with the original scores, some correlation will usually be found. This may make it possible to set a cut-off point below which there is little chance of an applicant being successful.

## SUMMARY

1. What aspects do we cover by the heading Qualifications?

Everything that the individual knows, his general education, his specialist training, and his experience at work. Another term for this heading might be Acquired Knowledge.

2. Can we set up a scale for general education?

The average person in this country at the moment leaves school at fifteen without a formal certificate of education. Upwards from this point we have C.S.E., G.C.E., and University degrees. Below this level, some estimate must be made of the stream, place in class, or other evidence of performance.

3. Can we set up a scale for technical training?

At the moment, the average person has no formal qualification under this sub-heading, though this may change. Above this are City and Guilds, Ordinary or Higher National, and membership of institutions which lay down specific levels of qualification.

4. What is the average for work experience?

In very general terms, the average is either a higher-level semi-skilled or a lower-level skilled job. Upwards from this point come highly-skilled, supervisory and management jobs. Downwards are lower-level semi-skilled, unskilled and labouring.

5. What is an intelligence test?

An intelligence test is a standardized mental task which does not depend upon knowledge and can be given to different people under the same conditions and scored objectively. Once it has been calibrated on a representative sample of the population the individual's score can be related to the distribution. When applied to children of different ages, an arithmetical device known as the "Intelligence Quotient" allows their scores to be compared.

6. What are the practical uses of intelligence tests?

They provide evidence of the individual's perceptual speed which research has shown to be reliable and valid within its framework. Tests usually provide a cut-off point below which there is little likelihood of success on a job. They also enable an indirect assessment of Motivation to be made by a comparison of test-scores with achievement.

7. What other types of test are available?

Intelligence tests can be made up of verbal, non-verbal, or numerical material. Tests can also be devised for aptitudes like mechanical ability, manual dexterity and the like. Sample tests for particular jobs can also be devised, but one must always remember that the standardization of a test is much more important than the test material.

CHAPTER XIII

# Differences in Motivational Patterns

We cannot be said to understand anyone until we have some idea of the sort of things he likes doing, the kind of aims he sets himself, and how persistent and successful he is in following them up. In other words, we must try to gain some insight into his Motivation. This is the aspect of personality in which we shall find perhaps the widest differences between people. So far as working life is concerned it is the most important of our five headings.

We have already discussed the subject in general terms in Chapters VI and VII and we have seen how human Motivation differs from the rigid, specialized, instinct-patterns of the animals. Human beings are flexible and adaptable, and while their basic needs may perhaps be summarized as food and shelter, companionship and self-respect, the methods by which they satisfy these needs vary enormously. The environment in which they live, its "culture-pattern" or accepted way of life; their own particular equipment of abilities, skills and habits; all these combine to present individuals with a variety of different ways in which to fulfil these simple primary urges. At the same time all kinds of intermediate goals will appear, as when young people who are basically seeking companionship and opportunities for mating, set themselves the task of becoming physically attractive and socially agreeable so that they will be accepted in the groups among which they wish to participate.

Motivation is a complex subject and obviously enough, differences between people cannot be reduced to test-scores or examination results as with Innate Abilities or Acquired Knowledge. We must nevertheless make some effort to understand this aspect of the individual's make-up, and if we think of it as a pattern we may find that the different elements fall into place to form a fairly coherent picture. This may be difficult and may require a lot of thought, but there are three main lines of approach which will help to show the essential threads which run through the pattern. These are, first of all, the *strength* of the individual's Motivation or the levels of achievement he characteristically sets himself, his consistency in following them up, the amount of initiative he displays in overcoming obstacles between himself and his goals, and his effectiveness in achieving results in action. Next comes the *direction* of his Motivation or the kinds of activity which he tends to seek out in preference to others. And third, there is its *reality-content* or the degree to which his goals are capable of attainment in the light of his own equipment of knowledge and abilities, and of the opportunities which are open to him in the circumstances of his life-pattern.

*Different levels of Motivation*

Dealing first with the strength of Motivation, it is not difficult to see differences in the levels of goal which individuals set themselves and the amount of drive they put in to achieve these goals. Once again the Normal Curve will make its appearance. The average man, when he comes in to work in the morning, will be prepared to carry out a fairly routine task, one which has been laid out for him by someone who has set the targets and provided the means of achieving them. If any difficulties crop up in the course of the day, the average person takes it for granted that there will be someone he can turn to for help in sorting them out. Similarly if the routine breaks down, he feels that it is up to someone else to tell him what to do. On this kind of job, the average person is a perfectly good worker and nothing that has been said should give the impression that he is lazy or inefficient. So long as the job is properly organized for him, the average man works hard and effectively. Where his limitations begin to show, however, is when he is expected to organize his own work, direct his own efforts, and show initiative in overcoming unexpected difficulties.

Outside of working hours, the average person will participate in activities which make the same sort of demands on him. The leisure pursuits which attract the largest numbers are, by definition, those in which the average man takes part. This is obvious enough, for there are more people in the average grade than in those above or below. A survey carried out in 1965–66 showed that— "active recreation is a minority activity. Television is overwhelmingly the most popular leisure occupation.

... No individual outdoor activity counts for much; but when all sports and games are lumped together with visits to the park and the seaside, they account for about a quarter of the men's leisure time and about a fifth of the women's "[1] All of this bears out the impression that the average person's ability or desire to direct his own activities and set his own goals is somewhat limited. This is not a moral judgment, nor does it carry any implication of criticism or disapproval. It is simply an attempt to set out as objectively as possible where the average lies under this heading, or where the pendulum hangs on the Motivational scale.

To push the pendulum upwards from its point of rest we need more evidence of self-direction, such as would be demanded by a job which involved taking charge of others and organizing their work. This would probably be supplemented by leisure activities of a more purposeful nature. Typical of these might be serious reading, where the individual notes the reviews in some critical journal and obtains the books from the library; going to concerts and appreciating music of a higher intellectual standard than that heard on pop discs and Radio One; adventurous weekends or holidays spent climbing or visiting far-off places; ambitious do-it-yourself projects which have been brought to a successful conclusion. These and similar activities would indicate that the individual sets his own objectives, aims at and achieves his own standards, and puts rather more drive and energy into everything he does.

There are, of course, higher standards still which would push the pendulum up into the A or "something extra" grade, 17 or above. These are the people with exceptional determination, who set themselves the highest possible standards and achieve them no matter what obstacles they may encounter. An interesting point to note is that these very highly motivated individuals are not always popular with the average person. This may be due, in part, to an awareness that by comparison, average Motivation is not very impressive. It may also be due to the fact that there is a certain ruthlessness and self-seeking about this top-level Motivation which is not very attractive when seen at close quarters. Nevertheless, these are the kind

[1] *New Society*, 2 October, 1969. Review of K. K. Sillitoe, "Planning for Leisure", H.M.S.O.

of people we need to start large enterprises and direct them successfully. In terms of the Normal Curve, there are not very many around, nor are there all that many opportunities for them to show what they can do. They do, however, represent the top end of our Motivational scale.

There are, inevitably, lower-than-average levels which are represented during working hours by individuals who cannot meet the demands of the normal routine job. Every first-line supervisor can recognize them, for they will take up a good deal of his time. Whatever they are given to do, something always goes wrong, some difficulty crops up which makes it impossible for them to achieve the objective. It is never their fault, but always something beyond their control which no one could expect them to anticipate. Such people need far more supervision than the average, for unless someone can nurse them along, sort out their little difficulties and give them the kind of support and encouragement they need, they will never get anything done. They present other problems too, for they make demands on other peoples' sympathy which bring out ambivalent reactions. At one time we feel that they haven't had a chance and that we have an obligation to help them smooth out their problems and try to make life a bit easier for them. At other times we can swing in the opposite direction, become impatient with them and withdraw our sympathy, feeling that the demands they make are unjustified and that they must make the effort to help themselves. Once again, we must emphasize that we are not making moral judgments. Such people exist and represent the below-average Motivational levels. If we can face up objectively to their existence, we may deal more successfully with the problems they present.

We also have an E grade, very-much-below average, 4 and below on this scale, including the vagrants and tramps, or the inadequate people in our community. They can be found in the Salvation Army hostels, in the prisons and the doss-houses. Life is just too much for them, for they cannot meet the demands of even the simplest job or hold it down for more than five minutes. Consequently they cannot earn a living or stick to anything for even the minimum time. They represent a social problem for, as they cannot look after themselves, someone else has to look after them. And there are very few dedicated individuals prepared to devote their lives to this hopeless task. Fortunately the proportions down at this bottom level are comparatively small, but the problem they present is out of proportion to their numbers. A further depressing note is struck by the fact that nothing much can really be done for them beyond providing them with care and shelter. By the time they arrive at this stage, the chances of their making anything of their lives are virtually non-existent.

*Differences in the Direction of Motivation*

Over and above these levels of Motivation, however, there is the question of which kinds of activity seem to give the individual most satisfaction. Most of us do some things which bring us into contact with other people, and most of us have to do something practical or active. Many of us also have to do a certain amount of reading or writing or similar intellectual pursuits.

But while all these activities will be represented in most peoples' lives, there will probably be one or more which seem to occupy more time and attention than the others. For example, a man may occupy a minor supervisory job in which he gives the work out to a dozen others. When one talks to him about his job, he may tend to emphasize the importance of suiting each one's task to his particular level of skill, and of trying to maintain a satisfactory team-spirit among the group by fostering good relationships and co-operative working. Suppose that in his spare time this man takes part in a number of local sports and social activities and seems in most cases to be put out on the committee and to find great satisfaction in taking charge of an outing or running a party for the club. It would be obvious that in this case, in addition to a rather higher-than-average level of Motivation, we have someone who finds his main satisfaction in doing things with other people, someone whose Motivation has a marked *social* trend.

When such an individual is contrasted with someone whose spare time is occupied entirely with solitary pursuits like fishing or stamp collecting, and who seems neither to seek out nor to find any pleasure in the society of others, either at work or in his leisure time, the difference between the two Motivational patterns will become apparent. These differences will be found sufficiently often in ordinary life for us to lay down "doing things with others" as one general direction in which peoples' preferred activities may lie. When we consider an individual, therefore, we may decide whether his Motivational pattern is likely to be *social* or *non-social* in nature and this will give some indication of the direction in which he is more likely to express himself.

Another general direction of preferred activities may be shown in a liking for *practical-constructive* pursuits. The traditional craftsman figure would illustrate this, for such a person gained great satisfaction from the exercise of his skill with tools and his ability to transform wood or metal into useful and beautiful objects. It is possible that a rather unreal halo of romance has gathered round the old-time craftsman who took a real pride in his work, but even at the present day it is quite clear that some people prefer such activities, even to the extent of devoting a proportion of their spare time to them. On the other hand, there are those to whom making things, working with their hands or with tools and machinery, is simply tedious.

Some people again, take great pleasure in the exercise of their physical powers; not only do they enjoy active games and open-air pursuits, but also they seek out work which takes them out from indoors and involves some exposure and possible hardship. This direction of Motivation might be called *physically-active*, and on a humdrum scale it can sometimes be seen among manual labourers, market porters and similar workers, some of whom seen to get a noticeable degree of satisfaction out of using their strength on such day-to-day tasks.

Another group of satisfactions might be labelled *intellectual*. Those who become easily bored with a routine job may do so because it presents no problems for them to solve. They might be happier if it gave them something on which to exercise their intelligence. To some extent, probably everyone gets some satisfaction out of the use of his intellectual abilities, but there are some people whose working life is taken up with planning or research and whose spare time is devoted to reading and study to such an extent that this becomes the main thread in their lives. While recognizing that the strength of their Motivation enters into this, we have another direction in which individuals can find a satisfying outlet. We might add another category of *aesthetic* satisfactions which would include pleasure in the appearance and balance of objects, but as we do not want to end up with an unmanageable number of classifications of the direction of Motivation, we shall stop here.

## The Reality-Content of Motivation

Living as we all do in a society with different habits and customs which is split up into various groupings each with its one way of life, individuals normally fit into a certain type of background. This is important from various points of view, but particularly as it makes certain types of activity easily available while certain others might cut across the social norms of the group. It has a bearing also in determining the way in which we should expect an individual to find his means of self-expression. A white-collar worker in his forties, for example, living in a suburban housing estate, would normally spend his spare time in his garden, cleaning the car, and doing a few odd jobs about the house. There would be some interest in television, an occasional visit to the local cinema accompanied by his wife, and perhaps some participation in local church or political affairs, or membership of a games club, a musical or other recreational association. These would be the activities locally available which people of his type would go in for, and while they may sound rather unadventurous, there is room for quite high levels of achievement in some of them.

But if we were to find someone like this appearing frequently in a white tie and tails and competing in the local dance hall for the title of the local ballroom champion, we should probably say to ourselves, "That's rather an odd thing for a man of this background to be doing in his spare time. I wonder what kind of satisfaction he's getting out of it?" In such a case we might be tempted to think that the spectacle of his rather humdrum life and approaching middle age had become too much for him, and that he was trying to find a slightly unrealistic compensation for the glamour and achievement he had missed.

When we come across elements in a Motivational pattern which don't seem to fit into the general picture, we begin to wonder if the individual concerned is seeking his satisfactions in the real world, or whether there is a certain element of phantasy in his Motivation. This is not to say that whenever we find anything unconventional we must leap to the conclusion that it is a retreat from the realities of life—many unusual pursuits are rather evidence of strong Motivation and self-direction. Moreover, with increased affluence, more people are having more opportunity to undertake a wider range of activities, while the former conventions are tending to weaken as a result. But when we find someone in whose life-pattern these phantasy achievements occupy a very large place, we are probably justified in thinking that the reality-content of his Motivation is a little low. This can present problems particularly with younger age-groups.

*The Assessment of Motivation*

Bearing these three aspects in mind, strength, direction and reality-content, it is not impossible to make some kind of judgment about an individual's Motivation. Once again, the pendulum will come in handy, for we can use the evidence of his performance in various situations to push it upwards or downwards along the scale. It we find that he has never risen above a routine sort of job but has coped successfully with these while at work, and that his spare time has been devoted to fairly passive, conventional pursuits, then we have nothing to swing it either way. If, however, we have evidence of progress upwards to more demanding jobs, coupled with more active leisure pursuits, then our pendulum will move almost automatically up the scale. A succession of failures, on the other hand, with evidence of inability to cope even on the average level, coupled with unrealistic aims and leisure activities, would inevitably tend to push it downwards from its point of rest.

The demands of jobs under this heading can be set out without much difficulty. There is, however, a problem in finding many which demand less than average Motivation. This rebounds on the supervisor, for his above-average Motivation must make up for the deficiencies of those under his charge. Thus, if we decide that there are some simple, undemanding jobs that could be allocated to those who are low down on this scale, we should make sure that the person in charge of them is adequately equipped from this point of view.

| 1-4 | 5-8 | 9-12 | 13-16 | 17-20 |

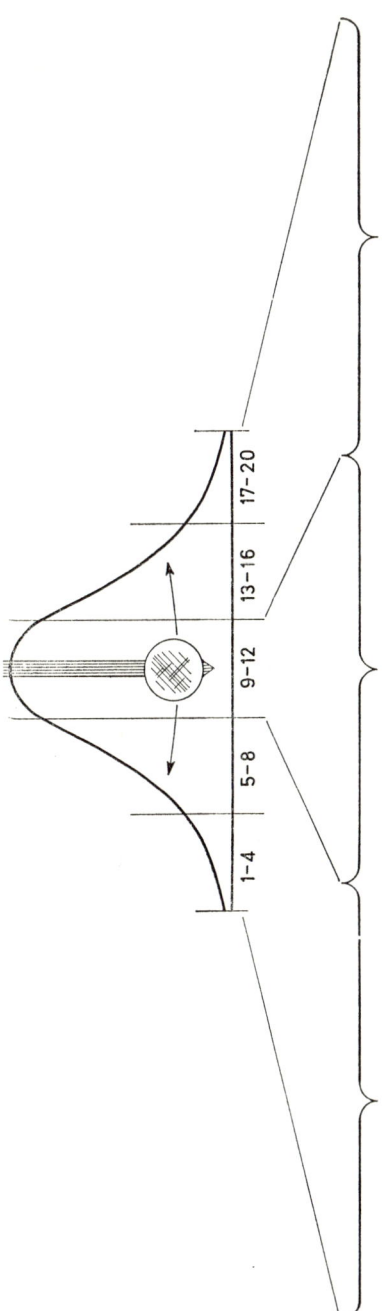

**1-4:** Finds it difficult to meet demands of normal jobs and has history of failures. Spare time completely undirected and at the mercy of others. Only capable of jobs which require no self-direction, and dependent almost entirely on supervision. At the bottom end of this scale we meet the drop-outs and other social problems.

**9-12:** Copes adequately with routine jobs which require only limited self-organization. Depends upon supervisor for help when the unexpected occurs. Spare time devoted to conventional activities in which he reaches accepted standards but does not strike out for himself. Perfectly adequate in meeting normal demands in familiar situations.

**17-20:** Evidence of self-direction in most of his activities. Capable of supervisory or management jobs or others in which routine element is limited. Spare time devoted to more individualistic activities which offer more scope but are still reasonably realistic. Suitable for jobs above the routine level which call for organization of his own and others' efforts.

FIG. 23. SCALE FOR MOTIVATION

As this is a very complex aspect of personality, these levels should not be taken too literally. The dangers of over-simplification must always be borne in mind. With these reservations, however, the above scale may be found useful in sorting out one's ideas about what can be expected of the individual.

Unless he is particularly well-motivated, he'll never get any work out of them.

Figure 23 sets out the different levels of Motivation in a simplified fashion.

## SUMMARY

1. What aspect of the individual are we considering under the heading of Motivation?

We are concerned with how he applies his efforts and how successful he is in finding satisfaction for his basic need to earn a living, be accepted by others, and feel that he has some significance as a person.

2. Can we set up a scale for different levels of Motivation?

The average person does what others expect of him, but his powers of self-organization and self-direction are limited. Above the average are those who set their own targets, direct their own activities, and are more effective in achieving results. Below the average we find individuals who cannot meet the demands of the normal job and who constantly come up against difficulties beyond their control.

3. Are there differences in the direction of an individual's Motivation?

Some people find certain kinds of activity more attractive and rewarding, and in consequence can express themselves more effectively in them. A rough classification could be Social or non-Social; Practical-Constructive; Physically-Active; and Intellectual.

4. What do we mean by the Reality-Content of Motivation?

This concerns the degree to which the individual can express himself and find outlets in the activities normally available in his way of life. When anyone appears to spend a large part of his time on unusual or unconventional activities with little or no practical result, then the element of phantasy may be making itself felt.

5. Is it possible to assess an individual's Motivation?

Every real-life situation makes demands and offers opportunities for the individual to express himself. How far he meets these demands and makes use of these opportunities is his Motivation in action in that situation. Once a repeating pattern becomes apparent, this will swing the pendulum one way or the other on the scale.

CHAPTER XIV

# Individual Patterns of Adjustment

WE have already suggested that, in everyday terms, living among other people makes the greatest demand on the individual's emotional Adjustment. Some people respond easily and constructively in the continuous interactions which make up their day-to-day life. Others find these interactions more of a strain and become emotionally involved in them. These differences tend to result in the individual gravitating into a characteristic role in most social situations. He can either become the helpful, co-operative chap on whom others come to rely naturally; he can be the awkward, difficult chap who can always find something to criticize or protest about; or he can be the silent, stand-offish person who never seems quite to fit in anywhere. Such characteristic responses to social pressures are quite easy to recognize in everyday life and they are the most significant indication of an individual's emotional Adjustment. Moreover, once they have become established, it is only too obvious that they will tend to repeat themselves in future situations. Every interpersonal experience makes this kind of demand on the individual, though some may be more difficult to meet than others.

Every human being has his built-in social or companionship needs which he can only satisfy by interacting with other people. Every community or way of life has its own pattern of roles and relationships by means of which these needs can be satisfied. In some communities such as the pre-industrial village, these were fairly simple and easily understood. The individual was born into the village community, he lived there all his life, he knew all the other members and they knew him. Perhaps even more important, however, the same values were shared throughout the village and everyone had similar ideas about right and wrong, or what was socially acceptable and what would be condemned by the rest of the village. In a small, self-contained community like this, the pressures on the individual's Adjustment were not too difficult for the ordinary person to meet. This is perhaps why there is such a sentimental attraction to the memory of the simple, pre-industrial way of life. However attractive it may have been, it has now disappeared into the past in the western industrial countries, and with it the very low material standards of living which accompanied it.

Our present-day urban, pluralistic society confronts us with a very different and much more complex picture. The modern city is no longer a community with shared values and a common sense of belonging. It is rather a structure of many different groupings, family groups, working groups, clubs, pubs, and other spare-time groups. Each of these has its own way of life, its own set of values, and its own ideas of the right thing to do. Each is capable of satisfying the individual's need to belong, but each will only do so on its own terms. The individual, however, finds himself a member of several different groups and must consequently adapt his behaviour from moment to moment according to the group he is in at the time. He must behave in one way if he is to be accepted in the family group, but in quite another if he is to be one of the boys in the local. He must meet certain standards if he is to remain a member of his work group, but he must adhere to quite different values if he is to be accepted as a loyal member of his trade union. Each of these groupings, in fact, offers him a social role in its own pattern of relationships. If he can express himself in that role he will find companionship in being accepted as a member of that group and at the same time will find some scope for achievement. But if he cannot adapt to the pressures of the role, he will find membership of the group an unsatisfying and frustrating experience.

To try to put this into rather more down-to-earth, everyday terms, let us consider a young man in his late teens who is within sight of the end of his apprenticeship. He will have a role at work, in which he is expected to show a certain amount of initiative and take a certain amount of responsibility. At the same time, however, he is still under the tutelage of his seniors and is expected to accept guidance and direction from them with good grace. At the local technical college he will have the role of a pupil or student and, according to how the relationships have developed with the staff, this may be passive or active, while the relationships may be more or less reassuring and supportive in quality. At home he will still be a son in the family and once again, this may allow him more or less scope. In his spare time he may be a member of the football team, "one of the boys" in the motor-bike group, a regular attender at the Youth or Folk Club, or someone who drops in quite frequently at the discothèque. In addition to all this he may have a few girl-friends, one of whom may regard him as her "steady" and look forward to a more permanent relationship. Each of these roles will make its own demands on him, some of which may conflict with the others. To expect our young man to switch around without difficulty and to meet all these various demands would be to assume a considerable degree of emotional maturity or Adjustment.

Inevitably there will be conflicts. In his leisure pursuits among his own age-group, he will have considerable liberty of action and scope for self-expression in the roles open to him. He may be accepted as quite a knowledgeable person whose opinions are worth listening to; he will be on level-terms relationships with the others and possibly treated with a certain degree of respect. At work, at home or in the college, however, a more subordinate role may be tacitly expected of him— "Your father knows best"; "You're here to learn"; "I've been on this job for twenty years and when I want your opinion I'll ask for it". Remarks like these may typify the kind of role expected of him in these groups and may conflict more or less directly with the self-image he is building up in his other activities. To defend this self-image he will be tempted to rebel against these subordinate roles, with the result that emotional pressures will build up on either side.

*Demands on the Individual's Adjustment*

Presented with this somewhat complex picture, how does the typical young man react? For most of the time, he probably adjusts quite well. He meets the demands of his work roles and his spare-time roles, and becomes "one of the boys" in these various situations. That is to say, he fits in with the group and meets the standards they accept as normal. He will not deviate very far from these standards, for this would make him stand out from the group. It might also involve him in the risk of rejection or criticism by the group, and this is where the limitations of average Adjustment make themselves felt. From this point of view the average person is very much under the influence of the groups to which he belongs. When he finds himself going against the group and being subjected to its disapproval, emotional stress tends to build up. This makes him less rational in his reactions and when it reaches a certain point he loses his temper. This is his "breaking point" at which his Adjustment can no longer meet the stresses to which he is subjected, and when his behaviour becomes irrational and controlled by emotion rather than by the realities of the situation.

Another approach to the "breaking point" is in terms of the individual's self-image. This can be understood as a vehicle for self-expression and, so long as it is adequate to the situation there will be no undue emotional pressures. If, for example, our young man thinks of himself as a practical sort of chap who can cope with his job, put up a good show on the football field, and give the girls a whirl in the evening, he will find plenty of scope in the life-pattern we have outlined. But if he is presented with too complex a problem at work; or he finds himself in a more fashionable or intellectual spare-time group which makes him feel a bit of a yob; or if his girl-friend transfers her affections to another more glamourous young man; then his self-image will be seriously threatened. Defence-mechanisms then come automatically into play, the most frequent and obvious of which is aggression. He must find some means of hitting back against the attack which threatens his self-image, the most natural being to give the attacker a smack in the kisser! If the circumstances do not permit this, he can resort to verbal aggression, or to taking the mickey out of him by a few sarcastic remarks.

By now a picture of average Adjustment should be building itself up. This is the individual who can fit in with others most of the time, who can meet the accepted standards and respond rationally to normal situations. In view of the different groups on which he must rely to satisfy his need to belong and be accepted, he may feel the stress of adapting to the various roles expected of him. Minor conflicts are therefore inevitable, but these will seldom provoke major crises. The point to emphasize, however, is the degree to which our average person is under the influence of the group. This makes it difficult for him to undertake a responsible role, for responsibility involves occasionally going against the group. This represents something of a strain on the Adjustment of the average person and consequently emotion may enter into the situation. His reactions may become less rational and there will be a danger of ill-tempered arguments which will bring him nearer to his breaking-point. The high incidence of stress diseases among supervisors provides evidence of this in practice.

Once again, we are not making moral judgments. There are plenty of roles in the work-situation, in family and spare-time groups with which the average Adjustment can cope without difficulty. Routine jobs which involve only limited interaction with others fall into this category, so long as there is someone in charge who can meet a rather higher level of demand. The supervisor's Adjustment must be such that he can settle the inevitable arguments and minor conflicts that crop up, without reacting emotionally to them. For emotion breeds emotion and if the supervisor is continually getting involved in rows, these will grow progressively more bitter. As soon as a job becomes more of a social role than a task, its demands on the individual's Adjustment will tend to move up the scale.

It is perhaps worth while to consider jobs from this point of view for a moment. Most factory floor and many clerical jobs are tasks, in the sense that the employee has been provided with certain equipment and is expected to produce certain results which can be measured, or at least estimated in a quantitative fashion. Interaction with others plays only a limited part in success in the job and consequently the demands on the individual's Adjustment are no more than the average person can meet without difficulty. When we look at the job of a retail salesman or saleswoman, however, the picture changes at once. Such a job involves continual interaction with customers, some of whom will be reasonable enough, but some will be awkward and difficult. With these latter, the emotional stress will tend to build up, and the salesman of no more than average Adjustment will sometimes be tempted to say "Well, that's the article and that's the price. If you don't like it, then get the hell out of here and stop niggling at me. I've got other things on my mind besides what you think you want!"

When we move upwards along the Adjustment scale, we shall find a proportion of people who can cope adequately with jobs which make these above-average demands. Foremen and supervisors who can spend the day sorting out difficulties and settling differences of opinion and go home in the evening without any feeling of strain; salesmen who can deal with a succession of awkward customers and remain perfectly calm and collected throughout; managers who can play a constructive part in discussions on future policy without making personal issues out of conflicting viewpoints; these and others represent a level of Adjustment in our B or 13–16 grade. Higher than this would be the comparatively small proportion of people who can stand the strain of really top management jobs which involve continual decisions on which large sums of other people's money and the future development of the enterprise may depend.

*Lower-than-Average Adjustment*

There will inevitably be a proportion of the population below the average from this point of view, and these present many of our day-to-day problems. As has been pointed out, living among others involves adjusting to various social roles, not all of which accord with our self-image. The person of less-than-average Adjustment tends to react emotionally to these challenges. "You don't expect me to put up with that, do you?" "What do you think I am? A bloody messenger boy?" "I told him straight. I'm not standing for that!" Responses like these to a request which might seem reasonable enough to anyone else, are typical and illustrate the difficulties involved in getting this level of person to collaborate in a work-situation. Most of us can call to mind examples of such awkward, difficult people who make excessive demands on the patience of colleagues and supervisors. Inevitably, of course, they build up a situation which cannot be resolved rationally and thus either leave the job, with a tale of unjust treatment, or they are dismissed after a series of increasingly bitter rows.

Below-average Adjustment can show itself in other forms besides simply being an awkward or difficult colleague. There are people who take the cares of the world on their shoulders and feel strongly about the injustices which are being perpetrated on fellow human beings at home and abroad. Such people are drawn into protests or demonstrations and are attracted by extreme political or religious groups. They are continually involved in "causes" and can talk endlessly about the unfortunate people who are being oppressed and exploited for the advantage of those who have them at their mercy. How much actual effect their protests and demonstrations actually have in practice, is a question on which different opinions may be held, but we are not advocating here a cynical attitude towards people who feel strongly on such matters. When we look around us, we can see many things which could be improved, and any generous-minded person must feel sympathy for those whose standards of life are degrading and whose opportunities are restricted. But when these tragedies begin to weigh so heavily on anyone that he cannot face up to the demands of his own life-pattern, then we suggest that his Adjustment pendulum is slipping down below the average.

Another way in which less-than-average Adjustment can show itself is in the qualities normally thought of in terms of ethics or morals. Looked at in simple elementary terms, these involve standards of honesty and integrity in one's dealings with other people. Meeting these standards, however, involves certain pressures, and it may at times be tempting to cut the corners and do what is more convenient to oneself. Those who cannot meet these pressures will tend to succumb to these temptations and work a few minor "fiddles' or disloyalties. They can always justify these to themselves if they get away with them by thinking that they harmed nobody and "what you don't know about, you don't worry about". In practice, of course, these are the people who cannot be trusted and should never be put in a position where they are exposed to such temptations. The more objective we can be about morals or ethics the better, for in actual practice this aspect is often affected by emotion which tends merely to confuse.

The bottom end of this scale is represented by mental illness, with which we are not equipped to deal. There is, however, a small minority in any community who cannot adjust to the demands of ordinary life, and for their own protection and that of the community, they have to be kept in a protected environment. Any mental hospital can provide examples of these,

| 1-4 | 5-8 | 9-12 | 13-16 | 17-20 |

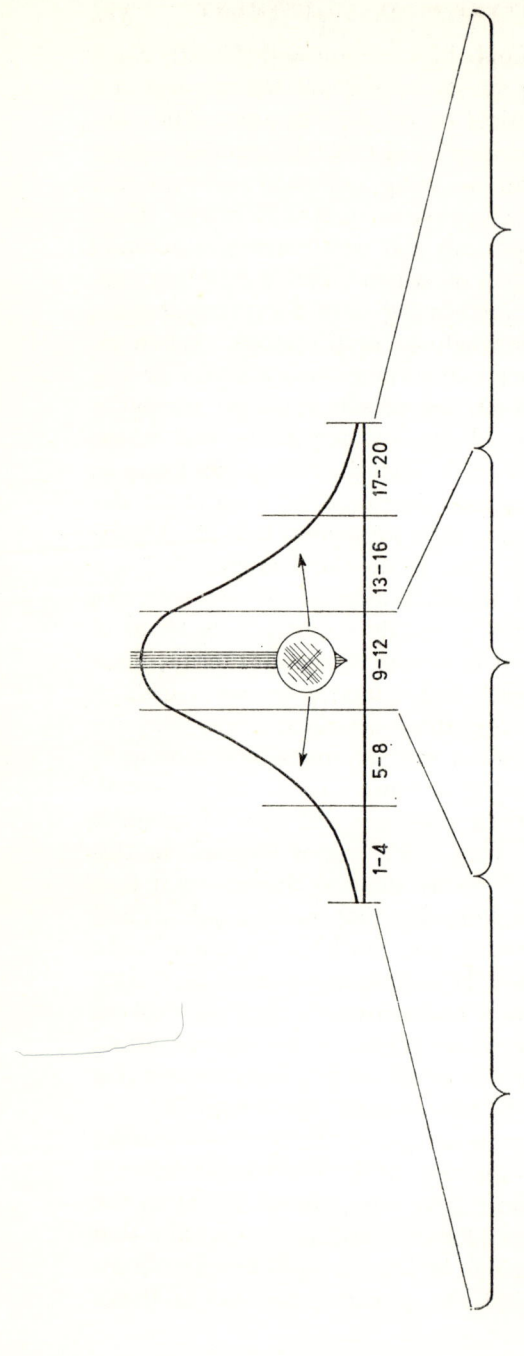

Finds difficulty in coping with the stress of normal interaction with other people and gravitates to the role of the awkward, difficult person. Problems arise in fitting him into the work situation and consequently the demands on the supervision become more apparent.

Capable of adapting to conventional roles in typical groups. Fits in with others in such situations but is very much under the influences of the group and its accepted standards. The threat of rejection involved in going against the group tends to bring out emotional reactions and thus makes it difficult to cope with responsible roles.

Higher levels of emotional maturity make it possible to go against group standards and thus become less under its influence, while still playing the expected role in it. This equips the individual for posts which involve responsibility and are rather social roles than routine tasks.

FIG. 24. SCALE FOR ADJUSTMENT

Once again the dangers of over-simplification must be emphasized, but the above may be helpful in organizing ideas about the emotional aspect of the individual's make-up.

and while some can be helped by psychotherapy or other means to return to a normal life, there are others for whom this represents too much of a strain. The numbers are comparatively small, but once again, they represent the bottom end of the scale.

Figure 24 may help to illustrate the different levels on the Adjustment scale. It may appear that Adjustment and Motivation have something in common, and indeed as they are two aspects of the individual's make-up there will inevitably be some overlap. It is, however, advisable to keep them separate in our thinking, for there are some people of high Motivation whose limited Adjustment ensures that they reach their objectives only after a heavy expenditure of emotional stress. There are, on the other hand, people of high Adjustment but lower Motivation who do not set themselves the targets they could be reasonably expected to achieve. Both these differences may be extremely important in terms of the kind of job for which the individual is fitted.

## SUMMARY

1. What aspects of the individual's make-up come under the Adjustment heading?

Mainly his reaction to emotional stress. As the most continuous source of stress is interaction with other people, this will show most obviously in how he gets on with others.

2. How do the demands on an individual's Adjustment manifest themselves in everyday life?

Mainly in his adaptation to the various social roles open to him in the different groupings which make up his life-pattern. As these are the means by which he can satisfy his need to belong and to be accepted among other people, there will be considerable pressure on him to meet the requirements of these roles. Different groups, however, will demand different roles, and some of these may conflict with each other. All of this will make a continuous demand on his emotional Adjustment.

3. What is the typical reaction to this situation?

The typical person fits in with the way of life of the group most of the time. He is, however, very much under its influence, because the threat of rejection represents a pressure on his Adjustment which he finds difficult to meet. Such attacks on his self-image will tend to bring him near to his "breaking-point" where his reactions become emotional rather than rational.

4. Can we set a standard for the average Adjustment in terms of jobs?

As has been said, the average person can adjust to the demands of the group and will consequently cope effectively with a routine job. His limited ability to go against the group, however, makes it difficult for him to stand up to the demands of a job which involves responsibility for others.

5. What kind of jobs demand more than average Adjustment?

As soon as a job becomes more of a social role than a task, the pressures on the individual's Adjustment begin to mount up. Supervisory and management jobs are the most obvious examples, though there are others, such as sales jobs, which make similar demands.

6. How does less than average Adjustment manifest itself?

Normally in the inability to adapt to the minor stresses of everyday life and the falling into the awkward and difficult personal role. Sometimes also in an unrealistic preoccupation with "causes" or "principles" and an attraction to organizations which represent extreme opinions. The bottom end of the Adjustment scale is represented by mental illness where the individual cannot cope with the demands of normal life.

CHAPTER XV

# Vocational Guidance and Selection

ONE of the practical problems in industry is that of getting the right person into the right job. It becomes very quickly apparent that some people are better suited for one type of work. They pick it up quickly, they do it well, and they find reasonable satisfaction in it. Other people on the same work may take a long time to train, they may never do it well, and they may feel continuously frustrated and irritated while they are on it. From the point of view both of efficient working and of individual satisfaction, therefore, it is advisable to avoid misplacements in work, and on this subject industry has a right to expect help from the psychologist.

Work on the subject has been in progress for a number of years, and while the problem is one and indivisible, it has tended to be approached in practice from two points of view. The first is that of the individual who wants to know which out of a number of jobs he is most likely to find success and satisfaction in. Most young people leaving school are in this position and the giving of advice to such individuals as to the course they should follow has come to be known as "Vocational Guidance." The other point of view is that of the firm which wishes to find the most suitable person to fill a particular vacancy. If a number of candidates present themselves the problem is one of picking out which will be most successful and satisfied in the job. This process has come to be known as "Vocational Selection."

While there is a difference in the two approaches, it is perhaps not quite so marked in practice as might appear at first glance. When conditions of full employment are the rule it is comparatively rare for a firm to be presented with a large number of candidates for a particular job, and it is not unusual for there to be a number of vacancies open at the same time. When an applicant appears, therefore, he will usually be considered not for one position only, but first for his general suitability for employment, and if he appears a useful person, then for a number of jobs in turn. In the same way, an individual is seldom in the position of being able to pick and choose among an unlimited number of jobs. Certain openings may be available, for each of which the standards may be more or less exacting. Among these he must make up his mind which offers the best opportunities from all the relevant aspects.

There has been a regrettable tendency to reduce both vocational guidance and vocational selection to a mechanistic process. Some years ago the expression "A square peg in a round hole" came into fashion and this has done a great deal of harm to thinking on the subject. It carries the implication that a human being can be reduced to measurable dimensions, and that these can be expressed in the same terms as would apply to a piece of wood or a block of metal. Similarly, that jobs are merely slots in an organization into which employees can be fitted and where they will operate, perhaps with a little lubrication, as automatically as a piston-rod or a propellor-shaft. We must dissociate ourselves from the whole idea of pegs and holes and face up to the fact that each human being is a unique entity, self-motivated and capable of directing his own efforts within the limits of the opportunities open to him. Jobs, on the other hand, are social situations where the individual must interact with others, meet various pressures from them and from the task, and apply his efforts to the achievement of certain results.

This is obviously a situation of some complexity, and with the continuance of full employment, these complexities are likely to increase. The object of vocational guidance and selection, therefore, can no longer be thought of as plugging anonymous bodies into slots whose dimensions fit with their aptitudes and training. It has now become a question of influencing a series of decisions so that human beings end up in work-situations the demands of which they can meet and which offer the opportunities which will enlist the maximum of their Motivation and provide the greatest reward in personal satisfaction and achievement.

### SPECIFICATIONS AND ASSESSMENTS

To achieve this matching up, we must have some means of summarizing the demands of the work-situation on the one hand. On the other, we must have a means of assessing the qualities of the individual. If these can be drawn up on similar terms, then the problem of relating one to the other becomes capable of solution. This is where the scales we have been discussing come in useful, for they provide a Five Fold Framework which serves the two purposes. We can lay out a *Specification* of the personal qualities demanded by any job on these five scales, and we can make an *Assessment* of an individual on the same terms. We can then consider whether the one fits with the other, and if they do, we have got the right man for the job.

A considerable amount of preparation will be necessary, of course, before this neat result can be achieved. To set out an adequate Specification we must know what the job involves, the conditions under which it is carried out, and the measures by which successful performance is judged. On the other hand, we must assemble a basis of factual data about the individual on which we can build up a satisfactory Assessment of his abilities and potentialities. The two processes have an essential similarity in that they both start with a study of the facts and proceed by logical inference from them, but this assembling of facts is not quite so simple as it might seem at first glance. Let us consider first the assembly of facts about a job.

### JOB-STUDY

When we first go into a factory to look at a job we are likely to see someone working on a machine or with tools which are unfamiliar to us. There may be a certain amount of noise and movement which tends to distract our attention, and we shall hear strange words which we do not understand applied to the materials and processes in common use. In such a situation we shall find it difficult to understand what is going on and if we stay for half an hour or so to study the job we may carry away a misleading impression partly because what we have seen in that limited time may not be typical of the work involved and partly because we may have failed to relate it adequately to the larger picture.

But if, conscious of these dangers and limitations, we apply for help to someone who is in daily contact with the work, we may not be much better off. Such a person may be so familiar with what is going on that he takes for granted many important details which are not immediately obvious to the outside visitor. For example, it frequently happens that on automatic machine-work the operator has no formal responsibility for mechanical adjustment and maintenance, this being under the control of specialists who have had suitable training and experience. But in practice it frequently happens that the difference between a good operator and a slow one is determined by the amount of mechanical trouble which the latter encounters while the former seems to manage long runs with only a very occasional stop for adjustment. Why should this be so? Usually because the better operator has more mechanical sense and, noticing the need for attention before serious trouble develops, can call the mechanic and point out the incipient defect. The difference between the two, therefore, may largely be a difference in the mechanical care they take of their machines, for which officially neither has any responsibility.

Those who are in contact with the work-situation usually have some responsibility for production and discipline, and they naturally think of operators from that point of view. If one is insolent or critical of authority he will be considered an unsatisfactory worker and his level of output, though it may be well above average, will be lost sight of. In the same way, those aspects of the job to which the supervisor's attention is normally called, such as the variations in quality or failure to conform to working instructions, will be considered of disproportionate importance. The same can be said for the dangerous parts of a job or those requiring assistance. A foreman who in the preceding week has had to cope with a serious accident, several mistakes which have led to a heavy proportion of rejects, and the provision of assistance in the manipulation of heavy objects, will have a totally different view of a job from one whose section has been running smoothly and uneventfully for the last month.

Many of the working methods and much of the training in British industry at the present day are still largely rule-of-thumb. One result of this is that traditional legends have grown up with the years which are accepted on a wide scale though they have little real foundation in fact. In some trades, for example, great prestige still attaches to the workman who superintends, say, a melting process and is supposed to decide by spitting into the mixture at the appropriate moment just when it is ready to run off. His knowledge and experience are of great importance in the daily working of the plant, but in many cases the actual control of the process has passed over to the laboratory and the decisions are in fact taken by a young man with a science degree. Such a change, however, is not understood in its full implications, and those in contact with the work would be very unwilling to admit that four years at a University could possibly lead to a better understanding of the process than twenty years on the floor of the shop. The accounts of a job given by those most directly in contact with it are frequently liable to be coloured by these traditionally accepted conventions which are becoming less and less realistic as industrial processes are brought up to date.

*The Need for an Effective Method*

To acquire an adequate basis of information about a job, therefore, we must devise a method of studying it which will avoid these pitfalls. This is, in part, a matter of a systematic approach so that all the details which concern one aspect are considered at the same time, and partly a matter of substituting objective facts properly observed for the opinions of those who are supposed to know, but in fact do not. For example, if we have a job which is supposed to involve "heavy work" it is advisable to find out what weights, in pounds, have actually to be lifted, how often, and with what mechanical aids. When this is done it may become apparent that while an object weighing as much as a hundredweight has to be lifted, this only happens on an average once during the working day and that there is always a block and tackle available with someone else to give a hand. The physical strain involved in such an operation may actually be negligible. When such factual information is assembled we can be sure that we know what we are talking about and that all the relevant facts are being considered.

When one thinks of a job-study in this manner it is surprising how much becomes susceptible to measurement. The physical strain of work can in many cases be expressed in the number of pounds weight to be lifted and the frequency with which this occurs. Exposure to heat can be expressed in degrees of temperature at the working point, and other trying conditions, such as humidity, fumes, poor light or the exposure to danger, can be expressed objectively in the appropriate units of measurement, or in terms of the frequency of accidents reported over a period. In the same way, the monotony or boredom involved in many types of work can be expressed in terms of the job-cycle and the number of changes of model in the working day. A job-cycle of ten seconds, such as would be involved in a very simple assembly operation, with only one change of model every three days, would be a very monotonous and routine kind of task, especially when compared with one where the job-cycle was three hours and a change of model occurred every day.

Collecting information of this nature may take time and may involve a special study; one must not overlook the fact, however, that a certain amount may already exist in production or wage records which only requires collating to be immediately available. Wherever possible, such records should be used, in intelligent relation to actual observation of the work, for it is only upon such a basis that we will ever know accurately what a job really involves.

*A Systematic Approach*

The information we require about a job can be conveniently arranged under the following four headings—

LIST OF DUTIES. This will comprise a straightforward description of the actual work involved. In a simple job it can be quite detailed and show the actual movements involved in each phase of the work. Such a minute account will not usually be necessary, however, and a more general statement may be of more practical use. In each case someone must decide the degree of detail which should be gone into, but it will usually be quite a safe guide to keep the statement as simple as possible. Under this heading all the devices mentioned in the foregoing section should be used to give objectivity to the description.

TRAINING AND SKILL REQUIRED. Before an operator can undertake a job he must be trained, and in some cases his failure to do the work is in actual fact a failure in training.

It is advisable, therefore, to deal in some detail with the knowledge and skill he must acquire before he can be considered fully proficient. Two categories will be found useful, one of which includes the qualifications he must have acquired before he begins, the other dealing with the training he must undergo on the job. The length and nature of normal training should be considered and where possible actual standards of proficiency should be quoted. It will also be useful here to deal with the kinds of difficulty which trainees encounter and also with the usual causes of failure. These latter can be most revealing in showing the kinds of people who find the work most difficult.

WORKING CONDITIONS. We turn next to the place in which the work is done and describe it under the appropriate headings. These will include whether it is indoor or outdoor, its heating, lighting and ventilation, and whether it is unpleasant through fumes, damp, heat, dirt, noise and the like. We should also note whether the worker works alone or in company with others, whether the social unit is large or small, and what kind of relationships prevail within it.

ECONOMIC CONDITIONS. Few things are more important about a job than the remuneration it offers, for that will determine its occupant's standard of living and probably also that of his wife and family. We must, therefore, have a clear idea of the wage or salary attached to the job we are studying and anything else, such as the incidence of overtime, paid holidays, sickness benefits or the like which determine the total material benefits an employee will draw from it. It is important to remember that the total income matters more than the actual rate of wages; consequently a job with a high hourly rate where employment is irregular and intermittent may be less remunerative in the long run than one with a lower rate, regular employment, and a certain proportion of overtime each week.

## THE SPECIFICATION

Once we have drawn up a complete and realistic description of a job we can work out from it a specification of the kind of person who is likely to do it satisfactorily. It is very important that this specification should be operational, that is to say, each quality laid down in it should be linked with some aspect of the actual duties shown in the job-description and should be set out in terms of those duties. Under the heading of turn-out, for example, it is rather meaningless to say merely that the successful candidate should be "of good appearance, speech, and manner." If we were drawing up a specification for the job of a dentist's receptionist, for example, it would be much more satisfactory to say that "her appearance, speech, and manner must be such that she will create a reassuring impression on patients, many of whom will be in a state of apprehension or possibly even in pain." If all aspects of the specification are expressed thus in operational terms they will be more convincing and accurate and will be much easier to work from.

The foregoing method can be very effective in studying factory-floor or office jobs. In higher-level jobs, however, the element of routine is less important and consequently the manner in which the supervisor or manager spends his time throughout the day may be relatively less significant. In these types of job it is the results that count, and consequently a more useful description may be obtained by listing these results. In some cases they can be laid out in quantitative terms, in standards of output, of quality, of direct and indirect cost, and the increasingly popular system of "Management by Objectives" is based on this. In other cases they can be laid out in "key tasks" by listing the longer-term results which are expected.

To build up an adequate specification of the personal qualities required, we must look at the Job Description from each of our five points of view in turn. First of all, how much interaction with other people does it involve? It is obvious, for example, the dentist's receptionist will be in contact with patients for most of her working day. This automatically sets out Impact pendulum well up in the B grade for the operational reasons we have described. Similar considerations will apply to salesmen's Job Descriptions, to those of supervisors, managers, teachers, lecturers and others which are largely social roles. They will have less importance in jobs which are mainly tasks, for however demanding these may be, they may involve no more than minimal interaction with other people.

Turning next to Qualifications or Acquired Knowledge, it should not be difficult to set the pendulum at the appropriate level from this point of view. In some jobs a certificate may be required, showing that the individual has reached a certain standard of knowledge or expertise after a systematic course of study. In others a certain level of experience may be necessary which could be set down in terms of months or years. As we are dealing here with matters that can be expressed in objective terms, few serious problems will arise. Much the same applies to the Innate Abilities heading for, as has been outlined above, cut-off points on suitable tests can be established, below which the chances of success on the job are very small.

Perhaps the headings which require most thought will be those of Motivation and Adjustment, but here again it should not be impossible to decide whether a job can be done effectively by someone in the average range from these points of view. As we have already emphasized, there are plenty of jobs which require little or no self-direction, and where the level of responsibility imposes no great pressure on the individual. To take charge of such jobs, however, is a very different matter, for supervision involves organizing the work of others, setting targets, providing resources, and making sure that results are achieved. Quite obviously, therefore, we must set minimum standards in the B grade for these and for higher-level jobs.

To illustrate the drawing up of a Five-Fold Specification, let us take as an example the job of a first-line production supervisor. The Job Description would be as follows—

*Title and Place in the Organization*

*Machine-Shop Foreman*, in charge of thirty semi-skilled operators working on power-driven machine-tools. These are pre-set by skilled tool-setters, one to every half-dozen operators, so that, with the addition of five labourers, the total personnel adds up to forty.

The Machine-Shop Foreman reports to a Superintendent who has four other foreman under his charge and who, in turn, reports to a Divisional Manager.

A patrol inspector is attached to the section, whose responsibility is to make periodic checks on quality. The Machine-Shop Foreman thus has a functional relationship with the inspector. He has similar functional relationships with representatives of the production planning and control department, the work-study department, maintenance department, cost control, and personnnel departments. There is also a recognized shop steward in the section with whom he also maintains contact.

*Duties and Responsibilities*

Targets of output representing 90 per cent of possible machine utilization have been agreed, also a standard of quality represented by no more than 2 per cent rejects. Budgets for direct and indirect costs have also been set and on these figures the foreman's performance will be judged from period to period.

In addition he is responsible for maintaining an adequate standard of relations with employees, the number of disputes which have to be taken to a higher stage being used as a measure of this aspect of the job. Labour turnover, lateness and absenteeism records, provide further measures of his success from this point of view.

Unforeseen machine breakdowns can be calculated as a measure of his collaboration with the maintenance department, while his standards of housekeeping can be estimated by the tidiness and cleanliness of his section.

*Working Conditions*

As the factory is relatively new, the physical environment is comparatively pleasant. The foreman has a small office partitioned off in a corner of the section, with a desk, telephone and filing cabinet. His working hours correspond to those of the operators.

*Economic Conditions*

The foreman is paid at the appropriate level on a salary structure which has been worked out on a job evaluation basis and which allows for merit increases dependent on his performance. He is entitled to three week's paid holiday a year, sickness benefit on a staff scale, and membership of a staff pension scheme. In the event of dismissal or redundancy he is entitled to the provisions laid down in the Contracts of Employment and Redundancy Payments Acts.

Such a Job Description could of course be elaborated in the case of an actual job, but the above outline may provide a general idea. From this the following FIVE-FOLD SPECIFICATION could be drawn up.

*Impact on Others*

The Machine-Shop Foreman will be interacting continually with other people throughout the working day. He must maintain close contact with his setters to ensure that production is being kept up to standard and he will also be in touch with the operators as occasion rises. His relationship with the Superintendent should be close and confidential and his contact with the other foremen on his same level should be frequent. He will have dealings with the inspector, progress chaser, and other representatives of the functional departments, and he will be accessible to the shop steward.

These continuous interactions will involve him in varying social roles and the effectiveness of his communication in each case will depend on his skill in handling the relationships involved. The demands on his ability to express himself and to draw out responses from others which are suitable to the situation will thus be considerable. Dress and appearance will not be of great importance, though if he is below average in this respect, it might prove something of a handicap.

It is therefore obvious that from the first of our five aspects, this job makes an above average demand. We could thus set a minimum of 14 on this scale in our Specification.

*Qualifications or Acquired Knowledge*

Some experience of work in a machine-shop would obviously be essential, probably at the setter level. A rather higher standard of mechanical understanding would be an advantage, possibly represented by a Workshop Practice Certificate.

In addition to these, however, the foreman must be able to collaborate intelligently with the functional specialists with whom he will be in continual contact. To do this effectively, he must have some understanding of their specialist function. This will involve training quite separate from that gained by experience on the shop floor, and the National Examinations Board for Supervisory Studies probably provides the most suitable and easily accessible courses. This N.E.B.S.S. Certificate can be obtained at most local technical colleges and covers Principles and Practice of Supervision, Technical Aspects, Financial Aspects, Industrial Relations, and Communications Aspects of Supervisory Management. We would be justified in laying down this certificate as a minimum Qualification and it would be represented by 14 on this scale.

*Innate Abilities*

The intellectual demands of the foreman's job may not be very high, for he will seldom be presented with abstruse or abstract problems. He will, however, be faced with new and changing situations to a far greater extent than his setters or operators. To appreciate these new situations he will have to be of at least average intelligence and this would be represented by a score of 10–11 on a conventional Intelligence Test. Before considering anyone for promotion from the factory floor, therefore, it would be advisable to apply such a test and to disqualify anyone who failed to reach this standard. The danger of promoting a reliable and experienced worker is that he may be taken out of his intellectual depth. In this way, we may lose a good operator and gain a bad supervisor.

*Motivation*

To be effective in this job, the foreman must be constantly aware of the targets outlined in the Job Description. These targets will never achieve themselves automatically, for things will be constantly cropping up which halt the production flow; which make it impossible for an operator to get on with his job; the inspector to pass a component; the progress chaser to check on priorities; the shop steward to agree on a change; the maintenance department to deal with an emergency, and so on. Each of these crises would provide the opportunity for someone of average Motivation to sit down and say "Oh well, there's nothing I can do about it. I'll just have to wait until somebody else sorts it out." Such a reaction, however, would simply illustrate a failure to meet the demands of the foreman's job. His Motivation must be of a standard that leads him to think "There must be some way out of this mess and it's up to me to find it". As a result, he will search around and show the kind of initiative that will get production flowing again with the minimum delay.

Another way to illustrate the standard of Motivation required will be to think of the forward planning needed to ensure that the above crises do not happen. And, going back for a moment to the methods of studying jobs, this is where the orthodox observations may be misleading. The foreman who is always busy, who rushes around dealing with one emergency after another, is not necessarily the effective foreman. Many of these emergencies might not have arisen if he had anticipated the difficulties beforehand and done something to prevent them arising. Another foreman who has done some more thinking ahead may seem to be less pre-occupied with detail and to have more time on his hands. It may well be, however that his Motivation is of a higher standard in that he makes more effective use of his time, plans work ahead and applies his effort where it is most needed. In terms of the achievement of targets, the latter will usually have a better record than the former.

Obviously this aspect of our Five-Fold Framework will play a most important part in successful performance of the foreman's job. We can therefore push our Motivational pendulum well into the B grade and set a minimum of 14–15. Below this it is unlikely that the demands of the job will be met.

*Adjustment*

The interaction with other people and the display of initiative we have tried to describe, will involve a considerable amount of emotional stress. To be effective, the foreman will have to remain calm and collected when discussing difficulties with his setters, with the shop steward, the inspector and the progress chaser. He will also have to avoid getting into a flap when one or other of the crises inevitably presents itself. If he cannot keep his temper, or if doing so involves him in a considerable effort of self-control, then at the end of the day he is likely to find himself in a state of emotional tension. We already know that the incidence of stress diseases is high among supervisors, which suggests that a certain proportion cannot easily meet the demands which the job makes on their adjustment.

It is therefore essential to set a fairly high minimum on this

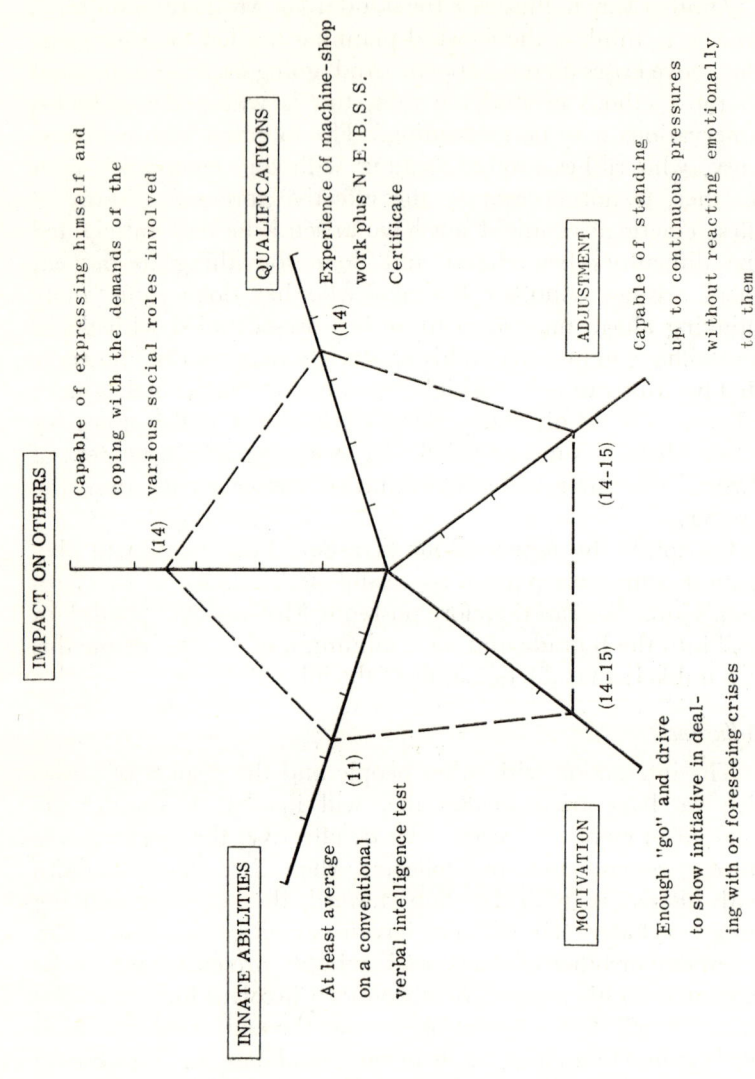

Fig. 25. Five-Fold Specification of a Machine-Shop Foreman's Job

**IMPACT ON OTHERS**: Capable of expressing himself and coping with the demands of the various social roles involved (14)

**QUALIFICATIONS**: Experience of machine-shop work plus N.E.B.S.S. Certificate (14)

**ADJUSTMENT**: Capable of standing up to continuous pressures without reacting emotionally to them (14-15)

**MOTIVATION**: Enough "go" and drive to show initiative in dealing with or foreseeing crises (14-15)

**INNATE ABILITIES**: At least average on a conventional verbal intelligence test (11)

scale. We must have someone who does not react emotionally to the pressures of the job, but who can remain objective and realistic in the situations we have described. This does not mean that he stays unaware of them or that he avoids them by keeping out of the way. It means that he is sufficiently mature in the emotional sense to be able to stand up to the pressures and not allow them to interfere with his effectiveness in action. Such a person would represent a relatively high level on our Adjustment scale, pushing the pendulum up to 14–15, or the middle of the B grade.

Figure 25 summarizes this specification and the resulting pentagon sets out the minimum standards required. It is hoped that the reader can see how a similar method could be applied to any job and a Five-Fold Specification drawn up to represent the kind of person required to cope successfully with it.

## SUMMARY

1. What do vocational guidance and vocational selection consist of?

Vocational guidance is the advising of an individual about which of a number of jobs he is most likely to be successful and satisfied in. Vocational selection is the picking out of the individual who is most likely to be successful and satisfied in one particular job. In practice a half-way stage between the two, which might be termed allocation, is frequently necessary.

2. What are the essential principles on which proper matching of jobs and individuals must be founded?

Individuals differ widely in their attributes and jobs are equally varied and diverse. Only if the two sets of variations can be reduced to a common standard is it possible to match one with the other. The Five-Fold Framework provides a series of categories by means of which the kind of person required to do the job can be specified on the one hand, and the individual applicant summed up on the other. On this common framework of reference the matching-up process can be approached systematically.

3. What is the aim of a job-study and what difficulties are likely to be encountered?

Only a thorough study of the job can provide the basis on which an operational job description can be built up. But unless the person who makes the study is familiar with the job and its setting he is likely to miss essential elements. Those who are in daily contact with the job, on the other hand, are probably so familiar with it that they may overlook important points. Moreover, what seems most important to the immediate supervisor may be less so when the total picture is considered.

4. How should a job-study be approached?

The job should be observed directly and as much factual information about it as possible should be assembled. An attempt should be made to obtain this in quantitative terms either by inquiry from those in contact with the job or from records. The information should then be arranged under the following headings—

  (*a*) List of duties
  (*b*) Training and skill required
  (*c*) Working conditions
  (*d*) Economic conditions

5. How is the job-specification related to the job-study?

The job-study provides a complete factual description of the job and the conditions in which it is carried out. From this it is possible to work out a specification of the person who will be best fitted to do it well. This specification will be in terms of the five categories already described, each characteristic being shown to be necessary by the actual circumstances of the job as made clear in the job-study.

CHAPTER XVI

# Interviewing

IN the last chapter we have considered how to match up jobs and individuals by expressing both the demands of the job and the attributes of the candidate in terms of the Five-Fold Framework. We have also thought about the method of studying a job and drawing up a description of it from which we can work out a Five-Fold specification of the kind of person who will do it well. We have not yet dealt with the method of summing up an individual in the same terms and it is to this that we must now turn.

How do we in fact get to know an individual, or come to understand someone with whom we have been acquainted for some time? Usually by seeing him so frequently that we come to know how he tends to deal with the various situations he encounters in life. We are in fact so familiar with his behaviour that we have had many opportunities of seeing the repetitions and regularities in it. With a friend of long standing, therefore, when someone tells us of something he has done, we can say with perfect justice "How like old so-and-so. That is exactly what he *would* do." With a stranger, on the other hand, we are often at a loss because we have not had enough experience of his characteristic behaviour to be able to know with any confidence what to expect of him.

In assessing a candidate for employment purposes we are, in effect, presented with a complete stranger and asked to predict his probable behaviour in a particular job-situation. The only way we can do this with any confidence is by providing ourselves with a sample of his behaviour sufficiently characteristic to serve as a basis for inference about what he will do in the future. There are several ways of doing this: one, for example, is to put him in a carefully controlled standard situation where he is presented with a number of problems, the solution of which calls for mental work. This is in effect what an intelligence test amounts to, and we have already seen how the behaviour it calls for, when assessed in the form of an objective score, shows us with remarkable accuracy what to expect of him in the future when he is placed in situations which call for the solving of problems by seeing the relationships between their elements.

Many of the "tests" for particular kinds of job consisted in putting the candidate into a controlled situation which called forth the same abilities and attributes as the job and where performance could be scored objectively. These have on occasion proved to have a limited usefulness, but we want to know much more about an individual than his problem-solving behaviour; hence we must study him from many more points of view. We may meet him in an interview situation and by personal contact with him provide ourselves with more behaviour to observe. As this is an almost universal means of studying individuals for employment it is advisable to consider it for a moment and to think how far it serves the purpose which we have laid down above—that of providing us with characteristic behaviour.

### THE AIMS OF THE INTERVIEW

Every word and action is to some extent characteristic of the individual from whom it comes. Thus, when someone comes into a room and says "Good morning" we shall learn something about him. If he goes on to talk about the weather and to give his views on the current political situation for twenty minutes or so, we shall learn more, while if he continues for half an hour and talks about business prospects as well we shall learn still more. But there is always the chance that the behaviour we have seen during this short period may be uncharacteristic of the person we are talking to. For example, a self-centred and irritable person can usually summon up enough surface affability to smile and say "Good morning." He can even make an effort to talk agreeably for half an hour if he judges it to be in his interest to make a good impression on his interlocutor. But one can imagine him leaving the interview and saying to himself, "Well, I managed to put myself across all right to that chap. Now that I've got what I wanted I can relax. There's no need to try to ingratiate myself any more."

Behaviour observed over a short period, therefore, may be uncharacteristic, and this is a serious danger when we have to make up our mind about someone during an interview of half an hour or less. Is there a way of ensuring that the behaviour presented to us during this short period will be more characteristic? Fortunately there is, because while the actual interview may only last half an hour, we can use it as a means of looking at twenty or thirty years of behaviour much of which cannot avoid being highly characteristic of the individual. The aim of the interview, therefore, should be to elicit the candidate's life-history, or as much of it as can be got out in the time available. Though it may be learnt at second hand, and though it can be no more than a survey, it is the best means of supplementing the behaviour which can be observed directly in face-to-face contact, by relevant and characteristic material.

We must, of course, get at the facts of the life-history, for vague generalizations about having worked here or there will be of little real use. We want to know in detail where the individual has worked, what were his actual duties and responsibilities, how long he remained, and under what circumstances he left. Once we are in possession of the facts we can build up a fairly accurate picture of what an individual has made of his life, where he has started from, and what use he has made of his opportunities. Provided it is factual and sufficiently detailed, such a case-history is the best source of characteristic behaviour we can have.

### RELEVANCE OF THE CASE-HISTORY

Why should this be so? Partly because we play a very large part in making our own lives and partly because we are to a great extent the product of the environment in which we live.

To take the former point: in most of the situations in life we can choose, within broad limits, how we shall behave. We can, if we care, be helpful and co-operative, doing the tasks assigned to us effectively and with good grace and showing a sense of responsibility for what goes on, over and above the actual details entrusted to us. If we set about the situation in this way it is probable that we may be invited to assume more responsibility, that we shall remain for a considerable time in that working unit, and that we shall improve our positon within it. On the other hand, we can choose to be unhelpful and irresponsible, doing the minimum necessary to complete the tasks actually assigned to us and showing no interest whatsoever in the larger aims and purposes of the job. This approach to the situation is unlikely to result in our being entrusted with positions of responsibility, and may cause us to be among the first to be dropped should there be any slackening of activity. By the final results, therefore, we may get some idea of how an individual has gone about such a situation.

But while it is true in a sense that we can choose how we shall behave in any particular situation, most people seem in fact to make the same choice every time. If in one situation they choose to be helpful and constructive, then within broad limits they will be helpful and constructive in another. This seems to be the behaviour that comes naturally to them and it will tend to show itself in their life-history by a series of characteristic patterns in the various situations in which they have found themselves. When we find an individual whose life-history shows that in every situation where he has been placed he has been on good terms with his associates and has been entrusted with responsibility, we can be sure that he in each case chose to be helpful and constructive and that this is in fact his characteristic behaviour-pattern. When, on the other hand, we find an individual who seems uniformly to have been on unsatisfactory terms with his associates, who has never risen to any position of trust, and who has always been the first to leave during a reorganization, then we can be certain, if the pattern has been repeated often enough, that an unhelpful and unconstructive type of behaviour is characteristic of him.

*The Effect of Environment*

Turning now to the influence of environment on an individual, it is common knowledge that people who have passed their lives in a particular type of community tend to possess certain mannerisms or conventions of dress and speech. Much of the comedy presented on the Variety stage used to depend for its point on the fact that Civil Servants were unimaginative when presented with individual cases, that senior officers in the regular Services tended to reminisce about happenings in different parts of the world, and that cockney street traders would begin their sentences with words like "Blimey, Guv'nor." But there is rather more to it than these superficial mannerisms, for each community has its own standards of acceptable conduct, its own ways of looking at events, and its ideas of what is desirable and undesirable. And one who spends a period in a community—and we must all live our lives in contact with others—will inevitably be affected by these common attitudes and standards; indeed he will be very strong-minded if he does not wholly accept them.

If we know, therefore, that an individual has passed most of his life among people whose standards of conduct were exacting and who maintained a code of values which was rather moral than material, then we should think it probable that his own standards and attitudes would make him trustworthy and reliable. If, on the other hand, we know that someone has lived for a long time among criminals and others who looked upon any moral scruples as a sign of weakness, then we should probably be justified in expecting that he would have some anti-social traits.

Environment can also exert an even more subtle influence on the individual, particularly in childhood and youth. We all depend to a greater or less extent on the approval of our associates for self-confidence and assurance, and we can only blossom out when we are surrounded by a certain atmosphere of encouragement. If we are conscious that those about us are disparaging our achievements and that they are taking every opportunity to criticize and belittle us, then it is highly probable that we shall feel lonely and insecure. Such a feeling will be very likely to result in aggressive and challenging behaviour, for we shall want to show the others—and ourselves—that we don't care a damn what they think of us. Reassurance and encouragement at home and in school are an emotional necessity to young people, and later they are no less necessary at work and in the other situations of adult life. If an individual has lived in an environment where these qualities abound he will have a chance of developing a reasonable degree of confidence in himself. But if he has lived only in "tough" environments, he is likely to be a fairly tough character and to seize every opportunity of proving to other people—and to himself—how very tough he is.

### HOW TO ELICIT A CASE-HISTORY

If we accept the fact that a candidate's characteristic behaviour gives us the best clue to his personal qualities, and if we agree that the best way to provide ourselves with an account of the candidate's characteristic behaviour is to use the interview to draw out his life-history, then the main problem in interviewing becomes clear. What we are setting out to do is to get a full and detailed picture of the candidate's background in the time, necessarily limited, during which we are in personal contact with him. This is not always easy, but it can usually be done, provided we pay attention to two things: the first of these is a systematic approach, and the second concerns our handling of the conversation during the interview.

An individual's life-history can easily present a confused and rambling appearance if we think of it merely as a series of disconnected events, but if we try to consider it under an adequate series of categories it will probably fall into order and become reasonably coherent. The following seven phases will cover most people's lives quite satisfactorily for our purposes.

*Home and Family Background in Childhood*

It is advisable to know where people started from, for only then can we evaluate their achievements. Gaining a higher education from a working-class home will often require more brains and determination than going up to university from a wealthy and cultured family environment. We want to know, therefore, the kind of opportunities presented by an individual's home circumstances and what the family tradition of education and employment has been. We also want to know something about the security of the home in the emotional as well as in the economic sense. Any breakdown in the family either through death or separation of the parents almost inevitably shatters the sure background of affection and stability which is so necessary for the developing personality. It is no coincidence that so many young people who find adjustment to normal life beyond them and turn to crime or other anti-social behaviour come from broken homes.

*School Life*

The home background is mainly important for its effect on the individual, but at school the young person has his first opportunity of showing what he can do when he finds himself among others on level terms. A satisfactory school provides a wide range of activities and should encourage the young person to do the best he can in as many of them as possible. If we find therefore that someone has done well in school work as shown by his place in class or by his results in examinations, that he has taken a distinguished part in school games and other activities outside the classroom, and that he has been selected for such offices as prefect or head of the school, then we can be sure that in comparison with his fellows he has been well above average. These achievements will in turn provide us with evidence about his personal qualities, for no one could reach them without being reasonably intelligent and hard-working and giving the impression of being a responsible and reliable member of the school community.

It does not invariably follow that those who have done badly at school lack the qualities mentioned above, for there are individuals who fail to adjust to the school situation and only do themselves justice when they reach the adult world outside. These, however, are likely to be exceptions and we may take it that in most cases an undistinguished record at school is evidence either of low ability, indifferent personal qualities, or a failure to adjust to the conditions and personalities in the school environment.

*Further Education and Specialist Training*

An increasing number of people continue their education beyond school or spend a period on some form of specialist training. This again provides opportunities for achievement and if in addition to the actual qualifications we can find out what part a person has taken in the social life of a technical college or university or whether he has passed through the course more quickly and with better marks than the average, then we shall have further valuable evidence about the personal qualities the individual has shown in that particular environment.

*Work History*

Few activities are more significant in the life of the individual than his work, for most of us spend more of our waking hours at work than in any other pursuit. If therefore we can provide ourselves with a complete record of the jobs an individual has held, how long he has been in each, and what were his actual duties and levels of responsibility, we shall have a very illuminating record of important behaviour. In some cases we may see obvious evidence of good adjustment to other people, increasing levels of responsibility, and steady and sustained progress. It will not be difficult, therefore, to gain an impression of very sound personal qualities. In other cases we may see a record of failure, short periods in jobs, decreasing levels of responsibility, and a series of rows with people. Again the personal qualities which have made themselves felt in this sorry history will not be difficult to understand.

*Service Life*

In a world where wars still seem to occur with depressing regularity, a number of people spend a period of their lives in the armed forces. Wasteful in some ways as this undoubtedly is, it does provide the individual with a new environment and a different set of opportunities to show what he can do. Under present-day conditions the services probably make it easier for anyone with ability and determination to rise to a position of responsibility than any other comparable organization. This phase of the case-history, therefore, can provide useful additional information, which may either fill out the picture gained from normal civilian life, or may, by its contrasts, draw attention to qualities which might otherwise not have made themselves apparent.

*Spare-time Life*

The pressure of earning a living restricts the freedom of action of most individuals during working hours, and the majority have to do what is required of them rather than what they would prefer for large parts of the day. During their leisure time, however, most people can to a great extent follow their own inclinations, and the kind of pursuits an individual chooses, the levels of achievement he sets for himself, and the relation of these to his abilities and opportunities are quite a significant element in the case-history.

*Present Circumstances*

To round off the picture we should know how the individual is living at the moment, what family responsibilities he has undertaken, and what he requires to keep up his present style of life. Not only will this be important from the point of view of the kind of job he will be suitable for, it will also provide a comparison with the circumstances from which he started.

### THE RELATION OF CASE-HISTORY TO ASSESSMENT

Once an individual's life-history has been covered in these seven phases, we shall have a considerable amount of information about his behaviour in a number of different situations. Each of these situations will make a certain demand on him, and each will offer certain opportunities. How far he has met the demands of these situations and how much use he has made of the opportunities they present, is simply his Motivation and Adjustment in action. Thus, when a biographical interview has been successfully conducted, we should have little difficulty in making an assessment of the individual under each of our five headings. His *Impact on Others* will have made itself felt in how well he has expressed himself and how much self-confidence he has shown in conversation with the interviewer. This, of course, will be affected by the manner in which the interviewer handles the situation, and we shall discuss this further in a moment. His health record should be seen in the various activities he has undertaken, but if there is any need for a more accurate assessment of this, then a medical report should be sought.

*Qualifications* can be assessed from the school and further education periods in the biography, while work experience will also be obvious from the posts he has held and the responsibilities with which he has been entrusted. It may be possible to estimate his *Innate Abilities* from his educational standards and the complexity of the tasks with which he has coped during his work history. In conversation also, he may latch on to what the interviewer says quickly and easily, or he may take rather more time to understand the questions he is being asked. All these will give some insight into his quickness on the uptake, but it is useful to have the result of an intelligence test as well. This provides additional information from another source and can sometimes give an insight indirectly into an individual's Motivation. A high test-score with a low achievement record suggests limited Motivation, while the reverse suggests that the individual has made exceptionally good use of his Innate Abilities.

Taking the different environments in which the individual has found himself, considering the demands and opportunities of these environments, matching the individual's performance against these standards—all this will provide evidence on which to move the Motivational pendulum up or down. Similarly the characteristic role into which the individual appears to gravitate in these situations, provides evidence on which to base a judgment of his Adjustment.

When a factual case-history has been patiently assembled about an individual it is usually surprising to find what a clear and consistent picture it presents and how easy it is to draw a logical and convincing assessment from it. Human beings run very true to form, both in the different aspects of their life at any one time and in the different periods and the environments in which they have lived.

A similarity must be noted here between the assessment process and that of drawing up a job-specification. Both start with a basis of factual information, the former about the job in the job-study and the latter about the individual in the case-history. Both proceed to interpret this information in terms of the Five-Fold Framework, ending up with a specification on the one hand and an assessment on the other. It is upon this similarity of method and of result that systematic selection must be based.

### HANDLING THE INTERVIEW

Now that we are clear about the aim of the interview, which is to provide a case-history of the candidate, we may turn to the method. It may seem a tall order to expect a candidate to tell you the story of his life during the time, usually quite short, which is available for the interview. Once a candidate is convinced that he has an interested and sympathetic listener, however, it is surprising how communicative he can become.

Conducting an interview depends essentially on two things. The first is the establishment of a relationship with the candidate which encourages him to talk freely, frankly, and confidently about himself. This cannot be done if the interviewer obtrudes his personality into the situation or uses the interview as an opportunity to show what a busy and important person he is. Nor can it be done by a series of standard formulae for "putting the candidate at his ease," such as shaking hands, or offering a cigarette, and the like. Each interview is a unique situation and the interviewer's attention must be fully absorbed by the candidate, encouraging every movement towards confidence and the forgetting of the strangeness of the situation, and counteracting so far as possible the feeling of being under examination.

The second element in the situation is to steer the candidate over the ground to be covered so that the essential facts appear as quickly as possible and the irrelevancies are cut down to a minimum. This depends on conversational dexterity, each remark guiding the candidate to talk about the right things without interrupting his flow of conversation. Every interview is first and foremost a conversation, and unless it is successful as such it will never be a good interview. Whenever an interview degenerates into a cross-examination it has been a failure, for such interrogations take an unconscionably long time, while they also tend to miss many of the important points.

Some people with a naturally sympathetic manner and a deftness in conversation can become good interviewers with a minimum of instruction. A few people are so insensitive to the reactions of others and so inept in their handling of social situations that they can never learn to conduct an interview. Between these extremes, however, most people by using a little tact and common sense can learn to handle most interview situations so that they gain quite an adequate case-history in a surprisingly short time.

### EXAMPLE OF A CASE-HISTORY AND ASSESSMENT

Suppose that by a skilfully conducted interview, the following case-history has been elicited.

*Home Background*

Father a builder's labourer earning good money while in work, but with fairly frequent changes. Eldest of five children for whom he appears to have taken some responsibility. No signs of breakdown in the home, but limited opportunities and encouragement.

*School*

Left Secondary Modern School at 15, having been about average in the "A" stream. Played football for the school and was runner-up to the school athletics champion. Prefect and vice-captain of his House. Ran a paper-round to earn some extra money and did errands for the local butcher on Saturdays.

*Further Education*

Was given day release in his first job and reached intermediate standard in City and Guilds Workshop practice examination. Continued after this to take the N.E.B.S.S. examination by part-time study.

*Work History*

Started as a capstan-lathe operator on leaving school as his parents couldn't afford to keep him on and as the money was good. Continued for a year or so, then was given the opportunity of setting his own machine and became a setter-operator. Acquired additional responsibility for setting the machines of some other operators, then was put on to some one-off jobs on which he was working from drawings. Though he has not served the traditional apprenticeship, he is now regarded as a skilled man. He is now in his twenties and is regarded as a possibility for further promotion.

*Service Life*

None. Compulsory National Service had been terminated before he reached the appropriate age.

## Spare Time

Has always been keen on football and has played regularly for a local amateur team of fair standard. Has occupied the position of secretary, arranging fixtures and planning games, and is now captain. Owns a secondhand car which he maintains himself and has undertaken some fairly large-scale repairs and re-fits. Was formerly active in a Youth Group but as he is now married, has given this up. Some do-it-yourself jobs in the house, but as this is Council property, the scope is limited. Little time for reading apart from his studies. Entertainment limited to occasional visits to the cinema and television at home.

## Present Circumstances

Married with one child and another expected. Wife formerly worked as a machinist but is now fully occupied with home and family.

From such a case-history, the following Assessment could be derived.

## Impact on Others

Dress and appearance average, and speech normal for the locality. Takes the initiative in conversation, however, and reacts quickly to other people. Self-confidence adequate to a fair range of situations and keeps his end up in discussions with other people at work. Likely to draw out appropriate reactions from others and from this point of view pushes the pendulum upwards to about 14 in the B grade.

## Qualifications

Has a range of experience in machine-tool work up to setter level and has formal qualifications in workshop practice. Has continued to the N.E.B.S.S. certificate, showing some knowledge of management techniques. 14 on this scale.

## Innate Abilities

Scores 11 on a conventional verbal intelligence test.

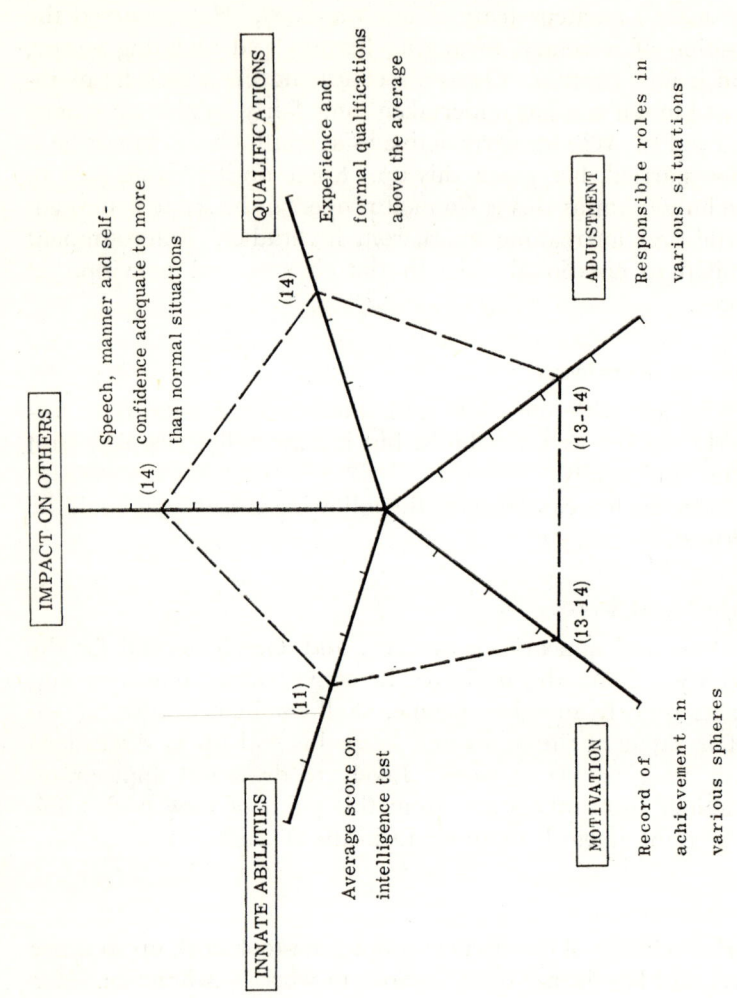

FIG. 26. ASSESSMENT IN DIAGRAM FORM

*Motivation*

Made the most of his opportunities at school and shows a record of sustained progress at work. Has spent some of his spare time on furthering his education and has shown initiative in the football club. Enough achievement to push the pendulum into the B grade, say 13–14.

*Adjustment*

Record of responsibility in his school offices and has apparently been found reliable and dependable at work. Has taken a leading role in the football club, so other members have apparently found him a suitable person for the offices he has held. This record of gravitating into responsible roles in various situations would push the pendulum up into the B grade, again, say 13–14.

This Assessment is shown diagrammatically in Fig. 26. It is obvious that he would be a possibility for the specification outlined in the previous chapter.

### THE APPRAISAL OF EXISTING EMPLOYEES

Another way in which the matching up of the Five-Fold Specification and the Assessment can be used is in the appraisal of existing employees. With personnel becoming an increasingly expensive item in the operations of an organization, it has become important to know how much value it is getting for the money it spends on wages and salaries. Reports on performance at regular intervals are thus making their appearance to an increasing degree.

These can be based on actual performance against the Job Description. If this is laid out in the terms we discussed, with targets for output, quality, cost control and the like, the appraisal can be quantitative and objective. But it may also be considered advisable to make an appraisal of the personal qualities which the employee has shown, and here the problems of subjectivity will present themselves. The two forms of appraisal should always be kept quite separate from each other, and the Five-Fold Framework used for the latter. Assessment can be based on available from the individual's behaviour in the work situation over the preceding period. If he has coped adequately with the interactions with other people which the job demands, he will have reached the requisite standard of Impact on Others. His knowledge of the job and management techniques can be expressed against the Qualifications heading of the specification, while his "quickness on the uptake" will be obvious in the degree to which he has understood new problems or situations. This again can be matched against the Abilities aspect. How hard he has worked and how effective he has been on the job provides the evidence for an assessment of his Motivation, while the number of avoidable rows and emotional crises occurring will be the measure of his Adjustment.

If such a Five-Fold appraisal shows that the individual is not matching up to the specification, the problem then arises of what should be done about it. If, in a counselling interview, the individual can be told how he is getting on and his shortcomings pointed out in such a way that he will appreciate that the counsellor is trying to help him, then he may make an effort to remedy the situation. The counselling interview is very difficult to handle, however, and if satisfactory contact is not made, it will simply be taken as an attack against which the individual must defend himself. When this happens it will have been a waste of time and may do no good at all.

## SUMMARY

1. How do we in fact learn enough about another person to be able to predict his future behaviour?

We can only predict what will happen in the future by finding out the main lines of development in the past. When we know someone so well that we have learned how he behaves in a large number of situations, the main tendencies and reaction-patterns will be quite clear and comprehensible. It is then possible to say with some confidence how he is likely to react to some specific situation in the future.

2. How can we sum up an individual in an interview?

We shall see a certain amount of his behaviour directly during the actual period of the interview, but this is likely to be too short to be fully reliable. We can, however, supplement this by encouraging the candidate to tell us about a much longer period of significant behaviour in his past life. This should enable us to see the main behaviour-patterns quite clearly.

3. How far is an individual's past life a reliable source of information about his personal qualities?

In the first place an individual's personal qualities play a large part in determining his level of achievement and the part he will play among other people. Broadly speaking, in the long term, most people make the circumstances of their own lives by the kind of people they are. In the second place, the kind of environment we live in has a hand in determining the standards we try to live up to, the opportunities we are presented with, and our powers of adjustment to other people. Though these two points of view may seem superficially contradictory, nevertheless from either one of them the case-history is the most important source of evidence about an individual's personal qualities.

4. How can we elicit an adequate case-history during the short period of a normal interview?

It will help if we think of an individual's life in the following seven phases—

   (*a*) home background in childhood;
   (*b*) school life;
   (*c*) further education or special training;
   (*d*) work history;
   (*e*) service life (if any);
   (*f*) spare-time life, and
   (*g*) present circumstances.

The main points under each of these phases can then be elicited to show how far the individual has been affected by it or how far he has shown his personal qualities in it.

5. What is the relevance of the case-history to the assessment?

The case-history provides the factual information on which the Five-Fold assessment is built up. Some of the points, such as Qualifications, can be got by a mere assembly or arrangement of the information available, while some will involve a little interpretation, such as the working out of the patterns to give the Motivational heading.

6. What are the main elements in the handling of the interview?

To gain the case-history as quickly and comprehensibly as possible it is essential that the candidate should be talking freely, frankly, and confidently. This depends on the interviewer building up the right relationship quickly with the candidate and taking him deftly over the ground so that he provides the information required.

CHAPTER XVII

# Training

UNTIL recent years, industrial training was almost entirely informal. The new entrant to a semi-skilled job was put with an experienced worker, who might or might not be able or willing to pass his knowledge on. After a period of observation and perhaps some practice under supervision, the learner was allowed to go on on his own and if he was lucky enough to meet no unforeseen difficulties in the early stages he might in due course work up to a satisfactory rate of output. Much the same happened with entrants to a skilled trade, except that the training took longer and the apprentices, being younger, spent a longer time standing round watching and were often employed on menial jobs whose actual training value was quite negligible.

Under such conditions any attention paid to systematic training was bound to yield dramatic results, and many firms who have provided formal instruction and graduated practice in the job have been surprised and delighted at the rapid progress which could be achieved towards the standard rate of output.

This state of affairs made it easy for anyone prepared to spend a little time and thought on training to claim, with perfect justice, that great improvements could be expected from his "system." Any training scheme will produce results if it is introduced where none existed before, and in vast areas of industry whatever was done to train workers or staff was bound to be an improvement on the haphazard and unsystematic methods which were practically universal. We should not take for granted, therefore, that every training scheme which we find in industry today is completely sound and effective, even though it has produced results. Training methods should be based on an understanding of the learning process, as set out in Chapter V, and if we can make proper use of this knowledge we should be able to make very significant reductions in the time required to learn a job, while at the same time we should be able to achieve much higher standards of performance.

### MOTIVATION IN TRAINING

We have already seen how large a part motivation plays in the learning process; in fact we can be quite sure that no one ever learns anything unless he sees good reason for doing so. In considering industrial training, therefore, it is advisable to turn first to the reasons for learning a job and to look at them from the new entrant's point of view.

At first glance this might seem far too simple to waste any time on, because it is surely obvious enough that people come into industry to earn their living and that unless they turn themselves into efficient workers they won't be paid and will have to look for another means of making an income. But this view of the situation presupposes first that the worker looks on his job simply as a means of earning money; secondly that he knows the standards of performance to which an efficient worker must keep; and thirdly, that he is unwilling to try an alternative means of making a living. And these three propositions are in actual fact misleading over-simplifications of the situation.

In the first place, all workers do not spend all day thinking about the money they are earning. There are too many things going on for any normal person to spend his day counting up the hours as they pass, saying to himself "That's twenty-five new pence I have earned, now it is seventy new pence and by lunch time it will be over three pounds." He may do so for part of the time, in fact he probably often does, but his attention will also stray to the work he is doing, the people round about, and the probable attitudes of the supervisor in charge. The money a worker earns is a very important element in his motivation, but it is not the only element.

In the second place, the standards of performance required to hold down a job are seldom definite and widely known. It may be generally accepted that a trained man ought to achieve an output of, say, fifty units a day, but there are generally a few in the shop who are only producing about forty-five and perhaps one who is producing as few as forty. Moreover, if someone fails to reach even that standard he will not necessarily lose his job; indeed he is more likely to be tried on some other work. Failure to reach a known standard, therefore, is seldom widely accepted as leading inevitably to dismissal.

In the third place, there are many other available ways of earning a living, particularly during a period of full employment, and if a man feels dissatisfied with his progress in learning one type of work he may turn to another without wasting time bewailing his lack of success. This picture of workers being motivated solely by a desire to earn their living through learning to reach a certain standard at a particular job is, therefore, much too simple to be realistic in the present-day conditions of industry. We must look a little more closely if we are to understand motivation sufficiently clearly to manipulate it intelligently during the learning process.

*The Reinforcement of Motivation*

We may get a clearer idea of the matter if we think of a young man beginning his apprenticeship at the age of, say, fifteen. On his first day he is probably very keen indeed, his new overalls and the unfamiliar routine of a workshop having enhanced the excitement he already feels at being away from school and among men at work. He probably carries in his mind a vague picture of himself as a skilled tradesman, sharing the prestige and security of employment which goes with that status and earning a rate of pay which is well above that of an ordinary labourer. During the first week or so he will be quite strongly motivated, but the goals at which he is aiming will be complex, including, as we have noted above, prestige, security of employment, and a certain level of income. They will also be rather indefinite, for he will be unable to describe exactly what he means by prestige and security; and they will be remote, for he will not be able to achieve any of them for five years or longer.

How long do we imagine that a boy of fifteen will continue to work conscientiously towards such a remote, indefinite and complex goal? Certainly not for the whole five years it will take him to reach it; in fact if we have any experience of young people we shall be quite prepared to find him larking about the shop and dodging the foreman in a few weeks' time—just as soon, in fact, as he is sufficiently familiar with his surroundings to recover his self-confidence. To keep a young man working throughout a five-year training course we must do something to bolster up his motivation before his initial enthusiasm evaporates completely.

How can this be done? Much will depend on the circumstances of each job, but in this case it is obviously necessary to do something about the complexity, indefiniteness, and remoteness of the goals. If his vague conception of a tradesman can be replaced by a reasonably precise idea of the knowledge and skill he is expected to acquire, then he will understand that he must learn to file and chip to certain tolerances before he can be considered proficient as a fitter. Likewise he must know something about drawings, which in turn will involve some familiarity with mathematics. In this way the apprentice can substitute a series of precise goals for his general aim of becoming a tradesman.

These precise goals will go far towards reinforcing his motivation, for they are more personal and more proximate. Instead of merely serving his time in the rather remote hope of being accepted as skilled in five years, he will be working to reach a certain standard in, say, the erecting shop during the six months he is spending there, while at the same time he is aiming to pass the end-of-term examination in mathematics in four weeks' time.

More will be said on the subject of motivation in Chapter XVIII, but from the training point of view it is always advisable to reinforce it by substituting short-term goals for remote ones and precise standards for vague levels of performance. In most cases this can be done by introducing intermediate levels of performance at which the trainee should aim during the learning process. The setting of these standards will be discussed later.

### THE DEVELOPMENT OF SKILL

In Chapter V we called attention to two different kinds of learning process. One of these was the slow and steady development of skill in a simple movement and the other was the quick intuitional comprehension of a situation. The former is characterized by a slow but consistent improvement in performance, while the latter leads by a rapid jump to near the maximum performance in the first few trials. As was pointed out at the time, most learning situations include both these elements so that in most cases a learning curve shows periods of rapid improvement interspersed with periods where performance improves very slowly or actually stays still.

These two elements point in turn to the two factors on which successful training will depend. One of these is practice and the other insight, and their effects alternate and overlap. The development of skill depends in part on the operator going through the same set of motions over and over again, while at the same time rapid improvements will be seen at times as habit-patterns integrate and as the process is more clearly understood. A successful training scheme must provide adequate practice and at the same time encourage insight, but there are at times difficulties in connexion with each.

Providing a learner with the opportunity to practise means in real life that he will spoil a certain amount of material, for he will inevitably make mistakes and produce sub-standard work in the early stages. In the training of sewing machinists this may not matter, for very little expense will be involved in the provision of waste fabric which can be stitched over and over; but if the material in use is a valuable metal, the prospect of a learner scrapping several pounds' worth before he turns out a single usable article may be more than management can face. Some means, however, must be found to get round this difficulty because, without practice, skill cannot be acquired and it may be quicker in the long run to provide a similar but less expensive material for a learner to make his mistakes on. It is no use trying to avoid mistakes by making the trainee watch a skilled worker instead of having a go himself.

*Insight*

Turning to the question of insight, we are aware of the limitations of our knowledge. Once we have studied a number of people learning the same job under similar conditions we should be able to build up a series of learning curves and observe their regularities. This might show us that between, say, the tenth and fifteenth trial there was usually a rapid improvement in performance which seemed to be due to the trainee's getting the hang of the job as a whole. Again we might find that between the fortieth and fiftieth trial there was usually a notable increase in speed though accuracy was still somewhat low, while between the hundredth and hundred-and-twentieth trial accuracy showed a rapid improvement. With this information at our disposal we might postulate three stages of learning—

1. An insight into the relationship of the various parts of the job between the tenth and fifteenth trial.

2. An integration of muscular habits leading to an increase of speed between the fortieth and fiftieth trial.

3. A further integration leading to an improvement of control between the one-hundredth and one-hundred-and-twentieth trial.

The next step might be to try to encourage these integrations by such measures as—

1. Explanation of the job as a whole during the trainee's first few trials.

2. Drawing the trainee's attention to speed from the twentieth trial onwards without paying much attention to accuracy, in the hope of achieving the improvement in speed by, say, the thirtieth to thirty-fifth trial.

3. Drawing the trainee's attention to accuracy from the fiftieth trial onwards, in the hope of encouraging the improvement in this aspect of the job by, say, the seventieth trial.

When we have made a close study of a particular training programme it may be possible thus to anticipate and accelerate every development, but few operations have so far been subjected to this close scrutiny. We must fall back, therefore, on a few general ideas, such as that improvement is usually very rapid during the first few performances due to the learner getting the feel of the job as a whole, so that any explanations which may facilitate this process should be provided at this point. In the later parts of the training explanations in greater detail may help to develop insight.

*Practice Periods*

It will begin to be apparent that we cannot expect good results by leaving a trainee to practise away on his own for long periods. This runs the risk of boredom and discouragement with a consequent falling off in motivation. Better results will usually be attained by splitting up the practice periods so that the trainee is never left alone for long periods at a time. This has several advantages.

In the first place it facilitates the actual learning process. Experiments in learning, which are designed to show in detail how performance improves, have made it possible to find out how much has been learned after a period of two hours of continuous practice. Comparisons can then be made with the amount learned after three forty-minute periods, six twenty-minute periods or twelve ten-minute periods. The results were as follows—

| No. of Periods | Length of Period (minutes) | Total Time (minutes) | No. of Letters |
|---|---|---|---|
| 1 | 120 | 120 | 135 |
| 3 | 40 | 120 | 195 |
| 6 | 20 | 120 | 255 |
| 12 | 10 | 120 | 265 |

The task on which these figures were worked out was the fairly simple substitution of letters for digits. Though this may not seem to have great direct relevance to industrial training, nevertheless it establishes the general principle that when the same amount of time is broken up into twelve practice periods, the performance achieved is almost twice as good as when it is spent in one period (see Fig. 27).

Distributed practice periods obviously reduce fatigue and they can be used to reinforce motivation. However, there seem to be three main reasons why they facilitate the learning process. In the first place we seem to forget wrong associations more quickly than correct ones and consequently when a gap is allowed between two practice periods it will enable us to forget our ineffective methods, while the effective ones remain. In the second place, older associations are strengthened more by practice than more recent ones; thus anything we learned yesterday will be more improved with practice than what we learned within the last half-hour. Distributed practice periods, therefore, facilitate learning by allowing habits to "age."

The second advantage in splitting up practice periods lies in the opportunity it provides for checking progress, by requiring the trainee to demonstrate his progress at the end of a period. Unsupervised practice over a long period is of little use in learning, as when a group of children were left to read over lists of syllables in an attempt to memorize them. The average score at the end of the period was seventeen syllables. Another group of children spent the same amount of time learning the syllables, but in this case 80 per cent of the period

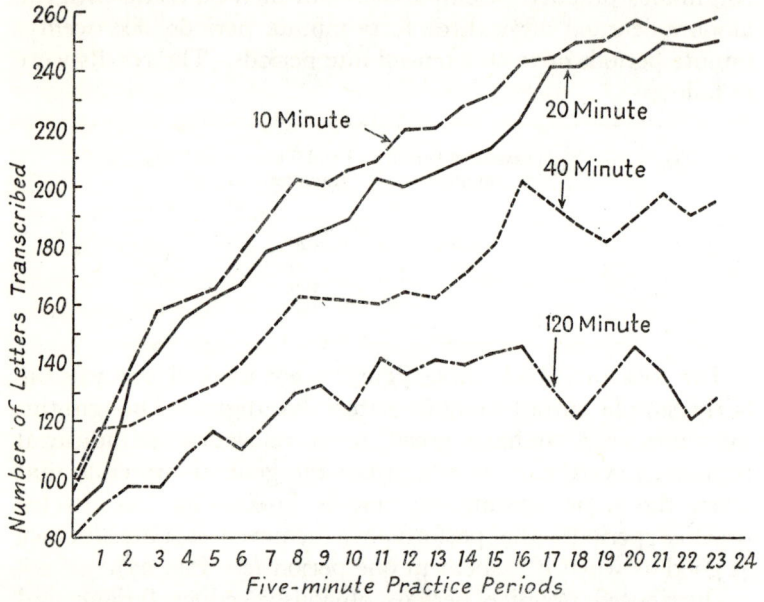

FIG. 27. INFLUENCE OF DIFFERENT DISTRIBUTIONS OF PRACTICE
(After Starch)

was devoted to repeating or reciting the syllables to a teacher. The average score of this latter group was thirty-five, or more than twice that of the first group. Each period of practice is directed to a definite end and, as one would expect from its value in reinforcing motivation, is very much more effective in enabling the individual to learn the material.

### STANDARDS

The third advantage of splitting up the practice periods concerns the setting of standards. Most of us accept certain standards quite unconsciously—standards of behaviour or standards of achievement. If our performance measures up to these standards we shall be quite satisfied with ourselves, but if we fall below these standards we shall be aware of it and shall seek an opportunity to do better and to rehabilitate ourselves in our own opinion.

These standards have an effect on the learning process, for we shall always be trying to measure up to them. The small boy at school tries to run as fast as the others and is satisfied with his performance if he is not left behind. A little later on he begins to match his performance against a more objective standard, the school record, say, and will be dissatisfied if he falls much below that. Later on still, if he continues to be interested in running, he may take as his standard the British record and aim at improving his performance until it can stand comparison with that. As anyone whose performance at running is better than the British record thereby reduces that record and so sets a higher standard for everyone else to aim at, we can be sure, in this field at least, of maximum effort and an ever-increasing standard of attainment.

But in most types of industrial work there are no British records, nor indeed are there any local records, so that the standards of performance which are accepted as adequate may often be much lower than they need to be. The new entrant, when introduced to a quite unfamiliar job and left to work away on his own, may find that it takes him an hour to make one not-very-satisfactory article. He may unconsciously accept this as a standard and spend the rest of the day at about the same level of performance.

At the same time, of course, a beginner's first attempt must not be compared straight away with the performance of an expert. Who would ever learn to play the piano if his early fumblings were recorded and played back after a performance by Rubenstein? Comparison with such a standard would emphasize the poorness of the learner's performance and would lead to grave discouragement by making the expert's standard seem quite unattainable. When faced with what seems an impossible standard most people give up trying. It is the standard which is a little above our present performance but which seems perfectly possible which calls out maximum effort.

Perhaps one of the most important elements in industrial training is this manipulation of standards. Set suitably low in the early stages they can be used to encourage trainees and provide the intermediate goals so important to motivation. Raised in accordance with the improvements which a study of the learning curve leads us to expect, they may help trainees to break through the flat periods sooner than they would otherwise do. Set finally at levels which indicate something near the best possible performance, they will ensure that there is no levelling off in the later stages of training at a standard which is below what it should be.

### THE APPLICATION OF THESE PRINCIPLES TO INDUSTRIAL TRAINING

W. Douglas Seymour, in his book *Industrial Training for Manual Operations*,[1] gives some striking examples of how these principles can be applied in the routine working of an industrial company. His first stage is to analyse a task into its sensori-motor elements, or to discover the "cues" which the experienced operator recognizes through the various senses involved in the task—sight, hearing, touch, etc. These cues trigger off muscular movements, which in the case of the experienced operator have become habit-patterns which spring effectively and economically into action as they are required for the smooth performance of the task. The main difference between the experienced worker and the trainee is that the latter does not appreciate the significance of these cues, while his muscular responses are neither smooth nor automatic.

To speed up the trainee's recognition of the cues and to develop his control of the muscular movements, a series of exercises can be devised, each of which is, in effect, a sensori-motor element in the complete task. These exercises are practised one at a time, the trainee aiming at a level of speed and accuracy in that element which represents that of an efficient operator on the complete task ("piece-work speed"). When each of two such exercises can be performed to this standard they are put together and practised until piece-work speed is attained on this larger portion of the task. In this

[1] Pitman, 1954.

way the complete job is built up, the trainee always aiming at a standard of performance which is within his reach and progressively mastering the job by a series of short practice periods.

These methods have proved to have two main advantages in practice. On the one hand they reduce training time, with its consequent under-utilization of equipment and risk of spoiled work. This alone would justify the not inconsiderable time and expense which the installation of such a system involves, for, if new starters can reach a standard of output equal to that of experienced operators in three weeks instead of three months, the savings will be considerable. But at the same time wastage among trainees, which is another source of loss, is also considerably reduced. Under the conventional methods of learning on the job by observation of a skilled operator (often characterized as "sitting next to Nellie") the risk of boredom and discouragement is very high indeed. There is so much standing around and watching, while the gap between the trainee's performance and that of the experienced worker is so depressingly wide and doesn't seem to be getting any less. This feeling of lack of progress leads many trainees to decide that they are not getting anywhere and they consequently leave to look for another job. If, on the other hand, they are always aiming at a standard which can be reached after only a few hours' practice, even if this represents no more than part of the complete job, then there is enough feeling of achievement to encourage the trainee to persevere.

Since the passing of the Industrial Training Act in 1964, more attention has been paid to training, and companies are making sure that the amount paid in levy is being returned in grants. Operator training, the training of technicians and specialists can be dealt with either within the organization or with the help of local technical colleges. Management and supervisory training presents additional problems and special external courses, planned experience and the like, play their part in extending the range and awareness of these levels of staff. The basic principles we have outlined, however, will play their part in making any training project more or less effective and should always be borne in mind.

## SUMMARY

1. How far has motivation to be considered in industrial training?

Motivation is all-important in training, to the extent that the strength of the motivation determines the efficiency of learning. In most industrial training situations the desire to become a skilled worker or to keep one's job is too remote and imprecise to be adequate. In many training situations it may be advisable to substitute short-term precise goals in order to stimulate the trainee's motivation.

2. What are the two main learning processes we have to consider in training?

The first is practice which enables the muscular habits on which manual skills depend to be built up gradually, and the second is insight which leads to quick improvements in performance as the various parts of the task are seen in relation to one another. Providing a trainee with adequate opportunity to practise may raise practical problems of spoilt work which must somehow be faced.

3. What can be done to facilitate insight in a training scheme?

Once we know enough about a particular learning process we shall see from the learning curve where the various insights develop. It then becomes possible to encourage these insights by providing the explanations and guided practice which may cause them to develop sooner. In most cases the first insight into the job as a whole can be encouraged by taking the trainee through the complete process in the early stages.

4. How should practice periods be arranged in training?

There is a considerable amount of evidence to show that a number of short periods of practice are more effective than one long period. This is probably due to the fact that short periods reduce fatigue and can be used to stimulate motivation, that they cause ineffective methods to be forgotten while effective ones remain, and that older associations are more strengthened by practice than are more recent ones.

5. Should progress be checked at the end of each practice period?

Nothing is more wasteful and ineffective in training than allowing trainees to potter along for long periods without supervision. Progress should be checked at each practice period by making the trainee show what he can do and how far he has got. This reinforces motivation, enables some control to be kept on standards, and gives direction to all the trainee's efforts.

6. How far are standards important in training?

Most of us work, consciously or unconsciously, to a standard, and are quite satisfied if we can keep up to it. If that standard has been set haphazardly and is below what it should be we shall be working inefficiently. Many standards during and after training have grown up by tradition and are in many cases well below what could reasonably be expected of a normal person. Unless care is taken to impose reasonable standards of progress and attainment throughout the training period, the pace will tend to be set much slower than it should be.

CHAPTER XVIII

# Incentives

THE word "incentive" is widely used nowadays and, when considering people at work, it generally means something which makes them work harder. There is some danger of confusion because "incentive" can be thought of in three different ways and the same word is frequently taken to mean any one of them at different times. The three uses between which we must distinguish are—

(*a*) Something external to the individual which he will strive to obtain, e.g. "Money is an incentive."

(*b*) Some manipulation of the work-situation which will encourage the individual to work harder, e.g. a "bonus incentive" system.

(*c*) Something within the individual which encourages him to do something.

To clear our minds on this subject it may be as well to revert for a moment to Chapter VI, where we discussed the subject of motivation. It will be remembered that human beings are subject in the last resort to a few simple basic urges, the satisfaction of which is necessary to keep them alive. Hunger and thirst, the need for clothing and shelter, the desire for companionship—these are universal in their application throughout the world. How we satisfy these urges, however, varies according to climate, geographical conditions, and state of development. One community may hunt and fish for its food, another may till the ground, while a third may make things and trade them with other people. The methods by which a community carries on its economic activities will vary from one place to another, being sometimes primitive and simple, and sometimes complex and highly developed.

If we consider any individual, therefore, we can trace his motivation through various stages, the first of which will be simple and universal, while the later ones will be more complex and peculiar to each person. The stages will be roughly as follows.

1. *Basic Urges Necessary to Sustain Life.* Hunger, thirst, the need for clothing and shelter, are universal among humans.

2. *Means of Satisfaction Available to the Community.* Determined broadly by geography, climate, and the level of development.

3. *Private Goals Set by the Individual for Himself.* Dependent on his abilities, upbringing, and interests, and infinitely varied according to each individual's preferences. (See Chapter VI on Motivational Patterns.)

Stage 1 is comparatively easy to understand, for it includes all that is necessary to keep a human being alive. Stage 2 depends on the community in which he lives, some account of which is necessary before we can approach Stage 3, which can only be comprehended in terms of the individual case.

### THE INDUSTRIAL CULTURE-PATTERN

When we consider the motivation of workers in industry, we must think of the means of satisfying their basic urges which the conditions in which they live make available to them. Standing aside from our daily lives for a moment, let us look at the community in which we live as though we were strangers from outside, and compare it with others in different parts of the world and at different times. How would we sum it up? As pastoral, where people feed and clothe themselves by tending flocks and herds? As agricultural, where they till the soil? Or as a community in which people hunt and fish?

All these elements are perhaps present, but they are hardly the main theme. Ours is a community in which most wants are satisfied by things bought in shops, these things having been manufactured or processed by the work of others from materials grown or extracted either here or abroad. The ordinary person has not to struggle with nature to feed or clothe himself, for all he may need is ready waiting for him and he may buy it with money which is equally exchangeable for shoes or sugar, trousers or tea. Moreover if he does not want to buy anything today, his money will be just as good tomorrow should he want anything then.

In an industrial community such as ours, therefore, money is the universally useful commodity. Everything can be valued by means of it, and its possession enables us to satisfy any reasonable want. The individual, in the vast majority of cases, tries to supply himself with money, and the most usual means of doing so is to find an opportunity of taking part in the process of manufacturing, transporting, and distributing goods, for a weekly or monthly payment.

Stage 2 in our consideration of motivation, therefore—that which concerns the means which the community makes available to the individual for satisfying his needs—is fairly distinct in a modern industrial state. There are, of course, exceptions, for a few people work on their own, like artists or writers. Housewives work within the family under conditions which are sometimes worse than are tolerated in any industrial company, and there is always a certain proportion of agricultural workers. A few people do not work at all. In the main, however, most of us have jobs of one kind or another, and though the complex pattern of activities which make up the economic life of the community produces many different kinds of job, nevertheless common elements can be discerned in practically all of them. One of these is that the individual works for a money payment. As we saw above, money is universally useful and with it we can satisfy any reasonable material want.

### THE WORKING OF THE MONEY INCENTIVE

If people work to earn money in the first place, then does it follow that they will work harder to earn more money? This is one of those questions which are so misleadingly simple in appearance that it seems as though only a born fool could give any other answer than "Yes" to them. The trouble is that while it is broadly true that people will work harder to earn more, it is not true all the time and in every case. There are exceptions to the working of this rule and we must understand them if we are to understand incentives. For the moment, however, let us put these exceptions to one side and consider how the money incentive works.

Having joined up with a body of people who are making, transporting or distributing something useful, the individual undertakes to work in return for a wage or salary. There are various kinds of work he may undertake, however, some of which are quite simple and can be picked up in half a day and some of which are very difficult and require months or years of training. Inevitably a kind of "supply and demand" situation will be set up, and as only a limited number of people will be able to undertake the more difficult jobs, they will come to command more money.

In this way a scale of payment will develop. The very difficult jobs which only a few people can do successfully will be paid the highest wages, while the simplest jobs which anyone can pick up will be paid lowest. The individual, seeing that one way to earn more money is to undertake more difficult or responsible work, will wish to get one of these better jobs because of the remuneration it offers. There will always, therefore, be competition for better paid work, even though it demands more from the individual who undertakes it, and consequently there will be a fairly universal desire for promotion to a better job.

On one particular job, however, this universal desire for money has made it possible to link up more effort with greater remuneration. Suppose a worker is taken on to peel potatoes, at a wage, say, of ten pounds a week. So long as his wage is forthcoming he can dawdle over the job and invent excuses for not having peeled more than a stone or so in a day. The responsibility for ensuring that he gets on with the job and turns out a reasonable number rests in this situation with the supervisor, as indeed it usually does when people are on a time rate.

Suppose, however, that the situation is arranged differently and the worker is paid 25p for every stone of potatoes that he peels. If he dawdles and only gets through a stone a day his wage will shrink to £1·25 for a five-day week, whereas if he works hard and steadily and gets through 10 stones a day his wage will increase to £12·50. Only the very simplest mind would fail thus to connect cause and effect and to make an effort to peel as many potatoes as possible during the working day.

This, of course, is a piece-work system and it has the advantage of transferring the responsibility for calling out effort from the supervisor to the worker himself by linking it up with his desire to earn more money. Straight piece-work systems are not usually practicable nowadays because in most trades minimum wages have been agreed on a national basis. Modifications of piece-work are widely used, however, the aim of which is to combine a minimum wage with extra payment for increased effort. Most of these depend on determining (usually by time-study methods) how much the worker can produce in a normal working day by the ordinary amount of effort. This is accepted as the standard rate of output and anything above it is paid for at an extra rate; the worker is thus told, in effect, that if he wants more money he must make an extra effort and produce more than a certain standard.

*Limitations to the Financial Incentive*

The working out of these bonus-incentive systems in practice is not always easy. The establishing of a standard, for example, depends in many cases on timing a worker on a specimen task at normal speed and using this as a basis. But what a "normal" speed consists of and what allowance should be made for rests and interruptions are questions which it is not always easy to decide on an objective basis. And when one side has an interest in getting the standard time set as high as possible, while the other has an equally strong interest in keeping it as low as can be managed, there is room for considerable argument which is not always amicable. In the same way it is difficult to ensure that the standards set for each job are strictly comparable and in practice some tend to be easier while others are significantly stricter. In normal working this means that on one type of work more money can be earned than on another which involves just the same amount of effort.

The need to "adjust" rates so as to reduce these inequalities means that changes have at times to be made. If any of these changes involves a reduction in what the worker earns there is a danger that he will react in a hostile manner and the suspicion will grow that the system is designed merely to call out maximum effort on his part without the slightest intention of allowing him to earn more than a certain standard of wages. From this it is an easy step to reducing effort to a level where something more than the time rate is earned but not enough to attract attention and cause the rate to be cut. The original intention of the system thus becomes vitiated and a kind of bargaining game takes place between those who set the rates and those who work them.

One reason why this happens is that such systems are based on the theory that the individual's desire for money is steady and continuous, and that he will always be willing to put forth an equal amount of extra effort to get an equivalent return in more money.

*The Point at which the Money Incentive Loses its Effectiveness*

But as any economist knows, this "infinitely elastic demand" is quite a rare occurrence, and it is rather more usual for a slackening-off process to take place after a certain point. In the case of water, for example, a man dying of thirst might be willing to give all that he possessed for a drink. Once his thirst was slaked he would be less willing to pay a high price, while we, to whom water is available out of the tap, would not be prepared to pay any price at all.

The position with money is rather similar. A man who has no money and who sees no prospect of getting any will seize any chance of work which offers him a wage and he will work very hard to hold on to that job. But the man who already has a job in which he feels to some extent secure will not necessarily put forth the same degree of effort to earn more. There is a point at which the incentive value of money drops off and in some cases this point may be reached as soon as the individual's most pressing needs are met. It is only by studying the individual on the lines laid down in Chapter X that we can get some idea of where this point will be reached.

Returning for a moment to consider the culture-pattern in which we live, there are a number of things which affect the individual's reaction to a money incentive, quite apart from this inevitable dropping off after a certain point. At the bottom end of the scale our social security services prevent anyone from falling below a certain minimum, so that people are protected from the desperate need to take any kind of work in order to escape starvation. Higher up the scale taxation begins to make itself felt so that when an individual begins to earn more than, say, ten pounds a week, the Chancellor of the Exchequer will take quite a substantial amount from him. Once he begins to earn very large amounts the situation can arise where the Chancellor appropriates 91p out of every pound and the individual is left with only 9p.

But besides these variations in the individual's desire for money, there is a further complication. Human attention seldom remains steady for long at a time and very few people continue to think about money all day and every day so long as their basic wants are reasonably satisfied. It is quite true that if we are hungry we shall always be thinking about food, but after a meal our attention will wander off to other matters. And as we have seen previously we have to be very near the bread-line before we spend all the working day calculating how much we have earned.

We have come to the point, therefore, where we understand that in an industrial community the normal way of satisfying our wants is by buying things with money, and that the primary incentive to work is to earn enough money to live on. So long as the individual's basic wants are unsatisfied the primary incentive to work is money and he will work harder to earn more money. After a certain point, however, the money incentive will become less effective. This point will vary with different people in different jobs, but as soon as an individual says "What is the good of bashing away at the job just for an extra pound a week?" or "Why should I undertake all this extra worry and responsibility for another hundred a year?" it has been reached.

### OTHER INCENTIVES IN THE WORK-SITUATION

The question then arises of what takes the place of the money incentive once this point has been reached? Will an individual then prefer leisure to money so that it becomes impossible to get him to take any interest in his work at all beyond that point? If this is so then we shall have the kind of situation which was alleged to occur in certain coalfields where miners worked four shifts a week because they couldn't make enough to live on in three, and it was only round Christmas and holiday times when they needed more money that output could be raised by working a full shift. The only remedy for this state of affairs would be to try to multiply the individual's wants so that he would always be in need of more money to buy the things he needs.

In some ways we shall find this process going on in industrial communities, for consumer goods advertising, the multiplication of goods, services and entertainment which can be bought, and all that is associated with our "rising standard of living" is suggesting new wants to the individual. Among ordinary working people, however, the effects are rather uneven, because the wants of most men for clothes, food and drink, and entertainment tend to be limited. It may be that this kind of reinforcement of the money incentive works best indirectly through the family, because it is when one turns to the provision of goods and services for a family that one becomes aware of a very large unsatisfied demand.

But this reliance on a reinforcement of the money incentive alone is not entirely satisfactory because it will be difficult to run most businesses if the individual workers merely come in to work until they have earned as much as they want and are then quite prepared to knock off and go home. What other satisfactions can be drawn from work which would encourage an individual to put out more effort?

*Satisfactions in the Immediate Task*

There are certain satisfactions which can be drawn from the actual work itself, or the immediate environment in which it is carried out. These have a certain importance as incentives, not always to the extent that they necessarily cause people to work harder at any one job, but they will certainly be effective in calling out more effort from an individual in one situation as contrasted with another.

There is, for example, a certain satisfaction to be gained from the exercise of skill. The pilot of an aircraft may well wish to fly even though he is not being paid for it, simply because of the pleasure he derives from controlling his machine and using the skill he has developed through many hours of practice. The same sort of thing may be found in those who sail boats, drive vehicles, or use tools, and in certain cases the opportunity to do the work will have a certain importance as an incentive because the individual will be glad of the opportunity to use his skill. Closely allied to this is the satisfaction to be derived from making things. Many people get considerable pleasure from being able to say "I made that," and while we are probably prepared to believe that this is part of the incentive to which an artist or craftsman responds in his work, we may be slower to appreciate that a semi-skilled worker operating an automatic machine may get the same kind of satisfaction from his job, though perhaps on a different level.

Possibly this is due to the fact that we attach different levels of prestige to the two kinds of work. We can imagine that someone might be proud of being a surgeon or an artist, and there is no doubt that the public recognition which attaches to jobs like these acts as an incentive to young people, causing them to work hard in the hope that in due course they may qualify for admission to that select and distinguished company. Few young officers have failed to repress a thrill of pleasure the first time they were saluted by an "other rank," and a newly qualified physician feels much the same way the first time he is addressed as "Doctor."

It is unrealistic, however, to confine this satisfaction in the prestige of a job solely to work which is recognized on that scale. The same considerations apply to the skilled ranks in industry and a fitter, carpenter, or electrician stands in much the same relation to other workers. A considerable level of prestige attaches to any "tradesman's" job, partly connected with the long apprenticeship involved, and partly due to the fact that his skill and experience enable him to cope with situations in which another person would be incompetent. Gaining and keeping this distinction of being skilful and knowledgeable where ordinary mortals cannot compete is an incentive to which many people respond in their working life.

One must always be prepared for irrational standards of prestige, however, for in industry it frequently happens that certain jobs, which seem to outward appearances little different from the remainder, come to be accepted as "better jobs." There will be competition for these, and even though management may not understand why they should be thought preferable, it should be aware of the fact that this is so. It is possible at the same time to enhance the prestige of certain jobs quite deliberately, by such means as giving them titles, providing a special uniform or taking steps to ensure that the importance of the work is more widely recognized. The jobs of cleaners in food factories have been made more attractive in this way by emphasizing the quite obvious fact that the purity of the product depends in great measure on how they do their work.

*The Effect of the Surroundings at Work*

Another group of satisfactions can be drawn, not perhaps from the work itself, but from the surroundings in which it is carried on. The dirty and unpleasant cellars in which some factory work was done had a "disincentive" effect, and indeed only those whose need to earn a living is very pressing could now be induced to work there. The movement towards better physical conditions at work has meant that in certain factories, with their colour-washed walls, pleasant lighting, good ventilation, comfortable seating, rest-pauses, "music while you work," and so on, it is at least no hardship to work, even though it is not a positive pleasure.

Closely allied to the physical surroundings at work is the social atmosphere, and here the incentive value can be very strong indeed. We all know the pleasure of being among agreeable people where encouraging and reassuring relationships abound and where a spirit of mutual appreciation and comradeship prevails. Such an atmosphere ought to be characteristic of the family group and it is frequently found in spare-time groups where people have come together spontaneously for some leisure activity. There is no reason, however, why such an atmosphere should not prevail at work, and if such a team-spirit can be built up individuals will make an effort to remain in such a working group in preference to another. It may be, indeed, that the opportunity of joining such a group will act as a strong incentive, particularly in a culture-pattern like our own where the opportunity of participating in groups where this quality of relationships prevails is severely limited.

There is, however, always the possibility that the immediate working group may have set itself standards of output and behaviour which are not those that management expects. There are examples of working groups where limitation of output is practised and where other forms of non-cooperation with management are the rule. In order to remain a member of such a group, the individual must conform to these standards. Thus, we may have a situation in which the worker may be pulled in different ways at the same time. The bonus or piece-work system may offer him more money for sustained and efficient effort on the job. His own disinclination to sustain this effort may grow as the day wears on and he becomes tired and bored with his task. Managers and supervisors may remind him that a certain level of output is an implied condition of his employment. His workmates may make it plain that anything above the standard of effort and output which is accepted as the norm of that group will be met with gestures of disapproval and even ostracism or ridicule. How these incentives work in relation to each other on the motivation of any individual at any one time is impossible to predict, so that any attempt to provide a simple answer to the problem of incentives at work is foredoomed to failure.

In trying to understand incentives, therefore, we must take a number of factors into consideration. The satisfaction to be drawn from the work itself or the surroundings in which it is carried out may act as an incentive through such things as—

(*a*) pleasure in the exercise of skill;

(*b*) the prestige of the job or the position it carries;

(*c*) appreciation of a comfortable physical environment; and

(*d*) pleasure in the agreeable atmosphere of the working group.

In certain circumstances all these may act as incentives once the basic incentive of money has begun to lose its effect. In certain other circumstances they may act the other way round.

*Awareness of the Purpose of Work*

Turning again to the work of such people as the physician, welfare-worker, or missionary, we may find a situation where the money incentive is not important, and where the individual is not getting any very active pleasure out of the actual work itself, or its surroundings. What makes such individuals work so devotedly as many of them do, if the incentives we have been considering are not effective? Probably in these cases there is a sense of responsibility to other people, an awareness of the social obligations of their work, that has either taken the place of normal incentives or has come in to supplement them. Think, for example, of the Dunkirk evacuation when some wounded had to be left behind and the doctors drew lots to decide who should stay with them. What incentive could be effective in that situation except a realization that these casualties needed medical attention which only a doctor could provide, and an acceptance of the responsibility for providing that attention as outweighing any considerations of personal safety or comfort?

Most people would probably agree that in certain types of work this acceptance of social obligation acts as an incentive, but they might feel that it had little importance in most industrial jobs. It is unfortunately true that in very many cases the hourly-paid worker's horizon is limited to the doing of a few routine operations in return for a weekly wage. This is probably one inevitable result of the subdivision of processes which makes each individual's job so small a part of the whole that his contribution to the final product is unrecognizable and meaningless. In a village economy it is easier for the baker, the blacksmith or the cobbler to see the results of his work being used by his neighbours and thus to be conscious of its social purpose. If the baker, for example, so far forgets himself as to drop a cigarette end in the dough, his neighbours will quickly recall him to a sense of his responsibilities to the community. But for an operative in a flour-mill to realize that the stuff passing through at high speed will be cooked and eaten by people like himself requires much more of an effort of the imagination. High-speed, efficient production inevitably increases the gap between the worker and the eventual consumer.

This is not to say that an industrial worker can never be inspired by the sense of social obligation of his job. In times of crisis the dependence of others upon him may be obvious, or the effort of imagination needed to realize them may be more easily made. The period in 1940 after Dunkirk illustrates this most graphically for then everyone understood that the danger of invasion was a very real one. Industrial or other work which had any connexion with our military preparations (and most of it had) was done with great devotion, long hours were worked, and production went up. The social obligation to help in the defence of the country was accepted almost universally and acted as a most effective incentive.

We cannot, however, live in a perpetual atmosphere of crisis, and indeed it would be most unfortunate if impending disaster of that magnitude could alone show the meaning and purpose of most industrial work. But steps can be taken, and in some industries are being taken, to show people in the company that the products on which they are working will be used by people like themselves for purposes they can understand and appreciate. Such measures are effective in fostering awareness of the social obligations of a job and these in turn constitute an incentive to which the best and most responsible individuals will most readily respond and which can supplement more selfish motives with something more altruistic.

### CONCLUSIONS ON INCENTIVES

How then can we sum up the subject of incentives? Not in a few simple words nor by a sweeping generalization, for people are moved to seek very many satisfactions in their work. We might think of a curve of distribution such as we discussed in Chapter X. At one end we should find those who look only for money in their work, either because their material needs press heavily upon them, or because they are insensitive to the other kinds of satisfaction which work can offer. At the other end we should find those devoted souls whose sense of vocation makes them so conscious of their duty to others that they live in poverty while working to relieve sickness and distress. In the middle we shall find those who, while working primarily to earn a living, respond also to the incentive of pleasant surroundings and meaningful, responsible work.

How far does this help those who have to think about the incentives in one particular work-situation? Not very much, perhaps, because it does no more than expose an already complicated picture and provides no simple answer to the problem of "increasing incentives." It does, however, suggest that to improve the incentive value of a job we must consider a number of factors, no one of which will be effective with all the people all the time, but some of which will be effective with some people part of the time and some with others at different times. The kinds of thing that can be done are these—

(*a*) to ensure that those working in the job earn an adequate living—adequate in relation to what they could gain in similar types of work, and in relation to their levels of material expectation (in standards of living);

(*b*) to ensure that the individual is remunerated for extra effort on a scale which makes him consider it worth his while to work as hard and as accurately as he can without undue fatigue and strain;

(*c*) to ensure that the individual finds satisfaction in the actual work he is doing and in the immediate physical surroundings in which he works;

(*d*) to ensure that the relationships in the immediate working group are so agreeable that the individual will consider it worth making some effort to remain with that group;

(*e*) to ensure that the individual finds that the prestige of the job is such that he will make some effort to keep it;

(*f*) to ensure that the individual finds enough meaning and purpose in his work to make some effort to live up to its social obligations.

A great part of the foregoing reverts to the question of fitting the individual into the right job. It also means that the individual must find some kind of incentive to meet his attention wherever it may stray throughout the course of the day or during the working week.

## SUMMARY

1. How are incentives linked to motivation?

Motivation is something within the individual which makes him strive for certain things. Incentives are those things external to the individual for which he strives. Human motivation may be reduced to its essentials in the striving for food, shelter, companionship, and the like, but the culture-pattern will determine the means available for securing these, while the individual's own motivational pattern will affect the private and personal incentives to which he will respond.

2. In an industrial society, what are the means available to the individual for satisfying his basic needs?

In this country we can buy anything we need in shops provided we have the money to pay for it. Money, therefore, is the universally useful commodity, for it is the means of satisfying any material want. It has, in consequence, a universal value as an incentive. The normal way of procuring money to satisfy our needs is to find an opportunity to take part in the process of manufacture or distribution for a wage or salary.

3. Is the money incentive universally and uniformly effective?

In the sense that anyone who has no money will be willing to work to obtain some, yes. In the sense that anyone who has some money will be willing to work correspondingly harder and longer to earn the same amount in addition, no. Once a certain standard has been reached, which will vary with the individual, the disinclination to make the extra effort, or the competing claims of leisure, will tend to reduce the effectiveness of the money incentive.

4. What means have been used to link up the money incentive with extra effort, and how effective are they?

Higher pay for more difficult and responsible work along with a limitation to the number of people who can deal with it effectively creates competition for better jobs. In addition to this, piece-work or bonus-incentive systems link up extra effort with extra remuneration. The establishment of standards for each job, however, being based ultimately on subjective estimates, tends to introduce an element of uncertainty and bargaining which may reduce the incentive value.

5. What other incentives can be effective in the work-situation?

There are certain satisfactions in the immediate job—in the exercise of skill, in the creation of useful or beautiful objects, in the prestige which attaches to a job or in the physical and social surroundings at work which can act as an incentive. These may frequently be sufficiently strong to encourage an individual to put out considerable effort to remain in a particular job or with a particular working group

6. Has the purpose of a job no importance as an incentive?

A great deal of the most devoted work is done because the individual is fired by its purpose or its usefulness to other people.

As an incentive this can on occasion outweigh the remuneration of a job, or the conditions in which it is done. In ordinary industrial work, however, this is not likely to happen, nor is it desirable that it should. Nevertheless, without some awareness of the purpose or meaning of his job, there will always be a gap in the individual's incentive-pattern.

7. What are the general conditions to be satisfied if we are to maximize the incentive in any particular job?

We must think, not in terms of one single incentive, but rather of a pattern to which different motivations in different people, or in the same person at different times, will respond. This pattern will include—

(*a*) Attention to the money incentive so that the individual's standards are fairly met and that he feels he is adequately remunerated for extra effort.

(*b*) Attention to the physical and social surroundings of the job so that the individual finds adequate satisfaction in the daily routine of work.

(*c*) Attention to the purpose and meaning of work so that the individual may derive satisfaction from doing something useful to other people.

A great deal of this depends on adequate vocational selection.

CHAPTER XIX

## Work Study and Working Methods

In 1878 a young American, born of middle class parents and apprenticed as a pattern-maker and machinist, was employed by the Midvale Steel Company as a labourer. After a time he was promoted to gang-boss or foreman and was put in charge of a machine-room. His name was Frederick Winslow Taylor.

When he was appointed the men said to him in effect—"Now you know how we work here. We have our own time for each job, which we reckon represents a reasonable day's work. We keep to these times and if anyone looks as though he wants to work a bit harder we tell him to slow down, and not show the rest of us up—or else! You're a sensible chap and you wouldn't want to make trouble by trying to get things done any faster than our usual speed, so you just keep to the rules and we'll all get along fine." But Taylor didn't see it like that. In his view the accepted speeds represented about a third of a reasonable day's work and as he now considered himself a member of the management staff he felt it his duty to try to raise the output to a higher level. "All right," said his men, "If that's the way you want it, don't say we didn't warn you."

The following three years saw a conflict between the two. Taylor would stand over a man and time the job he was doing to find out how long it should take. He would establish by close supervision what a reasonable day's output should be, but as soon as he moved away the operator would either stop work or fritter time away to keep his production down to the old rate. If he was prevented from doing this he would cause his machine to break down by a piece of sabotage, in order to prove that it could not be safely run at a higher speed. When Taylor found that he could not get the output he wanted from existing workers he took on new men and trained them himself until they were actually producing the output he thought possible. As soon as they came in contact with other workers, however, they were forced down to the old rates of output. Meanwhile Taylor himself was subjected to every kind of social pressure from his workers to give up trying to reach the standards he was aiming at.

### THE RESULTS OF TAYLOR'S EARLY WORK

At the end of three years, however, he had succeeded in raising the output substantially and in many cases doubling it. His success was due, in his own opinion, to two factors neither of which, rather surprisingly, was directly connected with the work-situation. The first was that he did not live in the working class district and that consequently the other workers could not get at him by bringing pressure to bear on his wife and children in the way they could do with other foremen. In the second place, as he was not of working class parentage he was better able to retain the confidence of the owners of the business when he asserted that breakdowns were due to sabotage and not to overdriving the machines as the workers claimed.

This early experience of Taylor's, which he has set out himself in some detail, throws rather a lurid light on the situation in an American company over eighty years ago. But though he had achieved his object, the bitterness and conflict it aroused disturbed him profoundly. Moreover, he was far from convinced that under the existing methods of piece-work payment it was to the worker's own advantage to raise his standards of production. He was led to reflect on the methods of management and the whole approach to industry on which they were based, and he concluded that it was unsatisfactory to rely on a worker to call out all his initiative, skill and knowledge in an effort to yield the highest possible return for his employer, even though a strong incentive was held out to him to do so.

Taylor felt that management must take much more responsibility for finding out the most effective way of doing a job, finding and training a suitable man in this method, and ensuring by adequate supervision and planning that he was able to put these methods into practice throughout the day. He began to put this new approach into operation and in 1898 he had an opportunity to put his ideas into practice on a large scale, in what has since become his best-known work, at the Bethlehem Steel Company.

## The Pig Iron Handling Study

Briefly the situation was this. Eighty thousand tons of pig iron had been lying in a field adjoining the works because the price was too low to make it worth while collecting for sale. The outbreak of the Spanish-American war, however, raised the price of metals so that it became an economic proposition to load these pigs on to railway trucks and sell them. This was being done by a gang of seventy-five handlers who were moving about $12\frac{1}{2}$ tons each per day on the average. The individual pigs weighed 92 lb. Following out his theory, Taylor made a study of the job and worked out what he thought was the most efficient and practicable method of lifting and carrying, and the best periods to work and rest. According to his calculations a man working on this plan ought to load 47 tons a day.

The next step was to find a suitable man and train him in the method. A strong and rather dull labourer named Schmidt was chosen and persuaded to follow out the detailed instructions of Taylor's assistant throughout the following day. The work then started with Schmidt being told "Now pick up that pig, walk to the truck, drop it, and walk back. Pick up another, carry it to the truck; now sit down and relax. Now walk back," and so on. This continued throughout the day and by knocking off time Mr. Schmidt had loaded $47\frac{1}{2}$ tons and earned 70 cents more than he had done before.

Now the whole point of this study is not that the amount loaded in a day rose to nearly four times the previous figure. It is rather the dramatic proof of Taylor's contention that if management undertakes what he considered were its proper responsibilities for methods, selection, training, supervision, and planning, the resulting levels of output will show how low are the traditionally accepted standards built up by workers finding their own methods and picking up the job by themselves. It also provided a starting-point for a whole series of developments in which departments were reorganized on a basis of adequate methods studies. An example will be found in the yard gang which was responsible for loading and unloading quantities of different materials—ore, coal, ashes, etc. It is unnecessary here to go into the details of Taylor's studies of the most economical loads, the designs of shovels, the detailed organization of work, and so on, but the following figures show the situation before and after he took over—

|  | Old Plan | New Plan |
|---|---|---|
| Number of labourers . . | 400–600 | 140 |
| Average tons moved per man-day | 16 | 59 |
| Average earnings . . . | $1·15 | $1·88 |
| Average cost per ton . . | $0·072 | $0·03 |

The last figure (average cost per ton under the new plan) includes the additional expenditure on tools, supervision, and so on.

### THE SIGNIFICANCE OF TAYLOR'S WORK

Many years have elapsed since Taylor opened up the subject of working methods and a whole literature has grown up about the methods of study. Not many people, however, have taken his point about the different approach and the new responsibilities to be accepted by management, and a rather unfortunate impression has been spread that he was a mere "efficiency engineer" only interested in speeding up work and quite indifferent either to the welfare of workers or to their share in the increased productivity. This is unjustified and one would do well to give more weight to Taylor's theories and less to the actual results that he achieved. This is not to say that his theories are necessarily correct, but they do represent one of the first attempts to think systematically about the methods and organization of work and consider where the responsibilities should lie.

If we accept, as is fairly widely agreed nowadays, that management should devise effective methods of work, rather than leave it to the operator to find out the best way for himself, then the first requirement will be a means of studying and recording working processes. Practically no work is static, for most jobs involve movement of some kind. If we want to find out what is being done, therefore, we may watch a series of more or less rapid movements, the earlier of which we may have forgotten before we come to the end of the task. Unless we have some means of recording the process we shall find it very difficult to consider the working methods, whereas if we can put down what is being done in some comprehensible form we can take our record away and study it at our leisure. There are many different kinds of task, on some of which the operator may sit still and perform fine manual movements while others may involve walking about and carrying out large movements of the arms and body. The same method of recording may not be suitable for both these kinds of job, so we must have a series of different methods which can be adapted to various tasks.

### FLOOR PLANS

The first and simplest method of recording is to draw a plan of the room in which work is done and to trace the movements of the operator as he walks about it. This may be done either by continuous or dotted lines, though an even simpler method is to stick pins in at the various positions taken up by the operator and to wind a coloured thread from one to the other to denote the movements. A very simple floor plan is shown on page 249, for the familiar task of laying a table for six places.

The black line shows the first journey when the operator lays out a mat at each place, the line of dashes shows a second journey when the operator lays out a glass at each place, while the line of dots shows a third journey when the operator lays out the cutlery: three journeys covering in all probably something over thirty yards, each with six stops, the whole process being laid out quite clearly in this simple diagram (Fig. 28.)

Now as soon as this process is recorded it at once becomes obvious that the same ground is being trampled over several times, and one can scarcely look at such a plan without saying "Are all these journeys really necessary?" The recording process at once shows up a simpler method which would be to put all the things required on a tray or trolley and lay out each place completely in one act, probably also making only one stop on the longer side of the table to lay out the two places from the same position.

Once we get such a job down on paper, therefore, it becomes immediately obvious that it can be done in one journey of, say, ten yards with four stops (Fig. 29.)

Floor plans can be used wherever the movements of operators of materials about a room have to be recorded. A more complex example is shown in Fig. 30 in which the progress of

——— 1st Journey  — — 2nd Journey  ----- 3rd Journey

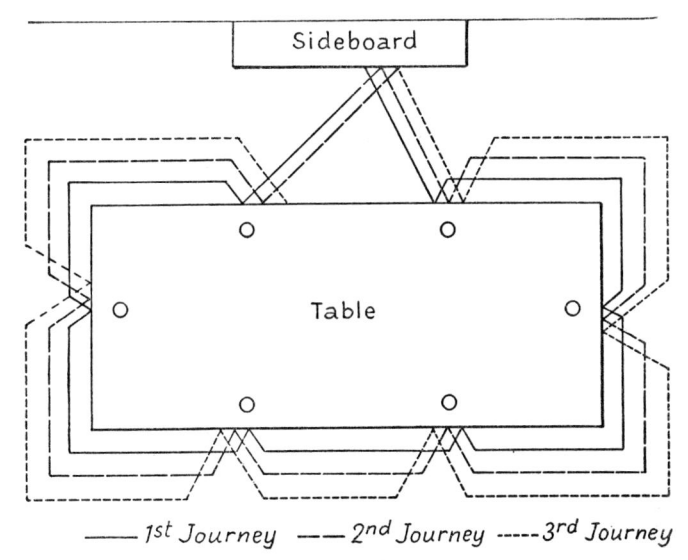

Fig. 28. Floor Plan for Laying a Table

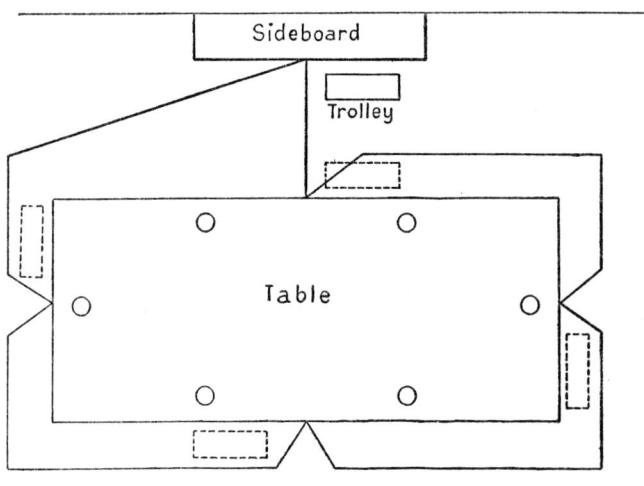

Fig. 29. Floor Plan for Laying a Table
(Improved Method)

9—(Man. 6/Man. 109)

a garment in an imaginary making-up factory has been traced. The reader may amuse himself by considering how many of the moves are unnecessary and how the distance travelled

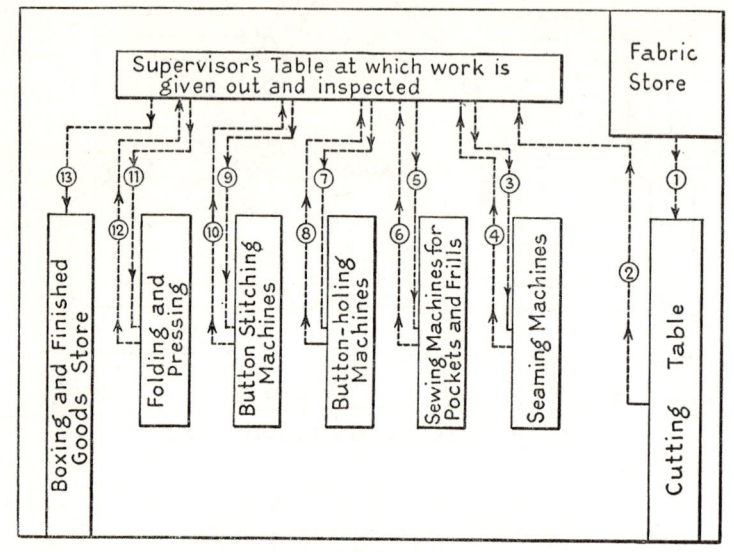

FIG. 30. FLOOR PLAN OF IMAGINARY GARMENT FACTORY

1. Fabric to cutting table for cutting out.
2. Cut out garments to supervisor's table.
3. Garments to seaming machines for main making-up process.
4. Back to supervisor's table for inspection.
5. Garments to stitching machines for pockets and frills.
6. Back to supervisor's table for inspection.
7. Garments to buttonhole machines.
8. Back to supervisor's table for inspection.
9. Garments to button-stitching machines.
10. Back to supervisor's table for inspection.
11. Garments to presses for finishing and folding.
12. Back to supervisor's table for inspection.
13. To finished goods store.

could be cut down. Such plans are essentially simple and need not detain us long.

### PROCESS CHARTS

By themselves, however, floor plans tend to be rather uninformative and at times they can become confused when so many movements have to be recorded that the lines become superimposed one upon another. Some form of legend is almost always necessary to describe the sequence of operations and perhaps to record times and distances in more easily comprehensible form. Such legends will develop naturally into process charts in which the use of a few symbols will be an aid to clarity. These symbols and a simple layout of a chart are as follows—

| Symbol | Meaning | Columns for | |
|---|---|---|---|
| | | Time | Distance |
| 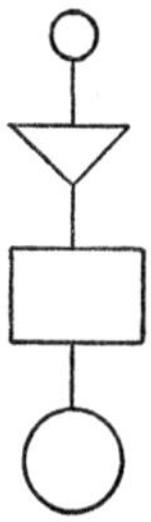 ○ | Transport | | |
| ▽ | Wait or Store | | |
| □ | Inspect | | |
| ○ | Operation | | |

FIG. 31. SYMBOLS FOR PROCESS CHART

The making-up process shown in Fig. 30 could be recorded by the means given in Fig. 32 (pp. 252–3).

Here again the recording method is essentially simple and can be adapted to most kinds of work. Whenever the symbols for "Transport" and "Wait" appear too frequently one's attention is immediately attracted and one begins almost automatically to ask whether these stages could be dispensed with.

### RIGHT- AND LEFT-HAND CHARTS

Floor plans and process charts used separately or in conjunction with one another will enable one to record most jobs where movement about a room is involved. They are of little use, however, in jobs where the operator is sitting still and doing a job by hand. In such cases we shall want to record what each hand is doing in some detail and we shall probably need a rather finer time-scale. A rough sketch of the layout of the bench will be found useful in such cases, accompanied by a right- and left-hand chart of

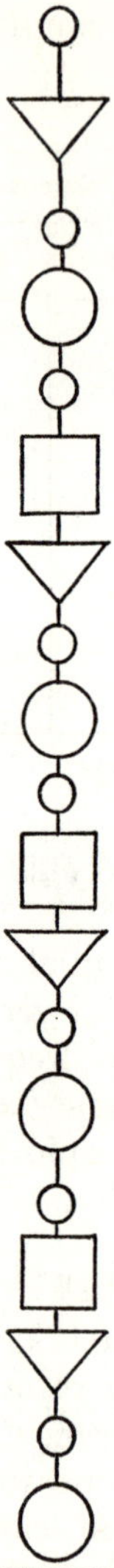

| Operation | | Description | Time | Distance |
|---|---|---|---|---|
| 1. | ○ | Fabric brought into fabric store | | 10 yd |
| 2. | ▽ | Remains till wanted for cutting | variable | |
| 3. | ○ | To cutting table | | 15 yd |
| 4. | ◯ | Laid out and cut to pattern | 20 min | |
| 5. | ○ | To supervisor's table | | 20 yd |
| 6. | □ | Checked before giving out for sewing | 5 min | |
| 7. | ▽ | Wait till machine ready | variable | |
| 8. | ○ | To seaming machine | | 15 yd |
| 9. | ◯ | Long seams stitched | 10 min | |
| 10. | ○ | Back to supervisor | | 15 yd |
| 11. | □ | Checked | 5 min | |
| 12. | ▽ | Wait for stitching | variable | |
| 13. | ○ | To stitching machine | | 12 yd |
| 14. | ◯ | Pockets, belt, trimmings stitched | 10 min | |
| 15. | ○ | Back to supervisor | | 12 yd |
| 16. | □ | Checked | 5 min | |
| 17. | ▽ | Wait for buttonhole | variable | |
| 18. | ○ | To buttonholing machine | | 10 yd |
| 19. | ◯ | Positions marked out | | |

FIG. 32. PROCESS CHART FOR MAKING-UP OPERATION
(See Fig. 30)

| Operation | | Description | Time | Distance |
|---|---|---|---|---|
| 20. | ○ | Buttonholes stitched | 3 min | |
| 21. | ○ | Back to supervisor | | 10 yd |
| 22. | □ | Checked | 3 min | |
| 23. | ▽ | Wait for button machine | | |
| 24. | ○ | Taken to button machine | | 12 yd |
| 25. | ○ | Marked out | 2 min | |
| 26. | ○ | Buttons stitched | 2 min | |
| 27. | ○ | Back to supervisor | | 12 yd |
| 28. | □ | Checked | 3 min | |
| 29. | ▽ | Wait for folding and pressing | variable | |
| 30. | ○ | Taken to folding table | | 15 yd |
| 31. | ○ | Pressed | 3 min | |
| 32. | ○ | Folded | 2 min | |
| 33. | ○ | Back to supervisor | | 15 yd |
| 34. | □ | Checked | 2 min | |
| 35. | ○ | Taken to finished-goods store | | 20 yd |
| 36. | ○ | Boxed | 2 min | |
| 37. | ○ | Labelled | 1 min | |
| 38. | ▽ | Wait in finished-goods store | variable | |

FIG. 32.—(*continued*)

which the following is an example, showing a clerk paging a report—

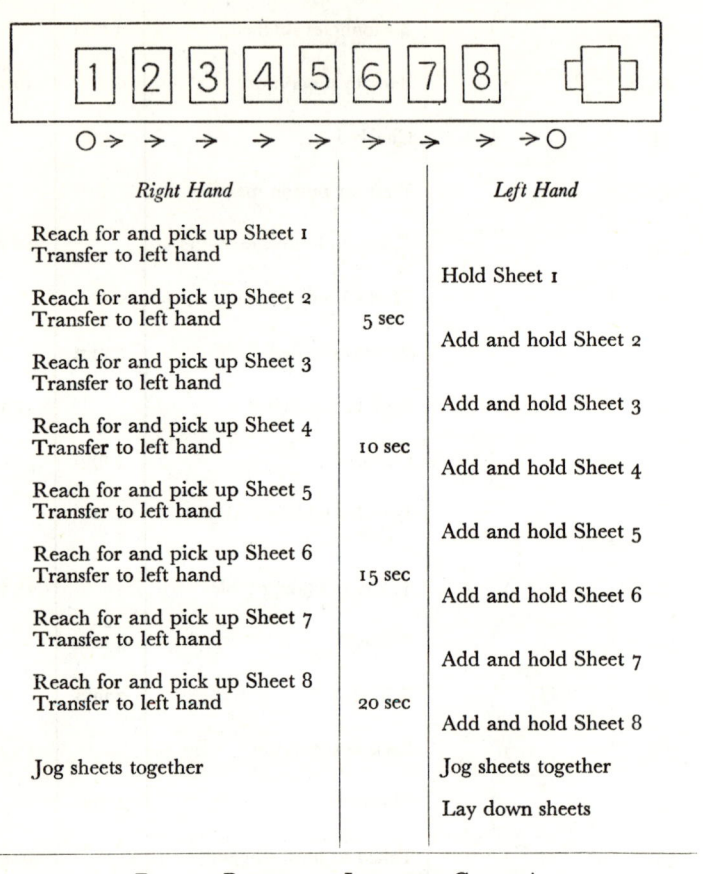

| Right Hand | | Left Hand |
|---|---|---|
| Reach for and pick up Sheet 1<br>Transfer to left hand | | |
| | | Hold Sheet 1 |
| Reach for and pick up Sheet 2<br>Transfer to left hand | 5 sec | |
| | | Add and hold Sheet 2 |
| Reach for and pick up Sheet 3<br>Transfer to left hand | | |
| | | Add and hold Sheet 3 |
| Reach for and pick up Sheet 4<br>Transfer to left hand | 10 sec | |
| | | Add and hold Sheet 4 |
| Reach for and pick up Sheet 5<br>Transfer to left hand | | |
| | | Add and hold Sheet 5 |
| Reach for and pick up Sheet 6<br>Transfer to left hand | 15 sec | |
| | | Add and hold Sheet 6 |
| Reach for and pick up Sheet 7<br>Transfer to left hand | | |
| | | Add and hold Sheet 7 |
| Reach for and pick up Sheet 8<br>Transfer to left hand | 20 sec | |
| | | Add and hold Sheet 8 |
| Jog sheets together | | Jog sheets together |
| | | Lay down sheets |

FIG. 33. RIGHT- AND LEFT-HAND CHART A

When we look at this diagram two things become obvious. In the first place the operator has to walk backwards and forwards to pick up the sheets, and secondly her left hand is doing little more than acting as a clip to hold the sheets. Now it would be quite possible to rearrange the sheets so that walking becomes unnecessary, and, of course, if the operator were standing still in one place, she might as well sit down. Likewise if she laid down the sheets in front of her she might use both hands to pick them up. Thus a short study of the first record suggests the following changes—

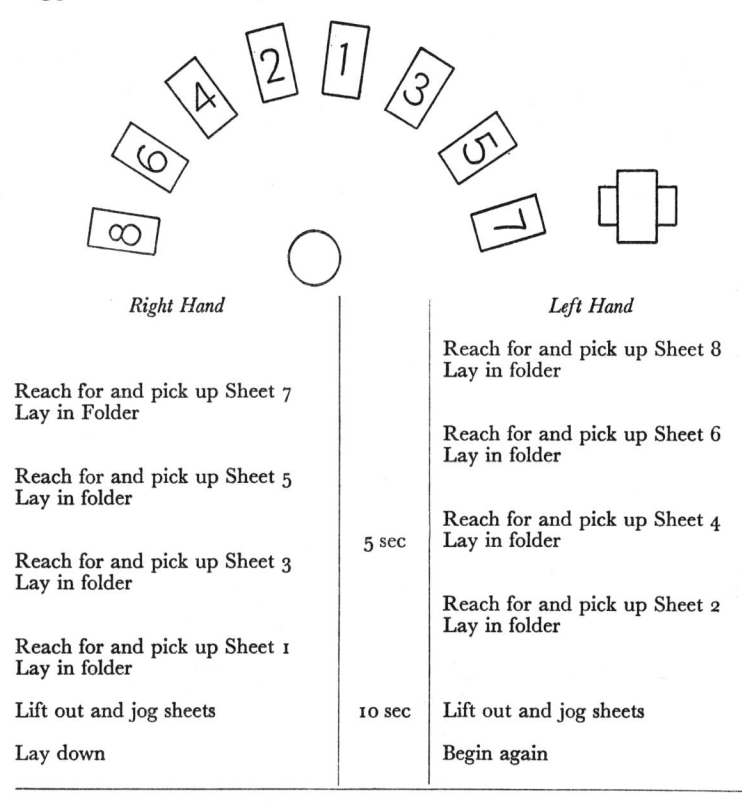

| Right Hand | | Left Hand |
|---|---|---|
| | | Reach for and pick up Sheet 8<br>Lay in folder |
| Reach for and pick up Sheet 7<br>Lay in Folder | | |
| | | Reach for and pick up Sheet 6<br>Lay in folder |
| Reach for and pick up Sheet 5<br>Lay in folder | | |
| | 5 sec | Reach for and pick up Sheet 4<br>Lay in folder |
| Reach for and pick up Sheet 3<br>Lay in folder | | |
| | | Reach for and pick up Sheet 2<br>Lay in folder |
| Reach for and pick up Sheet 1<br>Lay in folder | | |
| Lift out and jog sheets | 10 sec | Lift out and jog sheets |
| Lay down | | Begin again |

FIG. 34. RIGHT- AND LEFT-HAND CHART B

Right- and left-hand charts can be made much more detailed, the movements of the fingers included if this is considered desirable. There are very few cases, however, where it is really helpful to go into a great deal of detail and if this appears to be really justified probably the most effective method is to use a ciné-camera and record the actual movements on a film. With the addition of a flashing light bulb to provide a timescale this will give a complete record of the movements. Further refinements are to strap little flashing lights on the hands or fingers so that the paths of movement may be more easily traced.

## MAN-MACHINE CHARTS

In many kinds of job a large part of the work may be done by a machine which can work for periods with little or no supervision, the operator being only concerned with putting in the material, setting the machine, and starting it up. To find out the relative times when the operator and the machine are actually at work the following type of chart may be used. Idle times are shown by the shaded portions.

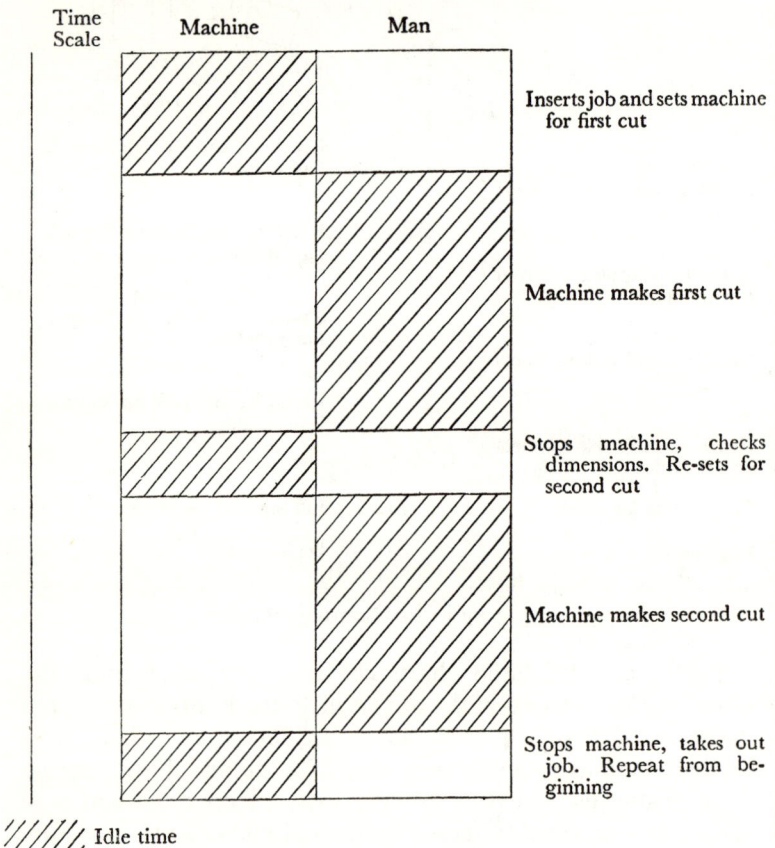

FIG. 35. MAN-MACHINE CHART

It is obvious here that more than half of the operator's time is unoccupied. Provided that the actual working of the machine does not require close supervision, the job could be laid out so that the operator looks after two machines.

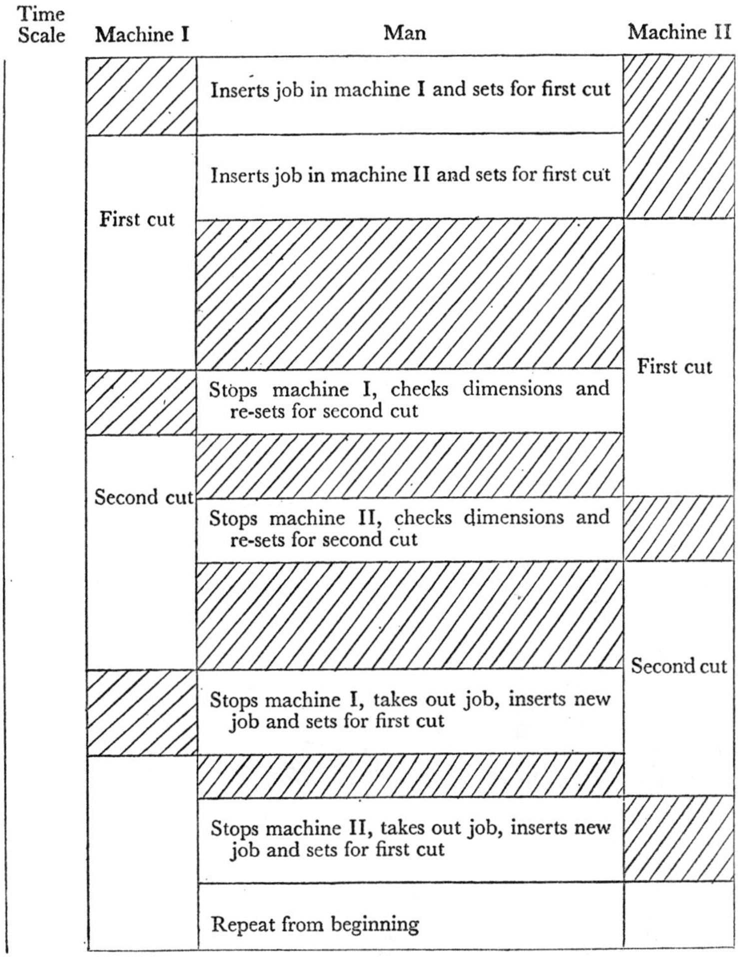

WORK STUDY AND WORKING METHODS 257

| Time Scale | Machine I | Man | Machine II |
|---|---|---|---|
| | ////// | Inserts job in machine I and sets for first cut | ////// |
| | First cut | Inserts job in machine II and sets for first cut | ////// |
| | | ////////////// | First cut |
| | | Stops machine I, checks dimensions and re-sets for second cut | |
| | Second cut | ////////////// | |
| | | Stops machine II, checks dimensions and re-sets for second cut | ////// |
| | | ////////////// | Second cut |
| | ////// | Stops machine I, takes out job, inserts new job and sets for first cut | |
| | | ////////////// | ////// |
| | | Stops machine II, takes out job, inserts new job and sets for first cut | |
| | | Repeat from beginning | |

FIG. 36. MAN-MACHINE CHART
(New Method)

By such a rearrangement two machines can be kept running at the same speed as one, while the operator's idle time is cut down, though it does not entirely disappear.

## MULTI-MAN CHARTS

Perhaps the most useful type of recording method is that which enables the work of several people on a common task to be put down. An example is given in Fig. 37.

| Seconds | No. 1 | No. 6 | No. 2 | No. 4 | No. 3 | No. 5 |
|---|---|---|---|---|---|---|
| 0 | To pump controls at A | To back of pump near A | To front of pump B | To front of pump C | To suction hose at D | To suction hose at E |
| T | Fix one front sprag | Fix other front sprag | Uncouple from lorry and fix near sprag | Help No. 2 uncouple and fix sprag | Lift 1st suction to position with No. 5. Go for 2nd suction at D | Lift 1st suction to position with No. 3 |
| M E | Get spanners, loosen suction blank cap and take it off | Pull out 2 delivery pipe blank ends | Go to E not D, see No. 5 later | Go to E | WAIT FOR NO. 5 | Go for 2nd suction at E |
| 10 | Set pump controls for start by No. 5 and regulate engine | Take hose ends from Nos. 2 and 4; plug in | Get 1 delivery hose, go to No. 1. Give him end of hose, run hose G to L | Get 1 delivery hose, go to No. 1. Give him end of hose, run hose F to K. (Cross to K, being ahead of No. 2) | Lift 2nd suction to position with No. 5 | Go to pump at B |
|  | Couple 1st suction to pump, and 2nd suction to 1st with help of No. 6 | Help No. 1 with suctions and tighten up | Run back to E for jet | Run back to D for jet | Get 1 delivery hose, run to L with it and couple to 1st length. (Cross to L because ahead of No. 5) | Start pump on crank |
|  |  |  |  |  |  | Go to D. See No. 2 |
|  |  |  | Take jet to J | Take jet to H |  | Get 1 delivery hose, run to K with it, couple to 1st length |
| 20 | WAIT | Suction end in water |  |  | Run hose L to J | Run hose K to H |
|  | Prime pump | Stand by to help anyone in difficulty | WAIT FOR NO. 3 | WAIT FOR NO. 5 |  |  |
| S | On valve to jet J |  | Give jet to No. 3 |  | Fit jet |  |
| C | On valve to jet H |  | Stand by with No. 3 on jet J | Give jet to No. 5 |  | Fit jet |
| A | On cooling water |  |  | Stand by |  | Stand by |
| L 30 E | Regulate pump and stand by |  | WATER ON J | WATER ON H | WATER ON J | WATER ON H |

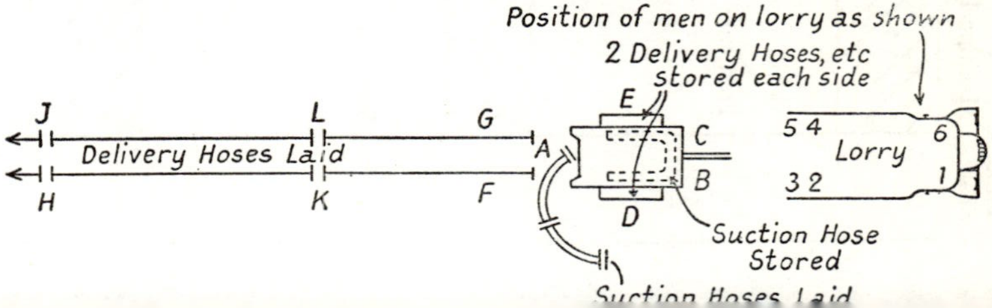

FIG. 37. MULTI-MAN CHART
Example—Six-man crew on a trailer fire pump.

## THE IMPORTANCE OF ADEQUATE RECORDING

It has already become apparent that when we make a record of what actually happens in many jobs we see at once that there is unnecessary movement, transport, or waiting. This is not due to idleness on the part of the worker or to any deliberate intention on his part to be inefficient. It is rather the result of seeing the job as a series of incidents which happen one after the other. This is the view that most of us get when we are actually engaged in a task, and it ensures that our attention is so absorbed by the actual detail of the operations that we do not notice how often we walk across the same piece of floor carrying one article and then another. It is only when we can get away from the details of a task and study it as a whole that we have any opportunity to observe the method rather than the end to be achieved.

When, by using the appropriate recording method, we can lay out the job in front of us and study it at leisure, ways of economizing time, movement and transport show up at once. Three separate journeys to carry articles which could be taken in one journey on a tray, goods piled up awaiting inspection while machines are idle, one-handed movements while the other hand is used to clip or hold—these and similar things force themselves on our attention and set us thinking of how they could be overcome. And once we start thinking we shall in most cases find that a very simple answer lies ready at hand.

Students would be well advised to concentrate first and foremost on these simple and obvious inefficiencies. There is a time for detailed study as we shall see in a moment, but it is important to remember that such studies tend to yield diminishing returns. Reverting to the example of paging a report, we found that a glance at the right- and left-hand chart of the first method showed two gross wastes of movement—the operator walking back and forth, and using her left hand as a clip. By dealing with these, the time required to do the job was reduced from 20 to 10 seconds and the operator was spared the fatigue of standing and walking. Dealing with the most obvious wastes, therefore, cut the time by 50 per cent—a very satisfactory saving. But it is possible still further to simplify the job by devising gadgets which enable operators to pick up two sheets at a time. These cost something to make and operators require a little training before they can use them efficiently. They result, however, in the saving of an additional three seconds—not a very impressive return for the time and material expended when compared with the ten seconds saved by ten minutes' thought and a simple rearrangement of the sheets.

It is very advisable, therefore, to concentrate on the opportunities for gross savings which many studies will reveal as soon as a record is made of what is actually being done at present. Only when one is fully convinced that all these simple and obvious savings have been made is it advisable to go into greater detail.

MOVEMENT STUDY

When we do turn to the detailed methods of work, however, we shall find that the human body has certain potentialities

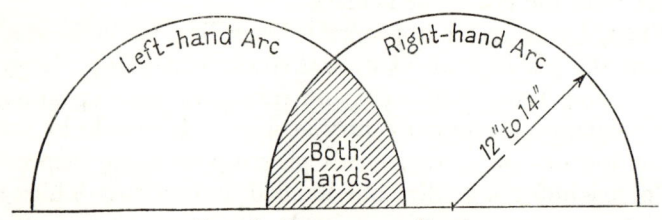

FIG. 38. COMFORTABLE REACH

and limitations and that tasks which fall within these limitations can be carried out much more conveniently than those which disregard them. Think, for example, of the cinema organist with his four keyboards, dozens, or perhaps scores of stops, and a set of pedals below his feet. He can bring all kinds of effects into play without difficulty because all these controls are arranged so as to be within easy reach of his two hands and two feet. The comedian, on the other hand, who makes us laugh by a series of comic mishaps while papering a room or laying a carpet, does so by attempting to reach tools which are too far away, by awkward movements when he is off balance, and by losing control of his material because he has failed to fix it adequately in the working position.

Looking, then, at the human body from this point of view, we shall find at once that the parts best adapted for most kinds of work are the hands. When standing or sitting at a flat table or bench the hands will rest naturally on it about fourteen inches apart. If the student will take a piece of chalk and draw the following lines he will learn at once the main limitations of his hand and arm movements.

1. Take the chalk in the right hand and draw a circle

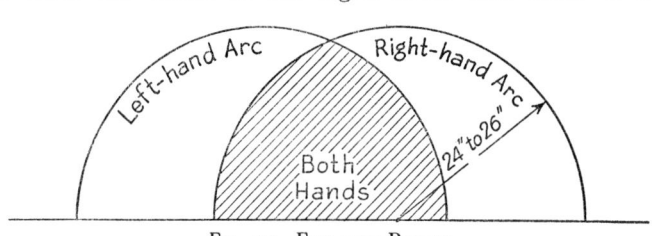

FIG. 39. EXTREME REACH

pivoting from the elbow, and keeping the upper arm motionless.

2. Repeat with the left hand.

This will result in two arcs roughly like those in Fig. 38, each with a radius of about a foot to fourteen inches.

Each arc shows what is a comfortable reach for the right and left hand while the shaded portion shows the area covered by both hands.

3. Take the chalk again in the right hand, and draw a circle at full stretch from the shoulder.

4. Repeat with the left hand.

This will result in two more arcs, each with a radius of about two feet, as shown in Fig. 39.

FIG. 40. ELEVATION

Each arc shows the maximum reach for the right or left hand, the shaded area being covered by both.

The next stage is to stretch the hands to the full reach of the arms on the bench and then raise them as high as they can go. The result seen in elevation in Fig. 40 shows another aspect of how the body can be most easily utilized.

*Bench Layout*

With these dimensions in mind it is easy to see how work to be done by hand can best be laid out on a bench. What has to be done by two hands should occupy the shaded portion, roughly triangular in shape, with a side of twelve to fourteen inches in front of the operator. The components and tools required frequently should be arranged along the right and left arcs at about a foot radius from the elbow, while those less frequently required should be laid out on the outer, maximum-reach arcs or perhaps on shelves above. The diagram below shows this in general outline. Differences of operator

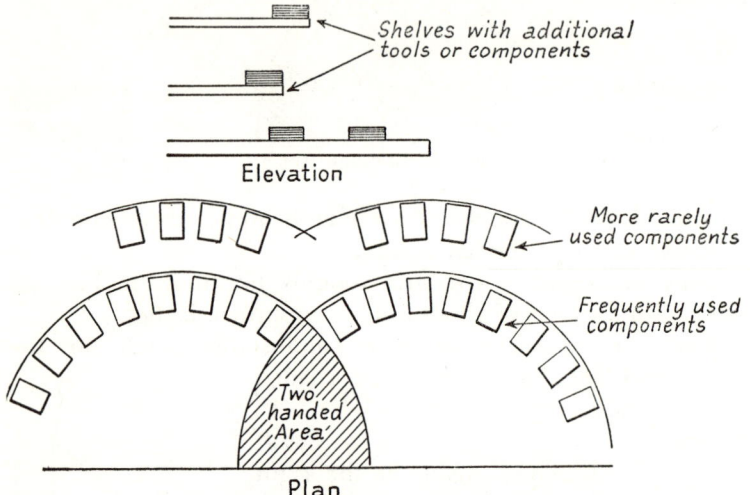

FIG. 41. BENCH LAYOUT FOR MANUAL OPERATION

size may have to be allowed for but these will rarely be more than a few inches.

Other dimensions such as the height of the bench from the floor for comfortable standing or sitting, or the location of pedals or foot controls will be important, but these can be ascertained by taking a few simple measurements. In this way a suitable layout for manual operations can be worked out from first principles in a very short time. The reader will probably already have been struck by the resemblance between the layout thus arrived at and the cinema organ, which we used as a starting illustration.

In considering other kinds of work, such, for example, as those which involve machine controls, we should always start with a consideration of the human body. If the operator has to stand he will have to rely on his hands and arms, and we have already seen something of the comfortable and extreme reach of these and hence the positions and distances within which controls should lie. If the operator sits he may use his feet and legs as well, provided the controls or movements he has to make fall within comfortable reach. Much the same applies to dials or other visual indicators; to be easily read these must be placed so that they can be seen without turning the head.

*Easy and Difficult Movements*

But once the layout of the work position has been adequately dealt with we still have to deal with the question of easy or

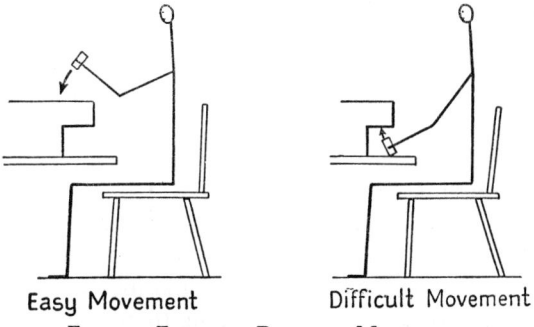

Easy Movement    Difficult Movement
FIG. 42. EASY AND DIFFICULT MOVEMENTS

difficult movements. Again the reader may provide himself with an illustration by placing a pile of books on the desk in front of him, with the top one projecting a couple of inches over the others. Take a pencil or rubber in the right hand and tap the top book. You will find this quite an easy natural movement and you will have no difficulty in exerting considerable force if you want to. But now try to tap the underside of the top book where it projects over the others. You will find this very much more awkward and it will be difficult to exert much force or hit hard.

We need not spend long considering why one movement is easier than another, for it is quite obvious that one gives a free swing, allows the operator to get the greatest "mechanical advantage" from his body, and so on. The fact remains that one is a natural, effective movement while the other is cramped and difficult and we only have to try them out to recognize at once which is which. This applies to any movement; if we try it we shall quickly find out if it is easy or difficult.

There are a few principles of effective movement which sum up the experience anyone may provide for himself with a few trials. For example—

1. Movements of the arms should be in opposite and symmetrical directions, and they should be made simultaneously. For example, take a book in both hands and swing it rapidly from left to right in front of you. Then take a book in either hand and swing them in opposite directions starting with both together in front of you, outwards and in again, rapidly several times. You will feel at once which is the easier movement.

2. Hand movements should be confined to the "lowest classification," i.e. don't use a hand if you can do the job with one finger, don't move your elbow if you can do it with a wrist movement, don't move your shoulder if you can do it from the elbow.

3. Momentum and rhythm should be encouraged wherever possible. Niggling little movements which involve continual starting and stopping and careful positioning are much less effective than the free swinging movements which a coal heaver uses when filling a cellar through a manhole. Such workers drop the first two sacks beside the hole, then swing the remainder down on them so that they empty themselves. In this way the weight of the sacks themselves does quite a lot of the work, and they can be thrown down without positioning while the operator has a series of swinging curved movements to perform.

4. Fixed positions should be provided for tools, materials, etc. We have already seen how these should be placed so as to be accessible with the minimum waste of motion. If in addition each item is located in a special place it can be picked up without searching or fumbling.

### THE DANGERS OF SPECIALIZATION

The detailed study of this subject has grown up in recent years into the science of "ergonomics," and an increasing amount of research is being carried out into the potentialities of the human sensori-motor equipment. Much of this is directed to the design of machines and equipment with the aim of making them easier for human beings to work. Dials and other forms of display can be laid out so as to make it easier for the human senses to take in the information they present, while levers and other controls can be so positioned as to require the minimum of movement and effort, or to facilitate greater sensitivity in their operation. But while these detailed and specialized researches undoubtedly have their place, it is important that they should not be allowed to obscure the contribution that can be made by the intelligent layman using no more than a simple method of systematic observation.

It is fatally easy to make movement-study sound difficult and complex by unnecessary theorizing, just as it is very tempting to devise impressive-looking gadgets which are supposed to make a task easier when in fact they complicate it. Work is at its most efficient when the tasks are simple and straightforward, the movements easy and natural, and the tools and controls handy and light to operate. One should always keep such an ideal in mind and direct one's effort and attention towards dealing with anything which interferes with it.

As has been pointed out above, the key to the situation is recording. Once we have a job down on paper we may study it at leisure and go over the various parts of it in as much detail as we wish. Once we do this it is almost impossible to miss the points where unnecessary, ineffective or fatiguing movements are taking place. There is no difficulty in recognizing such movements, for if one is in any doubt one may try them oneself. This will show at once whether they are easy or awkward.

Devising a better method is usually the easiest part of the task. The difficulties begin when one has to get it accepted and cope with the rearrangements necessary to fit it into the existing organization of production. People naturally dislike change, and quite apart from suspicion of the motives of management, disturbance of established routines will be unwelcome.

Finally, let it be emphasized again that the law of diminishing returns operates very markedly in this field. A simple rearrangement to cut out gross and obvious wastes of effort may effect a 30 per cent saving. An expensive gadget which involves long and difficult training of operators in its use may result in a 5 per cent saving. Only when one is convinced that all the gross and obvious savings have been made is it advisable to spend time and effort on the finer points.

## SUMMARY

1. What is the significance of F. W. Taylor's work?

By his experience in raising production rates from their traditionally low levels in the Midvale Steel Company in 1878, Taylor was led to reflect that management which relied only on stimulating the initiative of the worker by a strong incentive was wrong in principle. He contended that management should accept the responsibility for working out the best method, selecting suitable workers and training them in it, and planning the work so that these methods were actually put into effect on the job. His work in the Bethlehem Steel Company showed what can happen in practice when this theory is put into operation.

2. What is the first and fundamental step in any study of working methods?

It is essential to begin with a record of what is actually being done in a form which can be taken away and studied at leisure. Only then can we consider what actually happens and find out where unnecessary effort or delay is involved. So long as the job is only seen in progress we shall tend to miss important points because they are over before we have grasped what is taking place.

3. What are the uses of floor plans?

Floor plans enable a job to be recorded which involves much movement about the work place. Examples are shown in Figs. 28–30. Floor plans usually show that the same journey is being repeated more than it need be or that unnecessary journeys are being made.

4. What is a process chart and how is it used?

A process chart records a sequence of operations in detail with the times and distances involved. Examples are shown in Figs. 31–2. They are frequently used in conjunction with floor plans.

5. When are right- and left-hand charts necessary?

Whenever an operator remains in one place carrying out a series of manual operations, right- and left-hand charts are a useful means of recording. Examples are shown in Figs. 33-4. The most usual waste revealed by these charts is the underemployment of the left hand.

6. What is a man-machine chart?

Where an operator is tending a machine, a man-machine chart will show the relative times when each is occupied and at rest. Examples in Figs. 35-6.

7. What is a multi-man chart?

Wherever a number of people are involved in one task at the same time, a multi-man chart can be used to record the task of each individual and how it fits in with that of the others. Examples in Fig. 37.

8. What are the essentials of movement study?

The human body with its limbs and physical potentialities is equipped to carry out a certain range of movements within certain dimensions. These movements and dimensions are not difficult to ascertain. Movement study consists in so arranging a task that the movements it calls for are those which the human body is best adapted to make with the minimum of strain and fatigue.

9. What are the main characteristics of easy movements?

(*a*) Arm movements that are in opposite and symmetrical directions;

(*b*) movements in the lowest classification that will be adequate for the job;

(*c*) movements which make the maximum use of momentum and rhythm; and

(*d*) movements to and from fixed and known positions which are easily memorized.

10. What should be the characteristics of the ideal working methods?

They should be as simple as possible, free from strain and awkwardness. All gross wastes of time and effort should be avoided while at the same time complex gadgets which involve difficult re-training of operators should be refused unless they can be shown to contribute significantly to reducing effort and fatigue.

CHAPTER XX

# The Physical Conditions of Work

ONE aspect of work study which we have not so far touched on is the measurement of output rates. On a daily or weekly basis, of course, this is not difficult and in many companies such measurements are taken as a normal part of the wage-payment system. But if we can find out something about the fluctuations of output over shorter periods we shall provide ourselves with a means of studying the effect of different conditions in the work-environment. We may find that in certain situations the operator's speed increases while in others it tends to fall away. This will help us to determine the best conditions of work.

Where operators are on simple repetitive work with a short job-cycle, it is not difficult to establish a speed of output by noting the number of units produced in a given time. For example, with operators on a small assembly job which takes about thirty seconds we may check the output every five minutes. This will give us a rate, the number of assemblies produced per five minutes, as in the table below—

| 1st five minute period | 8 assemblies produced |
| 2nd ,, ,, ,, | 8 ,, ,, |
| 3rd ,, ,, ,, | 9 ,, ,, |
| 4th ,, ,, ,, | 9 ,, ,, |
| 5th ,, ,, ,, | 9 ,, ,, |
| 6th ,, ,, ,, | 10 ,, ,, |
| 7th ,, ,, ,, | 10 ,, ,, |
| 8th ,, ,, ,, | 11 ,, ,, |
| 9th ,, ,, ,, | 11 ,, ,, |
| 10th ,, ,, ,, | 11 ,, ,, |
| 11th ,, ,, ,, | 11 ,, ,, |
| 12th ,, ,, ,, | 12 ,, ,, |

Such a table will show the changes in the operator's speed of work during one hour, and it is obvious from a glance at the table that the speed is increasing. This will be made still clearer if we express the figures in the form of a graph (Fig. 43).

It is not always so easy to establish a rate of output because where the units produced take a considerable time, perhaps several hours, to complete, the period may be so long as to mask most of the fluctuations. In these circumstances we may have to subdivide the operation and use a smaller part as our unit of measurement. An example of this might be the weaving of a 50-yard piece of cloth. This may take too long a time to be useful as a measure of fluctuation in rate of output, but we can take instead each pick of the loom as our unit of measurement. Checking these each five minutes will show up any changes in speed of work.

But in other types of work the rate of output may be controlled entirely by the process and consequently the variations will be of little value in showing the effect of conditions on the operator. In flying an aircraft, for example, the speed will be controlled to some extent by the state of the wind, the altitude, the weight carried, and possibly also by instructions from the ground. The distance covered every five minutes will tell us very little about the pilot or his reaction to conditions. Such cases, however, can be approached from another angle and we may note the occurrence of errors or unsteadiness as the journey proceeds. We might find, for example, that in the early stages the pilot applied just the right amount of rudder and bank on each turn while in the later stages he tended to apply too much or too little and had to make corrections to compensate for these errors. With a little ingenuity they might be reduced to measurable form, and in fact during blind flying training on an artificial machine set up on the ground with recording apparatus (a Link trainer)

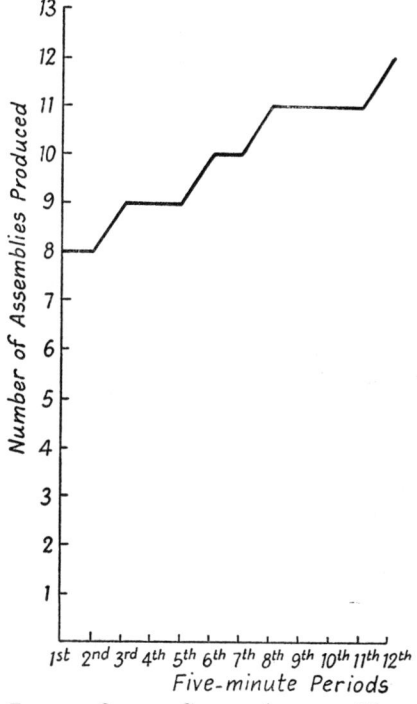

FIG. 43. OUTPUT CURVE—ASSEMBLY WORK

this has been done. Results like the following have been obtained—

| 1st Hour | | | 2nd Hour | | |
|---|---|---|---|---|---|
| 1st five minute period | 0 | errors | 1st five minute period | 2 | errors |
| 2nd ,, ,, ,, | 0 | ,, | 2nd ,, ,, ,, | 2 | ,, |
| 3rd ,, ,, ,, | 0 | ,, | 3rd ,, ,, ,, | 3 | ,, |
| 4th ,, ,, ,, | 0 | ,, | 4th ,, ,, ,, | 3 | ,, |
| 5th ,, ,, ,, | 1 | ,, | 5th ,, ,, ,, | 4 | ,, |
| 6th ,, ,, ,, | 0 | ,, | 6th ,, ,, ,, | 5 | ,, |
| 7th ,, ,, ,, | 1 | ,, | 7th ,, ,, ,, | 5 | ,, |
| 8th ,, ,, ,, | 1 | ,, | 8th ,, ,, ,, | 6 | ,, |
| 9th ,, ,, ,, | 1 | ,, | 9th ,, ,, ,, | 7 | ,, |
| 10th ,, ,, ,, | 2 | ,, | 10th ,, ,, ,, | 8 | ,, |
| 11th ,, ,, ,, | 1 | ,, | 11th ,, ,, ,, | 10 | ,, |
| 12th ,, ,, ,, | 2 | ,, | 12th ,, ,, ,, | 11 | ,, |

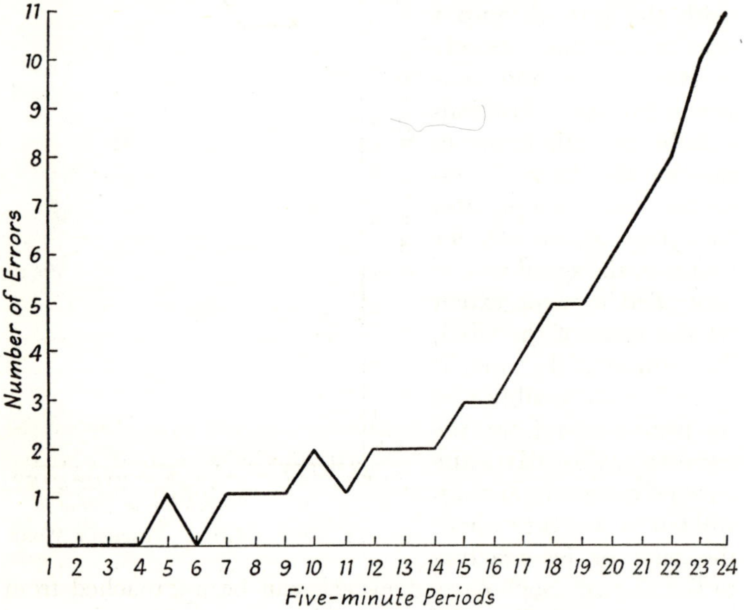

FIG. 44. CURVE SHOWING INCIDENCE OF ERRORS

Such a graph shows that during a two-hour period the rate of errors has increased, especially during the second hour.

### PHYSICAL FATIGUE

Having provided ourselves with a means of measuring the fluctuations in a rate of output, we can now study the effect of various conditions on the operator. The first of these is fatigue, which in its simplest form is not difficult to understand. If we take one small group of muscles, such as those involved in moving a finger, and exercise them alone by pulling a weight attached to a string while the rest of the arm and hand is strapped down, we shall find that we can only pull the weight up to its full extent for a limited time. After a little our pull becomes shorter until finally we are physically unable to move the weight at all. The reason is that this group of muscles is suffering from complete physiological fatigue and is quite unable to make any further effort. After a rest the muscles will begin to respond again and we can once more move the weight, though this time we shall only be able to go on for a shorter time than before. This kind of fatigue, while interesting from the laboratory point of view, is of very little significance in ordinary life, because we very seldom use such small groups of muscles so intensively that they "pack up" completely.

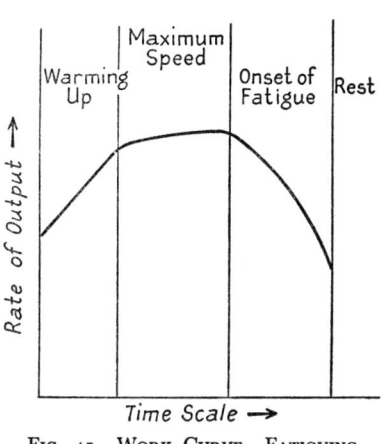

FIG. 45. WORK CURVE—FATIGUING WORK

What is more normal, however, in industrial life is the reduction of speed which occurs after a period of physical work, coupled with a disinclination to continue which never reaches a complete physical inability to do so. Take, for example, someone shovelling coal—a heavy, fatiguing task in which the speed could quite simply be recorded in terms of the number of shovelsful thrown per minute. The operator might start off fairly slowly, warm up as he got into the swing of it, keep going at his best speed for a period, then find the shovels becoming heavier and heavier. His speed would probably begin to drop a little at this point and the temptation to stop and rest would become increasingly strong until finally he knocked off for a little and leaned on his shovel while he wiped his brow. He would feel physically fatigued in the sense that he wanted to stop shovelling and rest for a period, but he would still be physically capable of going on as the appearance of a loud-voiced supervisor would quickly prove. The graph of fluctuations in the output rate is shown in Fig. 45.

If work was resumed after a rest the same process would be repeated except that this time both the warming-up period and the period of maximum speed would be shorter.

Such a graph is known as a "work curve" and the one in the diagram is fairly typical for heavy fatiguing work. It puts down on paper what anyone who has ever shovelled coal or sawn wood will recognize as the normal development of his feelings towards such an activity.

### MONOTONY AND BOREDOM

There are, however, many kinds of work which do not involve physical fatigue, but in which output tends to drop off after a

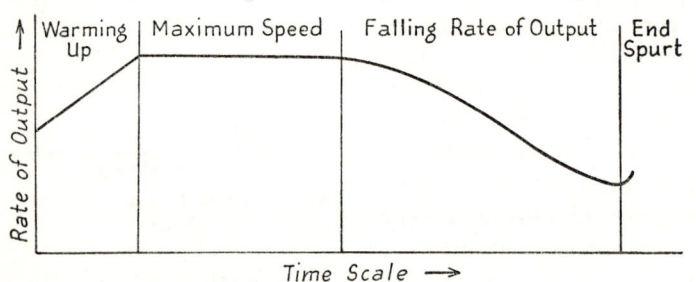

Fig. 46. Work Curve—Light, Repetitive Work

period. Repetitive, light assembly work is not fatiguing in the same way as shovelling coal, yet if we look at a work curve for this type of job we shall find a similar picture of falling speed though in this case it will be much more gradual, while we may find odd things like increases towards the end of the period.

A curve like this shows the incidence of boredom rather than fatigue, the "end spurt" being due to the operator brightening up when the end of the period is known to be within half an hour or twenty minutes.

Work curves will vary according to the kind of work, those for fatiguing work being usually different in shape from those where the work is light physically but monotonous and repetitive. It is never safe to generalize about any job and one should always construct a work curve, or a series of work curves, before committing oneself to an opinion about how output is likely to fluctuate. Work curves are also liable to fluctuate with different individuals, so that it will usually be advisable to construct several curves for one job and then to note any general similarities they may display.

### HOURS AND REST PAUSES

Once we have established a reliable work curve for a particular job we shall inevitably be led to consider whether anything can be done about the fluctuations. Think, for example, of the length of the working period. If the rate of

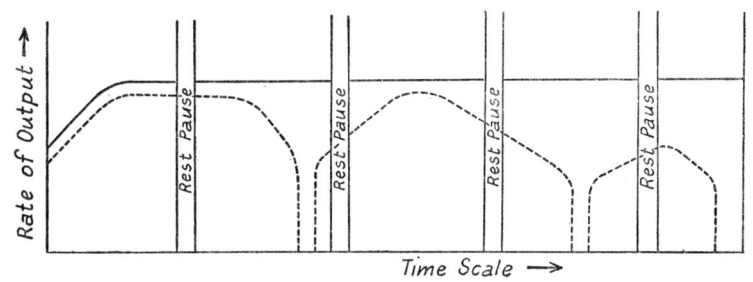

FIG. 47. EFFECT OF REST PAUSES—FATIGUING WORK

output declines after fatigue or boredom sets in, then we are obviously going to gain a diminishing return after a certain point. The fourth hour will almost certainly produce less than the second hour, while if we add a fifth hour the extra production will be still less. There will come a point where the rate of output is so low that it barely justifies the additional time on the job.

This decline in output rates as the work period lengthens can at times make long hours uneconomic. As far back as 1917 it was established that when excessive hours were reduced the drop in output was much less than had been expected, and in fact after a few weeks of readjustment the influence of the higher average tempo of production had caused total output to come back to the original figures. The same amount of work was being done, in fact, in a fifty-six hour week, as had been formerly done in a week of sixty-six hours.

Another example of the same amount being done in less time is provided by the introduction of rest pauses. If, on looking at a work curve, we note the point at which the output rate begins to drop and introduce a rest pause a short time before, we may offset the decline or postpone it. Fig. 47 gives an example of a physically fatiguing job of which the work curve normally follows the broken line, with unofficial rests being taken at irregular intervals. A new work curve with organized rest pauses is shown by the black line. The rate of work would thus be kept consistently higher by regularly spaced rests.

Next take the example (in Fig. 48) of a light job where the work curve shows the influence of boredom. The cross-hatched area represents the rest pause during which no

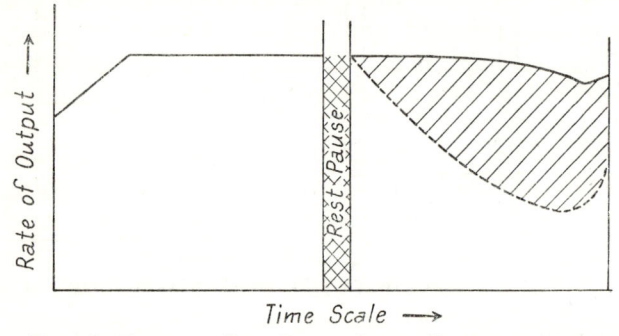

FIG. 48. EFFECT OF REST PAUSE—LIGHT, REPETITIVE WORK

work is being done so that the production rate drops to nil. It is thus lost time. The shaded area represents the gain in output which results from the higher speed of production. If the shaded area is larger than the cross-hatched area then the total output during the working period will be greater, even though ten or fifteen minutes have been lost through the introduction of rest pauses.

### OTHER METHODS OF DEALING WITH FATIGUE OR BOREDOM

The study of work curves will throw a great deal of light on the incidence of fatigue and boredom, and by calling attention to the points at which output rates tend to sag they lead one on to think about measures to offset these matters. Dealing with actual fatigue probably involves the reducing of the physical strain involved in heavy work by redesign of tools or equipment or by rearrangement of loads. Where such measures are not possible fatigue can be offset by the introduction of short rests as frequently as the work curves seem to indicate are advisable. Troops can march for very long periods when they are allowed a rest of ten minutes in the hour.

Dealing with boredom provides scope for a wide variety of expedients. Rest pauses, refreshments, "music while you work"—these have become accepted as normal at the present day, though thirty years ago they would have been regarded as immoral in many companies. Community singing goes on semi-officially in some workrooms and conversation may take place on a clandestine basis. Allowing operators to go home when the task is finished has in some cases had a very dramatic effect in speeding up the tempo and offsetting a sagging afternoon output rate by bringing forward and extending the influence shown in the "end-spurt." Reading improving literature used to be carried on in monasteries during working hours, and this might be useful in certain cases though it might cause some surprise at first, and would raise problems in the choice of literature. It is advisable, however, to keep an open mind and whenever a study of the work curves suggests that something might be done, experiments should be made and the results noted.

### NOISE

The hours of work have been considered for convenience as part of the physical environment which surrounds the worker, and this has probably some justification. There are, however, other conditions which fall more logically under the heading of physical conditions. One of these is noise, and some studies have been made of the effect of noise upon output. The question, however, is complicated by the fact that very many different sounds fall under this heading. Noise can vary in intensity or loudness, and this can be measured in units (decibels) by the use of a sensitive microphone with a recording device. It can also vary in quality.

In every large city there is a more or less continuous hum of traffic noises which many people hardly notice. In factories also there are usually machine noises which go on all the time at a certain pitch. Quite often these can reach a considerable degree of loudness without their having any noticeable effect on production rates, while workers say that once they have got used to them they fall below the conscious level and are never thought of. Some studies have been made in very noisy shops such as weaving sheds where the rattle of the shuttles approaches the noise of small-arms fire, and very little difference was found between the output rates of workers supplied with ear-plugs to reduce the noise and those who were not. Individual differences between workers, however, were noticeable here.

Certain kinds of noise, however, do have an effect which can be seen in the rates of output. Loud insistent noises such as are produced by pneumatic drills or steam pile-drivers do put a strain on those who work near them particularly if the noises are intermittent. Talk of which enough is heard to make sense will also fall into this category, though a buzz of conversation in which no words can be distinguished may pass largely unnoticed. Noises of these kinds will show an effect on the work curve either by startling the operator or by distracting his attention, and as a rough guide we might lay down these two criteria to work on: if a noise neither startles by its loudness or quality nor by being intermittent, and if people can get used to it so that it does not distract their attention, it will probably have little effect on output rates.

### LIGHTING

Another element in the physical environment is light. During the hours of daylight this will present few problems in workshops where there is plenty of window space and where the windows are kept clean. A guide to daylight lighting is to go to each workplace in a room in turn. If you can see the sky through some or all of the windows from each position then the daylight illumination is probably adequate. This is a very rough-and-ready guide and there will be exceptions, but in most cases it serves. To make a finer check one requires a light meter which registers in foot-candles the amount of light falling on its sensitive surface.

Artificial illumination, which may be called for during the hours of darkness, or where the natural lighting is insufficient, is however a different matter, one difficulty being the constantly rising standards. Some years ago it was possible to find factories where the overall illumination was dim and the light on the working point definitely inadequate, being perhaps as low as half a foot-candle. In those days five or ten foot-candles overall might have been considered very adequate illumination, and rises in the work curve were found when lighting was increased to that level. Nowadays, however, twenty foot-candles have at times been recommended as advisable and increases in output have been found when lighting was stepped up to that figure and even beyond. For certain jobs requiring fine discrimination, up to four hundred foot-candles (the equivalent of bright sunlight) have been tried and found worth while. For example, in the inspecting of soap tablets it has been found that with this amount of light on them any faults at once stand out, so that the strain on the operator is much reduced.

One element in the situation, of course, is the development of lighting apparatus. It was formerly quite an expensive business to raise the level of illumination with ordinary filament lamps. With modern fluorescent or mercury vapour lamps it has become possible to get a great many foot-candles for a comparatively small expenditure both in current and fixtures, and it seems likely that with improved facilities standards will rise still further, so that what is looked on as adequate artificial lighting today may in ten years' time be regarded as semi-darkness.

These same developments have also solved another problem, that of the quality of light. Very bright light from a single source tends to fatigue the eyes by its glare, while at the same time it casts very dark shadows. Modern fixtures cast a diffused light which does not glare nor throw dark shadows, so that these problems need no longer arise. Some fixtures, however, leave out certain colours in the spectrum, such as the reds and yellows, which has the effect of making human skins look remarkably pale and ghastly. Women workers at times object to this, particularly those who are unmarried and who bear in mind the possibility of a romance developing through social contact at work. When carefully applied make-up comes to look like black paint smeared on a corpse, as it does under certain kinds of lamp, they may get discouraged and try to move to a job where their looks, natural or artificial, have a chance. But these unfortunate effects will disappear as research into lighting fixtures shows how they can be avoided without loss of illumination.

### HEATING AND VENTILATION

The atmosphere of a workroom will remain comfortable so long as certain conditions are within the range of toleration. Outside that range there will be discomfort and grumbling, no matter whether they are above or below what is tolerable. There is a complication, however, for from this point of view comfort does not depend on one condition, but rather upon the interaction of three variables. These are—

(a) the temperature of the air;
(b) its humidity; and
(c) the rate of air movement.

Together they make up the "cooling-power" of the air and it is on this that our sensation of comfort depends. If it is too great, our bodies will lose heat quickly and we shall feel cold, whereas if the cooling-power of the atmosphere is too small it will not carry away the heat given off by our bodies and we shall feel uncomfortable.

Looking at the three components of cooling-power separately we need spend little time on temperature. This can be measured by an ordinary thermometer, and it can be raised by means of fires, radiators, and various heating systems with which we are all familiar. Lowering the temperature of a room when the outside atmosphere is very warm is rather more difficult though it can be done by various methods, such as air-conditioning. It is not a problem which crops up sufficiently often in this country, however, for us to deal with these methods in detail.

Humidity is the amount of moisture carried in the air in the form of vapour. It can be measured by wet and dry bulb thermometers.

Air movement means exactly what it says and is measured by a Pitot tube, the same instrument which is used for recording the speed of an aircraft by measuring the pressure of air against the end of the tube as it flies. Outside, the air is almost always in movement through the winds and breezes, while inside most rooms there are small draughts and eddies. When these rise above a certain speed they will cause us discomfort even though the day is quite warm. On a day which is actually cooler we may feel that the air is warmer simply because of the lack of movement.

A change in any of these three conditions will affect the cooling-power of the air. A drop in temperature will increase it and a rise will make it fall off. Low humidity means greater cooling-power while high humidity reduces it. Low air movement means low cooling-power while greater air movement results in higher cooling-power. The three conditions interact so that if the air is so warm and humid that its lack of cooling-power is causing discomfort this can be offset by increasing its movement artificially by means of fans.

Punkahs have been used for this purpose in tropical countries for many years. Conversely in cold countries, where the low temperatures make the air's cooling-power too great for comfort, people try to reduce draughts and eddies by double windows, stuffing up cracks below doors, and so on, in an effort to reduce the air movement and so cut down the cooling-power of the air.

Too high cooling-power and too low cooling-power will alike make themselves felt at work both in the operator's feelings of discomfort which will be expressed by grumbling, and in the low rate of output which will be seen in the work curve. The situation in most cases can be dealt with in common-sense terms by opening and shutting windows or turning radiators off and on as desired. There are, however, certain processes which require high humidity, as in the textile trade, or which involve uncomfortable degrees of heat as in certain types of metal smelting or foundry work. These may require special treatment, and the measures involved may be elaborate and expensive.

One method which makes it possible to deal with practically any atmospheric discomfort is to isolate the building from the outside completely and to circulate the air within it by mechanical means. In this way air can be warmed or cooled, dried or humidified artificially and blown through the ducts which lead to various rooms in the building by means of fans, at a given rate of movement. If the pressure within the building is kept a little higher than that of the outside air then the "used" air within the building will escape on its own and will prevent any outer air from coming in through the orifice by which it leaves. This system, which has been described in the merest outline, is known as air-conditioning, and it can be used to keep rooms cool in warm weather or warm in cold weather as may be required.

### FUMES AND DUST

There remains the question of unpleasant substances in the air itself. It was formerly thought that people breathed out "bad air" and that this caused rooms to be stuffy because of the reduced oxygen and increased carbon dioxide content. It is now known that, except in hermetically sealed compartments, ordinary breathing is very unlikely indeed to make enough difference in the oxygen and carbon dioxide content of the air to be at all significant. Discomfort is caused by loss of cooling-power and not by "bad air."

Some processes, however, give off fumes or dust which may remain in the air and cause discomfort or injury to the workers' health. When this occurs the only way of avoiding the unpleasant results is to draw away the impregnated air by an extraction system and to cleanse it by appropriate means of the noxious substances which it carries. The cleansing methods will vary according to the process and may be left to those who specialize in these matters. The extraction process is quite easy to understand, consisting as it does of a duct located at the working point so that it will catch all the particles or fumes given off by the process, and an extraction fan which sucks air down the duct and along it to the cleansing plant. The commonest examples may be seen in grinding or buffing wheels to carry off the dust from the process, or in fume cupboards in laboratories or where cellulosing or de-greasing is carried on. Should the process be dangerous, either through the amount or poisonous nature of the fumes given off, additional security can be given to the operators by the provision of a respirator. These, however, are not popular, and careful supervision is required to ensure that they are regularly worn.

### GENERAL

We have considered the hours of work and seen how they can be arranged so as to minimize fatigue and boredom, and we have seen how various elements in the physical environment, such as noise, lighting, heating, and ventilation can, if they are of an unsatisfactory standard, lead to grumbling or to lowered rates of output. No attempt has been made to deal with these matters in detail, for the changes in apparatus and technique are so rapid nowadays that whenever a problem arises it is better to call in a lighting or heating engineer and to follow his advice. The ordinary manager need only have a general knowledge of the subject and the appropriate methods of measurement.

Occasionally, however, someone breaks into print on the beneficial effect of cleaning the windows or painting the walls of a factory. These, of course, are mere matters of good housekeeping and it is surely obvious enough that a dirty, littered workshop is less likely to conduce to good work than one which is reasonably fresh and tidy. Slovenliness in these matters is an attitude of mind which can usually be seen in other aspects of management routine.

Standards of housekeeping in factories are constantly rising, and in some of the newest and best the conditions are extremely pleasant. Beyond dealing with these elements in the working environment which, when they fall below a certain level, can have an adverse effect on health and output, it is no part of our task to deal in detail with this question.

## SUMMARY

1. What is a work curve and how is it constructed?

A work curve is a graph showing fluctuations in the rate of output over a working period. It is constructed by laying out a time-scale on the horizontal axis and a speed of work along the vertical axis. In certain kinds of work it may be difficult to prepare a satisfactory estimate of speed, but in such cases some other measure, such as the incidence of errors, may be used.

2. How does physical fatigue show up in a work curve?

Fatigue shows itself in an increasing disinclination to continue with a heavy task, culminating in an irresistible desire to stop and rest. The characteristic work curve for fatiguing work shows a warming-up period, a short period of maximum output, and a fairly rapid decline.

3. What is the characteristic curve for a boring, monotonous task?

Boredom, which is distinct from physical fatigue, shows itself in an increasing difficulty in focusing attention on a repetitive task. The characteristic work curve shows a warming-up period, a reasonably long period of maximum output, lasting perhaps till more than half way through the working period, then a gradual decline sets in which will continue until within perhaps half an hour of the end of the period, at which point an "end-spurt" may be seen.

4. What light do work curves throw on the arrangement of hours of work?

In the first place they show that long hours yield diminishing returns in output because of the continuous falling off in the rate of production after a certain point. They also show that the introduction of a rest pause may, by lengthening the period of maximum rate of output, result in an increase in total production which more than offsets the time lost.

5. What is the effect of noise at work?

Continuous steady noise has little effect, even though it is quite loud, for after a period of habituation it may cease to be noticeable. Sharp, alarming noises which are intermittent, and human speech which is sufficiently distinct to be comprehensible, may have an adverse effect on operators by distracting attention, increasing nervous strain, and lowering rates of output.

6. What constitutes adequate lighting?

Standards are constantly rising, while the nature of the work calls for different degrees in intensity. Five to ten foot-candles overall, with at least ten at the working point, are probably adequate for all but the finest work. It is important that the quality of the light should be good, i.e. that there should be neither glare nor sharp shadows.

7. What constitutes adequate ventilation?

One's sense of comfort depends on the cooling-power of the air. If that is too low one will feel stuffy and uncomfortably hot, but if it is too high one will feel cold. Cooling-power is made up of three factors—

    (*a*) temperature;
    (*b*) humidity; and
    (*c*) air movement.

A change in any one of these will, unless offset by the other two, affect the cooling-power of the air.

8. What causes air to be "bad" and how can this be dealt with?

Provided that the cooling-power is adequate, normal human breathing cannot make the air bad. Bad air is usually caused by fumes, dust, or other noxious elements that are introduced into it. These can be removed by extraction plants.

CHAPTER XXI

# Accidents

EVERYONE knows what an "accident" is, but when we come to define the term as it is used in industrial studies we may have to think for a little. "Meeting someone by accident" means that there was no previous knowledge or arrangement about the encounter, but this use of the word is obviously different from what is meant when we say that someone "met with an accident" at work. In this latter case the essential meaning of the word includes some form of injury, unintentional or unexpected injury perhaps, but still injury.

A further complication might arise through difficulty in deciding on how serious an injury must be before it is classified as an "accident." In most kinds of manual work people suffer scratches, cuts, and abrasions which are considered incidental to the job and too superficial to be worth mentioning. While in a small number of cases these may lead to serious infections, they are normally not sufficiently serious to be thought of as "accidents." Only where the injury is bad enough to keep an employee off work for one or more days is it likely to be dignified by that name.

In this sense of the word, therefore, an "accident" occurs when an individual in the course of his work comes unexpectedly and unintentionally into a situation where he suffers a sufficiently serious injury to keep him off work for a day or more. Such situations can be of many different kinds. In some, the individual may be quite passive and the external environment active, as when he is standing motionless in a building which collapses about his ears. In others the external environment may be passive and the individual active, as when he falls off a quay or a dock. In others again both the individual and the external environment may be active as when he moves his hand in such a way that it is caught up in the machine.

It is obvious that accidents may be expected to occur more frequently in some environments than in others, but the dangerous situation may not always be recognized merely by observation.

Once careful records have been compiled and studied, however, it becomes clear which kind of environment produces accidents more frequently than others and that under certain conditions accidents may be expected to occur. Such records can also show something about the people involved in accidents, whether their actions have played a significant part in causing them, and whether certain kinds of people tend to have more accidents than others.

#### ACCIDENT RECORDS

Any study of accidents therefore begins with records, and we may turn first to these. The taking of particulars about an accident as it occurs presents no more difficulties than the recording of any other event, but once we start analysing these records in an attempt to classify these accidents complexities will arise. Some classifications may be quite simple and straightforward, but others may be more difficult to deal with.

As an example of a simple classification let us consider the place of the accident. In a factory, for example, we may take a ground plan and insert a pin on the location of each accident. If we have enough cases it is likely that the pins will tend to appear in clusters, each cluster calling for examination to see whether there is anything in the environment which might tend to bring about such accidents. In many cases this will be obvious, as, for example, in a wood-working shop when we found a cluster of pins around the circular saw. In other cases it might be less obvious and we might require to study the nature of the accidents a little before we realized that at that particular corner people tended to collide with moving trucks coming in a direction from which they could not be seen.

We cannot go into the various kinds of dangerous environment here in detail. A catalogue of places where there is danger of falling, being injured by moving machinery, or being overcome by noxious fumes, would be tedious and rather uninformative, whereas the limitations of space make it impossible to deal fully with the data available on this point. The reader is referred to the literature on the subject, either in the Factory Inspectors' reports or in other publications, for an adequate survey of the kinds of place where accidents tend to occur.

Many of these places, can, of course, be made safe once it is known that accidents tend to occur there. The provision of handrails and guards for moving machinery, and similar precautions, will help to prevent accidents and a code of precautionary measures of this kind has been drawn up in the Factory Acts and is enforced by the Factory Inspectorate. These are continuously being improved and extended, and once again the reader is advised to consult the literature.

What is perhaps best worth emphasizing here is the method by which the subject has been approached. Common sense tells anyone that a band-saw is dangerous but only records make it clear how often and under what circumstances accidents actually occur. When we have this knowledge we can set about devising precautionary measures to avoid those which are most common.

### PRECAUTIONARY MEASURES AND TRAINING

Making the environment safe, however, is not simply a matter of fitting appropriate guards and leaving it at that. In many cases these guards will involve a change in the working method and the natural dislike of change may tempt operators to leave them off, or in other ways render them ineffective. A great deal of ingenuity has been shown in the design of guards which are foolproof and without the proper use of which machines cannot be operated. For example, the controls of a press have been altered so that both hands must be placed on buttons well above the working point before it can be actuated. This means that it is mechanically impossible for the operator's hands to be near the position of danger when the press comes down. But even here a determined operator can rig up a piece of wood to depress one button while he works the other with his hand, thus bringing the press back to the dangerous one-handed method of operation which the new controls were designed to avoid. Without the intelligent co-operation of the operator, guards and safety devices may be of limited use.

This raises the question of training and, as in all other training schemes, a start must be made with motivation. Teaching a worker to use a method which seems more awkward than it need be will be an impossible task unless he can be brought to see some very good reason for it. Relying on a habitual set of movements learned blindly as a drill may be of limited value in the teaching of safe working methods. It is sounder to start by awakening a realization of the need for safe working methods, though this may conflict with the necessity for building up confidence in the early stages of training.

The matter is a delicate one and requires to be thought out carefully. Putting up gruesome posters showing mutilated bodies or wounded limbs may simply awaken an unreasoning fear that accidents are lurking round the corner and may catch one unawares. Such an attitude is unhelpful and unconstructive and will not result in adequate motivation to learn safe methods. Showing the dangers of an operation should always be linked up with information on how these dangers can be avoided, so that the individual is left with the impression that provided he understands the situation and goes the right way about it he will be quite safe.

In the United States during World War Two there was an interesting example of the irrational attitude to safe working methods. A well-known female star had appeared in a number of films with her hair hanging loose over her face in a style which was dignified by the name of a "Peek-a-boo bob." This style caught on and was adopted by numbers of young women workers in the war industries. The difficulty was, however, that such a loose coiffure tended to get caught when the workers bent over their machines, and a number who were on drilling machines or others with rapidly moving parts were well and truly scalped. Direct orders to wear caps were treated as infringements of their liberty, propaganda was ineffective, and quite a number of accidents ensued until the film star was persuaded to do her hair in a different style and declare the former one old-fashioned.

*The Role of the Supervisor*

The use of goggles to protect the eyes from chips and splinters, of respirators against fumes and of other types of protective clothing, raises the same kind of problem. No matter how carefully designed these may be they will in most cases involve a certain amount of minor awkwardness or discomfort when worn, and operators will be tempted to discard them or find excuses for not wearing them. Supervision will be necessary to ensure their continued use, and this will only be provided if the supervisor is aware of the dangers and is properly trained in the methods of avoiding them.

In some cases the regrettable tendency to short-circuit the supervisor has made its appearance here as elsewhere. Safety committees have been set up to encourage awareness of the problem among workers and safety officers appointed to supervise the working methods from this point of view. So long as these are properly related to the working of the firm as a whole they can do nothing but good, but if they tend to interfere too much at the working point they may dilute the supervisor's sense of responsibility on this matter.

### THE ACCIDENT-PRONE WORKER

The individual worker can contribute also to accidents. Even though the hazards in the environment are virtually eliminated and effective steps taken to make people aware of such risks as remain there is still the possibility that workers may injure themselves through what is usually described as "carelessness." This word can cover a multitude of sins.

Bad selection, of course, will make itself felt here. If a worker is not up to standard physically he is likely to become fatigued and inaccurate in his movements. This will increase the risk of accidents, in the same way as lack of manual dexterity or inadequate co-ordination on work which calls for these qualities. Similarly badly selected workers who get bored with their jobs may become inattentive and liable to accidents, while there is a minority of people who develop an irrational fear of machinery, which has the same effect. These feelings may spring from a low level of Adjustment or may be the result of putting someone on to a machine too complex for his level of understanding.

This connexion between selection and accidents has in the past led to an endeavour to detect "accident prone-ness" by means of tests. At times it appeared that a small number of workers were having more than their share of accidents. Tests of motor co-ordination and other qualities were applied and the workers with high accident records seemed to get significantly lower or higher scores than the remainder. It was argued, therefore, that such tests would be useful in showing beforehand which would be the safe workers and which would have accidents. These hopes, however, do not appear to have been borne out in practice, and it seems likely that if workers are properly selected and all their attributes taken into consideration, they should become, after training, safe as well as efficient.

## SUMMARY

1. What constitutes an "accident" in industrial work?

Probably the best definition of an accident is a situation, met with unexpectedly and unintentionally by an individual in the course of his work, in which he suffers an injury sufficiently serious to keep him off work for a day or more.

2. How may accidents be caused?

An accident may occur when an individual who remains passive is injured by something in the environment. It may occur when the environment is passive and the individual does something which causes him an injury. Or it may happen when both individual and environment are active, and their interaction leads to an injury.

3. How can dangers in the environment be detected and dealt with?

Adequate recording of accidents will show the places where they tend to occur most frequently. Steps can then be taken to provide guards or other appropriate means to reduce the risks at these points.

4. What can be done about accidents which result from interaction between the operator and the environment?

Such accidents are usually due to faulty working methods and their avoidance depends on training operators to use methods which are safe. This raises all the problems normally associated with training, in particular those of motivation and insight.

5. What happens when the operator contributes mainly to the cause of accidents?

If an operator is unsuited to his job, either by ability, aptitude, adjustment or any other of the points previously considered, he may by his inability to pick up safe working methods and adjust satisfactorily to his job, have more than his share of accidents. This, however, is a matter which adequate selection methods should take care of to a great extent.

# Part III

# Social Psychology

CHAPTER XXII

# Introductory

IN the preceding section we have been considering the individual in the work-situation and we have seen the importance of fitting him into the type of job which makes best use of his capacities and aptitudes, and which gives him the kind of satisfactions he is seeking. We have also dealt with other items in his adjustment to the work-environment, physical conditions, methods of work, and so on. But while all these matters are significant in the study of human behaviour in this particular area of activity they leave out one very important influence—that of the other people with whom the individual comes into contact throughout the working day. It is to this question, which has only been touched upon incidentally up to the present, that we shall turn our attention in the following chapters.

Most of our lives are passed among other people and from our very earliest days we are influenced by them or in other ways we interact with them. Many of our standards and attitudes are instilled in us by the people we live among and a great deal of our emotional life depends for its expression on having other people about us. In fact, from the social psychologist's point of view it is difficult or impossible to detach the individual completely from the network of relationships he has built up with other people. To a very great extent these relationships make up the life of the individual in the community.

We have pointed out above how an individual's life is made up of several different spheres of activity—his home and family life, his leisure-time pursuits, his working life, and so on. Each of these spheres involves activity with other people so that we can conceive of an individual's life as involving membership of a number of overlapping groups—a family group, a leisure-time group, a working group, and so on. To understand an individual's life, therefore, we must know something about the workings of social groups.

## THE STRUCTURE OF SOCIAL GROUPS

A social group is linked together by a network of relationships. When people come together by accident but remain isolated from each other without exchanging words or conversation—as in the normal railway compartment—they remain a mere collection of individuals. But as soon as anyone makes a remark and another answers, a new element has entered into the situation: a relationship has come into being between the two speakers, and also to some extent between them and the others. If the conversation continues and becomes general the network of relationships will grow larger and more complex until everyone in the group is included in it.

These networks of relationships are worth a great deal of study. In the first place they involve the individuals in social roles. The person who opened the conversation, for example, and who proves continuously garrulous and assertive falls quickly into the role of "the talkative man," for his place in the relationships within the group is an active and important one. The others who fall under his influence and who are interested and impressed by what he says fall into the role of listeners or followers. The taciturn gentleman in the corner who takes little part in the conversation but whose remarks are invariably disparaging or critical falls into the role of "the awkward type," and may form a little knot of unpleasantness in the network of relationships.

This last role brings up another point about the workings of a social group. The relationships of which it is composed vary in quality. In our railway-compartment situation the general tone of the conversation may be affable and agreeable and the relationships may be predominantly good in quality. In such a case the individuals in the group will see each other in terms of these good relationships and think each other rather pleasant people. But suppose the conversation starts with an argument about whether the window should be shut or open in which harsh words are spoken and recriminations exchanged. In such a case the quality of the relationships will be poor and the members of the group, seeing each other in terms of these poor relationships, will think they have fallen among a rather unpleasant lot of people.

#### GROUP STANDARDS AND ATTITUDES

Within a group which has been established for a long time there will also be certain common attitudes. It may be considered correct to talk with a particular kind of accent and disparage anyone whose speech does not conform to it. Certain kinds of behaviour may be considered "bumptious" or "pansy" according to the standards of a particular group, while someone who works hard may be thought of as a "rate-buster" in one group, or someone who does not work hard enough may be considered a "slacker" in another. Finding out the prevailing attitudes in a group is always an important and interesting study.

The structure of relationships on which a group depends for its existence varies from one to another. In certain groups one member is recognized as the leader. He decides what is to be done and the others carry out his directions. In other groups the leadership may shift according to what is being done, one member coming to the front when quick action is required, another when a more complex situation has to be handled. In other groups again there seems to be little or no formal leadership and everyone seems to work to a common plan with a minimum of direction. Each of these types of structure is best adapted to a particular kind of task, and different kinds of work will be done most efficiently by the group whose structure is best suited to it.

#### METHODS OF STUDYING SOCIAL GROUPS

These are some of the points which the social psychologist must take into consideration when considering a social group. His methods of approaching them are necessarily less precise than, say, in the study of perception, but nevertheless there are means of describing and classifying the structure of groups, the prevailing attitudes within them and the quality of the relationships between members. Many of these depend on encouraging people to express an opinion, either by means of a questionnaire or in a prepared interview situation. In other cases people may be encouraged to talk at random in an unguided interview while the investigator notes the points to which they seem to return in the conversation and about which they seem to have strong views or emotions. In other cases again a kind of voting procedure can be adopted which shows how each member of the group regards the others and from which diagrams can be constructed which give a very clear account of the structure of relationships within the group.

In considering an industrial organization from the social psychologist's point of view the first thing one must find out is what might be called its *social anatomy*. Every organization is built up of a number of interlocking groups from the half-dozen senior managers who report direct to the managing director down through department managers and supervisor groups to the actual workers on the factory floor. There is, or should be, an official scheme of organization but the actual groupings within the company do not always conform exactly to it. It is important to know how the individuals who make up the organization are actually grouped together in their day-to-day working. This subject is dealt with in Chapter XXIII.

Once the social anatomy is understood, two things must next be considered. First there is the *relationship between these groups*—how each regards the other and how easily communication can take place between them, remembering that the main function of many management groups is communication of information and instructions from the point where they originate to the place where action is to be taken on them.

Next comes the question of the *relationships within these groups*—whether they are of good quality and whether their structure is well suited to the particular task which the group has to undertake. From this we move naturally to the question of *leadership* and we must consider its nature both in the primary working group and in the larger organization. Chapter XXIV is devoted to this subject.

Most important of all in industry is the *primary working group* of a dozen or so workers who are daily in face-to-face relationships with each other under one leader. In the long run every organization, no matter how large it may be, boils down to a number of these primary working groups and the standards of efficiency and the quality of relationships which prevail within them will determine the efficiency and morale in the organization as a whole (see Chapter XXV).

The absorption of new members into an established working group does not always happen naturally and spontaneously. Frequently there is an *initiation period* in which the new member acquires a knowledge of the standards and customs of the group. This period is of supreme importance in determining the attitudes which the new member develops towards the organization and the role he accepts among his immediate workmates. In the *rehabilitation* of injured or handicapped workers this period is of special importance, for in many cases the actual physical injury they have suffered is less serious in the long run than the feeling of being cut off from the group of which they have so long formed a part. This is dealt with in Chapter XXVI.

Much of our knowledge of these matters in industry comes from a series of investigations (the Hawthorne Investigations) in one of the Western Electric Company's works near Chicago (see Chapter XXVII). These began as a study of the physical conditions of work but they came more and more to throw the intangible factor of *morale* into prominence. It soon became apparent that this factor by itself could override other conditions of work and the studies continued until by elucidating certain questions about the relationships and attitudes within groups they brought to light something of the psychological basis of morale. The subject is considered in the concluding chapter (Chapter XXVIII).

## SUMMARY

1. What is the subject-matter of social psychology?

Each individual's life is made up of different spheres of activity, in each of which he is usually in contact with other individuals. These work or leisure-time groups will be held together by a series of relationships which in turn will involve the members in social roles. We all of us depend for a great part of our emotional life on these groupings, and the study of what goes on in them is the subject-matter of social psychology.

2. Are there any significant differences between one social group and another?

Every social group has a life of its own which is quite distinct and characteristic. The relationships which hold it together may vary in structure and quality, and the commonly accepted standards and attitudes may vary so widely that what is acceptable behaviour in one group is considered quite intolerable in another. The purpose for which the group has come into existence will also have an effect upon it.

3. What are the methods of the social psychologist?

Probably the main preoccupation of the social psychologist is with attitudes, and the means of studying these are necessarily less precise than the methods of other sciences. Interviews, questionnaires, and various voting or ranking procedures are utilized from time to time as a means of observing what takes place when people are in contact with each other.

CHAPTER XXIII

# The Social Anatomy of an Industrial Company

ALL social life must take place within some framework of organization, otherwise men must revert to the law of the jungle. Before we can understand the individual's attitudes and relationships we must have an idea of this background.

Industrial companies vary in their structure according to the purpose for which they are set up. In general, however, they will fall into some kind of hierarchical organization, in which one man will be found in general charge, either of the company as a whole or of one of its sub-units. This general manager, managing director or whatever his title may be, will be responsible for the overall direction of the business either according to a policy laid down by a board of directors or according to his own ideas, if he happens also be to the owner of the business.

Beneath this chief executive the company will probably split into a number of vertical divisions each concerned with one of the principal aspects of its functioning. Once again an individual will be in general charge; the sales manager, for example, who is responsible for keeping in touch with markets and ensuring that the products are sold profitably; the production manager, whose job is to make them; or the development manager, whose job is to think ahead and consider new products, and new methods and processes.

Within each of these divisions the same picture will be repeated. The manager will have his immediate subordinates, each concerned perhaps with a department within the division or with one fairly separate aspect of its work. On the production side of the firm, for example, the production manager will be in general charge, while his immediate subordinates will be, say, six department managers. Each of these will have a number of foremen under his control, while each of these will have a number of charge-hands under him. Under the charge-hands will be found the actual production workers.

The conventional manner of representing this organizational framework is by a "T-chart" such as is shown in Fig. 49.

This shows up the hierarchical nature of the organization as it broadens down in a pyramid from the general manager at the top to the production workers at the bottom, and it is obviously in some such manner that human beings are usually organized when they work together. By this means it is possible to know who is responsible for what, and whom a person is responsible to. It provides also a means of control and co-ordination.

It is not certain, however, that such a diagram gives the clearest and most realistic picture of the workings of an industrial company. It does, for example, rather tend to concentrate attention on higher management and thence with diminishing emphasis on middle management and supervision until at the very last a few production workers appear, to fill up the picture as it were. But we must always remember that it is the production operatives who actually do the work, controlling the machines, using the tools, and making or transporting the finished product. In the last resort the management and supervisory staff only exist to facilitate and co-ordinate the efforts of the production workers. It might in effect be more convincing if we were to re-draw the diagram on the lines of Fig. 50.

Such a diagram might give the impression of the production workers being in the front line, with supervisors and management behind ensuring that everything they might need in the course of their work was easily available.

It is essential that this formal organization of management should be coherent and complete, for if this is not so there will be the danger that one individual or group may receive orders from more than one person. There is also the danger that individuals may be left out and may have an undefined power over others.

### COMMUNICATIONS FROM THE TOP DOWNWARDS

It is through this hierarchy of management that the communications pass on which the working of a company depends. Instructions must pass downwards from those who are responsible for the direction and management of the business. Their task is to understand the possibilities of the production and

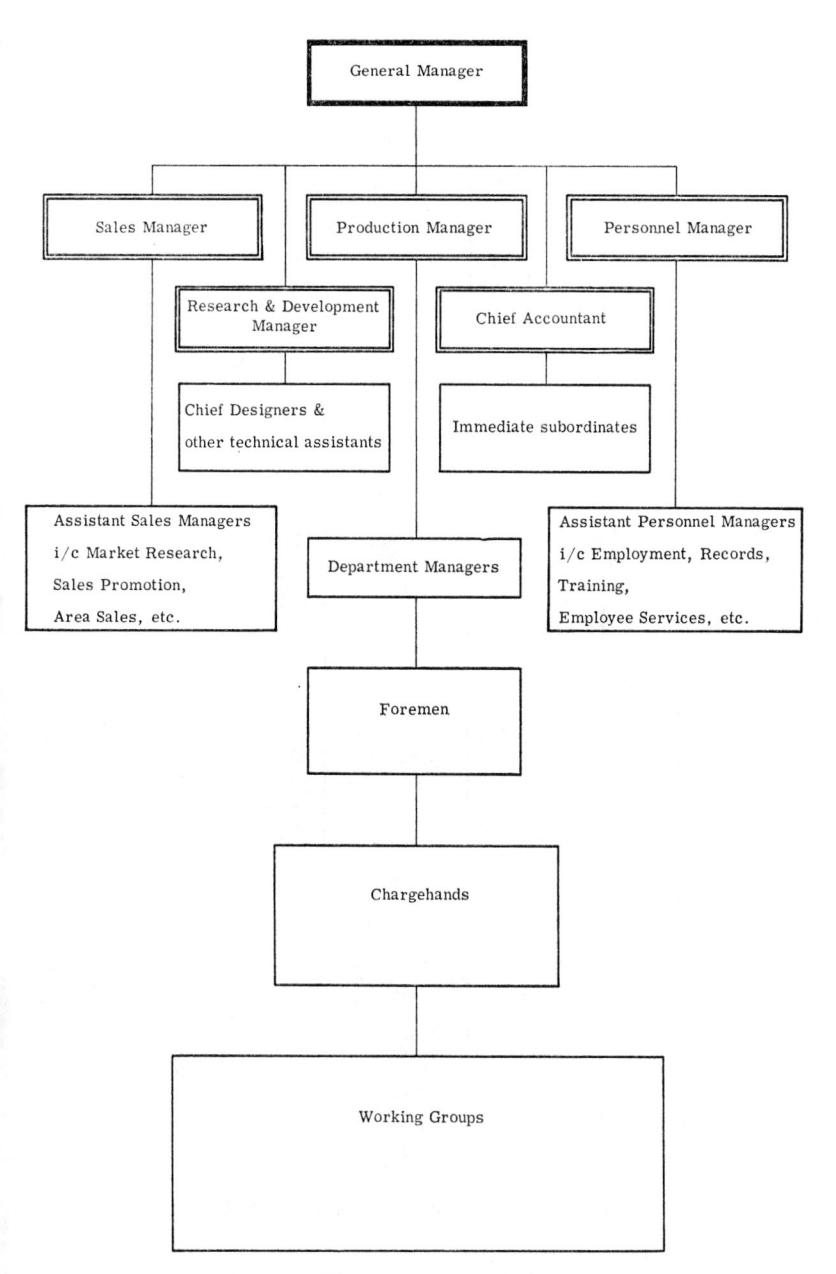

FIG. 49. CONVENTIONAL "T-CHART" SHOWING THE ORGANIZATION OF AN INDUSTRIAL COMPANY

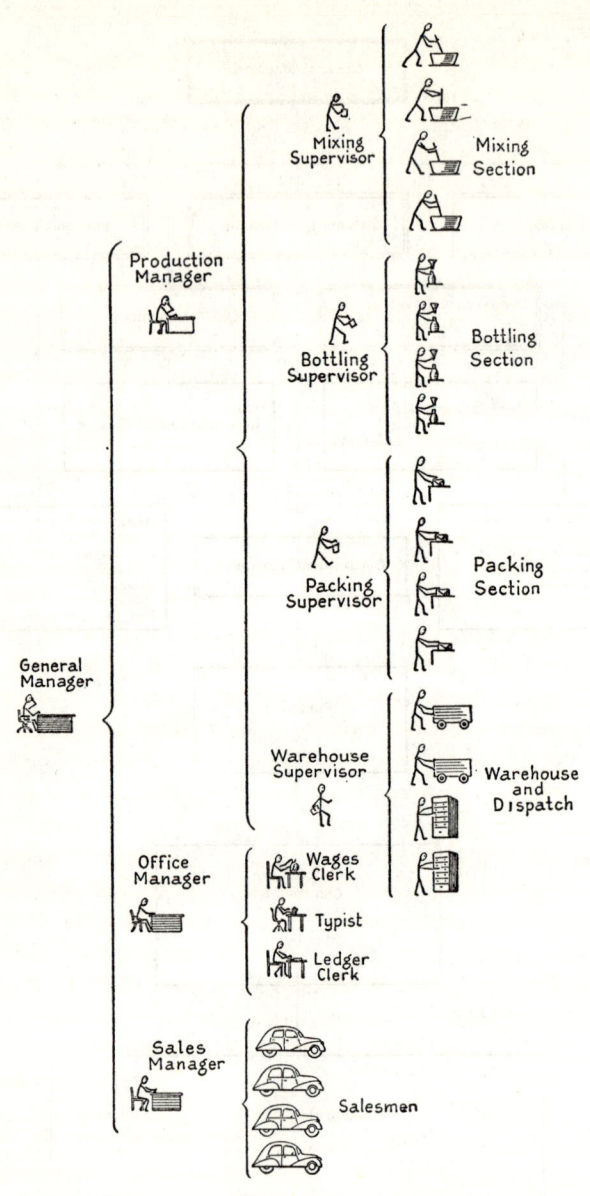

FIG. 50. IMPRESSIONISTIC STUDY OF A COMPANY'S STRUCTURE

marketing situation and to take whatever steps may be necessary to safeguard and develop the company in the immediate future. But no matter how well conceived these instructions may be and no matter how practicable and sensible, they will remain a dead letter until they are put into effect at the actual working point. Higher management, however, cannot follow each instruction down the line in detail and supervise its carrying out on the factory floor; this is the task of other people in the hierarchy. And unless the other people comprehend and pass on these instructions accurately and effectively they may arrive at the working point in a seriously distorted and impracticable form.

There are many opportunities for misunderstanding and distortion between the general manager and the production floor, for every individual through whom the instruction must pass can either omit some essential element or give it an unfavourable turn or twist. But it is of little use trying to short-circuit the normal chain of command because each section and level must translate instructions into terms which take account of their own duties and responsibilities and which can be understood by those below. Senior management, except on rare occasions which are carefully prepared beforehand, cannot communicate direct with production workers in the normal working of a company's business. If it has occasion to do so frequently this is probably a symptom that the normal channels of communication have been allowed to deteriorate to such an extent that they have become slow and unreliable. The remedy is not to hold more mass meetings but to improve the chain of command from the top downwards. Whatever starts from senior management as a practicable and obviously necessary development should reach every level affected by it in a form equally practicable, necessary, and appropriate to it.

## COMMUNICATION UPWARDS

But not all the communications will take place from the top downwards. A great deal of the information on which the working of the firm depends will come from below upwards—from the point, in fact, where the actual production work is done. And if the difficulties and maladjustments which inevitably occur in the course of normal working are not brought to the notice of those who are responsible for putting them right, they may drag on and on until what was quite a minor difficulty in the first place has become a major problem around which a dangerous amount of emotion and dissatisfaction has gathered.

There are inevitable difficulties in ensuring that information about things going wrong passes upwards as quickly as it should do. No one likes to be thought inefficient, and when anything goes wrong in a section or department the manager or supervisor may well be tempted to try to sort it out on his own and keep the knowledge of it to himself even though the situation may be beyond him. Added to this there is a dislike of troubling superiors with details they may think unimportant or unworthy of their attention, while the memory of having been dealt with sharply on a former occasion may prevent someone from coming up with a real difficulty the next time. Even with the best will in the world, the forces of inertia and procrastination will ensure that a complaint or request coming from a worker will be dealt with less expeditiously than one which comes from higher authority.

The danger is that the results of faulty communications from below upwards may remain unnoticed for a long time while the situation deteriorates until a serious crisis occurs. Dissatisfaction over some minor matter which could be settled in a few minutes may drag on for months while an accession of exasperation grows up around this small case. When the irritation has reached a point at which it is brought to the notice of higher management it is no longer a minor practical difficulty which must be dealt with. It is rather a problem of tackling six months' bad feeling and a number of people who have worked themselves up to the pitch of making a mass complaint and who may feel a sense of anti-climax when their crusading spirit shows signs of fizzling out with the replacement of a broken window or whatever was the original cause of dissatisfaction.

In addition to straightforward communication upwards and downwards, of course, there must be some provision for lateral communication as well. When a machine goes wrong it would never do for the news to travel from worker to chargehand, then through the foreman and department manager before it passed across to the maintenance department by means of direct contact between the production manager and the chief engineer. From the latter it would have to pass down through foreman and charge-hand before a mechanic could be put on to do a minor repair. In some organizations it may sometimes seem as though this is the only method of getting things done, but in practice it should be possible to communicate from one department to another at, say, the foreman or department manager level.

### THE NERVOUS SYSTEM OF THE COMPANY

This network of communications through the management and supervisory grades forms the nervous system of a company. In the human body the nervous system conveys information and instructions in much the same way. When we sit on a tack, the pain caused by the sharp point piercing our epidermis is conveyed by means of nerve fibres to the lower part of our brain. There a message is sent out on other nerve fibres to the appropriate muscles and action is initiated which will raise us off the offending point. Provided that our central nervous system is in working order these messages will pass rapidly and the process of feeling the pain and jumping up again will all happen in a flash. Where the nervous system is faulty, as happens in the case of certain diseases, the messages may pass slowly or not at all, and people with these diseases can suffer very bad burns indeed because the pain of touching a hot object is passed too slowly to their brain for them to take their hand away in time.

As an example of how this communications network or nervous system functions in the normal working of a company's business, let us think of a textile firm, one of whose salesmen gets an idea during a visit to, say, South America, for a line of merchandise which would sell in that market. He works out a rough draft of the design and colouring, notes the price range within which it should fall, and decides that it should be on the market there by the 1st of September. Now this idea will only become effective when the workers on the machines are actually making these goods in the right style and quality. Let us see, therefore, how many steps must be gone through before this can happen.

1. The salesman must pass his idea with the information on which it is based to the sales manager. He, with his wider knowledge of the company's markets and arrangements for distribution may make some modifications before he accepts the proposal as fully practicable. Assuming that he does so the next step will be—

2. The sales manager will discuss it with the general manager, who considers it in the light of the company's overall programme for the next few months. If he agrees—

3. The development manager will be called in and asked to produce designs and perhaps a prototype of the goods required.

4. The Chief Accountant may at the same time be asked to study the arrangements for selling to South America, along with any currency complications that may arise.

5. Within the development manager's department there will be further communications with the chief designer and others concerned, with the result that a design is produced which answers the requirements originally put forward. The next step will be—

6. The production manager comes into the picture and is asked to prepare for the output of the goods so designed. He may put forward some modifications to meet his own particular problems after which—

7. The department managers concerned with the different stages of production will be told of the arrangements which concern them. They in turn will pass these on to—

8. The foreman and charge-hands under whose immediate control the actual work is done.

9. The final stage in all this passing of information and instructions, which must be gone through before a single article is produced, will be for the charge-hands to tell the operatives what to do and how to do it. Now it will be possible for production to begin in its various stages and for the goods wanted in South America to start being made in this country.

Such a description is perhaps not entirely realistic, because it omits certain complications on the one hand and assumes an unnaturally tidy differentiation of function on the other.

Nevertheless it does represent something of the complexity of the communications involved in the working of a modern company and it does illustrate the number of different people through whom the matter must pass before appropriate action can be initiated. It is important to remember that at each of the links in the communications network there is an opportunity for a stupid, idle or uncooperative person to slow down or ruin the whole process.

### A PATTERN OF OVERLAPPING GROUPS

But when we look again at an industrial company and disregard its communications network or nervous system, we shall see that the people who make it up fall into a number of groups. Many of these groups are formed by the normal work of production, as when six or a dozen men are engaged on the drilling, shovelling, and so on incidental to digging a hole in the road. In fact when we walk through a factory we shall find that most productive work is done in fairly small groups of this kind. These little units in which people work in direct, face-to-face contact with each other can be thought of as the primary working groups, and they are the social cells of any organization. Because they are the smallest units of association among people they are of great importance in the working of a company. In some cases they are recognized and provided for in the organization, but in other cases they are not. This point will be discussed further in Chapter XXV.

Other groups, however, may not consist of people who are working in day-to-day contact with each other. The half-dozen charge-hands, for example, who are under the control of a foreman may all be working in different parts of the shop and may only see each other when the exigencies of the work make it necessary for one to walk over and talk to another. They may only meet all together in one place at the same time very occasionally when, for example, the foreman calls them together to discuss some question which affects them all. They are, nevertheless, a group, for the organization depends on their working together. Such groups of people who are not in face-to-face contact with each other in the normal working of the firm must obviously be kept in touch with each other. Practically all the management and supervisory grades of a firm will fall into groups like those shown in Fig. 51.

In fact, when we look at the accompanying diagram we shall see that an industrial company consists from this point of view of an aggregation of social groups. Beginning at the top, we have the general manager with his immediate subordinates. Together they form the nerve-centre of the management network, meeting perhaps in a weekly conference, co-ordinating and directing the activities of the business. Next downwards from this central group we have the general manager's immediate subordinates, now in the role of leaders, each the central figure in his own group of subordinates. The production manager controls his department managers, the office manager his section heads, the sales manager his assistants and so on. According to the size of each department we shall go through more stages outwards from the centre, each subordinate having his dual role, being also leader among his own group of subordinates. Eventually we shall reach the floor level where we come to those who have no subordinates to direct, but who are left with no alternative but to get on with the job themselves.

The kind of frog-spawn picture in the accompanying diagram shows the more obvious groups into which an organization may fall. There may be others superimposed on this, such as inter-departmental committees set up to deal with specific questions, or relations between different departments, such as maintenance and production, at the lower levels. Moreover the diagram may not represent any one company exactly, as it is drawn primarily as an illustration. Nevertheless if the reader thinks of any company with which he is intimately acquainted he will find that from this point of view it will break down into a somewhat similar pattern of interlocking groups.

*Relationships within these Groups*

Now, as is well known, the quality of the relationships or the team-spirit within different groups can vary widely. In some there may be pleasant relationships and a general atmosphere of friendliness and co-operation, things can be discussed constructively and it is not difficult to arrive at

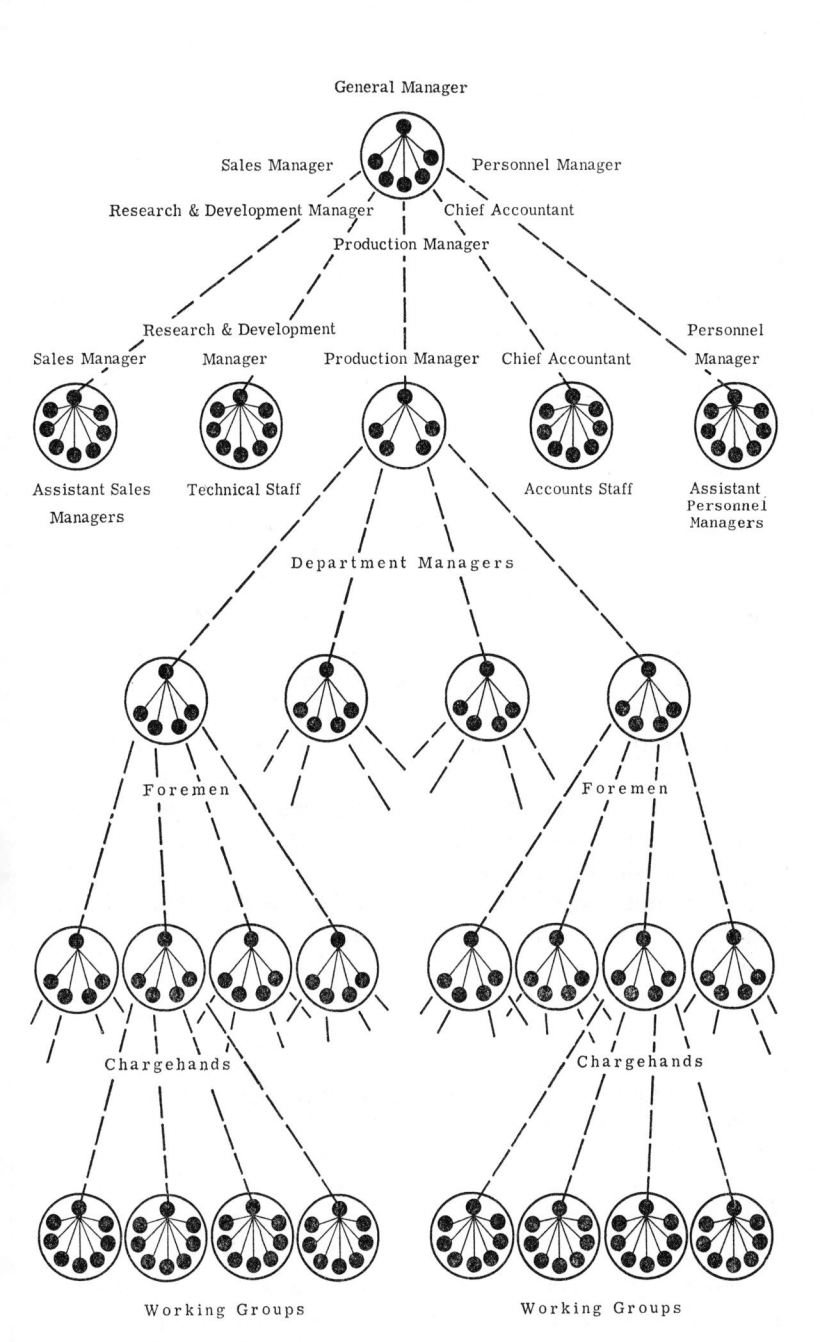

FIG. 51. ORGANIZATION SHOWN IN FIG. 49 REDRAWN SO AS
TO EMPHASIZE THE COMPONENT GROUPS

decisions on the merits of each case as it arises. Groups like these are usually effective working units as well as being very agreeable to work in. In others, however, there may be a spirit of distrust and suspicion, the relationships may be very bad, and only after prolonged argument and the unsparing use of authority can any decision be reached at all. Groups like these will usually be ineffective working units, because quite apart from the time they waste, the decisions they reach may often be the result of contending internal stresses rather than an objective consideration of the position.

Social groups are made up of human beings, who between them determine the quality of relationships or the social atmosphere. Some people who are very badly adjusted themselves will find it difficult or impossible to contribute to good team-spirit among others and will always tend to lower the quality of relationships of the people among whom they work. Other people, who may be outstandingly well adjusted, may have an opposite effect and may tend always to improve the team-spirit of the groups in which they find themselves. The majority will probably fall between these two extremes, sometimes joining in the maintenance of happy relationships and sometimes spoiling things by tactlessness or clumsiness, their contribution depending rather on the effort they make, on what they want from the situation, and to a certain extent on luck.

It will not have escaped the reader's notice that all the supervisory and managerial staff find themselves members of more than one group. They occupy one position in the group of subordinates of whom they are in charge and quite another in the group in which they themselves are subordinates. In both these situations different roles will be demanded of them, and they may find one or the other coming more naturally to them. Over and above the formal organization shown in the diagram they may find themselves members of other groups which demand different roles still.

### THE STRUCTURE OF COMPANIES

Let it be emphasized strongly that this pattern of interlocking groups is not something artificial which is theoretically imposed on a company by an outside observer. These are the actual groupings into which men and women fall in the normal course of their day-to-day work. The diagrams and examples given may not fit any existing company exactly and in detail, but that does not matter. Every company will fall into some kind of structure on something like these lines and will show a similar picture of interlocking groups. No collection of men and women who remain together for more than a few hours can remain "unstructured." Particularly if they work together they must develop some form of organization, and from our point of view that organization will comprise both a network of communications and a system of interlocking groups.

It is these groups that are interesting from the point of view of social psychology, because in them the standards of relationship and of working efficiency will be determined. Team-spirit within an industrial company is not a question of what the workers think of the managing director. It is rather a matter of what the different standards of relationship within the multifarious groups within the organization add up to, and if a significant number have very bad relationships, then the overall picture will inevitably be a discouraging one. In the same way the efficiency of a company is not simply a matter of how well the higher executives know their individual jobs. It is rather a matter of the working methods within these various groups and the communications between them, and if even a small proportion of these are bad the company will only be saved from serious difficulties by superhuman efforts on the part of the remainder.

When we are considering an industrial company, therefore, we must begin by looking beyond the hundreds or thousands of people whom it employs, because numbers of this size are rather meaningless when considered in the mass. We must begin by trying to understand the social structure of the organization, the network of communications within it, and the social groups into which people fall while at work. Only in this way can we begin to understand what is going on.

## SUMMARY

1. Is there anything in common between the organizational plan of different companies?

   In general, industrial companies and any other organizations which exist to carry out a definite purpose, fall into a hierarchy.

At the top will be found those who are concerned with the general direction of the company and immediately below, those who are responsible for one particular aspect of its working. These in turn will have a group of immediate subordinates each of whom will have others under his charge, until we reach the people who do the actual work of the organization—making, transporting, or distributing the goods with which it is concerned.

2. How do the communications, on which the company's working depends, pass through this hierarchy?

Communications must pass from the top downwards, as most of the instructions on which the direction of the company depends originate in the top groups of management. But many of the difficulties which are encountered in its day-to-day working will make themselves felt at the actual working point. Unless information about what actually happens at that point is passed quickly upwards these difficulties may not be dealt with. It will also be necessary for lateral communication to take place between departments.

3. How important are good communications in an industrial company?

The communications network may be looked on as the company's nervous system, and unless that nervous system works quickly and efficiently, the company's adjustment to the changing demands and pressures on it will be slow and ineffective. Ideally, any difficulty or friction at any point in the organization should be heard of at once by the person responsible for doing something about it. In practice, however, communications have to pass through so many individuals that there is always room for misunderstanding and delay.

4. Is there any other way of looking at a company's organization?

Any organization will fall into a series of groups, beginning with the primary working group where people are in face-to-face contact with each other day by day. Above these will come further groups of supervisors or managers reporting to one individual in charge. At the top will be found the senior management group which is responsible for running the business.

5. Are the relationships within these groups always of the same quality?

The relationships within different groups can vary widely in quality. In some there is a good team-spirit and people work co-operatively together. In others there will be poor relationships and it will be difficult to get anything done without arguments and bad temper. These difficulties will be due in part to the different levels of adjustment of the individuals who form these groups.

6. How should we think of an industrial company, then, from the social psychologist's point of view?

An industrial company may be thought of as a collection of individuals assembled for an economic purpose and held together by a structure of organization. This organizational structure can be thought of first of all as a communications network, and secondly as a means of subdividing the company into manageable groups. All the management and supervisory staff will find themselves members of at least two of these groups.

CHAPTER XXIV

# Leadership

If we accept the idea that an organization is structured as a series of interlocking groups, then an understanding of it as a social entity depends on an awareness of what is going on within these component groups. We must therefore look rather more closely at them and try to find out what holds them together and why one may be a happier and more effective group than another. This will bring us to the question of leadership, which is one of considerable delicacy in the present-day world.

In our discussion of the Impact on Others heading in our Five-Fold Framework, we touched on the processes which come into being when individuals begin to interact together. This, in fact, is the subject-matter of social psychology, but one cannot lay down clear-cut divisions between the social and the individual aspects of the subject. Human beings remain separate entities, obviously enough. But they must live and work together if they are to make anything of themselves. Thus the individual needs the group if he wishes to express himself, while the group is made up of individuals and depends on them for its existence. The processes which take place in a group can be recapitulated under the following headings.

### RELATIONSHIPS BETWEEN INDIVIDUALS

We have already discussed what happens when two strangers enter into conversation when they find themselves together for a period in an unfamiliar environment. This can be summed up as the emergence of mutual awarenesses and expectations between the two. When each begins to talk, he comes alive to the other as a human being. He becomes, in fact, a real person instead of a mere anonymous figure across the room. As the conversation continues, this awareness becomes more vivid, while at the same time it is supplemented by progressively confirmed expectations of what the other is going to say and how he is going to say it. If, for example, one expresses himself effectively, has a confident manner, and states his opinions in definite terms, the other will anticipate that he will go on doing so in a similar fashion. Depending on the others self-image, it is always possible that he may not look forward to this with any great enthusiasm and may say to himself "Do I have to spend the next hour listening to this self-opinionated character laying down the law on every subject under the sun?" If these expectations are further confirmed as the conversation proceeds, he may wish that he had kept quiet and not encouraged the relationship to come into being at all.

These mutual awarenesses and expectations which make up an interpersonal relationship can be very subtle, and will be affected by all sorts of factors including the Impact on Others of the individuals involved, their self-images, attitudes and background. They will always, however, have their own quality, and if one party is aware of the other as an amiable, considerate sort of person and feels justified in expecting courteous and well-mannered behaviour from him, this relationship will be of good quality. Conversely, if one becomes aware of the other as an ill-mannered so-and-so and feels justified in expecting discourteous and insulting responses from him, then the relationship will be of poor quality. It is thus easy to envisage a scale of quality, with very agreeable relationships at one end, very disagreeable ones at the other, and rather neutral, colourless interactions in between. Moreover, to find oneself interacting in good quality relationships will be a pleasant and satisfying experience in terms of one's companionship and ego needs, which one will be willing to prolong as far as is practicable. To be stuck in a situation where the interpersonal relationships are of poor quality will be a most frustrating experience, from which one will make every effort to disentangle oneself as soon as possible.

Any group or interpersonal transaction will have its formal purpose. This may be to work, have a meal, or play a game together, and this formal purpose will have its own significance to the individuals concerned. Over and above this formal purpose, however, and essential to its achievement, will be the creation of relationships as a means of communication, and these will inevitably be good, bad, or neutral in quality. These relationships will have an additional significance of their own, quite apart from the formal purpose of the group, and they may make the interaction a satisfying or frustrating experience to the individuals concerned. We can thus think of two groups, each with a formal purpose of equal significance to the members, in one of which the interpersonal relationships are of good quality, while in the other they are of poor quality. The former group will be a satisfying experience to the members, both in terms of its formal purpose and of the pleasant and agreeable moment-to-moment interactions which constitute its good quality relationships. The latter may be a satisfying experience in terms of its formal purpose, but its members will find the continual ill-tempered backchat incidental to its poor quality relationships, a source of continual frustration. They will therefore be in conflict as to whether they should leave the group and find some other means of achieving the ends which the formal purpose represents to them, or whether, because these ends are so important to them, they must put up with the continual bickering and bad-temper which makes several hours in the day a very frustrating experience.

Certain relationships also will contain within them expectations that one person will behave in a certain way towards the other. This may be illustrated when we enter an expensive restaurant to order a meal. In these circumstances we expect that the waiter will be considerate and helpful, possibly even a little deferential, as he takes our order and brings in our meal. It would come as a distinct shock if he greeted us with the words "Wotcher cock! Come in for yer bit o' dinner again eh?" and we would consider him insolent and familiar for thus failing to act up to our expectations. Many relationships to a great extent depend on the assumption that one person will give the directions and the other will carry them out. In some cases it may be quite explicit and formalized while in others it may never be put into words or formally recognized.

These relationships between people, therefore, which hold groups together and on which organized social life depends, can be extremely intricate and subtle. They are very difficult to describe and analyse, because they vary in quality and because they depend on a variety of expressed or tacit assumptions about the other person's behaviour or reactions. They are not, however, difficult to recognize, as anyone can prove to himself when he compares his feelings when he passes a stranger in the street with those when he sees a friend or acquaintance.

*Patterns of Relationships*

Among a group of people these relationships usually fall into some kind of pattern. In a simple case, for example, when one person is giving a lecture to a group of others, the relationships could be represented by a series of lines starting from the numbers and converging on the speaker thus—

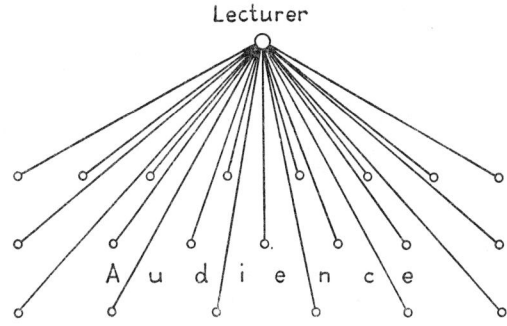

FIG. 52. PATTERN OF RELATIONSHIPS BETWEEN LECTURER AND AUDIENCE

A slightly more complex situation might be a play taking place in front of an audience. Among the players there might be a series of relationships built up by the circumstances of the plot, while in addition there would be relationships between the members of the audience and the actors as their attention centred now on one and now on another (see Fig. 53). These patterns will change according to the development of the situation, sometimes quickly, but sometimes leaving fairly stable and enduring traces behind.

Different patterns of relationships will develop according to what kind of task the group happens to be engaged in. The pattern shown in the first figure will obviously be the most suitable for a lecture; in fact it is difficult to think of a lecture being given without some such pattern of relationships being built up. The same pattern, however, would not be suitable for a working group, because if everyone sat around all day listening to the foreman holding forth, very little work would be done. A different pattern would be called for where the workers' attention was centred on their immediate tasks and where the appearance of the foreman did not cause a diversion of attention from the work to himself.

It is advisable to call attention here to what we might term different layers in the pattern of relationships. The momentary attention of a group of people may fasten on someone and for a small space this one individual may occupy a central position in this superficial pattern of relationships. Underlying this, however, there may be a deeper pattern of more significant

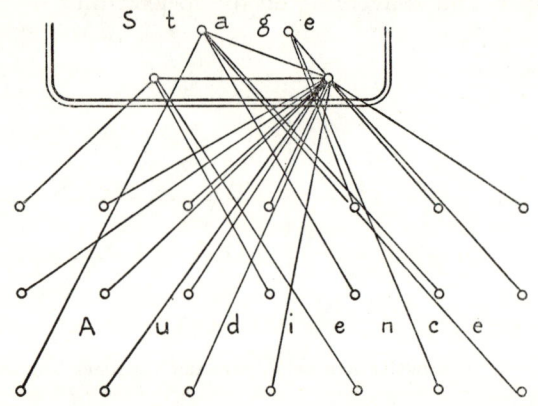

FIG. 53. PATTERN OF RELATIONSHIPS BETWEEN PLAYERS AND AUDIENCE

relationships which may continue in existence for a longer period. The situation might be illustrated at a works concert where one of the labourers who can sing a song and is a bit of a comedian entertains the audience and perhaps even leads them in singing popular songs. For a brief moment he is at the centre of the relationships in the group, and is quite an important figure, but as soon as the concert ends and he slips back into place no one would dream of taking orders from him. The underlying pattern in which the key points are occupied by the management and supervisory staff will be reasserted and people will expect and accept direction from them in everything that concerns the company's working.

*Social Roles*

The next thing we have to notice about this pattern of relationships which binds a group together is that it involves the members in social roles. In a lecture situation, for example, the pattern will only be maintained if one person talks for a given period, expounding a theme which the others have assembled to listen to with sufficient clarity and novelty to make it reasonably interesting. The others must maintain silence while the lecturer talks and must at least keep up the appearance of listening with attention. In other words the lecturer must undertake a certain role in the situation and the audience another. Moreover, unless all the members of the group carry out their roles with a certain measure of success the group situation will break down. No lecture has ever been really successful where the lecturer went out for a drink half-way through, or where the audience stopped listening and began singing popular songs.

The same will hold good of any group situation. At work, for example, the role of the operatives is to carry out certain tasks, while that of the supervisor is to tell them what to do and see that they do it properly. If one of the operatives objects to being told what to do and fails to carry out his task—i.e. if he refuses the role which the situation requires of him— it will be difficult for him to remain in the group. Similarly if the supervisor is idle about setting tasks and organizing the daily details of the job—i.e. refuses his role—the group will be ineffective and probably rather poorly disciplined.

It is possible to illustrate how group situations depend on individuals filling the roles which the pattern of relationships demand of them in all sorts of ways. When small boys play cricket, for example, there is usually a good deal of argument about whether the batsman is "out" or not, not infrequently terminated by the owner of the bat deciding that he will go home and not play any more. At such an age boys find it difficult to stand up to the roles that a team game demands, particularly when no older person is present to ensure that they abide by the rules. The difference between a game in the park and a game at Lord's is in part a question of the levels of self-control which the players display in assuming the roles that the game demands. Similarly a good party is one where everyone is able to join in the fun and be gay and amusing— i.e. where they take suitable roles successfully. A dull party is one where not enough people can be bright and entertaining or where too many "won't play" or join in the fun, i.e. where they cannot sustain suitable roles.

There are also cases where attempts are made to break up the pattern of relationships on which a group depends by people refusing to take suitable roles and insisting on taking unsuitable ones. For example, when a party of hecklers goes to attend a political meeting held by the other party they have no intention of taking the role of listeners, which involves sitting quietly during the meeting and applauding at the end, which the situation demands of them. They intend rather to interrupt the speakers, to ask awkward questions and to "boo" instead of applauding, in fact to undertake the most unsuitable role they can think of. If they are successful in this they may make it impossible for the speakers to be heard, and if they are not thrown out they may cause the meeting to break up in disorder. That is to say they will have disrupted the pattern of relationships on which the group situation depends for its existence, by refusing the roles which that situation demands of them and by taking up unsuitable ones.

This draws attention to the interdependence of social roles, which is a point of some importance in the understanding of relationships between people. When two people interact, the relationship between them arises out of the roles they adopt towards each other, or, to put it the other way round, the roles are simply the two ends of the relationship and cannot be separated from it. The manner in which one of the two parties plays his role, or indeed his willingness to accept that role, will affect the role of the person at the other end of the relationship. This may be illustrated by referring again to the political meeting. One person comes to the hall with the intention of taking a particular role in the pattern of relationships—the central role, that of speaker. But he will only be able to do so if the others present are willing to accept the reciprocal roles—those of listeners. If they are willing to sit quietly in the body of the hall and behave as an attentive audience, they make the speaker's role possible for him. But if one or more individuals has come with the intention of refusing this role of listener, the speaker's role can be made impossible for him. By interrupting, by heckling, by shouting rude remarks or by otherwise behaving in a manner which prevents the speaker from maintaining the even flow of his discourse, they can bring the meeting to a standstill.

This is where the competence of those who have arranged the meeting will be put to the test, for unless they can somehow maintain the pattern of roles and relationships on which it depends, the whole project will collapse. There are various courses open. Stewards can collar the interrupter and throw him out on his ear, saying "If you refuse to accept the role on which this structure of relationships depends, we cannot allow you to remain in the hall," or something else appropriate to the situation. Other members of the audience who find their roles satisfying may tell him to shut up. But the speaker, in the central role, can do more than anyone else to restore the situation. If he is experienced as a political figure, he may be able to maintain his role as a speaker by forcing the interrupter out of the disruptive role by means of which he is trying to sabotage the meeting. The ability to raise a laugh at the expense of a heckler, to score off him in a quick interchange, to confuse him and make him look ridiculous so that he subsides and keeps quiet from then on—these are essential weapons in the armoury of a political speaker if he is to deal successfully with those who attempt to "put him off his stroke" or to make his role impossible by refusing to accept the role which is its counterpart and on which it depends.

There is, therefore, a skill in handling our relations with other people, one part of which is to be able to recognize the role expected of oneself and to play it successfully. But another and perhaps more important element is the ability to draw other people into the roles which are reciprocal to that which one wishes to play and on which it depends. Thus, no one can be a speaker unless he can persuade other people to accept the role of audience; there can be no leader unless he can find others who will accept the role of followers, no order-giver without an order-taker, no bully without someone to cringe before him, no martyr without a persecutor, and so on.

Recapitulating what has been said about group situations, therefore, we have found that—

1. They depend on bonds between the members.
2. These bonds can be pleasant or unpleasant in quality

and can involve different expectations from and attitudes towards other people.

3. They will fall into different patterns, each of which is suitable for a particular kind of activity.

4. These patterns of relationships will involve the members of the group in social roles. Upon the adequate carrying out of these the pattern will depend.

### LEADERSHIP ROLES

Now it will already be apparent that the patterns of relationship in a great many group situations will tend to focus on one or two persons, whose roles will tend to have more influence in the general pattern than those of the remainder. So long as a lecturer continues to discharge his role, quite a substantial proportion of the others present can neglect theirs by dropping quietly off to sleep without the situation breaking down. Similarly so long as a supervisor is conscientious in his allocation of tasks and seeing that they are properly carried out, the working group may continue to be quite efficient even though the other members are not all entirely conscientious about carrying out their roles. These roles, on which the pattern of relationships depends to a greater extent than on the others, are the leadership roles, and in any group situation it is very important that they should be adequately filled. The pattern of relationships in most working groups will depend on a leadership role, and anyone who is put in charge of a working group will be successful or not according to how far he can fulfil the role that the situation requires of him.

Leadership is a social process: it depends on filling a certain role in a pattern of relationships in a group of people. That role will vary in different groups, and in different situations, some of which we shall look at in a moment, but it will always be at a focal point in the pattern. The quality of the relationships will depend upon it, for if all the bonds between the members of a group centre upon someone who is difficult, discourteous, and liable in most cases to arouse unnecessary resentment and bad feeling, these bonds will surely be disagreeable and unpleasant. On the other hand, if there is someone who is helpful, knowledgeable, well adjusted and mature at one end of most of the relationships between the members of the group, then these bonds are likely to be of much better quality.

In the same way the pattern of relationships will depend on the person who fills this role, for if he does not carry it out there will be a large gap at the most important point in the pattern. Other people will then begin to neglect or refuse their roles and in a very short time the whole situation will break down.

*Different Kinds of Leadership*

In certain group situations the pattern of relationships is laid down very rigidly and the roles of the individuals are defined in great detail and enforced to the letter. Quite obviously such a group will have an authoritarian character and considerable sanctions or powers of punishment will be necessary to maintain the pattern of relationships on which it depends. The slightest deviation from his role on the part of any individual must be effectively discouraged immediately it becomes apparent. Recruit training depots in the army were a good example of this kind of group situation, for minor infractions of discipline could be dealt with by a system of punishments enforced by N.C.O.s who understood exactly what was required of them.

The role offered to a leader in such a situation is in conformity with the rigidity of the pattern. He may maintain his position by using his powers of punishment and by insisting on the small details or gestures which mark the difference between himself and the rest of the group. Any failure to live up to the official pattern of relationships and roles might have a disintegrating effect on the group, for the rigidity of the structure is likely to make it unable to stand any severe strain. In actual practice, however, it is frequently found that this official pattern of relationships is supplemented by another unofficial and much more effective structure.

During a period of heavy unemployment it is possible to find these authoritarian groups in industry, for the power of dismissal or the threat of it is quite effective as a sanction to support the most rigid pattern of relationships. It is probable that in the late 1920's and 1930's, and perhaps as a hangover from earlier times, this situation prevailed, and the role of an industrial leader was thought of in terms of taking one's place in a rigid authoritarian pattern of relationships, supported by severe powers of punishment which were used ruthlessly to "keep others in their place" or ensure that they maintained their roles. The relationships in such a case would contain expectations of obedience on the one hand and domination on the other.

*The Situation in Industry*

For a number of years now, however, the situation in industry has been changing and with it the conception of a leadership role. Two main factors can be seen in action, the first of which is the quite simple and obvious change in the employment situation. Before the war there were well over a million unemployed and if a man were dismissed he could usually be replaced without much difficulty. Since the war there have rarely been more than about five hundred thousand unemployed, mostly for only short periods at a time, and if a man is dismissed he can often walk into another job the same day, while the employer may find a great deal of difficulty in replacing him. In these circumstances the principal sanction for discipline has disappeared, for apart from dismissal there are very few effective punishments available in industry. Without powers of punishment it is practically impossible to maintain a rigid authoritarian pattern of relationships.

The other factor is a change in outlook on the relationships between human beings in general. Sixty years ago it was quite natural to talk of "master" and "man," and the forming of relationships in which there was an expectation of obedience on the one hand and domination on the other was a normal thing. It was probably true also that the relationship carried an expectation and acceptance of the obligation to provide security of tenure at the same time, and that the breaking down of this element in the relationship led to the loosening of the whole. Be that as it may, however, the developments of the last sixty years have seen a gradual but definite movement away from the conception of "master-and-man" relationships in industry and very few employers have the self-confidence to expect implicit and unreasoning obedience from their workers. Very few workers, on the other hand, are prepared to put up with authoritarian discipline in a factory, simply because they happen to be employed there.

With this modification in the relationships within the working group there has come a change in the role of the leader. No longer equipped with powers of punishment, he is expected to elicit not so much obedience as collaboration from others. Unsupported by a rigid pattern of relationships, he is expected to maintain his position by his constructive handling of social situations and by his awareness of the needs of the group at any one time, for direction, planning, or the solving of difficulties. Provided that his workers are amenable to a reasonable approach this role may not be an impossible one and a sophisticated group structure, or one in which each member will understand and accept his role quite consciously, will be built up. In many cases, however, there is still a certain threat in the background in the shape of dismissal.

*A New Conception of Leadership*

In times of crisis, it is said, the moment produces the man; someone steps forward who can control the situation and everyone else turns naturally to him for direction. Be that as it may, we find more frequently that a leisure-time group, held together by no compulsion other than a desire to play some game together or promote some cultural activity, can produce from within itself people who can deal quite adequately with the leadership roles. Such groups are worth study for they show a voluntary acceptance of roles and a structure of relationships which is not at all rigid and which is maintained in existence by no sanctions.

Such groups might be called "sophisticated," because the members realize that a certain pattern of roles and relationships is necessary if the group purpose is to be achieved, and they accept this quite willingly without taking it any more seriously than the situation requires. This kind of situation might be illustrated by the captain of a local cricket club, who says to one player "Where would you like to field, Joe?" and Joe replies "I don't mind, Fred. Put me wherever you wish." Fred then replies "O.K. Will you go to cover point, then?" An easy, good-tempered relationship, with no show of authority on one side, and a willing acceptance of direction on the other.

In such groups the leaders maintain their position solely by their ability to fill the role which it demands. Having no sanction for their authority other than its acceptance by the other members of the team, they can be displaced at once if a small number of those members withdraw that acceptance.

It is not suggested that industrial leadership can ever approximate completely to this picture. The members of a working group have not come together voluntarily to work for the fun of the thing, nor can they ever be expected to identify themselves as completely with an industrial company as with their own sports club. Likewise it is probably impracticable to have the leaders of working groups appointed by popular election. Nevertheless, in these days industrial leadership may only be effective if it achieves some degree of acceptance from the led, and leaders may have to be chosen for their power to fulfil the role which is demanded of them under present-day conditions. This aspect of the leader's qualifications may come to bulk quite as large as his technical ability.

A new conception of leadership is therefore possible where the powers of punishment necessary to an authoritarian group-pattern are lacking. This will make serious calls on the leader, and it may make an equal demand on the led to accept their roles with only a minimum threat of coercion. In essence, however, there is no difficulty in putting such a conception into practice, other than the human limitations of the individuals concerned.

## SUMMARY

1. How is a group held together?

Whenever two or more individuals have any personal contact with each other a bond or relationship will be formed between them. It is these relationships which make the difference between a group in the proper sense of the term, and a mere collection of individuals who happen to be in the same place at the same time.

2. Are these relationships between people uniform in quality and content?

Relationships between individuals can vary widely. They can, for example, be of a pleasant quality when one person regards the other as an agreeable, reassuring companion. Or they can be distinctly unpleasant when one person thinks of the other as an object of fear and suspicion. Relationships between individuals can also contain expectations of different kinds of behaviour, such as the giving or receiving of orders and the like.

3. How are the relationships within a group laid out?

Among any group of people the relationships will fall into some kind of pattern. This will vary according to the task on which the group is engaged, but in many cases it will focus on one or more of the members. This pattern of relationships will involve the members of the group in social roles, and only if these roles are carried out adequately will the pattern be maintained.

4. Where does the leader fit into this pattern of roles and relationships?

The roles which stand at the focus of the pattern of relationships are the leadership roles and on them a great deal depends. Standing as they do where most of the relationships centre, they will have an important effect on the quality of these relationships. Likewise the maintenance of the whole pattern of relationships will depend on them. Similarly the encouragement of other members of the group to sustain their roles will depend to a great extent on how the leader discharges his role.

5. Are there different kinds of leadership role?

In a group situation where the pattern of relationships is rigid and is sustained by sanctions and punishments, the role offered to the leader will be a rigid, authoritarian one. Where punishments are lacking and roles are accepted voluntarily, the leader must maintain his position by discharging his role in such a way that he is accepted by the other members of the group.

CHAPTER XXV

# The Primary Working Group

Now that we have considered what goes on among people in groups and seen how a group depends for its existence on a pattern of relationships between its members, it will be apparent that the smaller groups where face-to-face relationships can be maintained are more likely to be significant than the larger groups where the relationships may be more distant. It seems to be generally accepted that the size of group in which these face-to-face relationships can exist is seldom more than about a dozen or so, and common sense tells us that in a group of this number individuals can work in intimate face-to-face contact with each other and get to know each other pretty well in the process. What goes on within these primary groups, therefore, is important from many points of view.

In the first place, these groups are the social cells of the organization, that is to say they are the smallest units in which people can work together. In the human body the biological cell is the smallest unit of living matter, and what goes on in the cell is of very great importance to the health of the body. If the cells are healthy the body will be healthy, but if the cells, or a proportion of them, are diseased, the body will be ill. In a company the social cells are of equal importance. If the relationships within the primary working groups are of good quality and the pattern into which they fall is suitable for the function of the group, then the team-spirit in the company as a whole will be a good one. But if the relationships within a significant proportion of the cells are poor then the team-spirit of the whole will be defective.

In the second place these groups form the immediate social environment of work for the individual, comprising the people with whom he is in contact for several hours at a time every day. Now our states of mind depend to a considerable extent on the circumstances in which we find ourselves and of these circumstances the other human beings are not the least significant. If we have to work throughout the day among people we dislike—with whom our relationships are of poor quality—we shall get little pleasure out of the hours we spend on the job and we shall look on it as irritating and tedious. The individual's state of mind, therefore, will be seriously affected by the relationships within the primary group.

Thirdly, working methods depend to a great extent on the administration within the primary group. This is a small-scale matter concerned with the minor arrangement of material, the allocation of tasks, and the day-to-day organization of work, but it is nevertheless important in determining the efficiency of the company as a whole. It is no use having methods worked out to fractions of a second if every time a batch is finished the operator has to wait half an hour before he is given another task. Such details do not depend on the planning department. They must be settled within the primary working group.

### PRIMARY GROUPS IN AN INDUSTRIAL COMPANY

Every organization, no matter how large, must come down in the last resort to primary working groups. The very large company tends to be thought of as employing thousands or people all herded together in a large anonymous mass. But when we go to visit one of the company's plants and look at the work actually in progress we shall find half a dozen men working on one process here, a dozen over there tending a large machine, eight or nine somewhere else engaged on a common task. Most industrial work falls naturally into small groups, and even on those processes where a hundred people seem to be working in one large unstructured group we shall find on closer inspection that there is usually some form of subdivision, either a setter or mechanic, a relief hand or an inspector who looks after every dozen or so workers.

These small face-to-face groups in which the pattern of relationships is so significant are worth a great deal of study. But quite frequently they are not provided for in the official organization of the firm. It is not unusual for the last step in the management and supervisory hierarchy to be a foreman who is left in nominal charge of fifty or sixty operatives, with no subordinate charge-hands to take charge of the primary groups. This is an impossible situation, for obviously no pattern of face-to-face relationships can form between fifty people and there can be no one central point at which anyone is offered a significant leadership role.

In such a case the official organization of the group is obviously unworkable except on a very artificial and unreal level. What happens in actual practice is that an unofficial form of organization comes into being, primary groups forming themselves spontaneously, and little patterns of relationships growing up unnoticed in the course of the work. The small groups into which people naturally fall in the course of work develop their own organization, while other unexpected groupings may also come into being. Now if these patterns of relationship remain completely unofficial a number of quite important things may happen which may remain beyond the control or even the knowledge of those who occupy the key positions in the company's official organization.

For example, the roles demanded by the unofficial pattern of relationship may be quite different from the official roles in the organization. Similarly the qualities of relationship and the expectations of behaviour they involve may be so different that they may in fact conflict. Most important of all, of course, is that the unofficial groupings will offer unofficial leadership roles to people who have no place in the formal organization of the company. These leaders, being purely spontaneous creations, will depend for their position on their ability to achieve the group's unofficial objective, but if they appear to be doing so at all effectively they will have a very real control over the rest of the group because of the face-to-face primary group relationships which hold it together.

*The Unofficial Primary Group*

Bringing all this down to practical terms, let us imagine that we have a department of sixty operatives under one supervisor—a number which is too large for any pattern of primary group relationships to form in. Suppose that ten of these people are working together on some process which involves some small collaboration between them and which brings them into some physical proximity to each other. Inevitably relationships will form between these ten people which are closer and more direct than those between them and the rest of the department. The pattern may be rather indefinite but it will be very unlikely to include the official supervisor of the department whose appearances will probably be relatively infrequent.

As the work proceeds minor difficulties will inevitably arise, and an impression may get around that the supervisor (official) is not doing as much as he might to deal with these and to facilitate the group's task. An opportunity is then provided for someone to say "Of course, no one cares what happens to us. We sweat our guts out to get production through in spite of difficulties and so long as the output keeps up we can ruin our health for all anyone else notices. *They* aren't bloody well interested in us as human beings." Everyone feels like that at times and there is bound to be some agreement from the others. The pattern of relationships will adjust itself for the moment to centre on the person who has thus expressed the common attitude of the group.

Now it is not impossible that the individual who comes thus into the centre of the pattern, however momentarily, may have an opportunity to express an official protest or in some way to contribute to easing the strain on the group or facilitating its work. If this happens he will tend to confirm his position of leadership in protecting the group from exploitation or in giving expression to its dissatisfaction. The pattern of relationships which centred momentarily around him will become more definite and permanent and some expectations will develop that he will continue to represent the group's point of view to the official hierarchy of management. This process has only to continue for a few weeks for this individual to become accepted in a leadership role among that primary group, and for another appointment, unofficial and carrying no responsibility, but quite real and effective, to be made within the company.

Primary groups of this nature, which form under unofficial leaders, tend inevitably to be to some extent in opposition to the formal organization of the company. Their purpose is usually self-protective, their relationships in a defensive pattern centring on the individual who can best carry out the defensive purpose, and their attitudes towards the company and its purposes rather suspicious and possibly hostile. The difficulty is, however, that being primary groups, the relationships within them have a face-to-face quality which is more significant in the lives of the members than the rather unreal official relationships expected by the unworkable formal organization. Moreover, such groups have come into being to fill a kind of social vacuum where a primary group was a necessity but had not been provided for.

It is not our purpose to consider intentionally subversive activity in industry, though a certain amount is usually carried on for one motive or another. One cannot fail to be struck, however, by the opportunities which are provided gratuitously for subversive elements when the formal organization of a company fails to take account of the necessity for recognizing the primary groups which must inevitably form at work.

### THE RECOGNITION OF LEADERSHIP ROLES

To cope with such a situation, which obviously has serious potentialities, it is necessary to carry a company's organizational framework right down to the actual working point. This might at first glance seem to involve a serious increase in the numbers of supervisory appointments. What is required, however, is not the multiplication of people who are supposed to "take charge" of others at work, but the recognition of the leadership roles which exist within the primary working groups in which the work is carried out. These will mostly be filled by working charge-hands, leading hands, setters, inspectors, and a host of other people who exist already but whose jobs have been recognized mainly for their technical or administrative content rather than for their social or leadership content. Quite a minor change could make a great deal of difference. This would be to recognize officially that such tasks involve a leadership role, and to make its satisfactory carrying out one of the duties of the job. The role will vary from one job to another but in every case the individual who occupies it should be held responsible for the quality of relationships within the group, for taking and keeping his proper place in the pattern, and for ensuring that the other members duly carry out their roles.

In certain cases the natural leaders of the primary groups are more willing to accept their technical responsibilities than the leadership duties which belong to the position. In the weaving trade in Lancashire, for example, the obvious primary group leader is the overlooker or "tackler" who takes charge of a manageable number of looms and operatives. But while accepting the responsibility for the maintenance and adjustment of the looms, the overlookers have refused to be held responsible for the discipline and management of the operatives, with the result that there is no one between the mill manager and perhaps a hundred or so weavers; the mill manager's job thus becomes an impossible one.

Where natural primary group leaders exist, as they usually do in most industrial situations, they should be held responsible for every aspect of the role. This will include not only technical and administrative duties in the care of machines and the handing out of work (allocating duties) but also a human element in the maintenance of the quality and the pattern of relationships. They must ensure that the other members carry out their roles adequately. They must be sure also that they do not overlook the protective aspects of the leader's role, because if they fail to represent the group's point of view or to play their part in gaining recognition for it and facilitating its duties, there will always be someone ready to step in and take over these more agreeable aspects of the role. This is what happened in the example quoted above, and in any dual-control situation like this it is usually the protective or "mother" figure whose role is the more significant while the authoritarian or "father" figure suffers by comparison and gradually loses significance, particularly in a situation where the powers of punishment necessary to authority are lacking.

Another aspect of this situation is that the leader of the primary group must accept a second role in another group—that of subordinate in the next above. Referring again to Fig. 51 on p. 309, which shows the component groups of which an industrial company is made up, dotted lines will be seen connecting each group with the next. But the same person appears at either end of these dotted lines, in one group occupying a leadership role and in the other a subordinate one. It is by playing these twin roles that managers and supervisors hold a company together, or form the essential links between the groups of which it is formed. Experience in the training of supervisors suggests that it is the subordinate role which in fact gives them most trouble. They do not seem to find their leadership roles too difficult, and, provided that a supervisor knows his stuff and is reasonably sure of himself, this is easy to understand. As a subordinate, however, he will find himself quite frequently the bearer of bad news in the shape of difficulties or delays on the job; he will have to put forward awkward requests and point out that unless they are met the job will suffer, he will have to tell his superiors things they do not like to hear. A little reflexion, therefore, will show why the subordinate role may easily have the more unpleasant aspects of the two. It is nevertheless quite as necessary to the effective working of the company as the leadership role.

When we really study what goes on in the primary group we shall find that unless the occupier of the leadership role carries out all the aspects of that role, the pattern of relationships which depends on it cannot be maintained. Some aspects of this role may be a little unwelcome, such as the necessity for the charge-hand to represent the group's point of view. There is a danger if he does so that he will be accused of "taking the side of the men"; but if he does not undertake this aspect of his role he is immediately leaving the way open for an unofficial competitor who may step into the vacant place and build up a new leadership role and a new and unofficial pattern of relationships.

### THE SELECTION OF LEADERS

Another problem which this approach to industrial organization poses is that of finding the right people for leadership positions. It is quite obvious that technical qualifications or experience alone will not enable a man to take charge of a working group, though he will be unable to do so without them. He must have all the qualities necessary to fulfil the different aspects of his role and these will include the ability to understand people and to establish and maintain the right kind of relationships among them; this in turn demands an ability to understand and control himself. In the specification for any supervisory position therefore, a high standard of motivation with a social slant and an above-average level of Adjustment will be essential.

In the past supervisors have frequently been selected for their technical qualifications and experience, and many people have been appointed to such jobs who clearly lack the other qualities required. This has obviously resulted in poor relationships and morale in the company as a whole and in the primary groups in particular, but nevertheless companies have continued to operate. How has this been so?

Partly because in the past the semi-authoritarian set-up backed by the threat of dismissal has kept many problems under the surface and enabled many otherwise unsuitable supervisors to maintain their positions; this situation has now changed and with the overall difference many problems are coming out into the open. The main reason, however, has been that in such cases supervisors reached some kind of working compromise between the aims of management and what the working group would accept.

Where the self-protective organization of the group is well developed it will be expressed in restrictive practices and customs, such as working to traditional standards of output, promotion to certain jobs by seniority rather than by merit, and the like. All these will provide means of frustrating any attempt to improve the efficiency of working. Where they are well established it will be impossible for a supervisor to get things done as he knows they could be done. He must content himself, therefore, with getting as near the desired level as he can.

If we revert for a moment to Taylor's early experience, as described in Chapter XIX, we shall see the kind of compromise which has to be arrived at when management stops short with its feet off the floor, that is when it does not reach down to the primary groups. Taylor's shop in the Midvale Steel Company was in the hands of unofficial leaders who, expressing the self-protective desires of the primary working group, had set up and maintained a set of working standards which represented in his opinion about a third of what could be achieved. His predecessors had acquiesced tacitly in these standards and were maintaining an uneasy compromise between the official purpose of management and the unofficial self-protective leadership on the floor of the shop. When Taylor appeared and refused to accept this compromise three years of bitter conflict ensued. This conflict will always occur when differences between the official and unofficial organization of a company are forced to an issue, particularly when the unofficial organization at the primary group level is well established.

## SUMMARY

1. What is the maximum size of the primary working group and why is it important?

The intimate, face-to-face relationships on which a primary group depends cannot be formed among more than, say, a dozen people. Primary groups are important in an industrial company because they form the smallest social units within it, because they are the immediate social environment of the individual worker, and because the methods and team-spirit which prevail there will determine the efficiency and relationships within the whole company.

2. Are these primary groups normally provided for in industry?

In the sense that most industrial work falls into small groups of up to a dozen or so, yes. In the sense that these groups are provided for in the plan of organization and provided with official leaders, no. Too often the official organization of a company comes to an end well above the primary group level.

3. What happens when the primary groups are not recognized officially?

Whenever the official organization of a company fails to provide for the primary groups, unofficial primary groups will spring up. These will usually have a self-protective purpose and they will offer roles to unofficial leaders whose aims will not necessarily be in harmony with the official aims of the organization.

4. Is it practicable to extend the official organization of a company down to the primary groups?

Most industrial work falls naturally into primary groups and there are a number of roles, such as those of setters, overlookers, and the like, which are in effect leadership roles. In many cases, however, these are recognized only for their technical content and not for their human content. If such people were held responsible for the whole of their leadership role—for the relationships and team-spirit among the group as well as for its technical working—management organization would extend to the primary working groups.

5. How far does this involve a change in existing methods?

The organizational changes need be very slight. It would however involve a serious change in the methods of selecting supervisors, for their personal qualities and their technical knowledge would have to be considered as of equal importance. Similarly they would have to be recognized in some degree as the spokesmen of their groups. In the present situation many charge-hands are having to acquiesce in an uneasy compromise between the aims of management and the self-protective organization of unofficial primary groups.

CHAPTER XXVI

# Entry into the Group and Group Attitudes

THE intimate life of a face-to-face primary group is probably the most significant aspect of the relationships of large numbers of people working together, and some understanding of it is essential to a proper appreciation of the problems of leadership and morale. But over and above these direct relationships, there are common ways of thinking among all the members of an organization which are essential to its functioning and which the individual who joins it must learn before he can become an effective member of it.

It is obvious that in any organization engaged on a technical job there will be a number of technical terms which are meaningless at first sight to the layman. Not only will he have to learn the meaning of the words, but also he must acquire some appreciation of the techniques and processes which they denote before he can take part in any useful discussions within the organization or even understand what people are talking about. So much would probably be accepted by everyone and the need for a period to "learn the language" would be recognized.

But even in non-technical organizations the newcomer will find himself at a loss until he learns his way about the building and something of its organization. He will want to find out whom to ask for certain things, who gives him instructions about what he must do, and the names of a host of people who at first sight will seem bewildering and strange. After a while he will gain some confidence in his knowledge and will find that he knows enough to be able to get through an ordinary day's routine without having to ask too many questions.

At this point, however, he may experience a rude shock, for he may find that there are certain ways of looking at things commonly accepted in this organization which are substantially different from what he has been used to. For example, he may have come from an organization where no one paid much attention to minor amounts of scrap and he may allow himself a certain margin of waste material. He will be very surprised, therefore, if in his new firm someone, not necessarily a supervisor, says to him "What do you want all that for? It's valuable material which somebody has to pay for. There's no point in wasting half of it just for the fun of the thing." From then on he may realize that the way of looking at scrap and other things may be quite different from what he has been used to.

### ATTITUDES

These "ways of looking at things" are known as attitudes. In most cases they are largely unconscious, people having absorbed them from those among whom they have lived. Take, for example, the word "nationalization." If one has lived in a traditionally Conservative business background this word will probably call into play a somewhat unfavourable attitude in one's mind, compounded of tag ends of sentences like "bureaucratic inefficiency," "stifling private enterprise," "jobs for the boys," "excessive centralization," all adding up to a general feeling that "nationalization is a bad thing." But if on the other hand one has been brought up in a traditionally Labour, Socialist or trade union background, one's mind will probably fill with phrases like "condition of economic justice," "protection against capitalist exploitation," "public ownership of the means of production," all adding up to a general feeling that "nationalization is a good thing."

If by chance you have thought seriously about the subject, reading the arguments for and against, trying to gather information about the relative efficiency and conditions in privately and publicly owned industries here and abroad, and reaching your decision after an honest effort to weight the advantages and disadvantages of nationalization, these words do not apply to you. But if they do have some approximate resemblance to your mental processes when the word is mentioned they will give you some idea of your "attitude" to that particular issue. You will realize also how far your thinking about many subjects is conditioned by your attitudes, many of which you take for granted, remaining unaware how irrational and unconscious they are.

In any group of people there will be common attitudes to most of the day-to-day issues which arise in the course of the normal routine. It may, for example, be unanimously considered a bad thing to work too hard (one remembers at school how offensive it was to call anyone a "swot"). Or it may be thought wrong to take orders with good grace and right to make difficulties and argue a bit before doing what one is told. Or it may be commonly held that this is a bad firm to work for, that workers are exploited, and that the new canteen is simply another means of "getting away" with something by making the workers think that they are better off. Even though the justification may be slender or non-existent, these views may pervade the group, being held with considerable devotion, and any refusal to agree with them may be courting extreme unpopularity and the risk of rejection. The strength of an attitude has little to do with its inherent probability or even its relation to the facts of the case.

### ENTRY INTO GROUPS

The existence of these attitudes raises a number of questions some of which are concerned with the entry of newcomers. A new entrant may be trained in the technique of the job and in the formal organization of the company but he will neither feel at home nor be accepted by his colleagues until he is familiar with the prevailing attitudes and until other people are confident that he shares them wholeheartedly. The most obvious social *gaffe* that one can make is to show enthusiasm for something in a social group where the prevailing attitude to the particular issue is negative and disparaging. Such a performance shows up the fact that the individual is either unaware of or indifferent to the group's attitude to that particular topic.

In some groups this kind of failure may entirely prevent the individual from being accepted. Such groups are rigid in their standards and particularly hostile to any suggestion that they are not universal and absolute. They will thus have a very low capacity for assimilating newcomers, as in the case of rather isolated village communities where new arrivals are thought of as "foreigners" for perhaps the first ten years of their residence. Certain industrial groups may be rather like this—very fixed and set in their ways and liable to make it difficult for new entrants for an unnecessarily long time and on quite irrational grounds. At times one may even find the hostility to a newcomer being expressed in unkind practical jokes (such as sending him to ask for a left-hand screwdriver) or even in a degrading initiation ceremony like those found among primitive peoples.

Some individuals, of course, make their own acceptance difficult because of the rigidity of their own attitudes and their low level of acceptability to other people. Not only are they insensitive to the fact that other people may react differently to certain events, they also take no pains to conceal the fact that they have their own ideas. If someone like this arrives in a group where rigid attitudes make it difficult to assimilate newcomers the stage is then set for a conflict which may be prolonged until one or other gives way, or until the community decides to accept the newcomer with reservations ("He's a bit queer, you know, but still . . .") and the individual makes a partial adjustment to the group ("They're pretty backward, one has to humour them a lot").

The ease with which a newcomer can fit into a group, therefore, depends on two variables. One of these is the group's capacity for assimilation which may vary from a very low level in the rigid and suspicious groups referred to above, to a very high level of sophistication. There are cases where a social unit on receiving a newcomer may say, more or less explicitly "Well here you are. We've got to live together so we might as well make the best of it. So long as you don't offend other people you will be accepted and we'll do our best to get along together." The other variable is the individual's level of acceptability. This may range from rigid attitudes and considerable suspicion of those who do not share them, which will make a person unfit for anything other than his own familiar background, to a high level of sophistication where an experienced person can refrain from showing surprise or disapproval at unusual attitudes and can make some kind of adjustment quickly to any social unit. In other words some groups will be able to assimilate almost anyone and some individuals can fit in almost anywhere, whereas some groups will regard any newcomer with hostility and some individuals will find it difficult to fit in wherever they are. In any particular case the speed of assimilation will depend on the relation between the group's capacity to take in new people and the individual's level and range of acceptability.

*Assimilation of the Handicapped Worker*

Among normal people of approximately the same background this does not usually present much of a problem, but there are certain types of people where some difficulties may be anticipated. Among these are the disabled or the physically handicapped, because in such cases there may be drawbacks on the part of both the group and the individual. There is an unfortunate tendency for physically normal people to have an aversion from anyone who shows outward signs of abnormality. Among primitive people, for example, those who are deformed are often treated with great harshness, or even put to death, and though in a civilized community we make an effort to treat such people with kindness and consideration we are not always as successful as we would like to be in concealing our distaste for, say, the sight of a man with no legs. When such a person is introduced into groups, therefore, there may be an increased difficulty in his assimilation because, however hard the other members may try, they may not entirely overcome their dislike of his abnormality; or what may be even worse, they may overdo their efforts to be kind and considerate to him and after making a quite disproportionate fuss in the early stages end up by being bored and irritated with him and with themselves.

On the other hand, however, the unfortunate individual who is disabled or handicapped may find it very difficult to adjust to his own limitations. It is not pleasant to feel oneself different from others and it is hard to avoid feeling sorry for oneself and resentful toward others because they do not suffer in the same way. This may result either in the handicapped individual demanding an undue amount of consideration from those among whom he lives or in his swinging to the other extreme—trying to show that he is just as tough and able as the next man and brusquely refusing reasonable offers of help and consideration. In addition, therefore, to the difficulties of assimilation on the part of the group there may be a lowered level of acceptability on the part of the disabled person which arises from the feelings of uncertainty and inadequacy which his disability has engendered in him.

Very often it is issues like these, rather than the finding of work for which they are physically fitted, which make it difficult to rehabilitate handicapped workers and fit them into industry again. The same problem arose after the war with the returning service man or ex-prisoner-of-war, who, though he was perfectly fit and healthy, yet found that his long absence and separation from civilian life made it difficult to settle down to a peace-time job again. Very great demands are thus made on the tact and sympathy of the supervisor and on his understanding of the situation when handicapped people join a working group.

*The Neurotic*

But there is one type of disabled person who presents a particularly acute problem because the very nature of his disability implies a difficulty in adjusting to other people. This is the neurotic, and an alarmingly large percentage of such people are said to exist in the modern world. Some account of the commoner emotional difficulties was given in Chapter VIII. Some people suffer from these and similar Adjustment handicaps to such an extent that they cannot build up stable and workable relationships with others, though they are in no way dangerous to themselves or their fellows, and no question arises of their being put into special institutions. People with very low intelligence (mental defectives), though not necessarily neurotic, raise similar problems.

In absorbing this type of person into industry it is necessary in the first place to realize that we are dealing with individuals whose level of acceptability is usually very low. Consequently it will only be possible for them to fit into groups in which the capacity for assimilation is very high. In practice this will mean that the supervision must be particularly sympathetic and the other members of the group capable of making allowances to a more-than-average degree. The kind of strain to which they will be subjected will not simply be that of having a "difficult" person among them, but rather one who may go out of his way to make fantastic allegations that other people are discriminating against him or even plotting to injure him. Not many people can continue to be sympathetic and reassuring in the face of this kind of thing and often the unfortunate neurotic has to take himself and his pitiful delusions back to the Employment Exchange in the hope that the Disablement Rehabilitation Officer's patience is more durable than that of his former colleagues.

It is for consideration whether the rehabilitation of neurotics in industry is not a problem where only a low level of success can reasonably be expected and whether special arrangements ought not to be considered for the more intractable cases. During the war, for example, it was found that men of very limited intelligence who had found their way into the army were making very little of it. They found it impossible to pick up the normal basic training of a soldier, they found difficulty in keeping themselves or their equipment in a satisfactory state—in fact the situation was quite beyond them. The people round about them, who were probably none too secure themselves, tended to make fun of them more or less unkindly, while the N.C.O.s showed no more patience than could be expected under war conditions.

Faced with such an intolerable situation there was a grave temptation to escape from it by going absent, thus adding a serious military crime to their already substantial list of minor offences. They found the conditions in the detention barracks even more intolerable than normal soldiering, as indeed they are designed to be, and thus a vicious circle of inability to cope with the situation, crime, punishment, and an increased inability to cope was set up. Such men were of no use either to the army or to themselves. They were bad soldiers, they were miserably unhappy, and under the existing conditions there was little or no hope of improvement.

Under the general direction of Sir Ronald Adam, the then Adjutant General, these men of limited intelligence were put into special companies, known as Unarmed Pioneer Companies. They were not required to complete the normal military training such as learning to handle weapons, and they were employed only on the simple tasks which were well within their limited capacity. They were commanded by specially selected officers and N.C.O.s and they were given welfare services on a scale rather above that of normal units. This last measure proved advisable because in many cases their home affairs were in a very unhappy and confused state.

Once these companies were formed the change was dramatic. Crime dropped and morale improved. The "King's hard bargains" began to take a pride in themselves and in their units, the difference being at once noticeable in their improved appearance and in the way they carried out their duties. In other words, having been placed in a situation which had been arranged to take some account of their limitations they were able to achieve a satisfactory adjustment to it. When the war ended and they returned to civil life, unfortunately, they found the adjustment to normal employment beyond them, and in many cases they slipped back into casual short-term jobs with the same wretched pattern as before.

### THE STUDY OF ATTITUDES

If the attitudes within a working group are so important, can anything be done to find out something about them? This is a problem which has occupied attention for some years and there are various methods available which can estimate more or less accurately what groups of people are thinking about certain things. The simplest of these is the opinion poll in which the whole group, or a large enough number to form a representative sample, are asked a series of standard questions by an interviewer. The published results of these polls which appear round about election times are probably familiar, but they can be, and are being, used to find out people's attitudes to a great many other things. The method is essentially simple, depending mainly on two things—

1. The sample must be large enough to be representative and it must include all the different categories of people in the group in the proper proportions. For example, if opinions on vivisection were being sought it would be unwise to invite people to come forward voluntarily to give their views, as this would almost certainly result in all those who felt strongly that vivisection was a bad thing accepting the invitation and thus overloading the sample with anti-vivisectionists. It is necessary to include men and women, older and younger,

better-off and poorer people in similar proportions to the numbers in the total group to be studied.

2. The questions must be devised so that they elicit an unbiased and honest reply. For example, if we say to a number of people "I suppose you go to Church fairly regularly?" many people would say "yes" whose attendance could only by the wildest stretch of imagination be called regular. A more reliable result would probably be gained by asking what the individual did last Sunday and perhaps the Sunday before. There is also the question of bias in the interviewer who may interpret the replies unconsciously in a manner which suits his own preconceptions. A great deal of experience has been gathered on these matters, however, and any reputable organization can avoid most of the pitfalls and produce very reliable results.

But while polling and questionnaire methods properly applied will provide an indication of people's attitudes to a few simple issues, there may be times when a more detailed survey is required. In such cases the non-directed interview may be used and a representative sample of the group interviewed at greater length. Interviews like this are permitted to take their own course, the interviewer simply encouraging the other person to talk while noting what he says and occasionally referring it back to him in the shape of a summary—"You feel that in this company too much attention is paid to so-and-so." Occasionally specific topics are raised in order to give the person interviewed an opportunity to say what he thinks about them, but for most of the time the interviewer is more interested in seeing what he talks about and what attitudes he displays on those subjects.

The results will be that at the end of, say, a hundred interviews, the position will be like this—

90 per cent of people have mentioned the canteen;

85 per cent of whom have shown a negative or disparaging attitude towards it.

70 per cent of those have tended to go on to say "Well, what do you expect? In this firm they're only interested in production. We don't count as individuals."

80 per cent of people have mentioned the supervisory and management staff in disparaging terms;

60 per cent of whom have said they don't know their job and have been promoted only by influence;

50 per cent of whom have said they never see the boss in person.

5 per cent of people only have mentioned the firm's products, none of whom have shown any pride in them.
 etc.

From such a result it will be apparent that the state of morale in that particular company is not very high. Moreover, there are indications of what is wrong—lack of any feeling of identification with the company or its products, poor communications within the firm, failure of supervisors to take their proper role in the primary groups, and so on.

The surveying of attitudes by non-directed interviews is a delicate matter and it requires considerable training and experience to interpret the results. The matter is complicated by the fact that in many cases people complain about inessentials, which can be shown quite convincingly to be perfectly satisfactory, thus making it appear that the actual complaints are frivolous. Such complaints, however, usually mask something much deeper and more significant, about which the person interviewed is unwilling to talk directly.

*Interpreting the Results of Attitude Surveys*

In this field of study it is not difficult to provide oneself with material. Anyone can put together a questionnaire or conduct a few interviews. What is difficult and delicate, however, is to be sure that the material collected is significant and reliable and that it has been properly interpreted. This requires a great deal of training and experience.

Complaints, for example, which can be shown to have no basis in fact, may in the hands of an experienced person be found to be symptomatic of unsatisfactory general attitudes to the company. Patient investigation, moreover, may show how these attitudes have arisen and what are their real causes. It is not unknown for a series of irrational grouses about the canteen food to lead to the discovery that the relationships centring round one badly adjusted supervisor were thoroughly unsatisfactory.

When a survey shows that the attitudes within a company

are unsatisfactory, can anything be done about it? In the short term probably very little can be done, for if a worker has come to feel after many years that he is being exploited it is useless to prove to him with a mass of figures that he is not. Specific difficulties or complaints can be dealt with at once, but lack of satisfaction in work or lack of any sense of identification with the company can only be tackled in the long term.

So many things can go wrong with workers' attitudes in modern large-scale industry. Many processes are so subdivided that the individual's job has little meaning for its own sake and the individual has no sense of doing anything useful. Gaps in the supervisory levels, such as were described in the previous chapter, interfere with the development of a sense of identification and community of purpose within the firm. Poor relationships within the primary group play their part, while over all broods the legacy from the last century when industrial relations and conditions were very unsatisfactory indeed and when unregulated exploitation of the workers' inferior bargaining power was far from uncommon.

A great deal can be done by improved induction training designed to show the new entrant what the firm does, how it works, and where he fits in. In the same way modern advertising and propaganda methods can do a great deal to inform the workers about current developments and their importance. Formal joint consultation also has a contribution to make in providing opportunities for workers to give their views through their representatives on matters of general concern.

There is, however, a danger that these methods may fail in their effect because they are artificially superimposed on an unsatisfactory structure and do not become an integral part of it. Good relationships start in the face-to-face groups of which a company is made up, and the major part of the information on which its happy and effective working depends must pass up and down its normal communications network. If either of these is unsatisfactory there is a danger that the situation may be made worse, not better, by substituting new networks of communication which may short-circuit the old, and new group relationships which may emphasize the unsatisfactoriness of the others.

## SUMMARY

1. Is there anything notable about the ways of thought within an established group?

In addition to specialist terms and processes, an established group will have its own values and ways of looking at things. These last may be termed "attitudes." In many cases they are implicitly accepted rather than expressed in definite terms, having grown up unnoticed and irrationally.

2. How do these attitudes affect entry into the group?

Until a newcomer is seen to be versed in the group attitudes, and until he gives evidence of sharing and accepting them, he will not be fully assimilated into the group. Groups where the attitudes are very rigid and irrational will have great difficulty in assimilating newcomers. Individuals, on the other hand, who are set in their own attitudes and insensitive to those of others will have difficulty in being accepted by new groups.

3. Are there any particular difficulties in the assimilation of handicapped individuals?

There is an unfortunate tendency for the normal person to dislike any form of abnormality. This may be expressed in a horror of the handicapped individual or in its opposite, an over-effusive attempt to overlook his disability. The handicapped individual, on the other hand, may be tempted by his difficulties into self-pity, or its opposite, an irrational attempt to do without help and to disregard his handicap. All of this will make it specially difficult to assimilate the handicapped person into a normal group. These difficulties are particularly acute in the case of neurotics.

4. How can attitudes be studied?

Polling methods, which involve asking a representative sample specific questions, will reveal the attitudes of a group to specific questions. Non-directed interviews may be used to investigate a wider range of attitudes. These latter will reveal a great deal that is irrational, and experience is needed to sort out what is significant and relevant. The interpretation of what is revealed by attitude studies is a matter of some delicacy.

5. What can be done to replace unsatisfactory attitudes by more positive ones?

Owing to the fact that attitudes are implicitly accepted rather than openly expressed, and that they are often irrational rather than based upon adequate information, not a great deal can be done to change them in the short term. Induction training and propaganda have some effect, but to build up a real sense of identification with a company there is no substitute for good communications and good relationships in the small face-to-face groups of which it is composed.

CHAPTER XXVII

# The Hawthorne Investigations

BETWEEN the years 1924 and 1932 a number of studies were carried out at one of the Western Electric Company's factories in the town of Hawthorne, near Chicago. These have come to be known as the Hawthorne Investigations; they have been very fully written up and are full of valuable information on the social psychology of industrial work. They are in fact a series of situations designed so as to bring under control all the known factors which might affect performance at work. Their main value lies in showing that the most important factor in each case was the unknown one which escaped control.

The investigations started with a study of lighting. It was known that better lighting had a beneficial effect on output, but there were some doubts as to what was the best level of illumination for particular kinds of work. To find out about this, "experiments" were made in which two parallel groups on the same kind of work were observed, one being kept under standard conditions of lighting while the other was subjected to variations. For a while all went according to expectations, the group in which the lighting was increased improving its output with each change in the lamps. But soon a few unexpected results came to light. The "control group" in which the lighting was kept standard and whose output was expected to remain constant, showed a tendency to increase its output also. This threw very considerable doubts on the whole procedure and these were more than confirmed when the lighting in the experimental group was decreased, with the result that output still went up. There followed a period in which lamps were changed more or less at random, being sometimes replaced with those of higher power, sometimes with those of lower power, and sometimes with those of exactly the same power. The trend in output showed no relation at all to the changes in illumination, except for a tendency to increase with each change in both the experimental and control groups. At one stage two operatives worked with an illumination intensity of 0·06 foot-candles, which is about the same as ordinary moonlight. There was no fall in their output.

It was quite obvious by this time that the "experimental" procedure was inadequate to the situation. It had been assumed that all the other conditions at work had remained standard while the level of illumination alone had been varied, but as no correspondence had been found between changes in the lighting and changes in output it seemed the obvious thing to bring all aspects of the work-situation more closely under control, to introduce changes one at a time and to try to find out more about the effect of these changes as they occurred. Consequently the best known of the Hawthorne Investigations was initiated—the Relay Assembly Test Room. This ran from April, 1927, until the summer of 1932—more than five years.

## THE RELAY ASSEMBLY TEST ROOM

Five young women were segregated into a separate room divided off from the production department by a high wooden partition. They were looked after by a service-hand who brought the materials and took away the finished work, and they were supervised by an observer who undertook to record what happened, maintain a friendly atmosphere, and exercise a general oversight. This observer was in fact a social scientist who had been mainly responsible for initiating and planning all these experimental studies. The work they were engaged on was that of assembling telephone relay units, which involves putting together a number of small components on a jig and fastening them with four screws. It was essentially a routine repetitive job of short cycle, that is to say each unit took about one minute to complete. A recording device was fixed up beside each operator so that when she dropped the finished relay through a chute in the bench a mark was made on a tape moving at a constant speed. Job, bench and working methods were the same as in the larger department from which the girls, who were all experienced operators, had originally been drawn.

The investigation started with the obtaining of records of performance of the five girls while they were in the ordinary department. This was done without their knowledge and served to provide a kind of base-line on which future performance could be evaluated. They then moved into the test room where they spent five weeks working under the same conditions of hours and rest pauses as in the ordinary department. The first change that was made was to form the five operators and the service-hand into a single group for the purpose of calculating piece-work. This was apparently more of an administrative change than an experimental one, for the whole department had hitherto been considered as one group for piece-work purposes, whereas it seemed more convenient to pay these six on the basis of their group output. The result, however, was to step up output which had already been showing signs of increasing ever since the girls had come together in the test room.

Then followed periods when rest pauses of various lengths were introduced. Details of these will be found in the accompanying table, along with notes on the changes in the level of output. They were eventually standardized at fifteen minutes in the morning and ten minutes in the afternoon, a snack being provided by the company (period VII). About this time an event happened which has received scant notice in most of the books written about the Hawthorne Investigations. Two of the operators who were not co-operating, who adopted rather an unsatisfactory attitude to the programme and who were failing to fit into the group, were returned to the ordinary department and replaced by two who were more satisfactory from these points of view. These remained until the end of the investigations.

The next few changes were concerned with shortening the total hours worked either by stopping earlier in the afternoon or by not coming in on Saturday morning. These were accompanied by further increases in production either in the total output for the week or in the hourly rate. Leaving aside the changing of two operators, therefore, the picture presented by this segregated group up to the present had been one of changes in hours and rest pauses, each accompanied by a rise in the level of output. Now, to find out whether these changes had been responsible for the increases, it was proposed to go back to the original conditions, cutting out the rest pauses and

## Relay Assembly Test Room

### Summary of Experimental Conditions and Output Changes
(from Urwick and Brech, *The Hawthorne Investigations*, pp. 35–7)

| Period No. | Date and Duration | Conditions and Special Features | Hours | Pauses | Output |
|---|---|---|---|---|---|
| I. | March–April, 1927 (Two weeks) | In ordinary department. Standard conditions | 48 | — | (Recorded individually without operators' knowledge, to give a base: 2400 per week) |
| II. | April–May, 1927 (Five weeks) | Transfer to Test Room. Standard conditions | 48 | — | (Period of adjustment to new conditions). Output rising |
| III. | June–August, 1927 (Eight weeks) | Group piece-work scheme for the Test Room alone (i.e. Group of 5 instead of 100) | 48 | — | Definitely increasing |
| IV. | August–September, 1927 (Five weeks) | Two 5-minute rest pauses. Overall hours unchanged | 47·05 | 2 × 5 min | Level |
| V. | September–October, 1927 (Four weeks) | Two 10-minute rest pauses. Overall hours unchanged | 46·10 | 2 × 10 min | Sharply up; bigger rise than in any period so far |
| VI. | October–November, 1927 (Four weeks) | Six 5-minute rest pauses. Overall hours unchanged | 45·15 | 6 × 5 min | Slight falling off. Girls complained of the "interruptions" |
| VII. | November, 1927–January, 1928, (Eleven weeks) | Two rest pauses; 15 min a.m. and lunch given by the company; 10 min p.m. | 45·40 | a.m. 15 min<br>p.m. 10 min | Output back to high level of V |

| | | | | |
|---|---|---|---|---|
| VIII. | January–March, 1928 (Seven weeks) | Stop work at 4.30 p.m. | 43·10 | ,, | Both sharply up |
| IX. | March–April, 1928 (Four weeks) | Stop work at 4 p.m. | 40·40 | ,, | Average hourly rose. Daily and weekly total fell slightly |
| X. | April–June, 1928 (Twelve weeks) | Back to 5 p.m. stop, i.e. same as in VII | 45·40 | ,, | Average hourly down. Daily and weekly up to highest level yet |
| XI. | July–September, 1928 (Nine weeks) | Saturday morning off | 41·40 | ,, | Unchanged from X except for slight recession in weekly total, but this still higher than any period except VIII and X |
| XII. | September–November, 1928 (Twelve weeks) | All previous changes withdrawn and return to conditions of period III, i.e. ordinary standard, but retain own group piece-scheme | 48 | Nil. | Hourly slightly down. Daily and weekly up to record high level (3000 per week) |
| XIII. | November, 1928–June, 1929. (Thirty-one weeks) | Back to conditions as in period VII but Company supplied coffee only (i.e. own food) | 45·40 | a.m. 15 min<br>p.m. 10 min | Increase to new high record (above XII) |
| XIV–XXIII. | June, 1929–July, 1932 | Continuing as for XIII | 45·40 | ,, | (Not relevant in present context) |

N.B. Period VII became virtually a standard of conditions for the rest of the experiment.

refreshments and lengthening the hours to the original standard. If the output dropped to its former level then it would be obvious that the increase has been due to the changes.

This was accordingly done. All previous changes were withdrawn (period XII) and the records were watched for the expected drop in output. It did not happen. Daily and weekly totals hit a new high level, while a very small recession in the hourly rate was not considered to be of any importance. It could confidently be asserted that output in this segregated group had increased and was increasing quite independently of hours and rest pauses. The factor associated with the increase had eluded the recording methods once again.

### OTHER TEST GROUPS

There was, however, one change which might have accounted for the improvement in output—that of the alteration in the method of calculating the piece-work payments. As has been pointed out above, this was a mere administrative convenience, by which the six operators were dealt with as a separate unit for calculation instead of being included in the figures for the department as a whole. It might, however, have had an effect and this effect could be investigated by setting up—

(*a*) another group which was not physically separated from the main department but which was dealt with as a distinct unit for piece-work purposes; and

(*b*) a group which was physically separate but which was not treated as a distinct unit for piece-work calculations.

To provide data on the first set of conditions the Second Relay Group was set up in which a small number of operatives were taken as a separate unit for piece-work purposes though they still remained within the main department. During the nine weeks they were kept under observation output rose some $12\frac{1}{2}$ per cent, but the other operatives objected to the arrangement and the group had to be disbanded.

The second of these sets of conditions was tested out in the Mica Splitting Test Room where five girls on a fairly skilled job were isolated in a separate room though they were not dealt with as a group for piece-work purposes. The result was a moderate but steady rise in the rate of output for the first few months. Here again, therefore, was an increase in production rates which seemed unrelated to changes in conditions. Whatever kind of test group was set up produced a rise in output no matter whether the light was increased or lowered, the hours and rest pauses were lengthened or shortened, the basis of piece-work calculations was group or individual. Was there any common factor which could account for the increase? All that was apparent was some undefinable "improvement in morale," but the attempts to reduce this to manageable terms were only partially successful.

What had happened, of course, was that manageable primary groups had been set up in which it was possible for good quality face-to-face relationships to be built up. In the Relay Assembly Test Room, for example, a group of six had been segregated. Two of the members did not fit in with the remainder and were replaced by others who formed better relationships. The supervision was taken over by the investigator who was responsible for designing and carrying out the experiment, someone who was interested in the girls as individuals, who discussed the changes with them and who encouraged the building up of a steadily improving relationship throughout this primary working group. The literature contains many references to girls going out together in their spare time, bringing cakes for birthday parties, and the like. It was quite obvious that a pattern of good quality relationships grew up over the period of the experiment, suited to the task in hand, permeating the immediate social environment of the operators, in which all the parties concerned played the roles demanded of them successfully and with satisfaction to themselves.

Few things could demonstrate the importance of the primary working group and the relationships within it better than the Relay Assembly Test Room. The same point is emphasized also in the other test groups which were set up for one purpose or another. The "experiments," while they mostly failed in their main purpose of showing what factor in the situation was associated with increased output, did provide the conditions where a primary group could exist and develop a workable and satisfactory pattern of relationships. Every time this happened, particularly in the later groups where some trouble was taken to place congenial individuals together, satisfaction increased and output went up.

### THE BANK WIRING OBSERVATION ROOM

Deviating from the strict chronology of the Hawthorne Investigations, to which we shall return in due course, let us turn to the attempt that was made to find out what actually happened in a normal working group. This was in the Bank Wiring Observation Room in which fourteen operators working on the connexions of rather complicated switchboard equipment were placed in a separate room. The internal organization of this group appears officially to have been as follows—

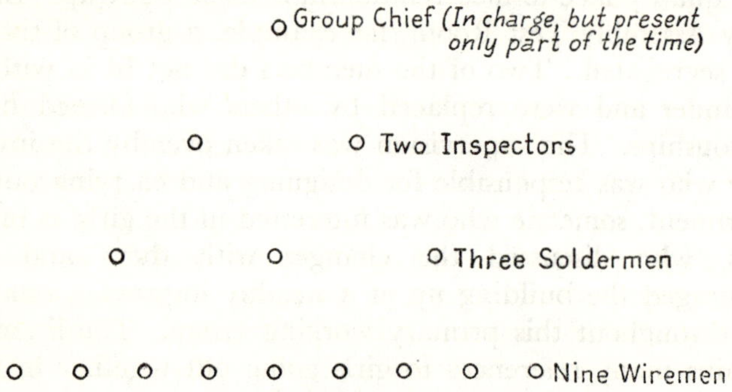

o Group Chief *(In charge, but present only part of the time)*

o      o Two Inspectors

o    o      o Three Soldermen

o o o o o o o o o Nine Wiremen

FIG. 54. THE BANK WIRING OBSERVATION ROOM

It is fairly obvious at first glance that this is rather an unworkable organization. The group was fairly large for a primary group and yet it had no full-time official leader, the group chief having other duties which kept him out of the room at least half the working day. And yet the group could not fall into two or three stable sub-groups because wiremen, soldermen and inspectors appear to have changed around from job to job while the last-named, though they were responsible for the quality of the work, appear to have had no responsibility either for administration or for human relations within the group. Moreover, the inspectors reported to their own functional chief. As one might have expected, the personal relationships within the official pattern were of low quality and the pattern itself was very poorly defined because the individuals did not carry out the roles required of them.

It is interesting to see what the actual situation in the group was in terms of—

(a) the organization of work;
(b) the pattern of significant relationships; and
(c) the relation of it to the official organization.

In the first place, the actual organization of work bore only the vaguest and most distorted resemblance to what it was officially supposed to be. There was organized limitation of output, most individuals turning out significantly less than they could have done, either by wasting time deliberately or by stopping before the appointed hour—it appeared, incidentally, that the most efficient workers wasted most time in order to keep their output down to the group standard. The departmental records were largely meaningless, the men reporting figures of output which bore no relation to the amount they had actually done. Claims for time-rate, which was paid when a stoppage occurred beyond the worker's control, were invented for no reason or lengthened when they actually occurred. The quality of output as checked by the inspectors varied for no apparent reason, some men being charged with more rejects by one inspector and less by another. In respect, therefore, of output, records, and quality, the "official" appearance of the department was little more than a fiction, the facts in each case being entirely different.

Secondly, the pattern of significant face-to-face relationships hung mainly on the group's unexpressed but very real intention to protect itself against change by keeping output at a standard level. Anyone who showed a tendency to produce more than the unofficial standard was subjected to social pressure until he fell into line. The leadership roles in this self-protective process were held by unofficial members of the group and a whole hierarchy of positions in this unauthorized pattern of relationships was found to exist. It is important to emphasize that these unofficial roles and relationships were the ones that mattered. They formed the immediate social environment of each individual, they were effectively enforced, and they were aimed at maintaining a state of affairs which was to a great extent opposed to the official aim of management.

The third and perhaps the most interesting point is the

relation between the "official" purpose and organization of the group, i.e. its production and remuneration in terms which the management of the company would recognize, and its unofficial but more significant and effective organization. Obviously there was a conflict between the two, but for the section to continue in existence some working compromise had to be found. This compromise was found in the role of the immediate supervisor. He had little or no place in the unofficial pattern of relationships within the group, certainly not a leadership role. He was aware of much that went on which was contrary to the established procedures but made no attempt to interfere and at times explained away shortcomings to his own superiors. So long as the standard day's work was forthcoming, even though this standard was lower than it need be, he appeared satisfied, and closed his eyes to other things. He thus personified a compromise whereby certain of the aims of management were satisfied and certain of the group's own unofficial purposes were carried out. Neither side got as much as it wanted for the two aims were not reconciled.

### THE INTERVIEW PROGRAMME

Along with the various test rooms which have been described, one attempt was made to find out more directly how a large number of workers thought and felt. This was the interview programme, which was initiated as soon as the Relay Assembly Test Room had made it clear that hours, rest pauses, lighting, and the like were much less important than the more intangible things like attitudes and relationships. It had not escaped notice that the different quality of supervision in the Test Room had made an important difference, and it was decided that an attempt should be made to find out something about workers' attitudes to the company and the people in charge of them, in the hope that the material thus obtained would be useful in training supervisors.

With this in mind a number of workers were interviewed by staff appointed and trained for the task. In the early stages they sought to find out what employees thought about certain topics, but as the programme developed the interview method became more informal and employees were encouraged to talk about whatever they thought important, while the interviewer listened sympathetically and took notes. Between 1928 and 1930 over 20,000 employees were interviewed for periods lasting from thirty minutes to an hour and a half.

The results were certainly effective in providing material for supervisor training. Added to the Test Room findings it quickly became apparent that the former conception of the supervisor's role as someone who told others what to do, and told them off if they didn't do it, was entirely inadequate. By listening sympathetically the interviewers were able quickly to build up a relationship with employees which inspired confidence and elicited co-operation to something like the degree that had been seen in the Test Room, and which it was now believed had contributed so much to the changed atmosphere there. All this pointed forward to a new role for the supervisor and though the full implications were not realized at the time, certain changes in the methods of supervisor training were made.

In other ways also, the results were illuminating. It soon became obvious that comments were in many cases unrelated to facts. In certain cases the employment conditions were adversely criticized when it could be demonstrated quite objectively that they were well above the average for the district. In other cases it was shown that the things employees considered important were not those which made the greatest material difference to them. The quality of supervision, for example, seemed to matter to most people quite as much as wages. Furthermore, it was apparent that many comments were coloured by matters outside the factory or by the employee's own state of health. The irrational element in employee attitudes forced itself more and more on the attention of the research workers until eventually it was recognized that what a worker felt about a particular topic was just as important as the facts about that topic, and that even though his view might be completely unjustified and mistaken it had to be taken seriously if a true appreciation of the human situation at work was to be gained.

The interview programme made it finally clear that the intangibles were more important than the actual conditions of work. Even though Western Electric were among the most enlightened employers in America—they would not have carried out such a programme if they had not been—it is fair to say that the interviewers uncovered a dismaying amount of dissatisfaction and frustration, much of it stored up for a long time and all of it capable of dissipation as soon as the employee had a chance of establishing good quality relationships with someone on the company's higher staff. It was perhaps unfortunate that that person had to be an interviewer with pencil and notebook who had been trained to draw him out and whose contact with him was shorter in term and more artificial in nature than that of his immediate supervisor. But this was due to a number of causes, most of which grew out of the mistaken idea that the economic relationships and the physical conditions at work were more important than the individual's attitudes and the immediate social relationships in the primary group wherein he passed his working hours.

## THE SIGNIFICANCE OF HAWTHORNE

The first series of investigations at Hawthorne petered out when the depression of the 1930's hit American industry. Two projects appear still to have been running—the Relay Assembly Test Room and the Mica Splitting Room. In both, the operators were aware of the looming danger of unemployment which indeed formed the background to the thoughts of most workers in those days. One might have thought that in these conditions the rational self-interest of workers would have encouraged them to work as hard as possible in the hope of being kept on or at least of making as much in piece-work as was possible while the job lasted.

Nothing of the sort happened. Output rates dwindled and earnings fell with them probably because the general attitude was that in the face of such an overriding anxiety individual effort was unavailing. In spite of the high team-spirit which had been built up in these primary groups the blow to their morale was too severe and their sense of purpose fell away with the rest of the economy. How far such a reaction spread and multiplied itself during those years must remain a matter for speculation.

No other series of investigations can compare with those carried out at Hawthorne in scope and depth. To them and to the writings of the late Professor Elton Mayo we owe much of our present understanding of the social psychology of work. This is not to say that the lessons of the Hawthorne studies were properly appreciated at the time, and indeed it is doubtful whether we have yet learnt all that we might do from the very full publications which have resulted from them.

Probably the first and most important lesson to be drawn is the supreme importance of the primary working group. It seems likely that the consistent improvements in production which were seen in almost all of the test groups were due to the opportunities thus provided for better integrations to take place within these groups. It is also probable that the astonishing improvements in production and morale which were seen in the Relay Assembly Test Room were due to the fact that, with the replacement of the two girls who didn't fit and the higher grade of supervision, a primary group in which the relationships were of very high quality and in which each member accepted his or her role wholeheartedly was set up.

The second lesson is probably that in the remainder of the company the relationships within the primary groups were unbelievably poor. The Bank Wiring Observation Room was quite probably typical of most departments in that the significant unofficial organization and purpose of the group bore no relationship whatsoever to the official organization and purpose.

The third lesson derives from this but was brought to light in the interview programme which showed that even in this socially responsible company the attitudes of many individuals showed little evidence of satisfaction in their work or identification with the organization. Lacking satisfactory relationships or any sense of common achievement in the course of their day-to-day work these individuals were apparently left in an emotional void during this significant aspect of their lives.

Finally it is obvious that the point to which attention should be directed is the supervisor of the primary working group. Given the right personal qualities and an adequate training in social skill, he can do something towards improving the situation within the primary group, always provided that he is given workers capable of adjustment to the situation. He can also do something towards keeping the group in touch with the rest of the organization provided he takes his proper place in the general network of communications.

## SUMMARY

1. How did the Hawthorne Investigations start?

In 1924 a series of studies on the effect of better lighting on output in the Western Electric Company's works near Chicago showed that production rates tended to rise as lighting was increased. These conclusions, however, were vitiated when it was seen that any apparent change in the lighting tended to result in higher output, even when the changes continued until lighting was reduced to very low levels. It became apparent that some factor other than lighting must be responsible for the improved output.

2. What was the significance of the Relay Assembly Test Room?

So that the situation could be further controlled and this missing factor brought to light, five girls on a repetitive job were put into a separate department specially arranged for observation. They were subjected to a number of changes in the arrangement of hours and rest pauses, each of which was accompanied by an increase in production rates. When these changes were withdrawn and the situation brought back to what it was originally, during a so-called "control period," production rates increased further still. The missing factor had eluded observation yet again.

3. What was the purpose of the Second Relay Assembly Test Group and the Mica Splitting Test Room?

In the first Relay Assembly Test Room the operators had been formed into a separate group for the purpose of calculating piece-work earnings. This was mainly a matter of administrative convenience, but to find out whether it had had any effect on the results two additional groups were set up. One, the Second Relay Assembly Test Group, was formed into a separate group for piece-work calculations but remained in the main department; the other, the Mica Splitting Test Room, remained as it was for piece-work calculation, but was placed in a separate room. In both cases improvements in production rates were noted, though the period over which observations were carried out was too short to be significant.

4. What was the purpose of the Bank Wiring Observation Room?

In order to gain a closer view of the actual situation within a working group an observer was introduced into this room to study the day-to-day relationships at work. He found that—

(*a*) the organization of work and the official records bore little or no relation to what actually went on;

(*b*) the significant relationships within the working group were quite unofficial; and

(*c*) there was a rather artificial compromise between what was supposed to happen and what actually happened, centring in the person of the supervisor.

5. What was the Interview Programme?

When the information from the various test rooms was studied it was decided that the company should try to find out more about what its employees thought and how they felt by interviewing a large number of them. It was thought also that the results would be useful in supervisor training. Over 20,000 interviews were carried out between 1928 and 1930 which disclosed that many of the employees, however irrationally, held very unfortunate attitudes to their work and the company.

6. What is the general significance of the Hawthorne experiments?

In the first place they drew attention to the importance of the primary group at work and the effect of the relationships within it on the individual worker and on production. Secondly, they suggested that the situation in a representative primary group was very unsatisfactory. Thirdly, they showed that many individuals were deriving little or no emotional satisfaction from their work or the relationships it involved. And finally they underlined the importance of the immediate supervisor both in his effect on the relationships within the group and on the communications between that group and the rest of the organization.

CHAPTER XXVIII

# The Object of the Exercise

THE justification for writing a book such as this is the possibility that it may give organizations some insight into the human problems with which they may be faced, and thus help to overcome them. For these are the problems which are going to require more and more time and attention. This is partly because, with full employment, increasing affluence, and a more egalitarian attitude now accepted as our normal way of life, authoritarian management backed up by the fear of the sack is as out of date as the feudal system. It is also partly due to the fact that human problems cannot be solved by the methods which have proved so successful in the physical sciences. In these it is possible to generalize with the assurance that once a principle has been established by rigid experimentation, it will apply universally. In the social or behavioural sciences, however, few generalizations are possible. They are concerned with human beings, who will always insist on remaining unique individuals, and who, whatever situation they may find themselves in, will still retain some freedom of choice and action.

Human problems at work will always vary according to the individuals concerned; the purpose of the organization in which they are employed; its technology; its structure; the current employment and trading situation; and many other factors. Large-scale generalizations will always be suspect, and no sensible person would expect a simple book of rules or a list of "do's and don'ts," that will settle any problem with which he may be confronted. All that Psychology or any other behavioural science can do is to study the underlying cause-and-effect processes that may be at work in a situation. Insight into these processes may make it possible to influence them in the desired direction.

The factors which may underly any particular situation may be considered under a series of headings. None of these can be separated from the others, for there will be a continuous interaction between them. Moreover, depending on the situation, one or other may exert a greater or less influence at any one time. Bearing this in mind, however, we may consider each in turn.

## THE INDIVIDUAL AND THE JOB

From this point of view, the ideal is to place the individual in a job for which he has the requisite personal qualities, which engages his Motivation to a reasonable maximum, and from which he derives the maximum satisfaction. This should always be regarded as an "effort-and-reward" transaction for, in the last resort, the amount of effort the organization gets from the employee is equal to the amount of reward he gets from the job. There is an obvious financial element in this, for everyone expects to be paid for what he does. But the other satisfactions which can be derived from work should always be borne in mind. We must think in terms of a pattern of satisfactions, in which money, a feeling of belonging, and a sense of personal achievement and significance, will all play a part. We must also bear in mind the level of the individual's Motivation.

What form this pattern may take in any individual case is a matter of considerable importance. Some recent studies have suggested that in technologically advanced, productively efficient enterprises, where sophisticated management techniques have taken most of the skill and knowledge out of many jobs, money plays the most important part. The worker feels little or no sense of belonging to the organization (nor, surprisingly enough, to his trade union) and has no feeling of identification with its purpose or its products. He works simply to earn as much money as he can, and looks to his trade union to make a series of increasingly favourable bargains for him in financial terms. These higher earnings go to provide him and his family with a better house, more domestic equipment, and more opportunities for his children.[1] Whether such a conclusion over-simplifies the situation is a matter of opinion, but it has the support of evidence in the form of attitude surveys.

Other patterns of satisfaction can be illustrated in which

[1] *The Affluent Worker*, Goldthorpe *et al.* (Cambridge University Press, 1968).

the sense of personal achievement, of social responsibility, of identification with the purpose of the organization, or even of dedication to a "cause," play a larger part. It is always dangerous, however, to close one's eyes to the part played by money in the effort-and-reward transaction. Certain "professions" which have been accepted as having a recognized social status, have been in trouble recently because their practitioners feel that their earnings are unjustifiably low. In the case of teachers, for example, this has manifested itself in strikes, demonstrations and other activities which were not in accord with the "image" which that profession had of itself and in terms of which it was regarded by the public. Similar situations can be illustrated among nurses, junior hospital doctors, ambulance drivers and others, all of whom have shown at one time or another that they feel they are relatively underpaid. What has gone wrong is that the pattern of satisfactions has slipped out of balance. Because of the better bargaining advantages enjoyed by workers in jobs where the social status and sense of personal achievement is recognized as being substantially lower, and to the continuing fall in the value of money, people in certain professions now have a sense of being exploited which cancels out much of the other satisfactions they derive from their jobs. If they succeed in improving their earnings, the pattern of satisfactions will change and may possibly settle down on a more stable balance—at least for a while.

This aspect of the effort-and-reward transaction depends largely on the individual finding himself in the right sort of work-situation. We have discussed methods of selection at some length and have put an end, we hope, to the "square peg and round hole" type of approach. Employment in industry is never static in the sense that the worker starts in a job when he leaves school and carries on for the next fifty years until he reaches the age of retirement. Products are constantly changing and with them production processes, plant, equipment and raw materials. If anything is being done in the same way five years from now, it will very probably be out of date. Constant re-training and re-development will demand continual re-appraisal and re-assessment of personnel. Well-motivated individuals will seek greater scope and advancement, and if they see no opportunities with their present employers, they will soon move elsewhere.

A dynamic situation like this presents many opportunities for the movement of individuals into work-situations in which the effort-and-reward transaction can balance out at a high level—that is to say, where those who are well Motivated and well Adjusted find themselves presented with an increasing range of opportunities for making the most of their potentialities. There is also the possibility, however, that those whose assessment on the Five-Fold Framework is less impressive may find themselves more and more at the mercy of these changing circumstances. From the point of view both of the individual and the organization, therefore, it will be essential for the latter to take control of the situation. People should no longer drift in and out of jobs in the haphazard manner characteristic of the past. Every appointment or promotion should now become a responsible decision based on a careful matching of the assessment of the individual and the specification for the job.

## THE STRUCTURE OF THE ORGANIZATION

One factor which makes a job satisfying or frustrating to the individual is the quality of relationships among the people with whom he spends several hours of the day. Over and above this, however, there are the commonly-accepted standards and attitudes which make up the way of life on the factory floor. Some studies have shown how these vary from one organization to another, and how widely they can diverge from the formal structure.[1] "Industrial Sociology" has come into being as a subject on its own, its aim being to study different factory-floor situations in the hope of understanding how they came into being and how they affect the working of the organization. Generally speaking, these studies have tended to reveal a very wide gap between what actually takes place on the floor of the shop and what management thinks is happening there. It may be nearly fifty years since the Hawthorne Studies were first initiated, but a great deal of the recent work has thrown up a picture very similar to that of the Bank Wiring Observation Room.

From our point of view, the key to the situation lies in the

[1] *On the Shop Floor,* T. Lupton (Pergamon, 1963).

individual's need to be accepted and to feel that he belongs among other people. No group will give him this feeling unless he conforms to its way of life, so that there will be considerable pressure to share the common attitudes and to work to its accepted standards. The average person's level of Adjustment makes him very susceptible to these pressures so that, as was pointed out earlier, he is likely to become "one of the boys." But what concerns us is which kind of group does he become one of the boys in?

Ideally this should be a primary group which is recognized and integrated into the formal structure of the organization. It would then be possible for him to satisfy his need to belong and to feel significant by identifying himself with the purpose of the group, which would be linked up with the overall objective of the organization. This ideal, unfortunately, is seldom realized in practice, and what actually happens is some kind of under-the-counter compromise between what management wants and what the unofficial organization will stand for. Such compromises can be recognized to any experienced supervisor, for he is usually the person around whom they centre. Quite obviously they represent a somewhat delicate situation, which can easily be upset by ill-considered moves on either side.

### THE EFFECTS OF TECHNOLOGY AND SUPERVISION

A series of studies aimed at finding out how the technology of the production process affects the structure of the organization has a certain relevance here.[1] Their original conclusions were that in flow production where jobs had been de-skilled, laid out by production engineers who had little or no insight into their human aspects, with standards of performance set by work-study specialists, there was evidence of maximum frustration and dissatisfaction. These were contrasted with one-off jobs which gave the worker some opportunity to put his skill into practice, to make some decisions on his own, and to obtain some sense of personal achievement during working hours, and with technician jobs in charge of automated processes which called into play some degree of theoretical knowledge.

[1] *Industrial Organization, Theory and Practice,* Joan Woodward (Oxford University Press, 1965).

Such a conclusion would fit in with what has been said above, for the effort-and-reward transaction in the de-skilled, repetitive jobs, while it might balance out at a high level in terms of money, would be at its lowest in terms of the other satisfactions. Skilled craftsmen or technicians, on the other hand, would find their work more satisfying from these other points of view.

It is not by any means certain, however, that the effects of technology can be separated out as the factor which exerts a dominating influence in the work-situation. It can be offset by the quality of the supervision, for the person immediately in charge of any work-situation will always play an important part. He is, or he should be, the one on whom the day-to-day relationships centre, and he can influence the quality of these relationships to a greater degree than anyone else. If he has too many people under his charge, of course, this influence will be diluted to the point of ineffectiveness, which brings us back to the structure of the organization. But if he is the central figure in a primary group, and if he has the right personal qualities, his influence should be considerable.

It may be objected that to have a full-time supervisor in charge of every ten operators would represent an unjustifiable increase in overhead expense. There are, however, many production jobs which involve central roles in primary groups, such as tool-setters, relief hands and the like. These have been described as "Semi-Supervisory Jobs," and they can be the key jobs from this point of view.[1] The semi-supervisor can be accepted as a member of the primary group, he can play the central role in it and exert an influence on the relationships among the members. At the same time he can be a member of the next group above, thus linking the primary group into the total organization. A major problem, however, is to select and train enough people to cope adequately with these extremely demanding roles.

### THE PLACE OF THE TRADE UNIONS

Industrial development began at a time when the "laissez-faire" philosophy was widely accepted in Great Britain. The belief was shared among those who had most influence in public

[1] Keith Thurley, **London School** of Economics.

affairs that if everyone were left free to pursue his own advantage with the minimum of interference, then the "greatest good for the greatest number" would be achieved. This outlook led to two results which can be considered separately, though in fact they interacted. On the one hand we went through a period of economic advance the like of which had never before been possible. Well-motivated entrepreneurs started businesses and made large profits which supplied that capital to start further enterprises and which helped to finance the technological developments which brought further industries into being. The rate of economic growth thoughout the 19th century changed the way of life substantially and made possible a standard of material living which up till then would have been inconceivable.

The other result was rather less attractive. Movements of population from the agricultural villages uprooted large numbers of people from a way of life in which they had some degree of security and certain established rights. In the new industrial towns, however, they were entirely dependent on their employers, as the public provision for sickness or unemployment was kept at an intentionally low and degrading level. Consequently the benefits of this economic advance were very unevenly shared. The recently-emerged middle classes, from which most of the iniatitive had come, did very well for themselves. The new industrial "proletariat" came off relatively badly for several reasons. Not only did the limited public welfare services make them dependent on their employers; the rudimentary legislation which governed the conditions under which they could be employed, permitted or even encouraged slum factories in which women and young children worked long hours among dangerous machinery under supervision which was not only unsympathetic but at times actually brutal. The "Dark Satanic Mills" were not a matter of legend but a very sad reality a century or so ago.

A progressive series of efforts were initiated to tidy up the mess, and to make of the industrial community something in which the rising standard of living could be more widely shared, and where the risk of damage to the employees' health and self-respect could be substantially reduced. Legislation in the form of Factory Acts played a part in this, as did a realization by employers that healthy and satisfied employees were more efficient than the near-slave labour of earlier times. A further part was played by trade unions which, after a long struggle to establish themselves, emerged as a means whereby workers could bargain collectively and thus represent their interests on approximately level terms with their employers. Trade union history is a long and somewhat depressing story which is not particularly relevant to our theme, but the current situation must be understood.

In the latter part of 1969 the then Secretary to the Department of Employment and Productivity, Mrs Barbara Castle, pointed out that the workers on the factory floor could now exercise an effective veto on any action with which they did not agree. This was not very well received in some quarters, but it was nevertheless a blinding glimpse into the obvious. When the employees of a company, organized in trade unions, are dissatisfied, they can go on strike and bring its operations to a standstill. Further, when a small proportion carrying out an essential operation in a highly-integrated production process decide to strike, officially or unofficially, they can not only halt the whole process, they can interrupt the activities of other organizations which supply components or which handle the finished products. The obvious example to take here is the car industry. Thus, the bargaining position of employees in a modern, fully-employed democracy is considerably stronger than that of the organizations which employ them.

This is a complex situation and has widespread implications ranging over the advisability of legislation to control the activities of trade unions, the complexity of trade union organization and the multiplicity of unions, the relation of industry-wide negotiation to in-plant bargaining and many other issues. What concerns us, however, is the problem which confronts the individual company.

We must accept as a starting point, that if we are to remain a democracy, employees must have the right to bargain collectively with their employers. We must also accept that some form of trade union organization is the only means by which this right can be made effective in practice. Recognition of this does not, however, justify wildcat strikes or a refusal to implement agreements which have been freely negotiated between representatives of both sides. As things stand at present, the employing organization has no redress against such actions, which in extreme cases could be described as sabotage. Is it possible to envisage a situation where the two sides can negotiate freely over issues where their interests clash, but when once an agreement has been reached, each side can rely on the other to carry out its share of the bargain? Some countries, such as Sweden, seem to have come some way in this direction, and while they have their share of strikes, these are mostly official and form part of the tough bargaining process. Their record of unofficial strikes is much better than ours. It is always a mistake to close one's eyes to conflict in industry, for conflict and competition are essential elements of a democratic society. The problem is to find means of making this conflict and competition constructive rather than destructive.

### THE INDIVIDUAL EMPLOYEE

When we return to the individual employee, the situation may simplify itself. He will be conscious of conflicting interests which might be described on the one hand, as some feeling of identification with the purpose of the organization which employs him, and on the other, as a desire to improve his standard of living by increasing his earnings. In theory, these can be resolved by improving the efficiency of the organization so as to provide a higher trading margin out of which claims for increased earnings can alone be met without the risk of inflation. In practice, however, it involves him in an alternation between two roles, one of these being his role as an employee of the organization, the other as a member of his trade union. He will be conscious of both of these in a vague sort of way most of the time, but at any particular moment, one or the other will enlist the major share of his Motivation. That is to say, if the effort-and-reward transaction balances out at a reasonable level in his role as an employee, he will be willing to discharge it in an adequate fashion. But if this role becomes unduly frustrating in any sense, he will turn to his role as a trade unionist. And the more frustrated he is as an employee, the more militant he will be as a trade unionist, willing to follow any leader who initiates the most extreme anti-management action.

This may seem an over-simplification of a highly complex situation, but it can be illustrated in everyday terms. Some organizations seem to hit the headlines every other week with strikes or walkouts, while others seem to steer clear of such troubles. Closer acquaintance usually reveals that the latter have shown more initiative in making the day-to-day roles of their employees a satisfying experience, by better supervision and more effective communication through the formal structure of their organization. They also anticipate claims for higher earnings and take the initiative in devising plans to meet these by better deployment of their personnel without adding to their overall labour-cost. They are, in fact, using their insights into the social psychology of their organization to exert constructive influence on the cause-and-effect processes which underlie it. The organizations which are continually in trouble remain unaware of these cause-and-effect processes, and in consequence control slips out of their hands into those of the militant shop-stewards.

## CONCLUSION

We suggested in the introductory chapter that in the social or behavioural sciences we are now at a stage comparable with that which the physical sciences had reached some hundreds of years ago. That is to say, we are beginning to glimpse some cause-and-effect processes which, while they may manifest themselves in different ways with different individuals in different circumstances, nevertheless go some way towards explaining why human beings act as they do. These essential processes we have outlined in Part I and they include perception, memory, thinking and other factors which help to determine how the individual interprets the world around him, and how he adds to his knowledge through the learning process. They also include the vital factor of Motivation, or what makes an individual direct his energies in one way rather than another. Perhaps most important of all, they lead us to the point where his powers of rational interpretation and self-direction break down, and his actions become governed by emotion rather than by an objective appreciation of the realities around him.

Part II is concerned with how we can apply this knowledge in the work-situation. It considers how individuals differ from each other and how an understanding of these differences helps to guide them into jobs whose demands they can meet and which give them a pattern of satisfactions which will enlist their Motivation. This involves drawing up a Five-Fold specification of the qualities required on the one hand, and making an assessment of the individual on each of the five scales on the other. It goes on to consider how our knowledge of the learning process can be applied to make training more effective, and how the individual's Motivation can be stimulated by the use of appropriate incentives. The systematic observation and recording of behaviour, which is the essential methodology or psychology, can be applied to making working methods more efficient, to the improvement of physical conditions at work, and to the prevention of accidents. In all of these areas steady progress has been made over the past 50 years and development is accelerating to such an extent that each has become a specialized field of study. Limitations of space have made it impossible to follow up any of these in detail, for each has been the subject of a number of specialist publications but it is hoped that enough has been put forward to make the reader aware of current and potential developments.

Part III takes up the question of social interaction and considers the roles and relationships which come into being when individuals begin to do things together. These fall into structures and it is these structures or patterns which make up the social anatomy of an organization. Some roles will be more central than others and will offer the opportunity of exerting more influence on the relationships which focus on them. These are the leadership roles, but they are not always effectively occupied by the people who have been officially appointed to positions of responsibility in the formal organization. When influence begins to drift away from this formal structure, unofficial groupings with their own roles and relationships and possibly their own objectives, come into being. When these can challenge and subvert the formal structure, the danger of its losing control becomes very real.

Perhaps the final point to emphasize is that until a comparatively short time ago, none of this mattered at all. A reservoir of unemployed, a rigid class structure, and a widespread acceptance of the authoritarian master-and-servant attitude, made it perfectly possible to disregard these cause-and-effect processes, or to simplify them and run an efficient organization on an orders-and-punishment basis. There were few human problems that couldn't be "settled" by sacking someone. The situation, however, has changed drastically and fundamentally, and we are unlikely ever to slip back into the past. When unemployment goes over the six hundred thousand mark, it is now considered to be almost a political crisis. State legislation has placed a series of limitations on the employer's freedom of action, while trade union and unofficial actions have drastically changed the bargaining relationship between employer and employee. Improved social services have spread a greater feeling of security throughout the community and have contributed to a widespread aspiration to higher standards of affluence. The old-fashioned phrase "Jack's as good as his master" has taken on a very real meaning, and is presenting new problems to those in charge of organizations. Nothing in our previous experience is of the slightest use in solving these problems. We must therefore start from scratch and use such elementary knowledge as we possess of pyschological cause and effect in trying to solve them. The future effectiveness of our organizations is going to depend very largely on our success in this field.

## SUMMARY

1. How does the study of psychology apply to industry?

It provides some insight into the cause-and-effect processes which go on within the individual and between him and other individuals. Such insights into human behaviour may make it possible to influence it in the direction of making an organization at once more efficient in achieving its purpose, and also a more satisfying experience for those who work in it.

2. Is there any point at which this should start?

Probably in the fitting of people into jobs which match their individual qualities and abilities, and in which the effort-and-reward transaction is likely to balance out at a high level. While money will always play an important part in this transaction, its relation to the total pattern of satisfaction should always be borne in mind.

3. What should be the next point to which attention should be directed?

The interpersonal relationships in which people find themselves throughout the working day. The most significant of these will always be found in the primary, face-to-face groupings, and it is important that these should be integrated into the formal structure of the organization.

4. Does the technology of the production process have any effect on these relationships?

There are indications that flow production depending on de-skilled repetitive jobs is more frustrating than one-off craft jobs or technician jobs which demand a higher level of theoretical knowledge. No one factor, however, seems to be decisive in every case, but the quality of the supervision will always play an important part.

5. How do the trade unions fit into the picture?

They provide a means of collective bargaining by which employees can now represent their interests on level terms with their employers. This situation, however, is somewhat confused, partly owing to the multiplicity of unions and partly because in-plant bargaining, for which union organization is not always well adapted, has become more important than industry-wide negotiation.

6. How does this affect the individual employee?

He now has two roles, one as a member of the organization which employs him, and the other as a trade unionist. According to the situation, one or other may enlist a larger share of his Motivation. If he is dissatisfied or frustrated in his employee role, he will be attracted to his militant trade union role.

# NOTES ON READING

*Part I – General*

If the reader wishes to delve further into the process of perception, any general textbook on psychology will provide the necessary material. M. D. Vernon's *Psychology of Perception* (Pelican, 1962) could be recommended. Recent approaches to the psychology of motivation have been made by F. Herzberg, *Work and the Nature of Man* (Staples, 1966) and Chris Argyris, *Integrating the Individual and the Organization* (Wiley, 1964). Raymond B. Cattell's *Scientific Analysis of Personality* (Pelican, 1965) covers all aspects of the subject in considerable depth.

*Part II – Industrial*

For the assessment of individuals in terms of jobs, *Employment Interviewing* (4th edition, Macdonald & Evans, 1966) by the present author can be recommended, while W. Douglas Seymour's *Industrial Skills* (Pitman, 1966) is perhaps the best book on operator training. *Principles & Practice of Supervisory Management* (Nelson, 1967) also by the present author, deals with supervisory training, while *Engineering Aspects of Supervisory Management* (Norton & Munro Fraser, Nelson, 1968) may be found useful for work-study and incentives.

*Part III – Social*

There have been a number of recent books on the *Social Psychology of Industry* but J. A. C. Brown's text of that name (Pelican, 1954) is still the most widely read. Tom Lupton's *On the Shop Floor* (Pergamon, 1963) is an account of day-to-day working in two industrial firms and might be read as a supplement to what has been said about the Hawthorne investigations. A series on *The Affluent Worker* (Goldthorpe *et al.* Cambridge, 1968) supplies some additional insights, while Joan Woodward's *Industrial Organization: Theory and Practice* (Oxford, 1965) describes some wider studies and the conclusions drawn from them.

# INDEX

ABILITY tests, 155
Accident prone workers, 288
Accidents, 284
Acquired knowledge, 126
Adam, Sir Ronald 344
Adjustment, 127, 171, 193
Aha experience, 64
Air movement, 278
Animals—
  behaviour patterns, 69
  reactions to conflict, 97
  speed in learning, 62
Anxiety, 100
Assimilation of the handicapped worker, 342
Attention, 24
Attitudes, 86
  in social groups, 295, 338, 345
Attitude Surveys, interpretation, 347
Awareness of purpose of work, 238

BACON, Sir Francis, 5
Balance, sense of, 17
Bank wiring observation room, 358
Basic urges or drives, 68
Behaviour patterns accompanying emotion, 74
Bench layout, 261
Binet, Alfred, 119
Boredom, 272
  measures to offset, 274
Brains and abilities, 126

CASE-HISTORY, 199
Charts—
  man machine, 256
  multi-man, 257
  process, 250
  right- and left-hand, 251
Communication, 49
  within an organization, 300
Companionship needs, 72
Concepts, 29
Conditioning, significance of, 55
Condition reflex, 54
Conflict, 96
Conversion hysteria, 100
Cooling power of the air, 278
Culture pattern, industrial, 229

DAY-DREAMS, 100
Deductive method, 4
Dissociation, 98
Downward communication, 300
Dust, 280

EAR, 17
Ego needs, 73
Emotion, 74
Emotional balance, 127
Entry into groups, 340
Environment, 200
Experimental psychology, 8
Eye, 14

FATIGUE, 274
Factory Acts, 372
Fear, 28
Financial incentive, 229
Floor plans, 248
Forgetting, 43
Fumes, 280
Fundamental urges, 68
Further education and training, 141

GALTON, Sir Francis, 115
Gestalt psychologists, 31
Groups—
  entry into, 340
  standards and attitudes of, 295, 338

HALLUCINATIONS, 40
Handicapped workers, 342
Hawthorn investigations, 351
  bank wiring observation room, 358
  interview programme, 360
  relay assembly test room, 352
  significance of, 362
Health of Munition Workers Committee, 109
Hearing, 16
Heating and Ventilation, 278
"Humours," 5
Hunger and provision of food, 69

ILLUSION, Muller-Lyer, 32
Imagery, 37
Impact on others, 125, 314
Incentives, 228
Individual and the job, 367
Individual differences, 114
Inductive method, 6
Industrial company, structure of, 299
Industrial culture pattern, 229
Industrial Health Research Board, 110
Industrial training, 224
Industrial psychology—
  development, 108
  methods, 109
  subject-matter, 110
Innate abilities, 146, 192

Insight, 219
Intelligence tests, 121, 152
Interview—
    aim of, 198
    handling of, 206
    programme at Hawthorne, 360
Introspection, 93

JOBS—
    and individuals, 367
    as a social role, 140
Job-study, 183

KINAESTHETIC sense, 19

LANGUAGE, 47
Leaders, selection of, 334
Leadership, 314
Learning, 54
Lighting, 276
    investigations at Hawthorne, 351

MAN-MACHINE charts, 256
Material needs, 72
Meaning, added to sensations, 48
Memory, 41
Mental set, 47
Methods of studying social groups, 295
Money incentive, 230
Monotony and boredom, 272
Motivation, 70, 89, 126, 192
    assessment of, 168
    basic drives, 68
    human patterns of, 161
Movement study, 263
Muller-Lyer illusion, 32
Myers, Dr. C. S., 110

NATIONAL Institute of Industrial Psychology, 110
Nervous system of an organization, 305
Neurosis, 96
Neurotics, 343
Newton, Sir Isaac, 4
Noise, 275
Non-measurable characteristics, 122

OLFACTORY cells, 17
Optic nerve, 15
Organization of bank wiring group, 358

PAIN, 19
Pattern of relationships, 317
Patterns of satisfaction, 83
Pavlov, 54
Pendulum gimmick, 121
Perception, 29
    of wholes, 31
    mistakes in, 32
Phantasy, 100

Physical conditions of work, 268
Physical fatigue, 270
Physiological accompaniments of emotion, 75
Pig-iron handling study, 246
Practice—
    in development of skill, 218
    periods in training, 220
Primary working group, 328
Private worlds, 48
Process charts, 250
Psychological methods, 93
Purpose of work, awareness of, 238

QUALIFICATIONS, 126, 146

RATING scale for appearance, manner and physique, 143
Rationalization, 99
Recall and recognition, 42
Recognition of leadership roles, 332
Recording of working methods, 259
Relationship of case-history to assessment, 205
Relationships, 131
    between and within groups, 308
    between individuals, 314
    pattern of, 317
Relay assembly test room, 352
Repression, 99
Rest pauses, 273
Retina, 19

SAFETY measures and training, 286
Satisfaction, 166, 235
    methods of, 72
    patterns of, 83
    variation in the means of, 69
Scale for different levels of job, 150
Scale for general education, 147
Scale for innate abilities, 152
Scale for technical education, 148
Scales of variation, 118
Science and value judgements, 11
Scientific method, 6
Selection of leaders, 334
Selection of sensation, 25
Self-image, 85
Sensation, 29
Senses, 10
Service life, 204
Sight, 14
Skills, development of, 57
Skin, 19
Sleep, 68
Smell, 17
Social anatomy, 296
Social roles, 132, 318
Standards of performance in training, 222

# INDEX

Structure of social groups, 294
Sublimation, 98
Suggestion, 33
Supervisors, 287
Surroundings at work, 237

TASTE, 18
Taylor, F. W., 244
    significance of, 247
Technology and supervision, effects of, 370
Test groups, 356
Thinking, 45

Touch, 19
Trade Unions, 371

UNOFFICIAL primary group, 330
Urges, 68

VENTILATION, 278
Vocational guidance and selection, 181

WEBER'S Law, 94
Welch, H. J., 110
Work history, 204
Work study and methods, 244
Worry, 100